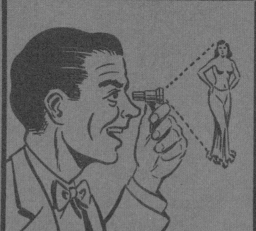

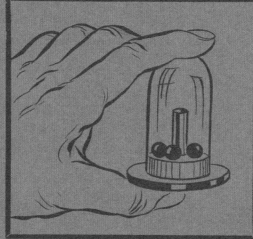

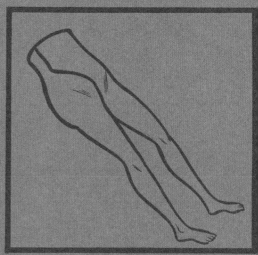

MAKE 'EM LAUGH

MAKE 'EM LAUGH

the funny business of america

Laurence Maslon

Based on the documentary film by
Michael Kantor

TWELVE

New York Boston

Twelve

Hachette Book Group

237 Park Avenue

New York, NY 10017

Visit our Web site at www.HachetteBookGroup.com.

Twelve is an imprint of Grand Central Publishing.

The Twelve name and logo are trademarks of Hachette Book Group, Inc.

Printed in the United States of America

First Edition: December 2008

10 9 8 7 6 5 4 3 2 1

ISBN-13: 978-0-446-50531-4

LCCN: 2008925836

To our wives:

To Kathy, who knows funny, but still loves me.
—MK

To Genevieve, three laughs a day, guaranteed.
—LM

Introduction 8

CONT

ONE

SLIP ON A BANANA PEEL

THE KNOCKABOUTS

Charlie Chaplin 16

Buster Keaton 22

Laurel and Hardy 28

Harpo Marx 32

The Three Stooges 40

Lucille Ball 44

Jerry Lewis 49

Jim Carrey 54

TWO

SOCK IT TO *ME*?

SATIRE AND PARODY

Will Rogers 68

Sid Caesar and *Your Show of Shows* 74

Tom Lehrer 80

Allan Sherman 86

Johnny Carson 90

Rowan and Martin's Laugh-In 97

Carol Burnett 100

Mel Brooks 106

Saturday Night Live 112

Billy Crystal 118

The Wayans Brothers 122

Jon Stewart and *The Daily Show* 125

THREE

**NEVER GIVE A SUCKER
AN EVEN BREAK**

SMART-ALECKS AND WISEGUYS

W. C. Fields 134

Groucho Marx 142

Jack Benny 150

Tim (The Kingfish) Moore 159

Phil Silvers 162

Paul Lynde 167

Redd Foxx 172

Joan Rivers 178

Eddie Murphy 182

Larry David 187

ENTS

FOUR
WOULD YA HIT A GUY WITH GLASSES?
NERDS, JERKS, ODDBALLS, AND SLACKERS

Harold Lloyd 198

Eddie Cantor 203

Bob Hope 208

Jonathan Winters 216

Phyllis Diller 220

Woody Allen 223

Cheech and Chong 230

Steve Martin 233

Gilda Radner 237

Robin Williams 240

Andy Kaufman 245

FIVE
HONEY, I'M HOME!
BREADWINNERS AND HOMEMAKERS

The Goldbergs 256

George Burns and Gracie Allen 260

The Honeymooners 268

The Dick Van Dyke Show 273

Norman Lear and *All in the Family* 276

The Odd Couple 284

Bill Cosby 287

Roseanne 292

Seinfeld 296

The Simpsons 300

SIX
WHEN I'M BAD, I'M BETTER
THE GROUNDBREAKERS

Mae West 310

Burlesque 316

Abbott and Costello 320

Moms Mabley 328

Fred Allen 325

Mort Sahl 332

Lenny Bruce 336

The Smothers Brothers 342

Richard Pryor 348

George Carlin 354

Bill Maher 360

Punch Line 364

Bibliography 366

Videography 370

Acknowledgments 371

Index 375

INTRODUCTION

So, these two Jewish guys go into a public broadcasting network . . .

"Laugh, and the world laughs with you" goes the familiar adage, but around the world people laugh at different things and for different reasons. *Make 'Em Laugh: The Funny Business of America* explores what has made America laugh over the past one hundred years, and why. It's not (necessarily) a collection of our favorite bits, nor is it an academic treatise on the nature of comedy; as the great essayist E. B. White once put it, "Analyzing humor is like dissecting a frog. Few people are interested and the frog dies of it." As early as 1931, Constance Rourke, in her pioneering study *American Humor*, wrote that "If the American character is many-sided, at least a large and shadowy outline has been drawn by its many ventures into comedy." *Make 'Em Laugh* is an attempt to fill in that outline with the trends and tensions that have exploded onto the scene in the subsequent eight decades.

What makes American humor particularly (or peculiarly) American? Different answers have emerged from the more than one hundred different artists and comedians interviewed for the series. Many of them pointed to the diversity of the "melting pot," our cheek-by-jowl interaction with so many different cultures, each one straining, in some way, to become assimilated into the dominant culture. Roseanne Barr sees comedy as the key to acceptance: "If you can make fun of your own in front of the dominant culture here, you can live next door to 'em." Other comedians look at the putative protections of the First Amendment; Jeff Foxworthy notes that "we have the freedom to talk about [issues] without fear of retribution. You can say, 'Hey, isn't this weird?' or 'Boy, I don't like what the leader of our government is doin'.' You can't do that other places." Norman Lear points to a larger cultural denominator: "Anywhere you look in America there's a tremendous amount of excess, so of course comics are working their hearts out to audiences who are demanding louder, more vulgar, more interesting excess." Comedy veteran Rose Marie echoes many comedians who, frankly, don't even consider the question worth asking: "Funny is funny. No matter what language. No matter who says it."

Still, comedy in America has evolved over five centuries; it remains an amalgam of cultural influences and comedic forms—many of which are derived from European art forms, such as the commedia dell'arte—that have melded with more homegrown entertainments such as the minstrel show or the vaudeville stage to create something distinctly American. In *Make 'Em Laugh*, we have identified six different categories of American comedy. Three of them are genres that have been reshaped or defined by American comedic geniuses—physical comedy, satire and parody, domestic comedy—and the other three categories identify archetypes that represent our national character: the wiseguy, the outsider, and the groundbreaker. What's truly fascinating is that, in each case, every generation and every new ethnic arrival to our shores absorbs the genre and adds to its complexion, evolution, and tradition.

Comedians are among our bravest individuals. Some of them have spent decades refining one unforgettable persona; others derive their strength from their transformative abilities as shape-shifters. Still, every night (sometimes both for the ten o'clock and the midnight shows) and every episode and every film—armed with only a nimble mind and a supple body—comedians have to face the monster with a thousand eyes that crosses its arms in front of its chest and demands: make me laugh. Tough stuff. But comedians are also the most generous of artists; every comedian, writer, or director interviewed for this series expressed gratitude to and admiration for someone who came before them. (Interestingly, the three most cherished comedians—by comedians themselves—were Jack Benny, Jonathan Winters, and Richard Pryor.)

Comedians, even the most misanthropic of them, are also optimists—"Well, if you didn't like that one, maybe you'll find this one funny"—and perhaps that, more than anything else, makes them quintessentially American. By telling their stories (and a few of their jokes), we hope to make you laugh.

Comics' comics: Jack Benny, Jonathan Winters, Richard Pryor.

CHAPTER ONE

SLIP ON A BANANA PEEL

THE KNOCKABOUTS

It is funnier to bend things than to break them.
If one comedian hits another over the head with
a crowbar, the crowbar should bend, not break.
In legitimate drama, the hero breaks his sword,
and it is dramatic. In comedy, the sword bends,
and stays bent.
—W. C. Fields

THE BIG(GER) PICTURE

It's not surprising that the world of physical comedy should have its own physics. The very word *slapstick*—synonymous with physical comedy—comes from a mechanical object created for the commedia dell'arte players of the seventeenth century. These knock-about comics realized that an exaggerated physical movement deserved an exaggerated sound—a slap worked better than a punch—so they created a wooden bat with a blade down the middle that would smack against the base, thereby creating a great whopping *whack!* And, proving that experimentation is the name of the game in physical comedy, gunpowder was added to the blades of the slapstick in the nineteenth century.

The vocabulary of physical comedy has not changed much since the commedia dell'arte: the pratfall, the kick in the pants, the tumble, the double take. What has changed, beginning with the American silent film comedies of the 1910s that revolutionized the world, is the relation of physical comedy to the world of modern mechanization. Henri Bergson, the French literary critic, wrote a famous essay, "Laughter," in 1900 in which he held the relationship of man to machine as key to comedy. He felt that audiences laughed at two basically interdependent ideas: that we are amused when comic incidents reduce human beings to mechanized objects, and when mechanized objects seem to take on an anthropomorphic life of their own. The history of physical comedy in America since Bergson wrote his essay can, in some ways, be seen as the tension between those ideas; the comedians who have found ways to make us laugh by mechanizing themselves (bending, not breaking) and their manipulation of the various mechanisms created by technology (film, animation) in the service of laughter.

A physical comedian is immediately divorced from the laughter of language; he carries his very best gag with him at all times, his own body. It's rougher that way—and requires more of a pioneer spirit—but it has its advantages, as the modern clown, Bill Irwin, puts it:

> A stand-up comedian, or an actor in a play, has to wait for that laughter to crest, and then say the next thing. When you've got something rolling as a physical comic, you can sometimes just keep going because people are laughing, so you can take the next iteration without having to wait for that laughter to die down. Now, that's useful when they're laughing. When they're not laughing, it's every bit as terrifying as stand-up.

While a verbal or stand-up comedian has to master content, the physical comedian has to master form. He or she has to know in which medium they are working, and how it can work to their advantage. Charlie Chaplin, Buster Keaton, Harpo Marx, and the Three Stooges had worked in live vaudeville for years before they ever got in front of the camera, so they knew what made audiences laugh; Lucille Ball just dove in, feetfirst. For some comedians, the short form has worked best—again, the Three Stooges were most comfortable in eighteen-minute segments, and luckily, that format was easily translatable to after-school television programs, thereby earning them an entirely new audience in the 1950s and '60s. Harpo could get away with a series of three-minute bits spread out over ninety minutes; audiences welcomed his appearances as a pleasant respite from Groucho and Chico's verbal assaults. But length would always be a challenge to these comedians—the sheer energy required of an extensive physical routine is enormous. When early silent two-reelers (about twenty-five minutes) segued to longer features in response to audiences' tastes, it required a radical rethink of the content of film comedy. As historian Jeffrey Vance put it, "When you went into features your stories had to be believable, otherwise it just wouldn't hold up, and that was true with all the clowns, Chaplin, Keaton, Lloyd. The cartoon gags, the impossible gags—gone. Everything had to work for the story."

Physical comedians have also been challenged by technology; they can either master it or be mastered by it. Chaplin preferred to keep the camera framed around him like a proscenium arch, so that his pantomime could be seen in its complete form; Buster Keaton was more interested in setting up gags that kept the strings hidden, as it were, in order to confound the audience. But just as the silent masters had figured out the transition to longer features, the technology of sound came in and asked them to rethink their comic strategies one more time. Harold Lloyd had a realistic assessment of the challenge:

Silents did have a wonderful quality, in that there was a certain relaxation in the theater: you could go in there and do your own imagining of what they would say and how they would say it. It had its own attributes. But of course, we all talk, we see things in color, and we see things in dimensions. That's progress. [Therefore], practically the whole procedure started to change. It was easier to sit down and talk, to make up verbal quips, to give dialogue instead of visual action, ocular business—gags, we used to call them, pieces of business. The spoken word seemed to be much simpler to get the laughs from, and much cheaper. They could make a picture for much less, because visual comedy is expensive. It takes comedy, it takes pacing, it takes rehearsal to bring it off correctly. As time went on, the comedians seemed to lose the art or knack of doing pantomime.

Chaplin, famously, refused to give up his art of pantomime for years, claiming, "If I did make a talking picture, I felt sure that when I opened my mouth, I would become just like any other comedian." He succumbed and re-created himself in a new and interesting way. For some comics, namely the Three Stooges, sound was a blessing—it enabled them to get away with the most violent slapstick, since it could be palatably denatured (oddly enough) by the addition of the most violent soundtrack. Jerry Lewis exploited his innate musicality by underscoring many of his most amusing sequences and letting his body language react and ricochet to the tune.

Sound also proved to be a boon to the world of animation, allowing cartoons to exploit their visual audacity to the fullest by underscoring them with equally outrageous music and effects. Even the addition of color—intense, shocking color—enhanced the animated experience. The art of animation turned a corner in the mid-1930s when inspired artists like Tex Avery realized that the mere duplication of reality was the very least of what cartoons could achieve: "We found out early that if you did something with a character, either animal or human or whatnot, that couldn't possibly be rigged up in live action, why then, you've got a guaranteed laugh." Still, as technologically progressive as cartoons could get, they still needed the human factor to connect with an audience. Film historian Leonard Maltin notes that "every animator I ever interviewed or read about in the twenties and well into the thirties, and maybe even beyond, studied Charlie Chaplin. The artists at Disney revered Chaplin, including Walt. They even traced some of his movements in some cases just to see how he did it, because his body language was so extraordinary."

Perhaps the threat of being mechanized out of existence is what has made physical comedians extremely protective—of themselves, of their gags, and perhaps most of all, of their props. One of the great ironies of physical comedy is watching a master comedian transform into a complete incompetent when dealing with the props of daily life: Keaton with a boat, Lucy with a blender, Jerry Lewis with a bunk bed. We laugh helplessly to see them undone by the simplest of appliances—but of course we've been in the same boat, as it were, ourselves. The supreme joke is that, in rehearsal, these comedians must attain complete mastery of their props in order to unleash such hilarious chaos.

Bill Irwin says that "Most of us physical comedians are prop comics. Most of us say, 'Mothers, tell your children to stay clear of prop comedy,' because it's all about stuff, and it's all about the stuff going well. And you're dependent on stagehands, some of whom, you know, really don't get it or really could care less sometimes." Harpo Marx would trust only his own son, Bill, to load and unpack his property case, and trust is a big issue for the physical comedian.

It makes tremendous sense. A verbal comedian can always get new writers, but a physical comedian writes his fate on his own body—he can't really send it back for a revision. The great physical comedians were always uncompromising, always in control. They had to be; they are the only comedians who work—figuratively and literally—without a net. What Harold Lloyd had feared in 1927 has come to pass, in a way; there are fewer and fewer comedians left with the knack of pantomime. Some of that may be because our modern age is so complex and so skeptical that it requires the full bore of verbal humor to produce any kind of effect. Some of it may be due to technology, after all; what Pixar can do with toy spacemen and wisecracking donkeys is far beyond the ability of human reality. The current state of computer animation allows audiences and producers to have it both ways; you can contract the voice and personality of a major comedian—Eddie Murphy, say—and attach them digitally to the limitless physical potential of an animator's imagination. And it's no use pretending that we don't laugh as hard at Robin Williams's Genie in *Aladdin* as we do at Buster Keaton.

But still, the pioneering work of the physical comedian lives with us every day. Maybe we don't laugh at every line of a late-night comic's monologue, but watching someone slip into an open manhole on the way to work in the morning is surefire. And it's not as if physical comedy isn't quotable, either.

JUST ASK SOMEONE TO "WALK THIS WAY" —AND SEE WHAT HAPPENS.

Pratfalls, Inc: (previous) Chaplin in *The Rink*; the Three Stooges, Jerry Lewis; Marty Feldman in *Young Frankenstein*.

"THE BEST DANCER THAT

CHARLIE CHAPLIN

The American is an optimist preoccupied with hustling dreams, an indefatigable tryer. He hopes to make a quick "killing." Hit the jackpot! Get out from under! Sell out! Make the dough and run! Get into another racket! Yet this immoderate attitude began to brighten my spirit. I began to regain confidence. Whatever happened, I was determined to stay in America.

–Charlie Chaplin

BALLET
EVER LIVED"

Balls in the air: (clockwise from above): Leading actor in Karno's company; monkeying around in *The Circus* (1928); *The Pawnshop* (Mutual, 1916).

Charlie Chaplin sailed past the Statue of Liberty for the first time twice; the first was as a featured comic actor traveling from England with the Karno American Company in the fall of 1910, the second time was as the Little Tramp in the spring of 1917, in the Mutual Films short *The Immigrant*. Within seven event-filled years, Chaplin had completely rewritten the Victorian rags-to-riches story for modern times.

Chaplin's goal in both of his American arrivals was to get laughs. With the 1917 short, it was immediate:

> Figuring out what the audience expects, and then doing something different, is great fun to me. In one of my pictures, *The Immigrant*, the opening scene showed me leaning far over the side of a ship. Only my back could be seen and from the convulsive shudders of my shoulder, it looked as though I was seasick. If I had been, it would have been a terrible mistake to show it in the picture. What I was doing was deliberately misleading the audience. Because when I straightened up, I pulled a fish at the end of a line into view, and the audience saw that, instead of being seasick, I had been leaning over the side to catch the fish. It came as a total surprise and got a roar of laughter.

His arrival in America in 1910 was part of a longer journey, and it wasn't all filled with laughter.

Charles Chaplin was born in London on April 16, 1889, in a working-class district, south of the river Thames. If his childhood was not exactly Dickensian, it was close enough to be miserable. His father was a second-rate music hall entertainer and his mother was an aspiring singer; neither parent's career was successful and they split up when Chaplin was a boy. Chaplin and his brother, Sydney, had to sit by and watch as their mother slowly degenerated into madness and went in and out of mental institutions. The Chaplin boys were thrown into a spiral of poverty and separation, often being sent to charity schools while their mother was recuperating.

But Charlie and his brother had inherited some of the performing talents that their parents had squandered; as a youngster, Charlie appeared in music hall skits and small parts on the West End. Sydney joined a successful music hall company called Fred Karno's Speechless Comedians in 1906 and two years later procured a role for his brother. Charlie did so well with Karno's pantomime style of humor that Karno promoted him to a leading role in one sketch because the previous leading man—named Stan Laurel—had moved on. Chaplin refined his comic style in front of live audiences for nearly six years under Karno's tutelage; despite his eventual success in film, he always felt grateful for the precision of his theatrical training.

Chaplin enjoyed a huge success traveling across America during the 1910 Karno tour; billed as Chaplin the Inebriate, he headlined in several sketches, including his great drunk act, "A Night in a London Club." He returned to the States in 1912, and while he was performing in Philadelphia a telegram arrived for the Karno company manager: IS THERE A MAN NAMED CHAFFIN IN YOUR COMPANY OR SOMETHING LIKE IT STOP IF SO WILL HE COMMUNICATE WITH KESSEL AND BAUMAN 24 LONGACRE BUILDING BROADWAY. Chaplin, thinking he had been left money by a dying relative, took the train to New York and found out that he was being made an offer by Mack Sennett's Keystone Studios. He signed his first film contract in December of 1913 for $150 a week and was off to California to become one of Sennett's legendary stable of comedians.

Sennett's Keystone films were boisterous, fast-paced, sloppy affairs, and Chaplin had some difficulty fitting into Sennett's schemes. He had made a few short films while trying to find a character or persona that he could latch on to. He thought a visit to the Keystone wardrobe department might give him an inspiration; it did more than that, it gave him his career. As Chaplin recounted in his autobiography:

> I had no idea what makeup to put on. I did not like my get-up as the press reporter. However, on the way to the wardrobe I thought I would dress in baggy pants, big shoes, a cane and a derby hat. I wanted everything to be a contradiction: the pants baggy, the coat tight, the hat small and the shoes large. I was undecided whether to look old or young, but remembering Sennett had expected me to be a much older man, I added a small moustache, which, I reasoned, would add age without hiding my expression. I had no idea of the character. But the moment I was dressed, the clothes and the makeup made me feel the person he was. I began to know him, and by the time I walked onto the stage he was fully born.

The Tramp character was first seen by the public in *Kid Auto Races in Venice* in 1914, a quickie not much better made than an amateur film, but he repeated the character in several more accomplished shorts. Chaplin moved on to direct himself in all of his pictures (with the exception of the first full-length comedy, *Tillie's Punctured Romance*) and quickly tired of Sennett's on-the-fly style. In 1915, after thirty-five short subjects with Keystone, Chaplin moved on to Essanay Studios, where he was given the unprecedented salary of $1,250 per week, as well as his own production unit and ensemble of actors. As Chaplin historian Jeffrey Vance put it, "If Keystone was his infancy, the Essanay film company was his adolescence. He slowed things down, he took more time, and he added pathos, irony, and fantasy to his comedies." Chaplin was now famous throughout the globe; according to one newspaper report: "The world has Chaplinitis. . . . Once in every century or so a man is born who is able to color and influence the world . . . a little Englishman, quiet, unassuming, but surcharged with dynamite is flinching the world right now." He had also further refined the Tramp character, with his unmistakable size-fourteen boots, derby, and wiggling mustache:

> You know, this fellow is many-sided, a tramp, a gentleman, a poet, a dreamer, a lonely fellow, always hopeful of romance and adventure. He would have you

If comedy is a man in trouble, Chaplin is up on the high wire with a monkey crawling on his face. When in danger of life and limb, he would always have some sort of preoccupation with dignity. —Bill Irwin

believe he is a scientist, a musician, a duke, and a polo player. However, he is not above picking up cigarette butts or robbing a baby of its candy. And, of course, if the occasion warrants it, he will kick a lady in the rear—but only in extreme anger!

Chaplin's contract with Essanay ended in 1916; his costly perfectionism disappointed the penny-pinching exhibitors, and there were lawsuits and recriminations. When Chaplin decided to sign with the Mutual Film Corporation, his salary was $670,000 (plus a

Comedy superstar: (l. to r.) Merchandising giant; before a bond rally; forming UA with Mary Pickford, D.W. Griffith, Douglas Fairbanks; behind the camera; *The Adventurer* (Mutual, 1917).

Charlie had one fault, I always felt. He'd milk his business, his gags too much. If he got something good, he never seemed to want to let go of it. But that's such a minor thing. We all have them.

—Harold Lloyd

$150,000 bonus), which was not only the highest amount of money paid to a performer in human history but the highest paid to any employee of any kind. He moved into his own studio, the Lone Star Studio, and over the next two years he created twelve short subjects, which critics believe to be his best, most essential work. Chaplin certainly thought so: "Fulfilling the Mutual contract, I suppose, was the happiest period of my career. I was light and unencumbered, twenty-seven years old, with fabulous prospects and a friendly, glamorous world before me."

The Mutual studio, with its ensemble of gifted comedians and full resources, was, according to Vance, "like Chaplin's comic laboratory. There he could experiment and could lavish the most precious thing in the world—time—on those twelve films. He was never more inventive." Film historian Leonard Maltin adds that Chaplin displayed another important quality at Mutual: grace. "He sifted out the crudeness that you see in his earliest films and sort of ennobled himself, but never so much that he wasn't still that little tramp man of the people." Chaplin's variety at Mutual was astounding. He alternates the Tramp with other characters, playing a daring escaped convict in *The Adventurer*, a beleaguered waiter in *The Rink*, and most impressively, an inebriated toff in *One A.M.*—for all intents and purposes, a solo film in which Chaplin tries, in vain, to enter his own mansion and put himself to bed (he winds up in the bathtub, snuggling with the bath mat). He keyed into the comic sensibilities of his drunken character:

> Even funnier than the man who has been made ridiculous, however, is the man who, having had something funny happen to him, refuses to admit that anything out of the way has happened, and attempts to maintain his dignity. Perhaps the best example is the intoxicated man who, though his tongue and walk give him away, attempts in a dignified manner to convince you that he is quite sober.

The tools available to Chaplin in his own studio appealed to the control freak in him. Most other silent comedy directors only shot another take if something catastrophic happened; Chaplin shot ten times the amount of footage he actually used in the Mutual films. His actors were trained to imitate his every suggestion to the letter. He frustrated his longtime cameraman by insisting that the camera capture him from derby to flatfeet as often as possible. Chaplin's framing followed his philosophical dictum that "Life is a tragedy when seen in close-up, a comedy in long shot." Yet all could be forgiven by his

immense grace on film, his physical mobility, his tiny touches, the flourishes that kept the roughhouse from being offensive and elevated his very essence into the realm of art, something the audience hardly thought possible from the knockabout world of silent comedy of the early 1910s. W. C. Fields saw one of the Mutual films, *Easy Street*, in a revival house in 1930 and famously ejaculated, "The son of a bitch is a ballet dancer. He's the best ballet dancer that ever lived and if I get a good chance I'll kill him with my bare hands."

Chaplin would move on once again, like a millionaire version of the Tramp. After his Mutual contract expired he signed with a company called First National, where he would create *The Kid*, and then left that studio to form United Artists with Mary Pickford and Douglas Fairbanks in 1923. Chaplin created five more feature-length silent comedies, and as the world—and sound pictures—got more complicated, so did his politics, his personal life, and his reputation. But within five years of his first visit to America, he had been transformed from a strolling player into the first, and perhaps best known, celebrity of the twentieth century, at a time when there were no road maps or precedents for such popularity. It was a heavy responsibility, and Chaplin made many mistakes along the way, but he knew that, in the end, what mattered most appeared on a projection screen:

> In my work I don't trust anyone's sense of humor but my own. . . . It isn't because I think I am so much smarter than those around me. It is simply because I am the one who gets all the blame or credit for the picture. I can't insert a title in a picture, for instance, and say: "People, I don't blame you for not laughing. I didn't think it was funny myself, but the fellows around me told me it was and so I let it go."

"I'D DOUBLE CROSS 'EM SOMETIMES"

BUSTER KEATON

Abbott and Costello—never gave the story a second thought. They'd say, "When do we come and what do we wear?" Then they find out the day they start to shoot the picture what the script's about. Didn't worry about it. Didn't try to. Well, that used to get my goat because, my God, when we made pictures, we ate, slept, and dreamed them! –Buster Keaton, 1964

Great Stone Face: as a vaudevillian toddler; with Fatty Arbuckle and Al St. John; the rest is silents. Far right: *Sherlock Jr.*; toying with sound.

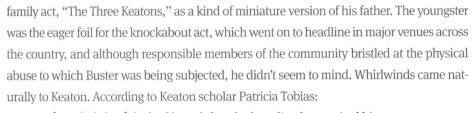

Buster Keaton's fevered dream of a film career—his silent classics—lasted a mere dozen years, but he had already been a show business veteran for seventeen years before he had even set his feet above his head in front of a camera.

Joseph Frank Keaton was born in 1895, in a small farm town in Kansas. According to him, "I was born with a tent show on a one-night stand in Kansas. My mother joined the show when I was two weeks old. It was called 'The Keaton & Houdini Medicine Show Company.' Now that's Harry Houdini, the handcuff king. He was the doctor and trickster of the outfit and my old man was the entertainer and comic." It was Houdini, Keaton always claimed, who gave him his nickname; at six months old, the boy fell down a flight of stairs and sat up unscathed. "That was sure a buster," said the master illusionist, and the elder Keaton said, "That would be a good name for him, don't sound bad."

At the age of five, Buster joined the family act, "The Three Keatons," as a kind of miniature version of his father. The youngster was the eager foil for the knockabout act, which went on to headline in major venues across the country, and although responsible members of the community bristled at the physical abuse to which Buster was being subjected, he didn't seem to mind. Whirlwinds came naturally to Keaton. According to Keaton scholar Patricia Tobias:

> [As a little boy], he had been left at the boarding house. And his parents were onstage when a tornado blew through town. They went running back to the boarding house and they discovered that Buster was not in his bed. And reportedly, shortly thereafter, after they had started searching all over, someone showed up at the door and knocked on the door and said, "Is this yours?" and handed them their child who had been sucked out the window and deposited, unharmed, about a half a mile away.

What had become more harmful, over the course of nearly two decades, was Keaton's father's alcoholism, which started lousing up the precision of the family act. At the age of twenty-one, Buster broke up the act and accepted an offer to move to New York and appear in a Broadway revue. Broadway audiences, alas, never got the chance to see him.

The theater's loss was the cinema's gain. One afternoon in 1917, Keaton went with an acquaintance to watch one of the screen's leading comics, Roscoe "Fatty" Arbuckle, film a two-reeler on East Forty-eighth Street. Arbuckle asked Keaton to join him for a scene or two in his short *The Butcher Boy*, and it was love at first sight. "Well, the making of a motion picture started to fascinate me immediately," said Keaton years later. "First thing I did was I asked a thousand questions about the camera and got into the camera. Then I went into the projecting room to see things cut. It just fascinated me." Keaton tore up his Broadway contract and joined Arbuckle's unit, eventually moving out to California to make movies with him. He had also discovered one of his great assets, his deadpan facial expression:

I just happened to be, even as a small kid, I happened to be the type of comic who couldn't laugh at his own material. I soon learned at an awful early age that when I laughed the audience didn't. So, by the time I got into pictures, that was a natural way of working.

By 1919, Arbuckle would get a contract to make his own feature-length films (and two years later, he would be washed up in Hollywood, due to a spectacular scandal not of his own making), and Keaton would be given his own studio by Metro and charged with putting out a half-dozen two-reelers a year. Before they went their separate ways, Arbuckle said to Keaton, "Here's something you want to bear in mind, that the average mind of the motion picture audience is twelve years old. It's a twelve-year-old mind you're entertaining." Keaton recalled, "I was only with him about another couple of months or something like that, and I says, 'Roscoe, something tells me that those who continue to make pictures for twelve-year-old minds ain't going to be with us long.'" He was right; silent film comedy was destined to grow in its ambitions. But Keaton had been a performer for nearly as long as silent films had been around, so he didn't need to experiment with who he was or what he could do. He just pulled the collaborators in his unit together, came up with a beginning gag and an ending gag—"we figured the middle would take care of itself," he always said—and started shooting the movie.

The first release that bore his unmistakable imprint, *One Week*, concerned a couple who buy a "some assembly required" home, only to be double-crossed when a rival mixes up the boxes. But Keaton the director double-crosses the audience, too. Keaton's character manages to assemble something vaguely resembling a house anyway, but, as Tobias describes it:

> At the end of the film, this house that he has built winds up having to get moved. It's on the wrong lot, so he's trying to get it across the railroad tracks, it gets stuck, and you see the train coming. And he and his wife stand back and cover their eyes and they know that the train's going to smash their house—but it goes by on a parallel track. Well, then just as they've breathed a big sigh of relief, another train comes from the other direction and demolishes the house.

"I always wanted an audience to outguess me," said Keaton, "then I'd double-cross 'em sometimes."

His fascination with film technology allowed him to work out brand-new gags in the most painstaking detail. In 1921's *The Playhouse* he exposed a sequence of film nine times to get the effect of him dancing onstage with eight exact doubles of himself. In his most adventuresome short film, *Sherlock Jr.* (1924), he invents a scenario where a movie projectionist falls asleep and dreams himself into the movies he projects. Keaton was insistent that the film's gags could only work within the context of a dream—he was a vocal proponent of the believability of a gag—but the dream allowed him to walk in and out of the action on a motion picture screen, something no one had ever done; luckily his crew had the skill to pull it off.

His body was as fearless as his imagination. His long tenure in vaudeville allowed him to do stunts no one else could accomplish. Dick Van Dyke, a fervent acolyte, recalled:

> He was an athlete. He could have been in the Olympics. I saw him do things that no human being should be able to do. I finally got to meet him in his later years. I

The average mind of the motion picture audience is twelve years old.
–Fatty Arbuckle

Roscoe, something tells me that those who continue to make pictures for twelve-year-old minds ain't going to be with us long.
–Buster Keaton

was asking him about how he used to put one foot up on the table and then the other foot and then seemed to pause in midair for a second before he'd fall. And he did it for me in his own kitchen at about sixty-eight years old.

On occasion, Keaton's luck might run out. While filming a sequence in *Sherlock Jr.*, Keaton was sprayed to the ground by the full force of an open spout on a water tank. He got up and finished the shot, unaware that he had broken a vertebra at the top of his neck—it wasn't until an X-ray pointed it out a decade later that he discovered the fact. But he always respected the audience's desire for a genuine thrill; as Tobias puts it, "He realized that if you're going to show something, you need to really show it."

Keaton's ultimate devotion to imperturbability came during the shooting of his last independent feature, *Steamboat Bill, Jr.* Forced by studio brass to change the framework of his scenario from a flood to a tornado, Keaton and his crew meticulously recrafted all their gags. One of them, perhaps his most famous, involves Keaton standing stock-still while a house falls down around him. In 1965, Keaton described the near-military planning that into the gag:

First I had them build the framework of this building and make sure that the hinges were all firm and solid. It was a building with a tall V-shaped roof, so that we could make this window up in the roof exceptionally high. An average second story window would be about twelve feet, but we're up about eighteen feet. Then you lay this frame-work down on the ground, and build the window around me. We built the window so that I had a clearance of two inches on each shoulder, and the top missed my head by two inches and the bottom my heels by two inches. We mark the ground out and drive big nails where my two heels are going to be. Then you put that house back up in position while they finish building it. They put the front on, painted it, and made the jagged edge where it tore away from the main building; and then we went in and fixed the interiors so that you're looking at a house that the front has blown off. Then we put our wind machines with the big Liberty motors. We had six of them and they are pretty powerful—they could lift a truck off the road. Now we had to make sure we were getting our foreground and background wind effect, but that no current ever hit the front of the building when it started to fall, because if the wind warps her, she's not going to fall where we want her, and I'm standing right out front. But it's a one-take scene and we got it that way. You don't do those things twice.

Supposedly, the nominal director of the action sequence started praying and looked away when the cameras rolled, but the sequence went off without a hitch. Sid Caesar remembers it as his favorite Keaton moment: "And he stood there with a smile and—boom!—you saw the dust come up from that, you went, 'That was *heavy*!' It took guts to do that! I mean, that's serious stuff." Although Keaton was fearless, he wasn't stupid. In *Sherlock Jr.*, he filmed one short dream sequence where he's in a lion cage with two supposedly trained lions. He did his shot and wanted to get out, pronto: "I don't know these lions personally, see. They're both strangers to me! I start to walk toward the side of the cage to slip out. Then the cameraman says, 'We've got to do that scene again for the foreign negative.' I said, 'Europe ain't gonna see this scene!' "

Keaton would have far more trouble with the MGM lion. When sound came in,

KEATON IS IN VOGUE MORE THAN CHAPLIN NOWADAYS BECAUSE KEATON IS COOL WHERE CHAPLIN IS WARM.

–Leonard Maltin

Keaton's independent studio was closed down and he was contractually obligated to work with MGM. Although Keaton was blessed with a pleasant baritone and could sing and dance, the studio denied him the opportunities to reinvent himself his way for sound. That restriction, coupled with a nasty divorce, kicked Keaton down the long staircase of alcoholism. He spent the next two decades doing what work he could get as an off-camera gagman for stars like Red Skelton, who couldn't hold a candle to Keaton. In the 1950s, however, television, with its shorter format, gave him a new audience, and the cognoscenti began to recognize the genius in their midst. His new projects and his reinvigorated reputation didn't make him much money, but he lived a simple life with his devoted third wife, Eleanor, in the San Fernando Valley, until he died of lung cancer in 1966.

"Keaton is in vogue more than Chaplin nowadays because Keaton is cool where Chaplin is warm," said historian Leonard Maltin. "We don't live in warm times, we live in more cynical times, and people are a little crueler, a little more aloof. But that doesn't mean that one is better than the other. Why can't we just agree that they were both brilliant?" Keaton always had the utmost respect for Chaplin, as he did for most comedians who worked hard, diligently, and honestly at their gags; aggression and vindictiveness were not in his nature:

There are certain characters you just don't hit with a pie. We found that out a long time ago. I remember a lot of people wanted to hit Lillian Gish so bad because she was always so sweet and innocent. But now for instance in television—Milton Berle hit Ed Sullivan with a pie, and the audience froze up on him, and Milton didn't get another laugh while he was on that stage. There are certain people you just don't hit with a pie. That's all there is to it.

Stuff of legend: (far left) *Steamboat Bill, Jr.*; (above) suffering as a gag man for the Marx Brothers, 1938; man of the times; (left) wrestling with celluloid.

"REMEMBER HOW DUMB I USED TO BE?"
LAUREL AND HARDY

MGMP-1268

Ollie was the dumbest guy in the room, and Stan was his stooge. It was zero sum intelligence. And these two guys teamed up to do what, for most of us, wouldn't be too difficult. Even in California, you can sell Christmas trees without destroying a man's house. But it's more fun if you destroy the man's house. It just is. —Michael McKean

In their films, Stan Laurel and Oliver Hardy seem incapable of succeeding with even the simplest collaborative task. As an off-camera comedy team, however, Laurel and Hardy proved to be the nimblest of jesters, juggling more elements than any comedians had before them—a double-act, pantomime, slapstick, dialogue, singing and dancing—with a deceptive grace. No other team could render effort (say, pushing a piano up a flight of 131 steps) more effortlessly.

They came from different parts of the world and were thrown together in the rough-and-tumble crucible of a Culver City film studio. Arthur Stanley Jefferson grew up in Lancashire, England, fascinated by toy theaters and puppet shows. Taking the stage name of Stan Laurel, he joined a traveling music hall troupe headed by Fred Karno, along with another young British farceur named Charlie Chaplin. When the troupe disbanded in America in 1914, Stan Laurel sought out his fortune in vaudeville and by writing and starring in silent comedies. Oliver Norvell Hardy was raised in an impossibly well-mannered household in Georgia; as a child, he loved imitating the guests at the hotel run by his family. He began his career managing movie theaters, then playing in short comic film subjects produced by a company based in, of all places, Jacksonville, Florida.

Stan and Babe, as Hardy preferred to be called, eventually found themselves in Hollywood, working separately at various studios (although, by chance, they had one brief scene together in a 1917 short called *Lucky Dog*). By 1926 both were working among the talented stock company at Hal Roach Studios in Culver City and were thrown together haphazardly, sometimes opposite each other, sometimes not, in almost a dozen silent shorts. Under the gaze of Roach himself, Laurel and Hardy had evolved as a team by 1927; their respective shapes—thin and wide—appealed to Roach's sense of comic geometry. Within the next two years, Laurel and Hardy starred in nearly two dozen silent short subjects and blossomed into an unforgettable duo.

For two such genteel and gentle souls, Laurel and Hardy wrought an awful lot of havoc in their silent pictures. Within the twenty minutes of each two-reeler, they could demolish, destroy, and decimate any dinner party, construction site, golf game, band concert, or traffic jam they blundered into. What made it all okay, in the eyes of the audience,

Mrs. Hardy and Mrs. Laurel: *Twice Two*—in drag for a gag.

were their basic characters. As ardent fan Dick Van Dyke put it: "They were like two children, two siblings who fought all the time, but who loved one another deeply and depended entirely upon the other one. They always made up. I loved that. There was a sweet relationship there that I had never seen in any other comedy team."

When sound came in, Laurel, a perfectionist who created most of their gags, was nervous about transferring their carefully controlled catastrophes from the silent screen. He

Several fine messes: *Lucky Dog* (1921), getting into *Another Fine Mess* (1930); *Brats* (1930); a tag team, wrestling with success.

I was looking through the phonebook during the early sixties in Santa Monica and just came across the name Stan Laurel. And I thought, It cannot be. So I called. And it was Stan Laurel. He was living on Ocean Avenue in an apartment. And my series was on, so he did know who I was. And I said, "Mr. Laurel, I've been such a fan all my life." I said, "I've copied and stolen from you very liberally." And he said, "Yes, I know."

—Dick Van Dyke

needn't have worried. Film historian and aficionado Leonard Maltin explained: "As much of a miracle it is that they teamed up, think of the serendipity of their voices. You couldn't have cast those voices. One from England, one from Georgia. How does that work? And yet it does. You just accept it as audiences did in 1929 and as we have ever since." Still, Laurel kept listening to the sound playback of their first talkie—wittily titled *Unaccustomed as We Are*—over and over again, trying to convince himself that the transition could work.

If anything, Laurel and Hardy played even better with dialogue, and they went on to dominate the era of sound comedy two- and three-reelers, making more than four dozen short subjects between 1929 and 1938. They were clever enough to orchestrate long passages of gifted pantomime with exquisitely ridiculous verbal and musical farragoes. Their 1932 classic three-reeler, *The Music Box*, won an Academy Award for Best Short Subject and is fondly remembered for the extended sequence in which the boys hilariously attempt the Sisyphean task of schlepping a player-piano up an immense flight of steps (which still exists, in the Silver Lake district of Los Angeles). But even better is the sequence once they eventually get the piano into the house; as the piano plays "Turkey in the Straw," Stan and Ollie do this flaky, delightful dance to the tune while cleaning up the damage to the living room, using the shredded lumber as percussion.

Such grace notes were possible because Laurel and Hardy existed out of time and space. They nearly always played characters named "Stan" and "Ollie" but still appeared in a vaster array of guises and identities than any other of their cinematic peers: detectives, French Foreign Legionnaires, fairy-tale characters, boxers, convicts, circus performers—even as their own wives (in drag) and their own children (through trick photography). They mastered their unique vocabulary and purposely slowed down the tempo of their pictures—in order, as Stan put it, to reflect the poky thought processes of their characters. Frequent director Leo McCarey captured their technique: "At that time, comedians had a tendency to do too much. With Laurel and Hardy, we introduced nearly the opposite. We tried to direct them so that they showed nothing, expressed nothing—and the audience, waiting for the opposite, laughed because we remained serious."

Sometimes their seriousness could verge on the macabre. In one film, *Block-Heads* (1938), Stan plays a World War I soldier who has never been told that the Armistice has been signed and is discovered still patrolling his fox hole twenty years on. Ollie, an old army comrade, ventures to a nearby veterans' home to visit his pal. Stan has, in the meantime, made

himself comfortable by tucking one of his legs underneath him; Ollie is shocked, believing that Stan has lost a leg in the war, and greets him solicitously.

STAN: Do you remember how dumb I used to be? Well, I'm better now.

(*Ollie, obligingly carries Stan to his car, huffing and puffing all the way, then Stan climbs out to get himself a drink of water.*)

OLLIE: Why didn't you tell me you had two legs?

STAN: Well, you didn't ask me.

OLLIE: (*witheringly*) You're *better* now . . .

Laurel wanted to end the film with the duo's two heads mounted on a trophy wall by a big-game hunter, to which Ollie would conclude: "Well, here's *another* fine mess you've gotten me into." Laurel was overruled by the studio.

As time went on, Laurel would get more frustrated by the changes and evolutions of the studio system: the demise of the short subject, the full-length feature with its overextended gags and romantic subplots, the lack of time and preparation, the exploitative contracts. Even into old age, when he was living in an apartment in Santa Monica, Laurel would write the local television station to complain about how Laurel and Hardy's films were being cut for broadcast, and he offered—in vain—to come in and re-edit them himself. Hardy rarely cared for the knuckle-bruising fights with the various studio executives; "Ask Stan" was his deferential refrain, and he busied himself instead with betting on the ponies with Chico Marx and winning amateur golf tournaments.

In one of their later films, *Swiss Miss* (1938), Stan and Ollie try to drag another piano through an impossible situation—this time across a rickety rope bridge suspended high above the Swiss Alps. They don't quite make it (something to do with a gorilla—never mind), but Stan and Ollie accomplished something even more impressive: They were able to drag their comedy across the seemingly unbridgeable gap between silent films and talking pictures, becoming a beloved and enduring legend in the process.

The relationship that Laurel and Hardy had was so delightful. And such a hard thing to do. There, if you watch them and start to analyze, is a love story between two men that never smacks of any homosexuality. You really feel a sincere love there. They slept together in bed, but it was a nice simple, light thing.

—Lenny Bruce

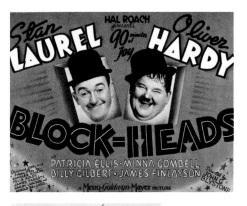

"HONK! HONK!"
HARPO MARX

Sweet, innocent, disarming. "Puck in a fright wig," was how *Time* magazine described him. They also said he was the warmest and most wonderful of the brothers, to which I also agree. The dames he chased were in no danger. He didn't know what to do with them once he caught them. In real life, however, he did.

–Groucho Marx

Most silent clowns were forced to stay silent because of their medium; yet when talkies came in, Keaton, Harold Lloyd, and even Chaplin gave voice to their characters. Only Harpo Marx kept a vow of silence throughout his career. It's not that Harpo *couldn't* speak—it's just that he *wouldn't*. It was more fun that way, and if anyone saw their comic destiny as one long playdate, it was Harpo.

Harpo came to his pantomimic skills through a process of elimination. Adolph Marx was born in 1888 (after his twenty-first birthday, he changed his name to Arthur), the second son of the Marx family. He joined his brothers in vaudeville when he was a teenager and proved proficient at singing and clowning around; he even picked up the harp, and although his technique was quite peculiar, his playing was effective. As the Marx Brothers' vaudeville act grew and refined itself in the early decades of the twentieth century, Harpo took on the character of an aggressive ragamuffin. When the brothers' uncle, a respected vaudevillian named Al Shean, revamped their act in 1914, he gave Harpo a couple of paltry lines and Harpo supposedly balked. Whether he was pushed or fell into a silent act is not exactly clear, but somewhere between the 1910 act "Fun in Hi Skule" and Shean's "Home Again," Harpo became a pure pantomime artist, communicating his desires through a pinwheel of flailing gestures, accessorized by shrill whistles, a honking taxi horn, and a plethora of preposterous props.

When the Marx Brothers hit the big time on Broadway in the 1920s, Harpo quickly became the critics' darling. That wasn't hard to do; he was a darling to begin with. Dick Cavett remembers Groucho telling him that Harpo "had all my mother's good qualities" and that "animals and children came to Harpo—and to nobody else in the room—wherever he was, automatically. He had some kind of mystical, saintly quality about him apparently." Harpo's appeal to less complicated beings makes sense; like children and dogs, he had an inexhaustible sense of play. In all of his plays and movies, whenever he has to perform some function—frisk someone, steal a document or a painting, play a round of bridge—Harpo embraces the sheer joy of the event, divorced from its purpose in the plot; he could go on forever, or at least until Chico implored him to "cut it out."

His personality onstage and offstage was much different from his brothers'. Groucho was eternally pessimistic; Harpo embraced life—games, painting, parties, music. (According to his son, Bill, his favorite radio show was a kiddie program that gave away birthday presents; when Harpo's wife forgot to send his name in for a birthday present, he sulked for days.) Chico was constitutionally irresponsible and a gambler; Harpo performed for whatever charity came his way, toured Europe, and was a dedicated husband and family man, adopting four children so that he could "have one in each window waiting for me when I came home." Onstage, he provided a welcome buffer from the chattering vocal antics of his two brothers; as film historian Joe Adamson put it, "Sometimes we get tired of hearing Groucho talk, and that's the point where Harpo comes in."

Harpo's copious bag of tricks came out of his battle-tested decades in vaudeville, his own inventiveness, and a good sense of who could create gags for him. A famous bit, where tons of stolen silverware pour out of the sleeve of his overcoat, had been around for years when George S. Kaufman and Morrie Ryskind drafted it into the stage version of *Animal*

Force of nature: Young Julius (top) and Adolph in vaudeville; what's that dog wearing?

Crackers (and added Groucho's "I can't imagine what's taking the coffeepot so long" right before—*boom!*—out comes the coffeepot). But in the draft of the script, there's a combination of carefully crafted bits for Harpo (usually with Chico), alternating with suggestions that Harpo simply do his "card business" or "hand business." Harpo trusted Kaufman and Co. far more than he trusted Buster Keaton. For the dreary 1938 comedy *At the Circus*, Keaton was employed by MGM to write gags for Harpo and concocted two bits, including one involving Harpo, a bunch of helium balloons, and a midget. According to Keaton, "When I acted this out for the Marx Brothers, Groucho asked with a sneer, 'Do you think that's funny?' Harpo and Chico just stared at me with disgust." Harpo knew what worked for him. Harpo could never be bothered with the mundane restrictions of the physical world. He worked with what comedians call "white magic"—an ability to produce or create objects on the whim of his imagination. Groucho tells Harpo that he can't burn a candle at both ends, and Harpo produces a candle burning at both ends. A bum asks Harpo on the street if he can help him out with a cup of coffee, and Harpo pulls one out of his voluminous, ratty overcoat—and the brilliant touch is that the cup is steaming hot. He embraces the joy of literal mindedness; in *A Night in Casablanca*, Harpo leans on the outside of a three-story building. When a cop accosts him and asks, "What you think you're doing, holding the building up?" Harpo nods, enthusiastically. When the cop yanks him away, the audience discovers that he was telling the truth, as the entire structure comes crashing down. Frank Tashlin, the Warner Bros. cartoon director who created that gag, once said:

> Harpo was fey and unbelievable; you could do anything with Harpo. Now I did, to me, what was one of the wildest jokes in the world. He was looking at a mirror and combing his hair and you saw the reflection of his face in the mirror. Now, he turned the mirror around, and now you saw the back of his head. He never moved. Well, it got a scream, but you could only do that with Harpo.

The total control that Harpo exercised over his surreal world becomes most apparent when one compares two versions of essentially the same bit: the mirror sequence, first performed by Harpo and Groucho (and a bit of Chico) in 1933's *Duck Soup*, and a reinterpretation by Harpo with Lucille Ball as his foil on a 1955 episode of *I Love Lucy*. Groucho and Harpo rarely had scenes with just the two of them in the movies because, as Bill Marx said, "Groucho doesn't have any idea what's going on with my dad—he can't figure him out at all." But in *Duck Soup*, both Harpo and Chico decide to impersonate Groucho in order to purloin some documents. With identical nightcaps, nightgowns, mustaches, and cigars, all three brothers look astonishingly alike (although Chico is a bit smaller). Harpo manages to get the documents, but Groucho is in hot pursuit; when Harpo breaks a full-length mirror in his getaway, he is immediately confronted by Groucho and his only salvation is to convince his brother that he is looking at his own reflection (somehow all the broken glass is magically swept away—who knows). Whatever trick Groucho employs to trip up his "reflection," Harpo manages to parry—he can mimic Groucho's funny dances, hat business, whatever. It's only when Chico bumbles into the scene—Harpo vainly tries to shoo him away—that the illusion, like the mirror, is shattered.

Twenty-two years later, Harpo returns to the bit, reuniting with Ball, with whom he

What's-a matter for you? Playing a version of himself onstage in *The Man Who Came to Dinner*; with Chico and Louis Calhern in *Duck Soup* (1933).

made *Room Service* in 1938: "With Lucy, he felt a kindred spirit there and wanted to do something absolutely ridiculous, and what could be more ridiculous than the mirror sequence?" said his son. But like a master painter, Harpo returns to the same subject years later from a different perspective; critics have often written that he reprises the routine, but other than the basic "Is that another person or is it me?" conceit, nothing is the same. Here, Lucy—dressed like Harpo to fool a nearsighted chum—is the impostor. When Harpo tries to catch

her out, Lucy proves extremely adept at countering his challenges, but whereas Groucho merely wondered what was going on, Harpo begins to question his own existence, pinching his cheeks, and so on. He tries out his own signature cross-eyed expression, which he called the "Gookie"—but Lucy can even reproduce that. Convinced that no one can take his identity away from him, Harpo rigs a string inside a dropped hat, pulls it back up, and foils Lucy. An excellent clown, Lucille Ball—but she forgot that Harpo is the master of time, space, gravity, and logic.

Harpo kept up his comic identity for more than half a century. Although age didn't necessarily improve his cherubic features, he seemed inexhaustible, performing well into his seventies (he had just recovered from a heart attack while filming *Lucy* and suffered another one soon after filming). He refused many lucrative offers to break his vow of silence on camera (although he played a stage version of his real-life self in Kaufman and Hart's *The Man Who Came to Dinner* in summer stock). In 1964, he performed on a bill with Allan Sherman, the parodist and a great friend, at the Pasadena Civic Center. During intermission, Harpo informed Sherman that it was going to be his final performance. Sherman, overcome with emotion, announced Harpo's retirement to the audience and brought him onstage to the microphone. No one in the audience—no one in the world—had ever seen or heard anything like it. "Now, as I was about to say in 1907 . . ." he began in his pleasant urban-sounding baritone, and the crowd went mad. Recounted Bill Marx, he gave a long speech and then finished, "And, in conclusion, I am so honored to know that you folks have the keenness and the perspicacity for recognizing monumental genius. I thank you." Harpo walked off and the audience gave him a three-minute ovation.

The rest, as Shakespeare said, is silence.

Party of the Life:
Harpo meets Satchmo; a tall drink (*Horse Feathers*, 1932); Dionysian cover boy, 1937.

Cartoons

The reason, perhaps, why most animated cartoons are funny is because it's in their pedigree; they came right out of the funny papers.

Windsor McCay was one of the most successful and technically brilliant newspaper cartoonists of the early twentieth century. His baroque, inventive *Little Nemo in Slumberland* series galvanized readers across the country as the title hero's adventures sprawled over an entire page in the Sunday morning funnies. Influenced by his son's "flip book," McCay tried his hand at animating Little Nemo for a brief cartoon—it took him four years of painstaking work. After a second attempt, he decided to create a character specifically for the movie screen, a gentle giant named Gertie the Dinosaur, whom McCay unveiled in 1914. It took 10,000 separate drawings, each hand-drawn by McCay on onionskin, to bring Gertie to life in a one-reeler. Audiences didn't know what hit them, but clearly the animated short was going to be an essential part of film vocabulary.

The early days of silent cartoons are filled with as many different experiments as their live-action counterparts. Animators had to find ways to get beyond the sheer novelty of the process and create something amusing and fluid, a particularly difficult chore considering the huge manpower required to churn out cartoons at a time when all the technology was done by hand. Transparent celluloid, or "cels," allowed for a more efficient way of reproducing each frame, and pioneer animators Max and Dave Fleischer invented a process called the Rotoscope in 1916, which projected live-action clowning directly onto a drawing board. Their Koko the Clown character was initially created by having one of the Fleischer brothers act out Koko's antics, while the other rendered the action frame by frame. Many early characters were simply transfers from newspaper strips—Krazy Kat, Mutt and Jeff—but in 1919, an original character appeared, a cat who was easy to draw because he was all black. His name was Felix, and his plucky resourcefulness led critics to compare him with Chaplin (who briefly appeared as an animated character himself in the 1910s). In 1923's

Felix in Hollywood, our hero actually unscrews his own tail and uses it as a cane for a Chaplin imitation. Felix was also the first animated character to be licensed for commercial products.

According to animation historian Leonard Maltin, as the 1920s ended, "more and more artists and cartoonists got the hang of animation and began to explore more and more with each passing year how you could do things in animation you couldn't do in a live action film. They created a whole new language for the animated cartoon which gave those characters abilities even beyond

Charlie Chaplin and Buster Keaton—and that's really saying something." But cartoon animation might have been stopped in its tracks without the invention of sound synchronization in the mid-1920s. There had been some crude "follow-the-bouncing-ball" shorts, which used music, but the industry was revolutionized in 1928 when producer Walt Disney reintroduced a character named Mickey Mouse in a short called *Steamboat Willie*. Mickey's previous two silent adventures had not even been picked up for distribution, but his new short subject had a synchronized sound score (and was delightfully illustrated by Ub Iwerks). Audiences loved it, and Disney built his empire on the little mouse—to whom he always gave credit.

Exaggerated sound fit exaggerated motion

to a tee—and it was just the element that cartoons needed to lift off the ground. Sound also accelerated the need for tempo; now it was even more crucial for a successful cartoon to have the right timing; it was a difficult trick to master. Pioneer animator Chuck Jones said that "animation is the art of timing . . . the difference between a huge laugh and a flop can be one frame." With the success of Walt Disney's short subjects (*Silly Symphonies*), movie studios in Hollywood set up full-time animation divisions (Disney's short cartoons were distributed by RKO); as every feature presentation at the time included several short subjects and cartoons, animation units became crucial moneymakers for the studios. Also, as with the creation of real live movie stars, studios needed to create characters with whom the audience could identify and would welcome back week after week. The creators of cartoons now had to expand their canvas dramatically—and that meant becoming part of the world of drama. As another pioneer, Walter Lantz (*Woody Woodpecker*) put it:

An animator is like an actor before the camera, only he has to act out his feelings and interpret that scene with his pencil; he also has to know how to space characters because the spacing of their movements determines the tempo; he must know expression; he must know feeling; he has to know the character and make him walk with a funny action.

Life as an animator for a studio division was chaotic, intense, frustrating, and often a heck of a lot of fun. Executives—other than Disney—rarely knew how to handle these strange men who drew cartoons, and animators, frequently fed up with one slight or

another, shuttled among the various studios with an alarming frequency; even the most ardent animation fan would have trouble keeping the scorecard straight. Warner Bros. started its own division in 1930 by animating songs from their vast musical catalog with the rip-off title *Looney Tunes* and soon added another series of one-offs called

Merrie Melodies. But these were initially conceived without successful characters; other studios were having better luck drawing their own stable of stars. Fleischer created Betty Boop in 1930 and brought the comic strip hero Popeye to the screen in 1931. Disney added Donald Duck to Mickey's menagerie in 1934, and the cantankerous waterfowl soon outstripped his friend's popularity. Disney outpaced all of his rivals during the Depression years, adding professional voice talent and Technicolor to his car-

toons. In 1937, he offered his competitors the greatest challenge of all: a feature-length adaptation of *Snow White and the Seven Dwarfs*, which used 750 artists who created a quarter of a million drawings at the cost of $1.5 million. It earned six times that amount in its initial release.

Yet for many aficionados, the most exciting animation of the period (and into the 1950s) was to be found at Warner Bros. In the years 1936 to 1937, the studio (which stuck their animators in a remote bungalow they dubbed "Termite Terrace") assembled the all-star team of cartoonists: directors Tex Avery, Chuck Jones, Bob Clampett, and Frank Tashlin, as well as voice professional extraordinaire Mel Blanc and musical director Carl Stalling. Working in deranged concert with each other, they demonstrated that classic comedy animation was a rare combination of design, voice, effect, character, timing, and point of view. Any combination of those would be amusing; to have all six at once, as Warner Bros. often did, was exhilarating. Their stable of two-dimensional celebrities was impressive: Porky Pig, Daffy Duck, Bugs Bunny, and, joining them after World War II, Sylvester and Tweety, Yosemite Sam, Pepé Le Pew, and Wile E. Coyote and the Road Runner. What the animators did with them was even better.

Each director had his own take on the material, and although the differences might be subtle for the average viewer, they were clear to the animators. Tex Avery is widely credited for taking a stock character, Bugs Bunny, and investing him with a definitive character for *A Wild Hare* in 1940. According to his biographer Joe Adamson, "Avery said, 'How about a character who just isn't fazed by anything? He comes up out of his rabbit hole, and he's got a gun in his face, and he

THE PICTURE FROM WHICH THE SONG SENSATION WAS TAKEN!

WALT DISNEY'S

donald duck

der Fuehrer's Face

IN TECHNICOLOR

DISTRIBUTED BY RKO RADIO PICTURES, INC

just chews his carrot and says, "What's up, Doc?"'" Avery was known as a keen gagman who wanted his cartoons to be louder, faster, funnier, and he was the first animator to have his characters talk to the audience.

Chuck Jones, on the other hand, was interested in subtlety and the release of a quiet moment or humorous aside. He saw Bugs Bunny as a cool cookie, a character who only reacted when provoked. The creator of Wile E. Coyote and Road Runner, Jones was a comedy purist and the Stanislavksy of animation, for whom motivation was key: "Daffy has the courage that most of us don't have. He will continue to try and try again where we would have given up, because failure is unknown to him. When Daffy pleaded with the studio head to put him in a serious part, to play the Scarlet Pumpernickel, he actually believed he could play it; it never occurred to him he couldn't. Daffy was one of the great comedians and I was lucky to be associated with him." Tashlin experimented with camera angles, blackouts, pace, and absurdity and

went on to become a highly valued live-action comedy director, working with stars like Bob Hope and Jerry Lewis. When, on his first nonanimated assignment, he created some dueling gags for a Bob Hope period comedy, Tashlin recalled that "It was full of cartoon jokes. I remember Bob saying—they must have told him I came from the cartoon business—things like, 'Jesus Christ, now I'm a rabbit!' "

However innovative the gang at Warner Bros. was, the fact remains that as the 1950s began, short cartoons for the movies were on the wane. The studio system had broken down and executives could no longer insist that exhibitors take two or three cartoons as part of the presentation package. Animation, which was always labor intensive, became more and more expensive to produce; even Disney was cutting back. New animation units were sprouting up, looking for new ways to do things. UPA was created in 1944 and cut costs by simplifying the visual depth of their characters and abstracting backgrounds. They called the process "limited

animation," and their new characters were Gerald McBoing-Boing and Mr. Magoo.

Television soon opened up a whole new market for cartoons; the Faustian bargain was a huge drop in quality and detail. It did little good for animators to wring their hands over the decline of artistry—the small black-and-white rectangular screen mercilessly dictated what looked good and what didn't. William Hanna and Joseph Barbera had burnished their reputation with the Academy Award-winning *Tom and Jerry* series at MGM; when they bailed out of movies to work in television, they were shocked by the meager budgets offered by the networks. To make the numbers work, they created an even more limited animation style, often pixilating only the moving elements of a character: the mouth, the hands (or paws). Beginning in 1958, Hanna-Barbera introduced new characters directly to television, such as Huckleberry Hound, Yogi Bear, and in 1960, created the first half-hour animated comedy series, *The Flintstones*, which was a huge ratings hit.

If you grew up in the 1960s, you had a nearly unlimited supply of cartoons available to you; every weekday afternoon, some local affiliate was repackaging old Bugs Bunny or Popeye cartoons, and every Saturday morning, there were nearly three hours of animated programming on each of the three major networks. Not to mention an entire menagerie of tigers, tunas, and toucans pitching products during the commercials. The quality of these candy-colored entertainments varied enormously, both as art and as literature, but they were omnipresent. Some shows broke out of the pack, such as Jay Ward's various Rocky and Bullwinkle incarnations, which were absurdist, witty indict-

ments of Cold War pieties (although Chuck Jones dismissed their visual crudity as "illustrated radio").

While television often lacked the virtuosity to create first-rate animated comic characters, the medium borrowed an astonishing amount of real-life comedy to prime the pump. *The Flintstones* were Stone Age versions of *The Honeymooners*, and another Hanna-Barbera prime-time show, *Top Cat*, was a feline adaptation of *The Phil Silvers*

Show. The creators of *Amos 'n' Andy* resurfaced after a decadelong absence to create an animated rip-off called *Calvin and the Colonel*. Bargain-basement animated versions of Laurel and Hardy, Abbott and Costello, Laverne and Shirley, Jerry Lewis, the Fonz, the Mask, and the Three Stooges (once as human beings, the second time as robots) made the Saturday morning rounds, but even the best cartoons borrowed from their three-dimensional progenitors—who doesn't recognize a shot of W. C. Fields in Mr. Magoo, a hint of Groucho in Bugs Bunny, a slather of Senator Claghorn in Foghorn Leghorn?

A combination of boredom with the limitations of television animation, computer technology, the freedom of cable networks, and some bright entrepreneurial thinking all helped to, well, reanimate the field at the beginning of the 1990s. Disney found a way to recapture its old feature-length magic by tapping into Broadway-style musicals with *The Little Mermaid* and *The Lion King*, two major blockbusters that spawned countless imitations both at Disney and other, often brand-new, studios. Cartoon Network was added to the cable system in 1992, eventually acquiring the Hanna-Barbera and Warner Bros. catalogs while developing some immensely creative cartoons, such as *Dexter's Laboratory* and *The Powerpuff Girls*. MTV took their freedom in another direction, using crudely conceived animation to deliver such counterculture slackers as *Beavis and Butthead* and *Daria* directly to the Generation X audience. First-rate comic talent was no longer reduced to Saturday morning purgatory; comedians such as Nathan Lane, Robin Williams, Eddie Murphy, Ellen DeGeneres, Billy Crystal, Woody Allen, Tim Allen, Mike Myers, Roseanne Barr, and Jerry Seinfeld gleefully leaped on the voice-over bandwagon, providing signature personalities of such dimension in animated cartoons that they were often billed above the

title for a film in which they never actually appeared. In 1997, *The Simpsons* beat *The Flintstones'* record for most consecutive prime-time cartoon episodes, and they keep on ticking. . . .

In the twenty-first century, animation has transformed, as *Aladdin*'s cartoon couple would put it, into a whole new world. Cartoons are more popular than ever, and they reach Americans in more ways, in more forms, with more resonance than ever before. It's a medium that achieves hair-raising technical brilliance on one level—say, *Shrek*—while making countless viewers giggle uncontrollably with products that could be just as easily created with construction paper and school paste—say, *South Park*. Cartoons now exist in a wide, tense universe bracketed by alpha and omega, and it makes some purists wistful for the glory days. As Leonard Maltin put it, "Television has reinvigorated animation, has created a new audience for animation, but sadly, has forgotten the history of animation. Modern cartoons couldn't exist without those [classic] cartoons, and yet they don't have the heart or originality or the organic humor of those cartoons." Cartoons remain a comic medium; no matter how detailed a computer can pixilate the green fuzz on an ogre's nose, it all begins with an artist brandishing a sharp gag and a sharp pencil.

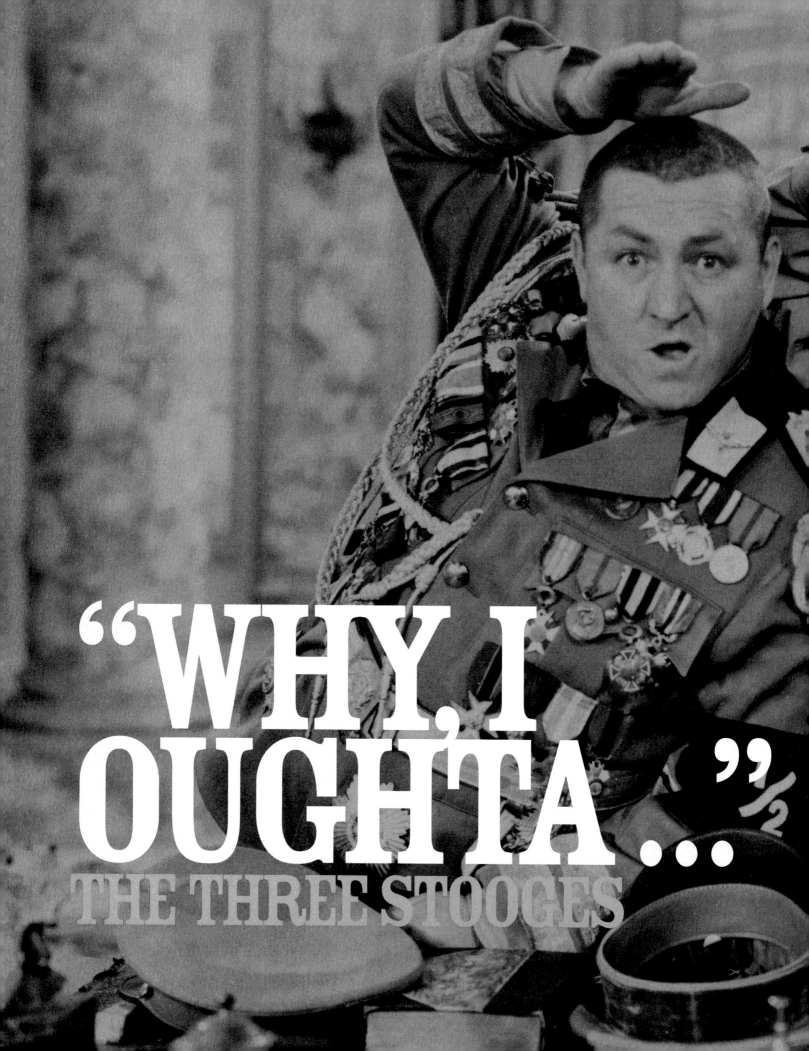

"WHY, I OUGHTA ..."
THE THREE STOOGES

It's going to be tough to give you a definition of a stooge in decent language, but here's a go. A stooge is a guy who never has a light for a cigarette he is trying to borrow. A stooge always comes in handy when you feel like throwing something at somebody. Whenever I'm in doubt or feel mixed up, I always hit the nearest stooge. But my stooges ought to get along fine in Hollywood. They have lots of company. —Ted Healy

MOE: Is that a musical saw?
CURLY: Soitenly! It plays "I Hear a Ripsody."

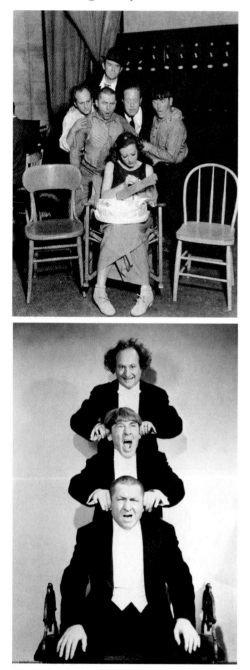

Clucks of a feather:
Larry, Curly, and Moe with Stooge founder, Ted Healy, director Robert Z. Leonard, and Joan Crawford on the set of *Dancing Lady* (1933); all dressed up.
Far right: Spoofing the Third Reich in *You Natzy Spy!* (1940); boys will be girls, *Nutty But Nice* (1940).

In 1934, when Ted Healy imparted his linguistic wisdom to *Movie Classic Magazine*, he was America's expert on stooges. Healy had been at the center of a vaudeville act that had been popular since 1922 called Ted Healy and His Stooges: a natty dresser with a brash charm, Healy has been superseded over time by the patsies and sidemen he always hit whenever he was in doubt, a conglomeration of various knuckleheads who would become legendary as The Three Stooges.

The eldest Stooge, Moe Howard, was born Moses Horwitz in Brooklyn in 1897, and he knocked around film studios, vaudeville, and even the Yiddish theater before playing second banana to Healy. Soon, Moe's younger brother Samuel, or Shemp, joined the act, as did a talented violinist named Larry Feinberg. Healy's antics with the Stooges made them very successful on the vaudeville circuit, and that led to motion pictures. A 1930 film called *Soup to Nuts* featured the Stooges as little more than comedic wallpaper, but they were far more appealing than Healy. The Stooges chafed under Healy's leadership; he was an alcoholic and they were little more than indentured servants, paid out of Healy's wages without a studio contract of their own. Shemp bolted from the act in 1932, only to be replaced by the youngest Howard brother, Jerome, who, in order to find some madcap identity, shaved his full head of hair and took on the moniker of Curly. After backing up Healy in some MGM features, Moe realized that the Stooges were going nowhere fast; they refused to renew their contract with Healy and went over to bargain-basement Columbia Studios in 1934 to start their own independent career.

Most comics would have been appalled to wind up at Columbia after the tonier studio halls of MGM, but the rough-and-ready studio was a perfect fit for the Stooges. Studio chief Harry Cohn enjoyed their knockabout humor and immediately assigned them to Jules White, who was head of Columbia's short subjects division; Columbia and the Stooges would enjoy a relationship that lasted for almost twenty-five years and two hundred pictures. White's job was to churn out dozens of shorts a year with the Stooges, so he hit upon a simple identity for their slapstick comedy: "I patterned the characters—the Stooges in particular—as living caricatures. . . . They weren't for real, so you couldn't take things seriously, like the eye-poking or the hand-slapping bits."

If White saw the Stooges as human cartoons, that was fine—the Columbia short subject unit was the perfect factory for them. Other comic teams, like the Marx Brothers in particular, always desired to do their comedy their own way, far from the restrictive formulas of the studio, but the Stooges blossomed under the Columbia assembly line. First of all, their humor could not have sustained a full-length feature (as their awkward color attempts in the late 1950s prove); eighteen minutes of them every other month, sandwiched between a couple of cartoons and a B-feature, suited audiences just fine.

Depending on which director from the Columbia stable worked with the Stooges, the violent mayhem quotient would rise or fall, but the major breakthrough for them was their use of sound. The emergence of sound in physical film comedy often made some gags uncomfortable, but the Stooges went in the opposite direction and ramped up their sound effects to accompany the myriad pie fights, eye pokes, mallet bashings, and nose twistings in their comedy. Sound editor Joe Henrie supervised the dubbing of their antics. White recalled that he and Henrie would "try to copy [the cartoons] as best we could. Cartoons had the greatest sound effects for many years. Anything in Columbia's sound library was available to us. I sat there day and night with the mixers while we put in the effects we wanted and got them just right." The pluck of a ukulele string when a strand of Larry's hair was pulled; the clang of a bell when someone was shot in the ass; the bass drumbeat that accompanied a sock in Curly's stomach; the bird twitter that signified a concussion—it was this silly symphony that made the Stooges' infantile violence palatable and popular. Even when the Stooges made one of their many popular live appearances over the years, there was a sound effects man in the wings.

Life as a Stooge was not easy. Moe was their ringleader on camera and off, supervising their contracts (which were never very lucrative), but the Stooges rarely showed much more than a passing interest in their scripts or productions, partly because they trusted the Columbia unit, partly because, at eight short subjects a year, they were just too darn busy. Even the fun part of being a Stooge had its occupational hazards. Larry Fine recalled: "Sometimes we would run out of pies, so the prop man would sweep up the pie goop off of the floor, complete with nails, splinters, and tacks. Another problem was pretending you didn't know a pie was coming your way. To solve this, Jules would tell me, 'Now, Larry, Moe's going to smack you with a pie on the count of three.' Then Jules would tell Moe, 'Hit Larry on the count of *two*!' So, I never got to three. . . ."

The Stooges could occasionally be quite brazen about their own Jewish background. They would frequently sprinkle their films with Yiddishisms, and comedian Robert Klein observed that "there is a direct link between the Three Stooges and Ellis Island—their shorts are completely awash in immigrant rhythms." In 1940, inspired perhaps by the resemblance of Moe's haircut to that of a certain fascist dictator, the Stooges became the first comedy team to parody Hitler and the Nazis in *You Natzy Spy!*, and they frequently bashed the Third Reich throughout the war. When the war was over, however, the Stooges faced their first major setback; the jovial nutcase Curly suffered a stroke in 1946 and retired from the team. He was replaced by Shemp, joining his brother Moe for the first time in years, but many fans felt the Stooges had lost their most gifted clown. Still, they clambered on for another six dozen short films and two more replacements, once Shemp suffered a heart attack in 1955.

Columbia was not quite through with them; they sold seventy-eight of their two-reelers to television syndication in 1958 and a whole new generation of kids grew up watching the Stooges after school. Although the Stooges were old men, and looked it, they kept making movies, cartoon, and stage appearances well into the 1960s. Stephen Cox remarks that "the Stooges mellowed when they knew their audience was kiddies. They had to tame their comedy because kids started emulating them and parents became furious." The fact that those same parents probably laughed themselves silly in the movie theater when *they* were kiddies is one of the ironies that attends the Stooges. People either think they're geniuses or an insidious form of torture—Lucille Ball, who had a tiny part in their 1934 *Three Little Pigskins*, said, "The only thing I learned from them was how to duck"—but Robert Klein gives them the benefit of the doubt: "A lot of people may not like them, and there are probably a lot of fractured skulls of children around the country because of them, but the Stooges have been around for eighty-five years and still going strong."

We subtly, the three of us, always went into an arena of life which we were not supposed to understand. If we were going into society, the picture would open with us as garbage collectors. We would take a man with a high hat, a monocle, and spats and bash him in the nose with a pie, thus bringing him down to our level. We did stupid things, but they were excusable because we didn't know any better.
—Moe Howard

"AND THEY CALL *ME* SUPERMAN!"

LUCILLE BALL

I am not funny. My writers were funny. My direction was funny. The situations were funny. But I am not funny. *I am not funny*. What I am is brave . . . –Lucille Ball

Lucy was a really brave comic because she always played the asshole—the person that has to be brought down—and that takes a level of skill that a lot of people don't have. Maybe, like, four people can do that. To make you like 'em still.

—Roseanne Barr

Among Lucille Ball's other considerable attributes, in addition to bravery, was ambition. Starstruck from a young age, Ball, born in 1911, dreamed of moving out of her upstate New York blue-collar dullsville town and making it big on Broadway. She moved to the city by 1928, and her early days were full of the pluck-and-luck clichés generated by the play *Stage Door* (Ball would eventually play a small role in the film version); she was an advertising and clothing model who was magically signed up in 1933 to be a Goldwyn Girl and shipped out to the West Coast. Ball's ambition brought her far—out of the ranks of the chorus, where she became a featured player for Hollywood's less grand studios—but not far enough. By her own estimation, she was "Queen of the B-pluses. I went from one-liners to these sorts of mediocre B-plus pictures. I would do anything."

There were small compensations. She had met a fiery young Cuban conga-drum player named Desi Arnaz on a picture together called *Too Many Girls* and married him in 1940. She had been befriended by two comedy veterans, Buster Keaton and director Eddie Sedgewick, who saw in Ball a potential comedienne of great scope, and they coached her and promoted her work. She landed the lead in a sitcom called *My Favorite Wife* during the waning days of radio, which allowed her to play a scatterbrained housewife. One contemporary review of a broadcast wrote that it was "too bad that Lucille Ball's funny grimaces and gestures aren't visible on the radio." Ball's two great passions in life were showbiz and her often errant husband; perhaps she could channel her ambition to bring the two together on a program for the new medium of television. It wasn't glamorous and it wasn't the movies, but it was a spotlight of some kind.

Ball, Arnaz (who had a fine business sense when he could concentrate), and producer Jess Oppenheim pitched a sitcom to CBS. There were many initial misgivings and false starts, but in October of 1951, *I Love Lucy* made its national debut. Although most viewers were hardly aware of it, the show displayed some important innovations. Since nationwide television transmission was a fragile thing, and since the Arnazes wanted to stay in Hollywood, they decided to put the series on film, shot by three cameras, in front of a live audience. According to producer-writer Garry Marshall, "Lucy said, 'I can be funny and fall down on television,' and Desi Arnaz said, 'If you want it to be funny physically, you can't do it more than once. Have three cameras—then the comedian can do the stunt once and you can record it from all angles and then it can be funny.' " Desi and Lucy, who had combined their names and fortunes into a studio called Desilu, also negotiated a deal with CBS to own the rights to all of the filmed episodes.

The premise of the show, centered around Ricky and Lucy Ricardo, was, as articulated by Oppenheim in an office memo, simple: "He is a Latin-American band-leader and singer. She is his wife. They are happily married and very much in love. The only bone of contention between them is her desire to get into show business, and his equally strong desire to keep her out of it." There was nothing Lucy Ricardo wouldn't do to have her way; likewise, there was nothing Lucille Ball wouldn't do to make an audience laugh. With no real training on Broadway or even in vaudeville, Ball taught herself to be a comedian through sheer determination. "Anything you wanted to do with Lucy she could do," recalled one of her directors, Herbert Kenwith. "She was very daring." Another director, Jay Sandrich, recounted that "One time she had to make pizza so we took her to a restaurant, and she'd go there every day or every night after rehearsal learning how to toss pizza. She had to know exactly what she was doing and break it down bit by bit so she could do it for the audience." Keaton continued to advise her, reminding her to take her comedy seriously and to get to know her props and treat them like treasures.

It was all good advice and the proof was in the ratings; *I Love Lucy* became one of the infant medium's first phenomena. Lucy Ricardo's weekly scrapes were eagerly eaten up by audiences across the country (perhaps because they were so beautifully captured on film and not on kinescope). *Time* magazine, in a cover profile on Lucy, put it very well:

> This is the sort of cheerful rowdiness that has been rare since the days of the silent movies' Keystone comedies. Lucille submits enthusiastically to being hit by pies; falls over furniture; gets locked in home freezers; is chased by knife-wielding fanatics. Tricked out as a ballerina or a Hindu maharani or a toothless hillbilly, she takes her assorted lumps and pratfalls with unflagging zest and good humor.

Part of her appeal was her beauty. It was rare for any clown to be so elegant in one scene and so gloriously spastic in another; for a female clown, it was nearly unprecedented. Joan Rivers points out, "Lucy knew you can't be accepted in comedy as a pretty woman, and she made the pretty woman funny-looking. I think she had the courage because she knew basically she was pretty—'Black out all my teeth, because I know when I go home at night I'm still gonna be a cutie-pie.' " Her physical anarchism was amusing enough on its own terms, but as a housewife in the 1950s, it was revolutionary. "Even though she was the well-meaning wife, she was rebellious," said Lily Tomlin. "She was always out trying to create her own situation, her own freedom, and that appealed to me."

RICKY: Lucy, this is the craziest stunt you've pulled in fifteen years!

SUPERMAN (George Reeves): Ricky, do you mean to say you've been married to her for fifteen years?

RICKY: Das right, fifteen years!

SUPERMAN: And they call *me* Superman!

I Love Lucy gave Ball the immense popularity she always craved, and even though she had to sacrifice her early dreams of glamour to get there, it was worth it. As she said herself:

> She's an exaggeration of thousands of housewives. She has always done things I feel other ladies would like to do with their husbands, their children, and their bosses. She goes the limit but is always believable. She's bigger than life, but just enough to make all her wild schemes seem perfectly understandable. While I was making pictures, I always had the feeling that I was waiting for something. I never found a place of my own and I never became truly confident until—in the Lucy character—I began creating something that was really mine. The potential was there. Lucy Ricardo released it.

Seeing redhead:
(far left): TV's most popular mom-to-be; (above) taking the plunge with mentor Buster Keaton; Queen of the B-pluses.

But there came a point when she had to release Lucy Ricardo. Her marriage with Arnaz—always a tempestuous and tenuous thing—was falling apart, and for a while, they could at least enjoy their presence together on the set. The day after shooting the last episode of the series (actually, the hour-long comedy specials that evolved from *I Love Lucy*), in April of 1960, Ball filed for divorce. There had been nearly two hundred episodes featuring the loving Ricardos until the off-camera reality set in.

In the next two years, she bounced back in her own series, *The Lucy Show*, with her old partner in crime Vivian Vance as her foil, and it, too, shot up in the ratings. Now, nearly fifty, she was still rolling up her sleeves to reveal her inner clown. Garry Marshall, who wrote for the new series, recalled one day on the set:

> With Lucy you started with the last scene: how can Lucy be funny? So, in this set piece, she came rolling in in a beautiful gown with roller skates because—there was some reason—she had the skates on. And the director had her roll in and two waiters were carrying a table, and as she was coming out, they lifted the table; she'd go right under the table—that was part of the entrance. And during rehearsal, the waiters carrying the table weren't sure what to do, and she came and she hit her head right on the table. Knocked down, and it was a mess. I remember saying to my writing partner, "I think we just killed Lucy. That'll be our reputation for the rest of our careers." But they helped her up and we went over and said, "We're so sorry! What stupid guys! What a dumb joke we wrote, that was no good." She said, "No, no, it was my fault; I mistimed it. You just keep writing 'em, I'll do 'em, don't worry. This is what we do here."

If she was tough on the set, she had to be even tougher off it. By the mid-1960s, she had bought out Desi's controlling interest of the Desilu studio and found herself to be not only the first female studio executive ever but an executive of a studio worth tens of millions of dollars. She befriended another loose-limbed comedienne, the young Carol Burnett, and confided in her the trouble and the tension of that kind of responsibility: "She said, 'I had a big talk with myself. And I knew that I could do it because I learned a lot from Desi. So, I went back and I became tough, you know. A guy can be tough but the woman being tough was a different thing then.' She said, 'But then, kid, that's when they put the S on the end of my last name.'"

Seeking double:
With kindred spirit, Harpo; braver than a speeding pratfall.

Lucy's last two decades were not pleasant (she died in 1989), mostly because she desperately wanted to keep working and it was difficult for audiences to take their beloved Lucy cavorting around in harmful situations when she was obviously a grandma. Her immense capacity for disguise had been thwarted by age. But throughout the monochromatic decade of the 1950s, she had pulled off one of the great deceptions of television comedy, that of a beautiful woman who was one of the most powerful figures in show business pretending to be a beautiful woman who often disguised herself in the most outrageous ways simply to sneak onto the fringes of show business. A tricky balancing act, but Lucille Ball's talents were forged out of an inner reserve of will power; for her to share her magic would require an awful lot of 'splainin'.

"THE PLAYBOY AND THE MONKEY"

JERRY LEWIS

HERBERT: "To whom it may concern: This is to introduce Herbert H. Heebert, a very bright, intelligent and smart and cute young man who is quite witty and kind and honest and works like a son of a gun—if he gets paid. He is willing and able and a swell kid and he does all the things that are expected of him besides he's also very smart and works like a son of a gun and he will do all he can to help, he has only the respect that's of the highest and he's cuter than anyone and smart as a whip besides being quite bright he can be considered a swell chap and works like a son of a gun."

KATIE: When did you write that reference?

HERBERT: Last night. I didn't have any so I figured I'd make one.

Appearances to the contrary notwithstanding, Jerry Lewis was always very smart and worked like a son of a gun. When he and his partner Dean Martin were making their first film, *My Friend Irma*, in 1949, Lewis was often missing in action when he was called to the set. He wasn't in his dressing room taking a nap, or on the golf links—as Martin longed to be—he was already *on* the set. It's just that he was hanging out with the crew. As Lewis told an interviewer in 2000:

> I had to learn everything. The guys in the camera department taught me to load a BNC camera, which was the biggest thrill of my life. . . . See, the thing that Dean depended on me for was "why do we do that again?" Our comic rhythm and timing was perfect, and now we hear a soundman say, we're going to have to do it again. And because of my voracious curiosity, I'd say to the soundman, "Why do

you need it again?" And he would say, "Well, we lost that line when Dean turns around." I said, "But the entire spontaneity of this scene—you want to throw that away to correct an upstage line that probably won't be used? We can cut that."

Lewis's knack for gizmos and technology launched his comedy career. Born Joseph Levitch in Newark in 1926, he grew up in a showbiz family. His father was a small-time borscht belt regular, a singer and comedian, who displayed little or no ambition; "He was so satisfied that it used to aggravate me," said Lewis. A class clown who was thrown out of high school for punching an anti-Semitic teacher, Lewis developed his own mechanical act—low-grade, but mechanical nonetheless—doing funny faces and pantomime shtick to someone else's prerecorded 78 rpm LP. It wasn't exactly Noël Coward, but it got him jobs throughout his teens in the Catskills and other low-rent nightclubs.

In July of 1946, Lewis found himself stranded in an Atlantic City joint called the 500 Club, when one of the singers on the bill quit. He remembered a guy whom he had run into on several occasions and with whom he even riffed once or twice. The crooner's name was Dean Martin, and Lewis had first met him in a hotel coffee shop:

> I was sitting at the counter having a very loose egg salad sandwich, and I bite the sandwich and most of the egg salad is now on my shirt and tie. And I look around and there's this handsome guy sitting there, hysterical. And I laughed because he laughed, and I looked down. He said, "Lick it." So I looked at the tie, I licked it, what else do you want? And I knew, the moment I looked at him, I knew I had found that big brother.

Martin joined Lewis on the bill for the first show, singing three songs, followed by Lewis miming three records—and they were a total bomb. The club owner threatened to bump them both off and chuck them in the ocean unless they came up with some real laughs for the second show. Lewis quickly scribbled some bits on a sandwich wrapper, and he and Martin just let loose for the second show. Lewis pretended to be a busboy, then his own brother, clowning with the band, with the audience, while Martin lobbed back every surprise ball that Lewis threw his way. "Dean was impeccable," recalled Lewis. "His natural sense of time was like nothing I'd ever seen in my life. He almost knew where I was going when I started. He almost knew when to pull back and when to go get me."

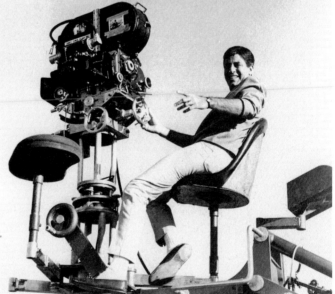

Anything for a laugh:
Young Joseph Levitch (left); with Dean; kissing and breaking up; finally in control.

Word-of-mouth caught on like wildfire and the duo zoomed ahead to become the most popular nightclub act of the postwar years, playing the country's best nightspots like the Copacabana and Slapsie Maxie's. Dick Van Dyke recalls seeing them: "There was never a better act like it. Something, the combination of those two guys, I don't know what it was, but it had class and it had pace. They bounced off of each other. You couldn't take your eyes off them." Beginning in 1949, the duo made sixteen feature-length films for Paramount—"automatic money," according to Lewis collaborator Bill Richmond—and hosted *The Colgate Comedy Hour* on television for five years. Radio was their only flop—critics said they had to be seen to be believed—and Lewis concurred: "We were so physical, and because it was the handsome man and the monkey." Lewis knew what made the act work: "I once overheard a woman in the audience saying

Chaplinesque:
Martin and Lewis; as director, writer, and star—
The Bellboy (1960).

how nice that boy looked—she was actually talking about me, not Dean. Right away, I got a crew cut haircut that made me look like a monkey."

By the mid-1950s, Lewis was successful beyond his wildest dreams—"I had fourteen [luxury] cars sitting in my driveway"—but the friction between him and his easygoing costar began to cause them both considerable strain, exacerbated by Martin's resistance to being a second banana and Lewis's ongoing serious ambitions. According to Bill Richmond: "The breakup was so obvious to anybody who really followed their career and knew about them. They couldn't possibly last, because in the first place, Dean was, like, 'We're making all the money in the world. Just relax, take the money and have a good time.' And Dean remarked that the worst thing that ever happened to Jerry was he read Charlie Chaplin's biography." The partnership came to an end exactly a decade after it began, this time onstage at the Copacabana. Martin went his way to become a pop music star and actor, while Lewis eventually signed the most lucrative contract ever offered to a performer as of 1959: $10 million up-front and 60 percent of net profits for a series of Paramount comedies.

The next stage of Lewis's career was a logical extension of his desire to control the effectiveness of his comedy. "Doing more than one thing is not that difficult if you want to protect something," he said. "And you have to learn all those other filmmaking chores if you want to protect your script." Lewis had already developed a good working relationship with Frank Tashlin, who directed and cowrote one of the bolder Martin and Lewis features, *Artists and Models*, in 1955. "Frank's reputation was wonderful for us, because he was a cartoonist turned director, and [producer Hal] Wallis was wise enough to know that Dean and I were cartoon characters on emulsion," said Lewis, and indeed, Tashlin contributed some first-rate physical comedy and surreal sight gags for Lewis's character. Tashlin's third film with Lewis under his new solo contract was *Cinderfella*, a distaff version of the fairy tale, which Paramount wanted to release in the summer of 1960, as all of Lewis's summertime releases did well with kids in particular. Lewis thought *Cinderfella* was better Christmastime fare, so he decided to produce, write, direct, and star in his own quickie slapstick farce in order to get something in the theaters by July. The film, written in eight days, was called *The Bellboy* and was filmed in Miami during the three weeks that Lewis was performing two shows a night at the Fontainebleau Hotel.

In many ways, *The Bellboy*—a plotless comedy about a silent bellboy named Stanley and his various antics—is the most successful home movie ever made (Lewis had actually made a number of extended home movies with plots and guest stars on 16mm film). Lewis strung together a series of blackout gags and displayed a real mastery of space and timing behind the camera; he was aided by his own invention, a monitor that allowed him to watch his own on-screen action, called the video assist, still in use on film sets everywhere. He made several allusions to the surreal world of silent comedy (his character, named Stanley, doesn't speak until the very end of the movie), referred to Stan Laurel on-screen, and even had the silent film veteran give advice on the screenplay: "I worshipped [Laurel's] knowledge of comedy, so I did everything he said. Naturally, I think the film is better because of it." *The Bellboy* went on to gross more than fifty times its original investment and provided liftoff to Lewis's career as a director.

His next effort, *The Ladies Man*, was even more ambitious. Lewis plays an infantile (surprise) but earnest young man named Herbert Heebert who gets a job as the caretaker in an immense mansion that serves as a boardinghouse for young women. Lewis combined two soundstages to construct the three-story mansion and ripped open the fourth wall, so that his camera (and the audience) could move fluidly from room to room. It was an audacious move, allowing Lewis to show off his mastery of camera movement. The setup, however, disappears or evaporates whenever something else surreal or just plain funny strikes Lewis's fancy; as cowriter Bill Richmond put it, "There were a lot of logic questions going on there, but Jerry often used this line: 'If people are concerned about that then we're making the wrong movie.'" It was the right movie for Paramount, which went on to produce seven more of Lewis's films: "If Jerry Lewis wanted to burn down the studio, I'd give him the match," said one executive.

Defying gravity:
The Ladies Man; early publicity shot.

Lewis starred in, directed, or wrote eighteen pictures in the 1960s. He may have earned money, but he was squandering some of his respect. Writer Hal Kanter observed that "He got to the point where he decided he could do everything—that he was the new Chaplin. He didn't realize that when Chaplin did it all himself, he took months and months to do a picture. Jerry wanted to do it quickly, quickly, quickly, quickly, fast, fast, get it done." His movies, which are an extreme matter of taste, may have worn out his audience. Steve Martin, who counts himself a Jerry Lewis fan, said, "Careers are really film clips when they're all said and done. Fred Astaire has the greatest collection of film clips in the world, but you don't necessarily want to sit through the whole movie. And Jerry Lewis is a guy who has great, great film clips."

If Keaton and Chaplin were minimalists, Lewis was a maximalist; he wouldn't mug three times when six times would do. Friend and foe alike agree that there was nothing he wouldn't do for a laugh. That often meant he would switch styles at an alarming rate, or stop playing by the rules if they no longer suited him. His work was better in the short haul than in an extended narrative, but his connection with an audience was elemental. Richmond observes that "His greatest talent is that he's international—he was a total variety act. Joe Blow off the street could go see him and just laugh his head off. Jerry was totally physical; in his words, he was a dumb act."

Lewis always thought of himself as schizophrenic; he could easily describe himself as torn between what he called "Serious Jerry" and "Idiot Jerry." When it comes to his film career, he says, "I'm a dichotomy; I love progress and I hate change." But when it comes to his comedy, he takes his idiocy very seriously:

> I have a philosophy that I dealt with that was very, very important. [I'd tell my crew] Let me make my own mistakes. Let me score and don't get in the way of my taking the bow. If I go on my ass I'd like you to hang around then, too. . . . What I got from my dad was, if you're going to go out on the stage, sweat. Don't go out there unless you're going to sweat. And in everything that I've ever done, the hands-on [control] was to protect, defend, and live or die with the outcome.

"FRED ASTAIRE ON ACID"

JIM CARREY

When Jim Carrey was growing up in Ontario, he'd act out his favorite cartoons in the living room, little knowing that one day he'd become a cartoon himself—and transform himself into a multimillionaire.

> Mr. Carrey is a barbed original: a golem of grotesque comic energy who obsessively presses his foot to the emotional floorboard. His characters are aggressively manic—leaping, spinning, thrashing, thrusting and mugging through nut-ball riffs, swallowing the world.
>
> *–The New York Times, 1998*

Man of a thousand faces:
The Mask (previous); Fire Marshal Bill; Ace Ventura; as Andy Kaufman; and just plain Jim, on *The Tonight Show*.

There was a point in Carrey's adolescence when a $20 million paycheck would have seemed even more ridiculous than the animated antics of Daffy Duck or Bullwinkle. Carrey was born in 1962 in a small Canadian town, the son of a frustrated saxophonist and his hypochondriacal wife. When Carrey's father lost his clerk's job, the family spiraled into a near-Dickensian existence; to make ends meet, Carrey's family—parents and kids—worked the sanitation night shift in a local factory. Soon the family packed up and lived out of a van; for months, they were parked in the backyard of an older sister's house. Years later in a stand-up routine, Carrey joked about his life as a teenager: "I know a lot about the poor, because we were homeless for a long time. It was in Canada, so I thought we'd just gone camping."

This was a grim punch line for a kid who had become popular in the third grade for imitating all Three Stooges in a school assembly. Before his family's descent, Carrey loved watching Jerry Lewis and Dick Van Dyke and was so adept at impressions that he sent his résumé to Carol Burnett at the age of ten. "While the neighborhood kids were all playing in the field," Carrey said, "I'd be in my room getting Johnny Mathis down." When he was in his late teens, his family became stable enough for him to forage on his own, and he hit the various stand-up clubs in Toronto, honing his impressions, before finally striking out for Los Angeles. "Jim had this loose body and this plastic face, but when a comedian just sticks primarily with impressions, most of them hit a wall. He hit a wall and then he went back to Toronto, and he was kind of discouraged," said manager George Shapiro.

After watching fellow Canadian Rich Little do a devastating imitation of Cary Grant while Grant was in the audience, Carrey had an epiphany: "At that moment, I realized that . . . the best I could ever hope for was to go onstage with someone I impersonated, and do him. I thought, God, I want to be the guy being impersonated, not some pilot fish living off whatever star is hot." When he returned to Los Angeles in the early 1980s, he cast about, trying to find an original voice. Director Judd Apatow remembers: "When I met Carrey, he had no act. So he would go onstage with nothing and improvise for twenty minutes. And it was truly the funniest live experience that I ever had, because half of it would kill and half of it would bomb as bad as anything you've ever seen. He would lose them as much as you can ever lose an audience, then somehow he'd climb out." Carrey worked best when he tapped into his unique loose-limbed body; he'd pretend to be Cockroach Boy, squirming on his back as a roach eluding a vacuum cleaner, or he'd give his penis a life of its own, allowing it to drag him across the room to meet a girl, as he cantilevered his torso parallel to the ground:

"Hi! My penis and I would like to meet you."

Carrey was briefly delivered from stand-up purgatory by a role in a 1984 sitcom called *The Duck Factory*, but it tanked, leaving him to alternate between comedy clubs and some interesting film cameos. In 1990, he was cast as the sole "white guy" in Keenen Ivory Wayans's groundbreaking satire variety show, *In Living Color*. Fellow cast member Tommy Davidson was blown away: "His physical gifts alone will overwhelm you. He's so in touch with what he's gonna do, he's like a grown-up toddler—there's no in-between. He can get there and he can get there fast." Carrey elaborated his repertoire of impressions while also creating new characters on the weekly series, such as Fire Marshal Bill, a deranged safety inspector who should be trusted by no one. Comedian and actor Bill Irwin remarked that

"What Carrey used to do when he was on the Wayans brothers' show looked like film tricks, like 'somebody's doing something with the image there'—but it would just be him."

After actor Rick Moranis turned down the lead in an adolescent comedy, *Ace Ventura, Pet Detective*, Carrey nabbed his chance for big screen recognition. His cocky, eccentric hero was a hit with audiences, and the 1994 film made him a star, earning nearly ten times its original budget. It proved to be an amazing time for Carrey, who released two more films that year and leapfrogged directly into superstardom. *The Mask* was a strange property; based on an independent comic book, it was the tale of a small-time loser who becomes a fantastical maniac by donning a mask with strange powers. *Ace Ventura* hadn't opened by the time Carrey was signed to play Stanley Ipkiss and his alter ego, the Mask, so the casting was considered to be a risk—Carrey soon taught the filmmakers a new meaning of the word *risk*.

The Mask character, untrammeled by time and space, allowed Carrey to exploit his inner cartoon. The creators of the film were inspired by the aggressive, explosive cartoons of Tex Avery from the mid-1940s and sought a new way to bridge live action with a new sophistication for animation. The 1988 film *Who Framed Roger Rabbit?* had also exploited the relationships between reality and cartoons, but *The Mask* wanted to take it to the next level—3-D animation—and hired Industrial Light and Magic to create the Mask's surreal farragoes. It was the dawn of the digital age of computer animation, and the film's creative staff had found the perfect Columbus in Jim Carrey. In transforming himself into the Mask's physicalized imaginings—eyes shooting out of their sockets, tongue rolling out of his mouth like a carpet, even homages to the Tasmanian Devil and an Avery character called The Wolf—Carrey met the animators more than halfway. "I had never seen anyone who could move that way," said Russell. "Jim gave the animators less work to do—we scrapped some optical effects because Jim was already stretching like a cartoon." The animation staff was amazed that Carrey had cartoon rhythms in his body—like ratcheting himself backward before zooming forward. Carrey even got to slip in some of his best impressions: Clint Eastwood, Elvis Presley, Sally Field. Carrey himself referred to his character as "Fred Astaire on acid."

By the time Carrey had signed for his final 1994 movie, *Dumb and Dumber*, his salary had shot up more than ten times to $7 million. It seemed worth it; five of his first six major films made over a hundred million dollars in their initial releases, and Carrey became the first comedian to command a $20 million salary for *The Cable Guy* in 1996. Having attained superstardom, Carrey developed the "Patch Adams syndrome"—a tendency to stretch himself as an actor by picking serious and often sentimental film roles. But he threw himself headfirst into the world of comic eccentricity by playing Andy Kaufman in the unsuccessful biopic *The Man in the Moon*, and in the year 2000, he displayed more of his rubbery charm by impersonating yet another green-skinned cartoon character, the Grinch. Bill Irwin, who also acted in *The Grinch*, said, "Carrey does this thing of having a heart attack and then he stops and sort of comments on it. There's a lot of bringing the audience in. That's one of Jim Carrey's things, like wild, physical abandon and then close into the camera: 'You see what I'm doing here?' If you overuse it, it sometimes gets predictable but, with Jim—oh, my God."

Carrey achieved a new level of modern slapstick by throwing himself around the room, but he was also a throwback to another generation—perhaps two—the comedians who relied not on the effects manipulated by a computer but on the elastic talents that God gave them.

I'm happy to see somebody doing the kind of broad things that Jim Carrey is doing, simply because it seemed to be going away. Disappearing. He would have been a big star in the twenties, in silents. He really has that ability, he's that brilliant.
—Dick Van Dyke

CHAPTER TWO

SOCK IT TO ME?

SATIRE AND PARODY

An ad that's bad
Will end up spoofed in *MAD*!
–"My Fair Ad-Man," *MAD Magazine*, 1957

THE BIG(GER) PICTURE

The White House Correspondents Dinner has been an annual institution since 1920, giving both the president and the press corps a chance to drop their boxing gloves for one evening and trade them in for tuxedos. It has always been a tradition to invite a comedian to roast the incumbent and for everyone to engage in some good-natured topical satire. In 2007, the guest host was impressionist Rich Little, a good-natured comedian who had been in the business for more than four decades. "I want to tell you that I'm not a political satirist," Little told the crowd up-front. "I'm just a nightclub entertainer who has come up here to tell some dumb, stupid jokes."

Little had a tough act to follow. The year before, the speaker was Stephen Colbert. Colbert is a comic actor who takes on the persona of an intolerant, blinkered, right-wing television correspondent. Having graduated from success on *The Daily Show*, he had been given his own phony news show on Comedy Central, *The Colbert Report*. His act is a subtle blurring of reportage and satire, a kind of comic *truthiness*, a term he coined on his first show. Not everyone gets his jokes:

> Ladies and gentlemen of the press corps, Madame First Lady, Mr. President, my name is Stephen Colbert, and tonight it's my privilege to celebrate this president. We're not so different, he and I. We get it. We're not brainiacs on the nerd patrol. . . . So don't pay attention to the approval ratings that say 68 percent of Americans disapprove of the job this man is doing. I ask you this, does that not also logically mean that 68 percent approve of the job he's not doing? Think about it. I haven't.

Apparently, President Bush did not get the joke—or at least find it very amusing. Nor did many in the audience at the dinner. The dismay over Colbert's intense skewering of Bush led to Rich Little's anodyne remarks the following year. Around the country, it was a different story: Colbert's address is one of the most popular Internet downloads of all time, following a long American tradition of satire and parody.

When Americans get sick and tired of their politicians, they can either vote or send a letter to the editorial page of their local newspaper. If there's a television show or a pop singer they think is foolish or pretentious, they can just turn off the TV. But Americans have also exercised an additional option for decades: make fun of something. The Constitution does not guarantee Americans the right to satirize or parody, but it does guarantee freedom of expression and the right to bear arms. When those last two items are put together and sprinkled with a heavy dose of wit, Americans have created a form of humor that both ennobles and destroys its subject at the same time.

Political satire stretches back to 1789, when, supposedly, a satirical woodcut of the new president, George Washington, riding into New York on an ass was circulated on broadsheets. Not even today's most outrageous news parody or late-night remark can compare with some of the lithographic lampoons of Andrew Jackson or Abraham Lincoln in their day. Cartoonist Thomas Nast almost single-handedly brought down Boss Tweed and the Tammany Hall ring with his pen-and-venom illustrations in the late 1890s. Throughout the ensuing decades, political satire has been our way of wrestling with authority—"speaking the truth to power" in a more contemporary phrase—and frequently, the satirical swipe has become more memorable than the offense, or the politi-

We are not amused:
Stephen Colbert and President Bush at the 2006 White House Correspondents Dinner.

cian, it was created to ridicule.

Parody is a much more difficult form of ridicule to master. Oscar Wilde once said that parody was the tribute that mediocrity pays to genius, but he was writing (or quipping) decades before the advent of electronic media, which gave comic artists not only prose but images, voices, and physical characteristics to parody. (For the sake of argument, *satire* uses wit to criticize content; *parody*, while often critiquing content, uses wit to make fun of form as well. In parody, one must not only get inside one's subject, one has to get outside it—or "get" its "outsides"—too.) In the performing arts, parody debuted on the American stage about the same time as lithography raised the level of the cartoonist's art. From roughly 1830 to 1880, the minstrel show was the most ubiquitous form of comic entertainment; with their blackface makeup, minstrel entertainers spoofed books, politicians, musical fads, and so on, by burlesquing and exaggerating their qualities. The minstrel show was largely buffoonery, but literary artists like Mark Twain could elevate satire and parody to a high art. Twain coupled genuine outrage with a mighty pen, realizing that you can open more minds with a laugh than with a cudgel. In his famous 1895 essay "Fenimore Cooper's Literary Offenses," he destroyed the author of *The Deerslayer*, concluding:

> A work of art? It has no invention; it has no order, system, sequence, or result; it has no lifelikeness, no thrill, no stir, no seeming of reality; its characters are confusedly drawn, and by their acts and words they prove that they are not the sort of people the author claims that they are; its humor is pathetic; its pathos is funny; its conversations are—oh! indescribable; its love-scenes odious; its English a crime against the language.
>
> Counting these out, what is left is Art. I think we must all admit that.

Next in line to Twain was Will Rogers, whose terse but gentle comments of opprobrium made him an idol to millions of Americans, including—often especially—those public figures whom he criticized. "Rogers would go visit presidents, he would a couple of times a year just go to Congress and just walk around through the halls," said Ben Yagoda, his biographer. "The funny thing was that the Congresspeople themselves, they loved it too, they loved to be kidded by him, they loved to hang around with him, they knew he wasn't personal, so to be seen on a platform with Will Rogers, kidding back and forth, that was the best thing a politician could do."

Rogers had honed some of his gifts for satire on the Broadway stage during the 1910s and 1920s, performing in a series of comic sketches poking fun at current trends, personalities, and preoccupations for the *Ziegfeld Follies*, an annual revue. It was the very brevity of the revue sketch—say, ten minutes tops—and its quick turnaround time (sketches would be retired every year, or sooner, if they became stale) that made them an influential staple of parody to this day. The great American comic playwright George S. Kaufman was famous for saying that "Satire is what closes on Saturday night," but, in fact, many Saturday nights on Broadway featured full houses of audiences enjoying a Kaufman satire. Or they might enjoy the parody sketches he and oth-

We, the people:
Thomas Nast dresses down Abraham Lincoln; Helen Broderick and Leslie Adams spoof the departing Hoovers in *As Thousands Cheer* (1933).

ers—Moss Hart, Abe Burrows, Comden and Green—concocted for dozens of Broadway revues from the 1920s to the 1950s; the best of them was probably *As Thousands Cheer*, created by Hart and Irving Berlin in 1933. That revue took as its "concept" the form of a daily newspaper, and this allowed Hart to parody such wet-ink-fresh subjects as Gandhi and Aimee Semple MacPherson, the building of Rockefeller Center, the divorce of Joan Crawford and Douglas Fairbanks. The most modern of the sketches was "Franklin D. Roosevelt Inaugurated Tomorrow," a spoof of the departing Hoover administration, where the ex-president and his wife run up a huge last-minute long-distance phone bill. It was the first time an actual president was parodied in front of a live audience.

Broadway audiences demanded a high level of sophistication and topicality in their parodies, but Hollywood was not always willing to oblige. Although the silent era featured a large number of amusing screen parodies, they were usually short subjects, and seemingly of no harm to anyone. When the studio system came of age in the 1930s, Hollywood executives were reluctant to parody the genres that audiences took seriously. Instead, they might drop their hottest comic down in a serious Western, period film, gangster picture, or horror film and let audiences laugh at the fish-out-of-water stories. The breakout smash *Abbott and Costello Meet Frankenstein* was the perfect example, as film historian Leonard Maltin points out:

> Someone came up with the idea of putting Bud and Lou in a Universal horror movie. And Universal owned all those monsters. And they played it just right, because the monsters are not funny and are not trying to be funny. They're straight, they're serious, they're played by Bela Lugosi and Lon Chaney, Jr., and it's Bud and Lou who do the comedy against that backdrop.

Beyond the infringement:
Charles Boyer and Ingrid Bergman in *Gaslight*; Jack Benny and Barbara Stanwyck in their parody, "Autolight."

It would take another medium entirely to give the art of parody the nationwide audience it deserved: television. Satire and parody were never truly major parts of radio's comic vocabulary—the closest thing was perhaps Fred Allen's "Mighty Allen Art Players"—and the few parodies that were broadcast on radio vanished into the ether without creating much damage. Television would be a different story; the speed of television, its insatiable maw for comic material, and the sheer visual impact of actors making fun of personalities brought the art of parody into dangerous territory. In 1952, Jack Benny parodied the movie thriller *Gaslight* (as "Autolight") on his CBS television show and was promptly sued by MGM, which had produced the original film and owned the copyright on the material. (Benny had done a similar but briefer parody of the movie on his radio show in 1945 and gotten away with it.) Three years later, the California Supreme Court ruled against Benny and CBS, claiming that there wasn't enough new material in the parody and that the hunks of dialogue and character names borrowed from the original source constituted copyright infringement.

Yet no single television show took on more parodies in the medium's infancy than *Your Show of Shows*—and took on many of the concomitant complications. As Sid Caesar recounted, when the show was about to parody *On the Waterfront* as *On the*

Copyright © 1999 by E.C. Publications, Inc.

What, me worry?
MAD Magazine spoofs the competition, 1953.

Docks, a phone call came:

> Sam Spiegel, the producer, called me personally. He said, "Now look, I just opened this picture *On the Waterfront* this week, and we're starting to do very fair business. And I don't want you making fun of it. I'll come down and I'll sue you." The staff panicked and I said, "Wait a minute. Let's not get crazy here. Let's do it. If he wants to sue, he's gonna sue. We're not taking the story; we're not taking anything." So we did it. Sam Spiegel called me up the day after the broadcast. He said, "Mr. Caesar, if you need anything, I will help you." A hundred thousand degrees different. And he said, "I tell you what, I have a picture that I'm making now called *Bridge on the River Kwai* and I have the cast here, we can send them in, we can give you this or give you that." And I said, "Okay." All I knew was that he wasn't going to sue me.

Caesar had just discovered the complicated relationship between parody and publicity, and both he and Benny had smacked up against the boundaries that were the natural extension of the 1950s, with its famous culture of conformity. The movie industry, the television industry, the music business, the advertising industry—even the comic book publishing industry—all had rigid codes of conduct, designed to promote decency and conventional morality. These rules were destined to be broken, and in 1952 the task had become easier, because a new gold standard for parody and satire among the younger generation had slouched upon the scene.

MAD Magazine was itself a product of a 1954 Senate investigation into juvenile delinquency, a delicious irony. Publisher William Gaines ran the EC Comics empire, and its more offensive horror comics roused the ire of various public officials and the media during the Senate hearings. As a result, Gaines had to cancel the titles and was nearly bankrupt. Besides, the other comic book publishers had instituted a self-regulating Comics Code Authority. This would affect the last remaining viable title in Gaines's stable: *MAD*, a comic book that spoofed other comic books ("Superduperman," "Batboy and Rubin," "Wotta Woman," and so forth). "The rest is history," said one of its premier satirists, Frank Jacobs. "Gaines changed *MAD* from a color comic to a black-and-white magazine instead, twenty-five cents instead of a dime, simple as that. They didn't have to have that little symbol on it which said they subscribed to the Code, so they were able to do what they did."

Soon, *MAD* stretched its range of targets to include movies and TV programs, along with a favorite whipping boy: Madison Avenue. The younger generation took up *MAD*'s challenge to the hypocritical world of their parents' materialism with a vengeance. By 1960, *MAD*'s circulation had reached one million, and it was read by nearly half of all high school students and more than half of all college students in the country. One of them was Jerry Seinfeld: "When we grew up, poking fun of commercials or television or movies, that was not something everyone did. But *MAD Magazine* was the first place where you found that going on, and it was, like, can we *do* this? And we did." Frank Jacobs saw a wider cultural context:

> One of the reasons for *MAD*'s incredible success was the fact it had no competition. It came during a repressive era of House hearings and Senate hearings about this and that. It opened up a door and suddenly there was humor and

satire regularly produced for people to look at and in a form with a lot of pictures that made it easy. They didn't even have to read it.

One well-received *MAD* parody in 1957 satirized the inanities of Madison Avenue with a musical spoof called "My Fair Ad-Man," based on *My Fair Lady*. That encouraged the magazine to expand into the musical parody business with a 1961 insert called "Sing Along with *MAD*"—forty-six parodies of standard Tin Pan Alley songs. Veteran songwriter Irving Berlin was particularly incensed by the ditties that took off his venerated classics—"A Pretty Girl Is Like a Melody" became a spoof of hypochondria:

> Louella Schwartz
> Describes her malady
> To anyone in sight.
> She will complain!
> Dramatize every pain!
> And then she'll wail
> How doctors fail
> To help her sleep at night!

Berlin got together with other injured songwriters and promptly sued *MAD* (and the writers of the parodies, including Jacobs) for $25 million. The legal action took three years to resolve, but in March of 1964, the U.S. Court of Appeals decided that no actionable harm had been done. Said the opinion written by Judge Irving R. Kaufman (who, incidentally, was the judge who sentenced the Rosenbergs to the electric chair):

> Through depression and boom, war and peace, Tin Pan Alley has lightheartedly insisted that "the whole world laughs" with a laugher, and that "the best things in life are free." [The suit against *MAD* is] an apparent departure from these delightful sentiments. We believe that parody and satire are deserving of substantial freedom—both as entertainment and as a form of social and literary criticism.

"This was a landmark case," said the relieved Jacobs. "It meant that so many things could be parodied and satirized as never before because of this one thing, 'Sing Along with *MAD*.' " *MAD Magazine* achieved even a kind of exalted status as a major influence on several generations of iconoclasts of all stripes in all media.

On the political front, the decade that spawned *MAD* also presented the American public with figures so objectionable and partisan that satire seemed to be the very least they deserved. Walt Kelly, the cartoonist behind *Pogo*, put Communist hunters Joseph McCarthy and Richard Nixon both into his strips, reconceived as animals in the Okeefenokee Swamp. It seemed more and more permissible to tackle public figures directly and, with the passing of the revered Franklin Roosevelt, even the presidency was considered fair game. At the same time, the nature of theater (and theater training) was shifting, and improvisational groups like Second City in Chicago were developing more limber, more intuitive satirical performers—Nichols and May, to give but two examples—who could take on a range of topics. Funny voices and impersonations of old movie stars would no longer cut it.

Not that funny voices were entirely out of the picture. In 1962, Vaughn Meader made a long-playing comedy album titled *The First Family* in which he spoofed the

Sock it to *whom*?
"Nixon looked like his policies. His nose told you that he was going to bomb Cambodia," said political cartoonist Doug Marlette. Here's impressionist David Frye bombing his favorite target.

newly installed President Kennedy and his clan (by today's standards, it was incredibly good-natured); it sold an unbelievable 7.5 million copies and ushered in a new wave of satirical material on records and on television: Tom Lehrer, Allan Sherman, Fireside Theater, David Frye, and so on. The counterculture rebellion of the 1960s threw the floodgates wide open—what was the revolution for, if not to mock one's elders and other figures of authority?

The conflicts of the late 1960s and the early 1970s were too intense to be expressed by, say, *MAD Magazine* (although they pulled their own kind of weight). In 1970, the *National Lampoon* came along, formed by three colleagues from the *Harvard Lampoon*, hot on the heels of their J.R.R. Tolkien parody, *Bored of the Rings*. If *MAD* was high school (sophomore class), the *Lampoon* was college fare. *National Lampoon* had a different, more rigorous standard—"no one had flies buzzing around their head in the illustrations," said one of their best writers, Anne Beatts. It employed a tenacious realism; an infamous ad for the Volkswagen Beetle (which could float on water) used the tagline "If Ted Kennedy had driven a Volkswagen, he'd be president today" and, aside from its open-grave humor, the ad was indistinguishable from the real thing. When a new publisher pushed the *Lampoon* to compete with *Hustler* on the newsstands in the mid-1970s, it lost a lot of its edge (the recent movies bearing the *National Lampoon* imprimatur are but a tedious shred of its former self) and many of its best collaborators.

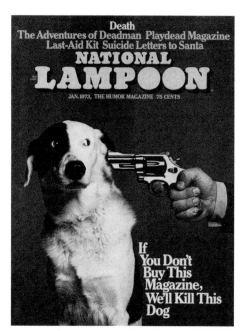

Luckily for the world at large, however, two of those writers were Beatts and Michael O'Donoghue, who went straight to the writing staff of *Saturday Night Live*. The staff and ensemble of that show were part of the first generation to grow up with *MAD Magazine* and Sid Caesar; they were mad as hell, to boot. When Chevy Chase used slapstick to satirize then President Gerald Ford, he didn't even deign to imitate him, really (well, how could you?). In Robert Klein's view, "Chevy falling down on the most popular television show cost Gerald Ford the election. It labeled him as kind of stupid and inept. If it's of any comfort to the Ford family, Chevy has arthritic injuries like an ex-NFL player from all these falls." Ford had to answer back with a brief appearance on *Saturday Night Live*; he didn't look very happy to be introducing the show. Such "good-natured" self-immolation seemed obligatory, and by the early 1980s, that kind of forced geniality between the parodist and the

Darker territory:
National Lampoon cover, 1973; Christopher Guest in *This Is Spinal Tap* (1984).

parodee was happening more and more. Chase even went to the White House and became somewhat cordial with the Fords, much the way that Dana Carvey did with George H. W. Bush a decade later. As long as the elected official and the comedian stood across the fence from each other, it was fine; when the line was crossed, it got messy, and the whole point of satire—the genuine expression of anger—was oddly denatured.

What *Saturday Night Live* also accomplished, with its expert parodies and expert actors, was to unleash a slew of parodies in all forms, *of* all forms. A barrage of genre parodies appeared in movie houses during the 1980s and 90s. Some, such as *Airplane!* and *The Naked Gun*, were clearly inspired by the grab-bag philosophy of *MAD Magazine*. Others, such as *Scary Movie* or *Top Secret*, were homages to the homages of

Mel Brooks; many more were derived from the imaginations of artists who had come up through *Saturday Night Live*, such as Mike Myers's hugely successful *Austin Powers* trilogy. Still other parodies came from *SNL* alums who had cultivated a more subtle approach to comedy. Christopher Guest and Michael McKean collaborated with Rob Reiner on the seminal improvisatory documentary spoof *This Is Spinal Tap* in 1984. McKean distills the film's appeal:

> Rock and roll takes itself very seriously. It shouldn't. But there is something about the self-importance of this kind of bubble mentality. When bands are on the road and making money, and scoring chicks, and doing all this stuff, they don't really reference anything else in the world except themselves. I think that the films that Chris has done subsequent to *Spinal Tap* all have that in common; They're all about people taking themselves very seriously. If you're not riding high, then your fall's not amusing.

Another reason for the spate of parodies was technological: the introduction of the VHS tape and, later, the DVD format. Allusions to this movie or that performer were previously gleaned from what we remembered from reruns or revival houses; now an entire database of pop culture can be constantly and consistently mined for comedy. What our ancestors knew about classical mythology or what Mark Twain's readers knew about James Fenimore Cooper's prose, the current generation knows about *Star Trek*, Hitchcock films, and Sharon Stone's crotch. Is there even such as thing as an "in-joke" anymore? Isn't everybody "in"?

At the end of the day, however, the skill or perceptiveness of the parodist or satirist matters less than the audience's ability to hear their criticism and make constructive use of it. No less an expert on this subject than Tom Lehrer said, in 2002: "I think the people who say we need satire often mean 'We need satire of them, not of us.' I'm fond of quoting Peter Cook, who talked about the satirical Berlin cabarets of the 30s, which did so much to stop the rise of Hitler and prevent the Second World War."

Today, even though we have more venues for parody and satire than ever before, the emergence of absurd personalities outpaces our ability to mock them. During the 2008 presidential campaign, when *Saturday Night Live*'s Tina Fey was able to get laughs with her imitation of Republican vice-presidential candidate Sarah Palin simply by recycling Palin's own tortured syntax verbatim, it's hard to tell, exactly, just who has socked it to whom.

I Spy:
Mike Myers takes on a much-parodied topic as superspy Austin Powers.

I don't think I've seen anything, in my lifetime, more fearless and more ballsy than Stephen Colbert doing his routine with President Bush five feet away. If you're talking about the president and he's right there, it does not get any better than that.
—Richard Lewis

"I'M NOT A MEMBER OF ANY ORGANIZED POLITICAL PARTY"
WILL ROGERS

Most actors appearing on the stage have some writer to write their material. Congress is good enough for me. They have been writing my material for years. –Will Rogers

Two months after President Herbert Hoover proclaimed that "prosperity was just around the corner," he was forced to admit that the Depression had delivered a severe shock to the American system. On October 18, 1931, Hoover went on the coast-to-coast national airwaves for a special broadcast to address unemployment relief. For his "warm-up act," he chose the most popular man in America: Will Rogers.

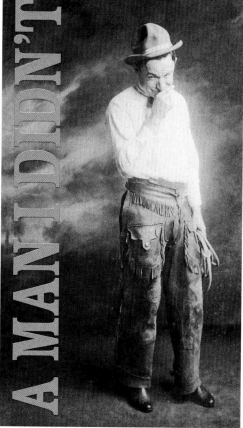

Ropin' fool:
Rogers in his vaudeville days. Right, as America's most successful columnist; with an Oklahoman's best friend.

Hoover assumed that Rogers would tell a few jokes, reassure the country, and sugarcoat his administration's ineffectual plans for recovery. He had underestimated the country's comic conscience:

> We got more wheat, more corn, more food, more cotton, more money in the banks, more everything in the world than any nation that ever lived ever had, and yet we are starving to death. We are the first nation on earth to ride to the poor house in an automobile. . . . I don't suppose there is the most unemployed or the hungriest man in America that hasn't contributed in some way to the wealth of every millionaire in America.

Rogers had made a career out of poking fun at both sides of the aisle, as it were, but the depredations of the early Depression made it impossible for him to stay neutral, at least for this one broadcast. For another performer, perhaps, biting the president's hand in such an overt way might have spelled career suicide, but Rogers was treasured by the public because he was never a product of any party, politician, president, or partisan; he spoke to, and for, the heartland of America because his folksy proclamations came straight from the heart. He was, according to a contemporary reviewer, "what Americans think other Americans are like."

As his principal biographer, Ben S. Yagoda, put it, Will Rogers was both a cowboy and an Indian, which is a neat trick. He was born in 1879 in what was then the Oklahoma territory, in a log house without running water or indoor plumbing. "I was born on November 4, which is Election Day," he said. "My birthday has made more men and sent more back to honest work than any other days in the year." Rogers was more than one-quarter Cherokee, and his father was a successful but imperious rancher who put him on horseback before he could learn to walk. Rogers was no backwater hick, as many assumed; he had ten years of formal education, but his most important schooling came from Dan Walker, a black cowboy who taught him the rudiments of lariat handling. When Will was ten, his mother died, and friends said it broke his heart forever; to cheer the boy up, his father gave Will a beloved horse name Comanche. "A fellow that don't love a horse," he said, "there is something the matter with him."

At the age of thirteen, Rogers saw the exquisite rope handling of a Mexican roper named Vincente Oropeza. With a flick of the wrist, Rogers was transformed forever. When he failed as an actual cowboy, he took to performing as one in various Wild West show tours around the world, brandishing his skill with a lariat. When he returned to the States, he was vaulted to fame when, performing one night in Madison Square Garden, he roped a wild steer that had made a mad dash into the audience. This publicity was a conduit for Rogers's entrée into the venue that would make him as an American performer: vaudeville. While many vaudeville entertainers traded on their ethnic backgrounds, Rogers gave an eager public all the cornball cornucopia of the Wild West. He managed his vaudeville act of lariat derring-do down to the last twirl, often sharing the stage with his old pal Comanche, and started adding one-liners as early as 1905, sometimes to cover up a rare botched effect. "I'm handicapped up y'har, as the manager won't let me swear when I miss," he'd drawl, and bring down the house.

By 1915, Rogers had snared a top spot in one of New York's most prestigious venues: the rooftop nightclub Frolics, with floor shows produced by none other than Florenz

Ziegfeld. But however much the repeat customers at the Frolics admired Will's rope tricks, they were quickly getting bored by the same terse witticisms. Ziegfeld dispatched an associate to fire Rogers, but Rogers surprised him by countering with a request for a fifty dollar a week raise. Will also had a suggestion: "My wife says I ought to talk about what I read in the papers. She says I'm always reading the papers, so why not pass it along?" So began Will Rogers's lifelong immersion in the topical subjects of his day, turning the rope twirler into a yarn spinner, a town crier railing in a gentle Oklahoman drawl against America's dim-witted hypocrisies:

A man to run second in any other event in the world it's an honor, but any time he runs second for president, it's not an honor. It's a pity.

Rogers got his material by voraciously reading every edition of the dozen or more New York newspapers: "All I know is just what I read in the papers" became his trademark line. When an occasional line bombed, he'd tell the audience, "I guess I'm a couple of editions ahead of you folks." He struck such a chord with audiences that Ziegfeld brought Rogers downstairs to star onstage as a headliner in the *Follies*. Between 1916 and 1925, Rogers would star in six editions of the *Follies*. To Will, the job description was simple: "I go out and entertain the audience while the chorus girls change from nothing to nothing." (And despite W. C. Fields's curmudgeonly remark, he and Rogers were great comrades in their *Follies* appearance, both on Broadway and on tour.) But Rogers's knack for poking fun at people at the top made him a celebrity in and out of the *Follies*.

THAT SON OF A BITCH IS A FAKE. I BET A HUNDRED DOLLARS THAT WHEN HE GETS HOME, HE TALKS JUST LIKE EVERYBODY ELSE.
—W.C. Fields

> A big shot, a major industrialist type, was not a confirmed tycoon until he had been kidded by Will Rogers, and there was a great deal of snob value to a Rogers rib.
>
> –John O'Hara, 1920

By 1920, Rogers was so successful that the next step was inevitable; film producer Samuel Goldwyn offered him a motion picture contract. His short silent subjects made him a star all over again, but Rogers was unimpressed with both the movies and his work in it. Hollywood did, however, provide him with one of his best lines: "I am the only man who came out of the movies with the same wife I started with." In 1922, Rogers added what may have been the most successful string to his bow. He was recruited to write a syndicated Sunday newspaper column. Over the next thirteen years, he wrote 666 Sunday columns, subscribed to by forty papers nationwide. Three years later, he was offered a daily column—a series of observations and one-liners that went out under the title "Will Rogers Says." In the next ten years, Rogers wrote 2,817 daily columns; at its height, he was read by 40 million people every day. The columns made Rogers the most widely read writer in America.

> As a matter of truth, no nation wants any other nation exerting a "moral leadership" over 'em even if they had one.

Well, they finally stopped us from sending Marines to every war that we could hear of. They are having one in Afghanistan. This thing will be over before Congress can pronounce it, much less find out where it is located.

The Democrats are having a lot of fun exposing the Republican campaign corruptions, but they would have a lot more fun if they knew where they could get their hands on some of it themselves for next November.

As the Roaring Twenties moved to a close, Rogers's career took an unprecedented turn. The general populace was always clamoring for his views on politics, but now, even the politicians wanted a piece of him. President Calvin Coolidge invited Rogers to the White House in 1926, and he went straight from the White House to Carnegie Hall, where he became the first comedian to play that honored auditorium. It was only a matter of time before Rogers's name was bruited about as a political contender—his name was entered into nomination at the 1928 Democratic Convention. "There is no inducement that would make me foolish enough to ever run for political office," he responded. "I want to be on the outside where I can be friends and joke about all of them, even the president."

The stock market crashed just two weeks shy of Rogers's fiftieth birthday. By then, he was conquering every modern medium. He had a weekly fifteen-minute Sunday night radio show and his contract stipulated that no sponsor could or would restrict or censor his broadcast. He had signed a contract with Fox to make twenty talking feature films; within three years, he would be the number one box office attraction in America. "Look at the man," wrote H. L. Mencken. "He alters foreign policies. He makes and unmakes candidates. He destroys public figures. . . . I consider him the most dangerous writer alive today." One Washington diplomat put it more simply: "You can never have another war in this country unless Will Rogers is for it."

The fact remained, however, that Rogers was never for or against anything; that was part of his credibility with his audience: "I'm not a member of any organized political party. I'm a Democrat" went one of his more famous lines. But in 1932, Rogers's equanimity shifted conspicuously when he appeared at the Chicago Democratic Convention and demanded that the delegates support their nominee, Franklin D. Roosevelt. Roosevelt appealed to Rogers's populist instinct and he went on the campaign trail for the candidate. When FDR was elected, Rogers commented, "The whole country is with him: If he burned down the Capitol we would cheer and say, 'Well, we at least got a fire started anyhow.' " Roosevelt, no stranger to the allure of the mass media himself, returned the favor by inviting Rogers to the White House and, shrewdly, scheduling his second fireside chat radio broadcast following Rogers's regular Sunday night show. *He* wasn't about to share the same bill with Rogers.

Rogers usually handled the immense exposure afforded by his newspaper columns and radio broadcasts with perceptive discretion, but occasionally he could get tripped up. One night in 1934, an offhand reference to a "nigger spiritual" on his radio show brought NBC a deluge of telegrams and phone calls. Rogers was stunned by the outrage and wrote a long letter to a black listener:

> I reverted to the word I had used since childhood down home, with never a thought of disrespect. . . . If you or anyone else can find a [black man] that will say that I ever by action, or word ever did one thing to humiliate or show in any way that I was antagonistic to them, I will, ah, well, I would do anything, for you can't find 'em, for I never did.

This rare misstep didn't dent Rogers's popularity—nothing could. On Friday, March 18, 1934, he was asked to enliven the Academy Awards as its first master of ceremonies. "You'll see great acting tonight, greater than any you will see on the screen. We'll all cheer when somebody gets a prize that every one of us in the house knows should be ours. . . . That's acting," he said at the podium.

Whenever such earthbound concerns as censorship or celebrities got to Rogers, he took to the skies. Rogers had become enamored with the possibilities of commercial flight in the late 1920s, and although he never piloted a plane himself, he became known as the Patron Saint of Aviation. When aviation pioneer and fellow Oklahoman Wiley Post announced in August of 1935 that he was exploring a new passenger and mail route from the West Coast to Russia, Rogers asked to come along— he needed new material for his column and a jaunt to Alaska seemed just the thing. As Post and Rogers were setting off for the remote Point Barrow, their plane's engine back-fired and quit, then the plane nose-dived into a lagoon three feet deep. It took the nearest federal marshals half a day to arrive, but when they did, it was clear that Post and Rogers had died instantly.

Enemy territory:
Rogers crosses the line by supporting FDR in 1932.

> When I die my epitaph or whatever you call those signs on gravestones is going to read "I joked about every prominent man of my time, but I never met a man I didn't like."

The entire country went into mourning. Businesses were closed and NBC and CBS went off the air during the funeral services. President Roosevelt spoke directly to the nation:

> He loved and was loved by the American people. His memory will ever be in benediction with the hosts of his countrymen who felt the spell of that kindly humor which, while seeing facts, could always laugh at fantasy. That is why his message went straight to the hearts of his fellow men.

When Florenz Ziegfeld died in 1932, Rogers was devastated. Rogers had endured similar losses in his lifetime—his mother's death, the death of a two-year-old son—but he never turned to any conventional religious comforts. Will Rogers always saw Heaven as a kind of happy theater of hardworking angels. In his daily column, Rogers wrote movingly of Ziegfeld's legacy—and surely of his own as well:

> Ziegfeld left something on earth that hundreds of us will treasure till our curtain falls, and that was a "badge," a badge of which we were proud and never ashamed, and wanted the world to read the lettering on it, "I worked for Ziegfeld." So, good-bye, Flo, for you will put on a show up there some day that will knock their eyes out. Save a spot for me.

WHEN YOU GET INTO TROUBLE FIVE THOUSAND MILES FROM HOME YOU'VE GOT TO HAVE BEEN LOOKING FOR IT.

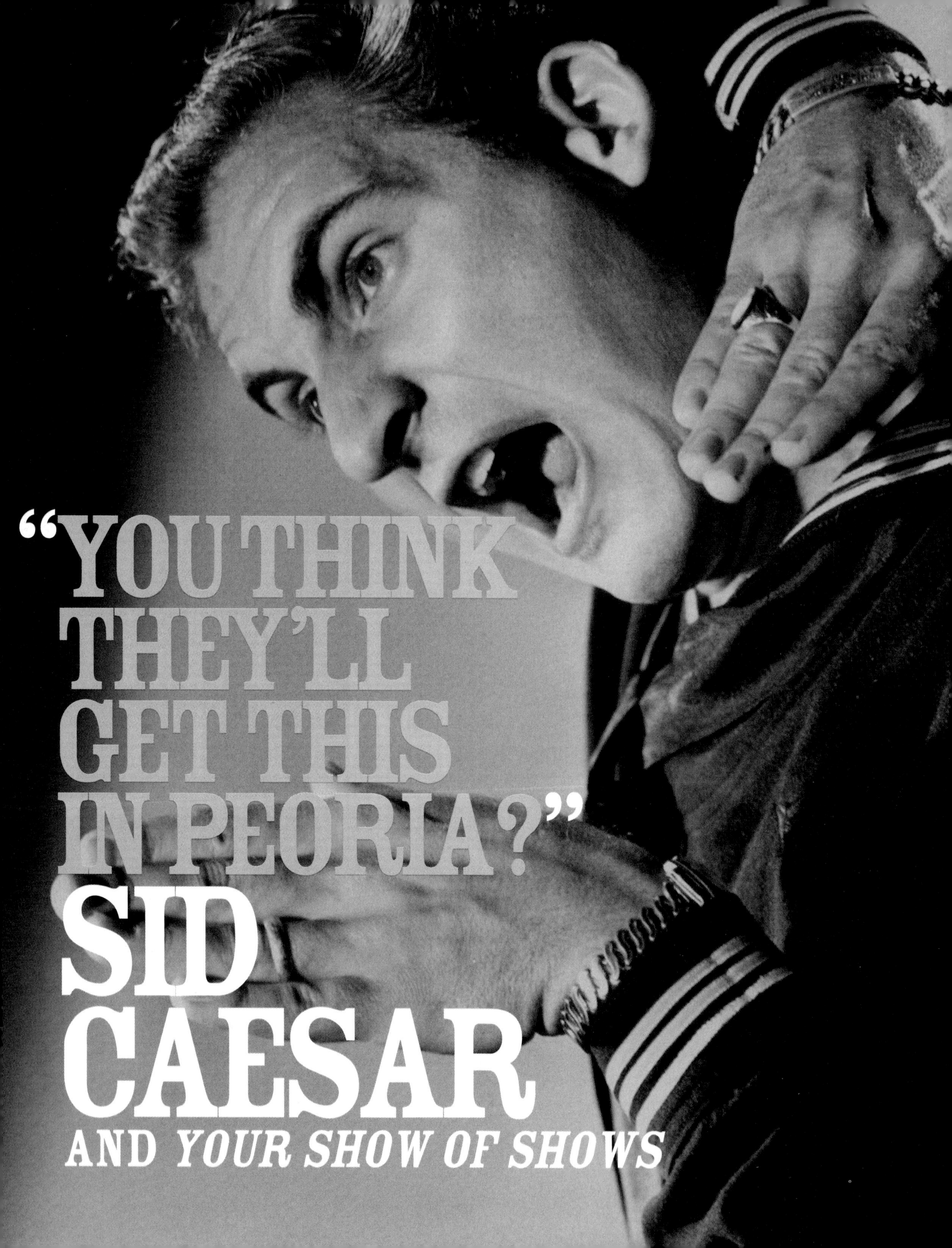

"YOU THINK THEY'LL GET THIS IN PEORIA?"

SID CAESAR

AND *YOUR SHOW OF SHOWS*

First of all, Sid was wildly talented. There was nothing you could write that he couldn't play, except the simple sentence like, "Good evening, ladies and gentlemen." That he could not say. So we laid off that. –*Your Show of Shows* writer Larry Gelbart

In 1949, there were only two million television consoles in homes across the United States—and nearly half of them were in New York City. The network executives were also in New York, and they struggled to figure out what to put on the airwaves for the forty-two hours a week they were broadcasting. One early solution was the variety show, such as Ed Sullivan's *Talk of the Town*, which showcased an evening of different acts. Another kind of entertainment show was a revue, but revues took more work; they required original material, original songs and dances—and an original point of view. The sponsor, Admiral Television, found an original mind in producer Max Liebman.

Liebman had worked magic at Camp Tamiment in New York's Catskill Mountains, putting on three separate professional-level revues a season. Liebman agreed to produce the hour-long *The Admiral Broadway Revue*, to be broadcast by both NBC and the DuMont networks, and it was to be exactly what it sounded like—a Broadway-quality evening of sketches, songs, and dances performed by an expert ensemble. There was only one problem, as Carl Reiner later pointed out: "Liebman knew how to put on a show every three weeks. He didn't realize that putting on thirty-nine shows is not the same as putting on three." It would be a herculean task, but Liebman's savior was not Greek at all; he was a Jewish saxophonist from Yonkers with a Roman name and a Roman nose.

Sid Caesar had worked for Liebman before; while in the navy, he had appeared in the coast guard revue *Tars and Spars* (Liebman, on hearing Caesar's inspired improvisations, promoted him from musician to featured comic), then in a 1948 Broadway revue called *Make Mine Manhattan*. Caesar could play a mean sax, he could do knockout impressions, he could do pantomime, he could do double-talk in foreign languages, he could riff off any comic premise. There was one thing he couldn't do: "He couldn't tell a joke. I don't think I ever heard Sid tell a joke," said Reiner.

HE COULDN'T TELL A JOKE.
I DON'T THINK I EVER HEARD SID TELL A JOKE.

"But Sid had a kinesthetic sense. He knew intuitively how people behave—he had a perfect pitch about the human condition. He just knew." *The Admiral Broadway Revue* would demand all of Caesar's skills. Unlike Ed Sullivan, who simply hosted a show, or Milton Berle, who shared the stage with other acts, Sid Caesar would be his own three-ring circus, appearing in almost all the sketches, supervising the writers, and eventually producing his own programs.

The first seventeen weeks of *The Admiral Broadway Revue* were so successful that Admiral dropped the show—they were getting more orders for television sets than they could produce. So Liebman, Caesar, and their crew moved to Saturday nights to create a ninety-minute weekly revue that would set the standard for television comedy over the next four years. *Your Show of Shows* would prove to be the ultimate trapeze act without a safety net—all of the 160 shows were broadcast live. "A live show is a different animal altogether than what they have

Naval contemplation:
Young Sidney Caesar, as the top comic of coast guard revue, *Tars and Spars*, 1947.

now on tape," said Caesar. "It's different because in live, the performer is the boss. Whatever you say is going to be out on the air in the next second." It would be crucial, then, to make sure that whatever Caesar and his talented ensemble were going to say would be of the highest quality.

It was. Caesar presided over the greatest writing talent in television history. The Writers' Room, as it would be called (and immortalized in various fictional plays and films), was originally inhabited by Mel Tolkin as head writer, Lucille Kallen, Reiner, and Mel Brooks. They were eventually joined by such first-rate comic writers as Larry Gelbart, Neil Simon, Joseph Stein, Bill Persky, Sam Denoff, Sheldon Keller, Gary Belkin, and Michael Stewart. Each of them would go on to create or write some of the best and most important comedy films or sitcoms of the next two decades. (Woody Allen joined very late in the game, in 1958, for one of Caesar's last series.) The weekly grind was the same; the team would meet on Monday morning and toss out ideas and segments. Caesar, who had no writing background at all, was the final arbiter of what went on the air; with a pantomime machine gun, he would shoot down ideas he didn't like: "*Rat-a-tat-a-tat-tat*!" Caesar would go, playing off a routine he did in the navy. "Never say that one again! That's the way I shot them down, because then it wasn't insulting and it wasn't embarrassing, it was funny."

There was a unique combination of aggression and affection in the Writers' Room. "Everybody was very territorial about their own work," recalled Reiner. "Everybody really fought for their jokes—they would go home and say to their wives, 'That's my joke.'" But there was also a certain urban Jewish consanguinity among them. "We were able to be urbane," said Gelbart. "Between us we read every book. Between us we saw every movie. Between us we saw every play on Broadway. You could make jokes about Kafka or Tennessee Williams. We also had dinner together. We went to movies together. We were all friends. And that was very important. We appreciated each other a lot."

What they appreciated most was Caesar, and so the writers laid on a series of sketches, songs, parodies—even extended mime sequences—that could be served up brilliantly by Caesar and his ensemble; the impish, pert Imogene Coca, whose demure gooniness was the perfect foil for Caesar's explosive energy; Carl Reiner, the slightly crooked straight man; and eventually, Howard Morris, the scrappy character actor extraordinaire. There were recurring sketches, such as "The Commuters," one of television's first glimpses of a domestic suburban couple, and recurring characters, such as the Professor, Caesar's double-talk virtuoso, and Progress Hornsby (originally Cool Cees), "the ultimate smoker-upper"—a stoned bebop jazz musician who gave Caesar the chance to play the sax and gave the writers a chance to show what hip New Yorkers they were. "And then we have Nikto Barada on the radar—he's the one who warns us in case we approach the melody," drawled Hornsby. (To show you how hip the writers were, "Nikto Barada" was an allusion to the 1951 science fiction film *The Day the Earth Stood Still*.)

Harder than it looks:
Caesar, being pitched to by writers Mel Brooks, Woody Allen, and Mel Tolkin; Hail, Caesar!

Your Show of Shows was hippest, however, when it came to parody. "When you're doing a television show, you need forms to fill. And one of the forms we filled every week was a parody," said Reiner. The show borrowed from its Broadway roots and parodied every genre cliché: espionage movies, Westerns, backstage musicals, gangster films, silent movies. Eventually, however, they moved into new territory—*new* is the word—by parodying movies current at the box office. Most famously, the crew spoofed the overheated wartime soap opera *From Here to Eternity* as "From Here to Obscurity," with Caesar and Coca aping the film's beachfront love scene by getting doused with buckets and buckets of water.

There were times when the writing staff drifted off into Obscurity themselves. As bright young New York intellectuals, the writers would attend some foreign art film and then go sample the food from that country afterward; a De Sica film would be followed by some Italian food; a Kurosawa festival would be the prelude to a Japanese steakhouse. Inevitably, these movies would become fodder for the weekly parody. "Ubetchu" was *Ugetsu* in disguise, produced by the fictitious Take-A-Kuki ("take a cookie!") film company. In that spoof—which ran nearly ten minutes—Caesar played a bellicose samurai warrior, barking all of his dialogue in pidgin Japanese. It was outrageous—in every sense of the word. Reiner recalled, "We had to be brought to reality by somebody saying, 'Hey, fellas, you think they'll get this in Peoria?' We didn't care. We realized that we had people of a certain ilk in every part of the country—not a lot—and they didn't have foreign movie theaters in Podunk. And so we were aware that we were doing something that tickled us and may not tickle other people."

Even Caesar was often perplexed by the choice of parody. "He was parodying movies that he had never seen, but based on his faith in his writers, he went ahead and performed them," said Gelbart. "If you thought it was funny, he would join the crapshoot." Caesar, clearly, came up sevens. He was not comfortable in his own skin—

the writers will attest that Caesar would go for days speaking in the persona of one of his characters—but he was fiercely committed to the show. He oversaw every detail and his off-camera habits were equally prodigious; to fuel his overpowering comedy furnace, he would often eat several dinners a night, frequently washed down with a fifth of Johnnie Walker.

Inevitably, the tempo within Caesar's empire would prove exhausting. In 1954, NBC broke up the *Your Show of Shows* team, thinking they could make more money by splitting Caesar, Coca, and Liebman into three separate shows. Only Caesar hung in there, starring in three seasons of *Caesar's Hour*, using many of the same writers and formats (Nanette Fabray joined him as the distaff foil), followed by an unsuccessful attempt to reunite him with Coca called *Sid Caesar Invites You*. By that time, Caesar had been on the television treadmill for a decade and had held down the lead in over four hundred live hours of broadcasting, a feat unmatched since. In the ten years since *The Admiral Broadway Revue*, the two million television sets in the U.S. had increased by a factor of twenty-one—and, of course, half of them weren't in New York anymore. As Larry Gelbart put it, "When we started, television sets were expensive, so we had a very, very sophisticated audience. As the price of sets went down, so did the IQ of the watchers, and we were finally knocked off the air by Lawrence Welk."

Still, in television's infancy, no one ever worked harder—or more hilariously—to raise the bar for comedy than Sid Caesar. He made Saturday evenings a very special—and irreplaceable—time. Carol Burnett recalls her own required viewing back in 1956:

> *My Fair Lady* had opened on Broadway and I won two tickets in a lottery to see *My Fair Lady* on a Saturday night. I gave the tickets to my roommate because I said, "*Fair Lady*'s gonna be running for a hundred years. I know I'll get to see it, but Sid Caesar is live and I'll never see *that* again."

Caesar played the Gary Cooper part in a High Noon *parody:*

I was supposed to have a sponge on my chest to pin the badges on, but I had to put on so much stuff: cowboy boots, pants, and then the vest and then this and that—as I walked out of the dressing room, I saw the sponge laying on the chair, and I didn't have time to go back, because they were playing the opening music. And I walked out and I tried to say to the other actors, "Take it easy, you know, *easy*." Three guys came back and said, "I'm sorry, sheriff, I'd like to help you out but my wife wants to go to the dance tonight," and they would go *boom!* with the badges. I said, "Holy jeez!" And they're long pins. And there were three of them. And they knew that they were putting the needle into me and, after the skit, as I'm changing costumes I said, "Get some tetanus shots ready!"

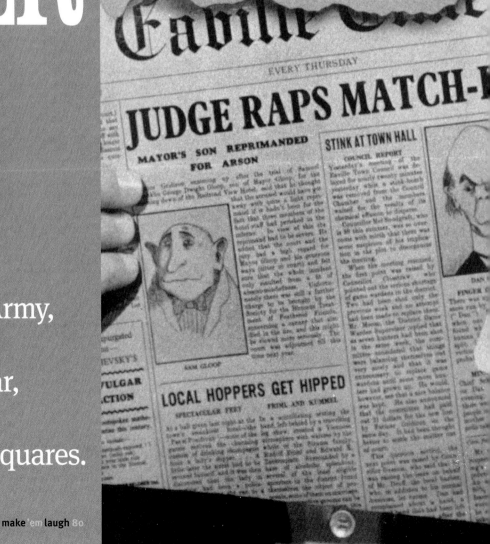

"UNLIKE THE REST OF YOU SQUARES"
TOM LEHRER

We are the Folk Song Army,
Every one of us cares.
We all hate poverty, war,
 and injustice,
Unlike the rest of you squares.
– Tom Lehrer, "Folk Song Army"

Tom Lehrer was one of America's most unlikely folk heroes—if nominated as one, he probably would not run; if elected, he certainly wouldn't serve. Still, Lehrer did serve to crack open the buttoned-up, deferential reserve of the American electorate in the 1950s. His weapons of choice were a keyboard and a ten-inch disc made of vinyl.

Lehrer was born in 1928 to a well-to-do Manhattan family, ethnically but not religiously Jewish. " 'God' was primarily an expletive, usually preceded by 'oh' or 'my' or both," he said. He was a genius at mathematics with a passion for the tricky wordplay in songs written by Gilbert and Sullivan or sung by Danny Kaye in the 1940s.

> There's sulfur, californium, and fermium, berkelium,
> And also mendelevium, einsteinium, nobelium,
> And argon, krypton, neon, radon, xenon, zinc, and rhodium,
> And chlorine, carbon, cobalt, copper, tungsten, tin, and sodium.
> These are the only ones of which the news has come to Ha'vard,
> And there may be many others, but they haven't been discavard.
> –"The Elements"

In 1952, while studying at Harvard's Graduate School of Arts and Sciences, Lehrer was persuaded to go onstage at a Boston nightclub to perform some of the satirical songs that amused his Cambridge classmates. Although the novelty of performing eventually wore off, he became a local sensation. His songs were unconventional, to say the least, dealing with dope peddling, masochism, incest, dismemberment, and—perhaps worst of all—pacifism. Pop singer Tony Martin's sultry "Kiss of Fire" inspired Lehrer to take romantic self-abnegation to new depths in "The Masochism Tango":

> I ache for the touch of your lips, dear
> But much more for the touch of your whips, dear
> You can raise welts like nobody else
> As we dance to the masochism tango.

While continuing with his studies, Lehrer decided to put a dozen or so songs on a ten-inch long-playing record. *Songs by Tom Lehrer* came out in 1953 when he was still teaching undergraduate math. It became an immediate sensation on college campuses throughout the country. Anyone who wanted bad reviews of Lehrer's work had only to look at the liner notes, where he had each pan painstakingly reprinted. "Mr. Lehrer's muse is not fettered by such inhibiting factors as taste," wrote the *New York Times*. Lehrer took it all in stride, with a healthy disrespect for the obsequiousness of celebrity, and responded in kind on his second album:

> Any ideas expressed on this record should not be taken as representing Mr. Lehrer's true convictions, for indeed he has none. "If anyone objects to any statement I make, I am quite prepared not only to retract it, but also to deny under oath that I ever made it."

Lehrer would only write about three dozen songs in his career—and few radio disc jockeys would dare play them—but record buyers were so wild about his first two albums, they demanded his appearance onstage. He agreed—for a while. His concert and nightclub career essentially lasted only from 1957 to 1959; he never thought much of his celebrity and went back to Harvard to resume his studies and teach classes at MIT. "It isn't as though I have to do this, you know. I could be making, oh, $3,000 a year just teaching," he told audiences. Still, Lehrer was becoming the perceptive and skeptical voice of a generation, often quoted, frequently admired, despite all of his attempts to discourage a breakout career. "Lacking exposure in the media, my songs spread slowly—like herpes, rather than ebola," he later recalled.

MR. LEHRER'S MUSE IS NOT FETTERED BY SUCH INHIBITING FACTORS AS TASTE.

The Lehrer Retort:
(previous) Biting the hand that feeds him; (above) one brief shining moment—Tom Lehrer onstage.

Tom Lehrer is one of those guys that when you get their record, you've found gold—"We've got it. We've got it. Let's go listen to it." The songs were brassy, bold and perfect for my college head. We just loved him, still do.

–Steve Martin

The early sixties—with their plethora of social and political issues—brought Lehrer out of retirement briefly to exercise his satirical skills. He submitted some material to a new television show devoted to spoofing the news, *That Was the Week That Was*. "[It] was supposed to be satiric without offending anyone, which is a contradiction in terms," he said. After watching the program cut and alter his songs, Lehrer showed up to sing his own material, in his own inimitably snide fashion. By 1965, there was so much more to sing about. His songs from this period, recorded in his album *That Was the Year That Was*, are a veritable time capsule of everything disturbing, disappointing, and just plain wrong about the 1960s. In "Pollution," he pointed out that "You can use the latest toothpaste/And then rinse your mouth with industrial waste." And if you needed to pinpoint where the *real* tensions were in the world, all you had to do was drop the needle on "Who's Next?," Lehrer's extrapolation of nuclear proliferation:

> We'll try to stay serene and calm
> When Alabama gets the bomb.

Liberal preoccupations had no safe refuge in Lehrer's hands; he was an equal opportunity destroyer. He skewered the naive aspirations of the mid-sixties' National Brotherhood Week:

> Oh, the Protestants hate the Catholics,
> And the Catholics hate the Protestants,
> And the Hindus hate the Moslems,
> And everybody hates the Jews.
> But during National Brotherhood Week, National Brotherhood Week,
> It's National Everyone-smile-at-one-another-hood Week.
> Be nice to people who
> Are inferior to you.
> It's only for a week, so have no fear.
> Be grateful that it doesn't last all year!

Lehrer retired a second time in the mid-1960s to pursue his teaching career. Although fans and reporters seem disinclined to believe him, Lehrer simply embraces a happier life as a teacher than as a celebrity. His healthy skepticism extends even to his own fame: "I don't think this kind of thing has an impact on the unconverted, frankly. It's not even preaching to the converted; it's titillating the converted." Even while exiting the stage of his performing career, he dropped a zinger on the way out: "I've said that political satire became obsolete when Henry Kissinger was awarded the Nobel Peace Prize." The freedoms of expression experienced in American culture since his retirement have not exactly thrilled him:

> Alas, irreverence has been subsumed by mere grossness. . . . Irreverence is easy—what's hard is wit. And the nature of forbidden words has certainly changed. When I was in college, there were certain words you couldn't say in front of a girl. Now you can say them, but you can't say "girl."

Lehrer unleashed his own satirical song army. "Weird Al" Yankovic, the premier song parodist of today, considers him "the J. D. Salinger of demented music." A half century later, his satirical bite remains as topical—and as sharp—as ever. As he told an Australian reporter in 2005, "I'm not tempted to write a song about George W. Bush. I couldn't figure out what sort of song I would write. That's the problem: I don't want to satirize George Bush and his puppeteers, I want to vaporize them."

Clubs, Camps, and the Catskills

"Follow the money," went the refrain in *All the President's Men*. When it comes to charting the influence of nightclubs and resorts on American comedy, the refrain might be "Follow the martini."

Conviviality and comedy have gone together for centuries. In the nineteenth century, music halls allowed workingmen to enjoy a pint or two watching a couple of lowbrow baggy-pants comics hammer it out with each other. When Prohibition was enforced in 1920, it created a new venue where covert imbibers could drink and be entertained: the speakeasy. Speakeasies often had hosts, like the legendary Texas Guinan, who served up the perfect cocktail of hooch and hilarity, confirming the basic fact that, for many consumers, a drink went down better with a joke as a chaser.

After the federal government restored the legal procurement of alcohol to the American public in 1933, it seemed unlikely that profitable speakeasy owners—or their clients—would give up their postprandial amusements. Organized crime had discovered a lucrative source of income and therefore backed many nightclubs—as they were now known—in cities across the country. In 1940, the mob invested in the Copacabana, a Latin-accented club on New York's East Sixtieth Street, and it quickly became not only one of the most successful nightclubs in America but one of the premier venues in which to watch ascending stars of comedy. Typically, in the 1940s and '50s, a club like the Copa offered dining, drinking, and dancing, which were temporarily halted three times a night, at eight and ten p.m. and then at two a.m., to provide a fully produced floor show. There would be an orchestra, a bevy of dancing girls, a crooner, and, more and more frequently, a comic. According to producer Bernie Brillstein, "On Friday night at the Copa, it was the gangsters and their dates, and the comics would do a different show than on Sunday night when it was the gangsters and their wives."

A high-profile nightclub like the Copa (or Los Angeles-based clubs such as Ciro's or the Cocoanut Grove) could provide a unique launching pad for a comedian. In 1948, Dean Martin and Jerry Lewis were signed, against their better instincts, for a two-week engagement at the Copa. They thought working in a nightclub was a step sideways on their career paths and were displeased to open for a singer, Vivian Blaine. But they were such a sensation that the Copa management extended Martin and Lewis's engagement for eighteen weeks, raised their salaries to $5,000 a week, basked in the rave reviews from the gossip columnists—and sat back and watched as the duo was snapped up by Paramount Pictures. The Copa provided a showcase for other comics, but the club was practically synonymous with Martin and Lewis; they played there every year, and it was at the Copa that they played their farewell engagement as a team in July 1956; it was the hottest ticket in the country.

The nightclub life was not the easiest one for a comedian. Usually the comedian opened for a singer (only with a great comedian was it the other way around), and three sets a night, seven nights a week, four weeks an engagement (not to mention the travel) was grueling work. That kind of gig was, of course, not helped by the whispered drink orders or tinkling silverware that formed a distracting accompaniment to the act, but with a weekly salary that often cracked five figures, such annoyances could be endured. Hecklers were an occupational hazard, but they kept a comedian on his toes and each had their preferred way of dealing with an obstreperous drunk: "Oh, I remember when I had my first beer," was the way Steve Martin dispatched hecklers in the mid-sixties.

Catching a comic in a major nightspot such as the Copa would be the kind of thing out-of-towners would consider the height of postwar urban sophistication. However, there was also another place to catch some of the best comics in America, although it was as far removed from city life as possible (well, an hour and a half, anyway): the Catskills. The Catskill Mountains, located northwest of New York City in Sullivan and Ulster counties, had been a popular resort area since the 1880s; the hotels, bungalows, and campsites there provided relief to a largely Jewish population fleeing the city for the summer. The Catskills resorts catered (and that is the word) to Jewish sensibilities in terms of food, socializing, and entertainment. The entertainment, in particular, included seminal work by some of America's most successful comedians. They, too, were defined by the heavy Jewish food offered in mammoth proportions at these resorts, specifically the cold beet soup smothered with sour cream—the borscht belt.

The Saturday night show was the major social event of the week, and hotels such as the Concord, Kutscher's, Brown's, and Grossinger's built larger and larger rooms for the headliners to play for their eager, well-dressed, well-behaved audiences. Needless to say, the comics who played there traded on Jewish clichés and Jewish jokes. ("The food is terrible here." "Yes, and such small portions," ran one famous joke.) Like the city nightclubs, it offered opportunities for comics to find their voice: Red Buttons (who changed his name from Aaron Schwatt at the Catskills), Buddy Hackett, Jerry Lewis, and Alan King joined such Jewish comic stalwarts as

Myron Cohen and Henny Youngman.

The Catskills resorts, so desperate to keep their
clientele amused, often employed full-time
jester/social director/cheerleaders called tummlers.
Mel Brooks famously got his start in this
capacity; one might say he never stopped.
Tummlers, however, were not welcome at all
resorts. Camp Tamiment, located in the nearby
Pennsylvania Poconos, prided itself on being a
social meeting place for Jewish singles, but with
a high ethical component. Beginning in 1921,
Tamiment provided weeklong vacations in the
summer, the highlight of which was a highly professional
Saturday night revue. The revues at the
Tamiment Playhouse have become the stuff of
legend, especially during the regime of the social
director and producer Max Liebman, from 1933 to
1949.

Liebman was in charge of putting on a brand-new
revue every week; he had an excellent eye
for talent and recruited, among many others,
Sylvia Fine and Danny Kaye (who began their
personal and professional partnership at
Tamiment), Imogene Coca, and choreographer
Jerome Robbins. When television came along in
1948, Liebman was hired to produce the first
original revue for broadcast, *The Admiral
Broadway Revue*. After Liebman left Tamiment to
concentrate on producing television full-time, the
camp still brought in major young comic talent to
churn out its weekly revues: Carol Burnett, Danny
and Neil Simon, and Woody Allen, who made
both his directing and acting debuts at
Tamiment, when he felt the staff wasn't doing

justice to his comedy material. But the camp
closed in 1962, a victim of television and air-conditioning,
which made the urban nightclub a
comfortable fixture fifty-two weeks a year.

Nightclubs were part of the diurnal rhythm in
big cities across America well into the early sixties,
before crime and the call of suburbia made
catching the 7:21 to Scarsdale a higher priority
than catching Joe E. Lewis's act at two a.m. New
York's best clubs were the Copa, the Latin
Quarter (run by Barbara Walters's father, Lou),
and the Basin Street East. Le Ruban Bleu, the
Blue Angel, the Village Vanguard, and Julius
Monk's Upstairs at the Downstairs catered to a
more intimate, cabaret crowd. Chicago had the
Palmer House and Chez Paree for the expense
account crowd, Mr. Kelly's Mill for those who
liked their comedy a little on the raw side. Los
Angeles had the Cocoanut Grove for the movie
stars and the Crescendo for the hipsters. Miami
was building fancy hotels at an expansive rate—
the Fontainebleau, the Eden Roc, and the
Diplomat—to accommodate the older generation
who were fleeing the Northeast. Lou Walters
established a Latin Quarter down there, and
headliners like Milton Berle and Jackie Gleason
were packing them in; at a tiny club called Murray
Franklin's, one could catch a balding barracuda
named Don Rickles.

Then Vegas, fittingly, raised the stakes. With the
addition of major hotels like the Desert Inn, the
Sahara, and the Sands (the last two opened in
1952), the modern age of Las Vegas entertainment
had begun. Vegas had its own rules; no
comic could play a set longer than ninety minutes,
recalled Bob Newhart, because management
wanted the audience back at the gaming tables.
There were lounges, open all night, where comics
could get their start, and the main rooms, which
featured headliners, often earning five to ten
times what they could make in New York at the
Copa. Rickles, a feature at the Sahara's Casbah
lounge, remembered the thrill when his reputation
grew there: "For the first time, they've even

slapped on a cover charge. It's only five bucks, but
it makes me feel good. I'm no longer free. You
have to buy me." Vegas dealt a fatal blow to the
tonier clubs in cities across the country; their payroll
simply couldn't compete anymore.

Luckily, there were places springing up around
the country where you could get a few laughs
without being a high roller. In fact, some of the
best and most interesting nightclubs of the
1950s and '60s were in direct contrast to Las
Vegas—small, intimate, and definitely geared to
the counterculture. The tone of these clubs followed
the tune of the musicians who played
there, usually jazz musicians and folksingers.
The pioneer was the hungry i in San Francisco,
which opened its basement doors in 1951. Its legendary
owner, Enrico Banducci, created a venue
in complete opposition to a place like the Copa;
customers were not allowed to order drinks during
the show, tabletop candles were placed in
soup cans; and hecklers were forcibly ejected,
often by Banducci himself. Still, although there
was a heavy focus on folk music acts, the hungry
i was a career-making showcase for Mort Sahl,
Shelley Berman, Tom Lehrer, Bob Newhart, and
Nichols and May, among many others. (Lenny
Bruce often tried out material there in the wee
small hours, but generally considered the club
too "square" for his purposes.) The Purple
Onion, also in San Francisco's North Beach,
shone an early spotlight on Phyllis Diller and the
Smothers Brothers.

The bohemian life of Greenwich Village was the
perfect incubator for the kind of club that flourished
in San Francisco. The Village Gate, the
Bitter End, the Café au Go Go, and Café Wha?
allowed comics from off the beaten track to try
out a newer kind of material—hipper, more political,
more sexual, more idiosyncratic—and certainly
without a tuxedo. Comedians such as
Lenny Bruce, Joan Rivers, Woody Allen, Robert
Klein, Bill Cosby, Richard Pryor, and George
Carlin found receptive audiences among the
Bleecker Street crowd, and their careers flour-

ished at these clubs.

Chicago had an identity all its own by the 1960s. A group called the Compass Players based at the University of Chicago introduced ensemble improvisations to the club world in 1950; their alumni included Nichols and May and Shelley Berman. That group evolved into the Second City in 1959, continuing a more disciplined version of the comedy improv group. Second City set a very high bar, as comedians such as Robert Klein and Joan Rivers passed through the ensemble in the 1960s, and it continues to provide a fertile training ground for comedians to this day.

Perhaps the oddest but most interesting nightclub in Chicago was the Playboy Club. Opened by publisher Hugh Hefner in 1960, the Playboy Club was members only, with stiff drinks served by cottontailed waitress with a décolletage. A key to the club was, in the words, of comedian Dick Gregory, "a status symbol, like a Mercedes is now." In 1961, Gregory was a black comedian struggling in segregated clubs on Chicago's South Side. While Gregory admired routines like Shelley Berman's airplane bits, he knew such material was off-limits to his crowd: "I could never do that back then in the black nightclub, because less than one-tenth of one percent of the patrons had been on an airplane! But I could do the same thing about a Greyhound bus." One evening in 1961, when Professor Irwin Corey canceled on Hefner at the last minute, he brought Gregory across town to do his material at the Playboy Club: it was the first time a black comedian played in a white club. Gregory was a hit, the evening received national attention (and made Gregory's career), and the Chicago Playboy Club became a groundbreaking venue for artists like Lenny Bruce, Moms Mabley, and Redd Foxx, who required a hip audience that appreciated blue material but not cheap material.

With the greater presence of comedy on tele-

vision screens—talk shows, variety shows—comedians became much more in demand in the 1970s; also, the popularity of rock music made it difficult for the old-time crooners and saloon singers to attract audiences. It also proved a tough time for the borscht belt. The New York urban population had fled to other parts of the country, and air-conditioning and cheap airfare allowed customers to go somewhere else for their vacations.

Something new and different was needed. In 1963, impresario Budd Friedman opened a nightclub on West Forty-fourth Street called the Improv; initially, the club followed the traditional alternation between singers and comedians, but soon its stage hosted only comedians.

The Improv was the first comedy club in the country, and it offered important crossover spotlights on David Steinberg, Robert Klein, Jimmie

Walker, and Andy Kaufman, among many others. The concept of a two-drink minimum to watch comics, young and old, experiment with their craft proved surprisingly appealing, and "open mike" nights allowed a lot of beginning comedians to work on their material. New York soon played host to such groundbreaking clubs as Catch a Rising Star and the Comic Strip; comedian Rodney Dangerfield inaugurated a club of his own in 1970, Dangerfield's, which presents comedians to this day.

The elimination of the singer in a standard nightclub and the concurrent spotlights shone

exclusively on comedians behind a mike gave rise to a new and ubiquitous term: stand-up. Robert Klein observes:

"Before you knew it there were more young people standing in front of brick walls with microphones than you could shake a stick at—if that's your idea of a good time, as Groucho would say. And what happened is that comedy clubs began to open, specifically comedy, and there were no longer elegant nightclubs with martini glasses."

The middle ground of the sophisticated nightclub of the Copa days is a thing of the past. The lure of gambling casinos has increased the number of hotels across the country—Lake Tahoe, Atlantic City, Foxwoods—that need a big-attraction floor show. The performers—and their performances—become a commodity. For those audience members with hundreds of dollars to blow, Vegas and the other casinos will continue to offer impressive floor shows featuring top-notch, if undemanding, comics.

The nightclub and cabaret life of the postwar era is as nearly extinct as the Catskills resorts; it's nearly impossible to maintain a high-class boîte for the very best singers anymore. Standing on top of the heap—on many heaps, actually, all over cities in America—is the stand-up comic. The quality of stand-up comics at these comedy clubs varies enormously; you might get stuck with a college sophomore up there, but, hey, you never know when Jerry Seinfeld or Chris Rock is going to try out some new material. Comedians should enjoy their newfound triumph in comedy clubs while it lasts—they certainly put up with enough crooners and combos over the years. As Budd Friedman put it, "Stand-ups have become stars. Stand-ups get the women now. Except for a handful of Milton Berles and Sid Caesars, stand-ups were basically opening acts and the singers got the girls. Well, comics are getting the girls now."

"PILE THE COLD CUTS HIGH" ALLAN SHERMAN

To this day, at performances of Ponchielli's 1876 opera, *La Giaconda*, even at the Metropolitan Opera, an odd phenomenon occurs during the Act Three ballet sequence, called "The Dance of the Hours." Despite the august surrounding, as the orchestra takes up the first eight notes, a murmuring sound can be heard bubbling up from all corners of the house: "Hello, Mudduh . . . Hello, Faddah . . ."

"Dance of the Hours" had also been used in Disney's *Fantasia*, as the background music for the blithely dancing hippos, but in the early 1960s, a hippo-sized, bespectacled, Jewish television producer from Westchester danced into the national spotlight and became one of the most unexpected phenomena—and the most successful parody act—in American comedy.

Allan Sherman, like Tom Lehrer, was born in the mid-1920s to middle-class parents who divorced when he was in his teens. Sherman also became the class clown in college as well, gaining popularity through his wit and knack for parody. He went into television production in the 1950s, creating the concept for *I've Got a Secret* and serving briefly as a producer on *The Steve Allen Show*. But unlike Lehrer, Sherman, né Allan Copelon, wore his Jewishness proudly and loudly on his husky-sized sleeve. He had a gift for parodying songs from the classic Broadway scores, which he performed for friends at parties. "This is what the songs would be like if the Jews wrote all the songs—which, in fact, they do," he'd begin, and then regale the crowd with his ditties from *South Passaic*.

His satiric inversion for *My Fair Lady* was to have a Yiddish-speaking professor on the Lower East Side teach an articulate WASP flower seller to "speak as good as me." Inevitably, one lyric ran:

> I'm getting married in the morning.
>
> Ding-dong, the bells are gonna chime.
>
> I'll make some whoopee under the huppie—
>
> Get me to the temple on time.

Sherman was lucky enough to have Harpo Marx as his next-door neighbor in California for a brief time, and Harpo enjoyed his work so much that he threw numerous parties to allow Sherman to demonstrate his skills; he also arranged an audition for Sherman at Warner Bros. The producer there was thoroughly amused by Sherman's Broadway parodies but turned him down, mindful of the ruling that protected *MAD Magazine* because only the lyrics, and not the music, could be freely parodied.

Sherman borrowed his melodies from the public domain instead, and in doing so managed to take on his suburban Jewish preoccupations and the folk song movement at the same time. In a pleasant, if overtaxed, tenor voice, Sherman rendered his creative reimaginings of the world's great Gentile classics through the prism of a Jewish sensibility. "Frère Jacques" was the melody for one of the most memorable phone calls of the 1960s:

> Sarah Jackman, Sarah Jackman.
>
> How's by you? How's by you?
>
> How's by you the family?
>
> How's your sister Emily?
>
> She's nice too, she's nice too.

A dozen of these ditties appeared on Sherman's debut album, *My Son, the Folk Singer*. Released in October of 1962, it became one of the fastest-selling records in history. By Christmas, it had sold a million copies. A second album, called *My Son, the Celebrity*, released only three months after the first, also went number one.

For decades, Jewish American songwriters had changed their names or written about Gentile holidays and preoccupations as a way of crossing over. Sherman turned the whole thing inside out, giving Middle America short, sharp doses of *Yiddishkeit*. The fact that his roly-poly persona also folded in affectionately shared aspects of Jewish culture

Elvis, Schmelvis...
Allan Sherman, superstar.

My Son, the Media Sensation:
Cover boy; by the beautiful Westchester pool;
happy camper.

made him beloved by the Jewish population, while intriguing everyone else in the country. Sherman was the perfect transitional figure between first and second generation American Jews; he could drag in the familiar tropes of the Bronx and the Lower East Side: seltzer, delicatessens, the Garment District, traveling salesmen, and vacations in Miami:

> Do not make a stingy sandwich.
>
> Pile the cold cuts high.
>
> Customers should see salami
>
> Coming through the rye.

At the same time, his satirical targets included the accoutrements of middle-class success in the early 1960s: crab-grass, diet fads, mothers-in-law, and rebellious teenagers. Like Tom Lehrer's, his songs could capture a cultural moment better than any issue of *Time* or *Look* magazines. But Sherman transcended the boundaries of borscht belt humor, or singing to the converted (or, more accurately, the unconverted).

By the middle of 1963, Sherman was a national celebrity, playing nightclubs and amusement parks around the country, and selling out concerts at Carnegie Hall. It would be hard to provide an encore, but he did:

> Hello, Muddah. Hello, Faddah.
>
> Here I am at Camp Granada.
>
> Camp is very entertaining,
>
> And they say we'll have some fun if it stops raining.

"Hello, Muddah. Hello, Faddah" came from Sherman's third album, and when it was released as a single, the song was the number two song in the country for three weeks; this, in an era dominated by rock and roll. It combined Sherman's easy way with highbrow culture—"And the head coach wants no sissies / So he reads to us from something called *Ulysses*"—with something more accessible.

But tastes changed very quickly, and by the end of 1964, Sherman's genially exasperated criticisms started to seem like harangues. "Pop Hates the Beatles" was typical of latter-day Sherman:

> My daughter needs a new phonograph.
>
> She wore out all the needles.
>
> Besides, I broke the old one in half—
>
> I hate the Beatles.

The Beatles were, of course, the big competition. Sherman tried to remain in the game by parodying rock 'n' roll songs, but the gag had gone on too long. A score to a failed Broadway musical didn't help, and by the end of the 1960s, Sherman's suburban irritations paled before the greater outrages facing the country. He died in 1973, after a precipitous rejection by show biz.

> Somewhere overweight people
>
> Just like me,
>
> Must have someplace
>
> Where folks don't count every calorie. . . .

Sherman's star burnt out as quickly as it flared into being. Inevitable, perhaps, but for a couple of years his crossover dreams of acceptance for a fat, bespectacled, henpecked Jew really did come true.

IF BLUEBIRDS
WEIGHED AS MUCH AS I
YOU'D SEE SOME BIG FAT BLUEBIRDS
IN THE SKY . . . !

HARVEY AND SHEILA Allan Sherman

Sung to the tune of *Hava Negeila*

Harvey and Sheila, Harvey and Sheila, Harvey and Sheila,
Oh, the day they met.
Harvey and Sheila, Harvey and Sheila, Harvey and Sheila,
No one will forget.

Harvey's a CPA.
He works for IBM.
He went to MIT and got his PhD.

Sheila's a girl I know,
At B.B.D.& O.
She works the PBX,
And makes out the checks.

Then came one great day when
Harvey took the elevator,
Sheila got in two floors later,
Soon they both felt they were falling,
Everyone heard Sheila calling,
"Ring the bell,"
But they fell,
Harv and Sheila fell in love.

Harvey and Sheila, Harvey and Sheila, Harvey and Sheila,
Chose a wedding ring.
Harvey and Sheila, Harvey and Sheila, Harvey and Sheila,
Married in the spring.

She shopped at A&P,
He bought a used MG,
They sat and watched TV
On their RCA.

Borrowed from HFC,
Bought some AT&T,
And on election day,
Worked for JFK.

Then they went and got a
Charge-A-Plate from R. H. Macy's,
Bought a layette, pink and lacy,
Then they had twin baby girls,
Both with dimples, both with curls,
One named Bea,
One named Kay,
Soon they joined the PTA.

Harvey and Sheila, Harvey and Sheila, Harvey and Sheila,
Moved to West L.A.
Harvey and Sheila, Harvey and Sheila, Harvey and Sheila,
Flew TWA.

They bought a house one day,
Financed by FHA.
It had a swimming pool,
Full of H_2O.

Traded their used MG
For a new XKE.
Switched to the GOP,
That's the way things go.

Oh that Harvey he was
Really smart, he used his noodle.
Sheila bought a white French poodle,
Went to Europe with a visa,
Harvey's rich, they say that he's a
VIP!
This could be,
Only in the USA!

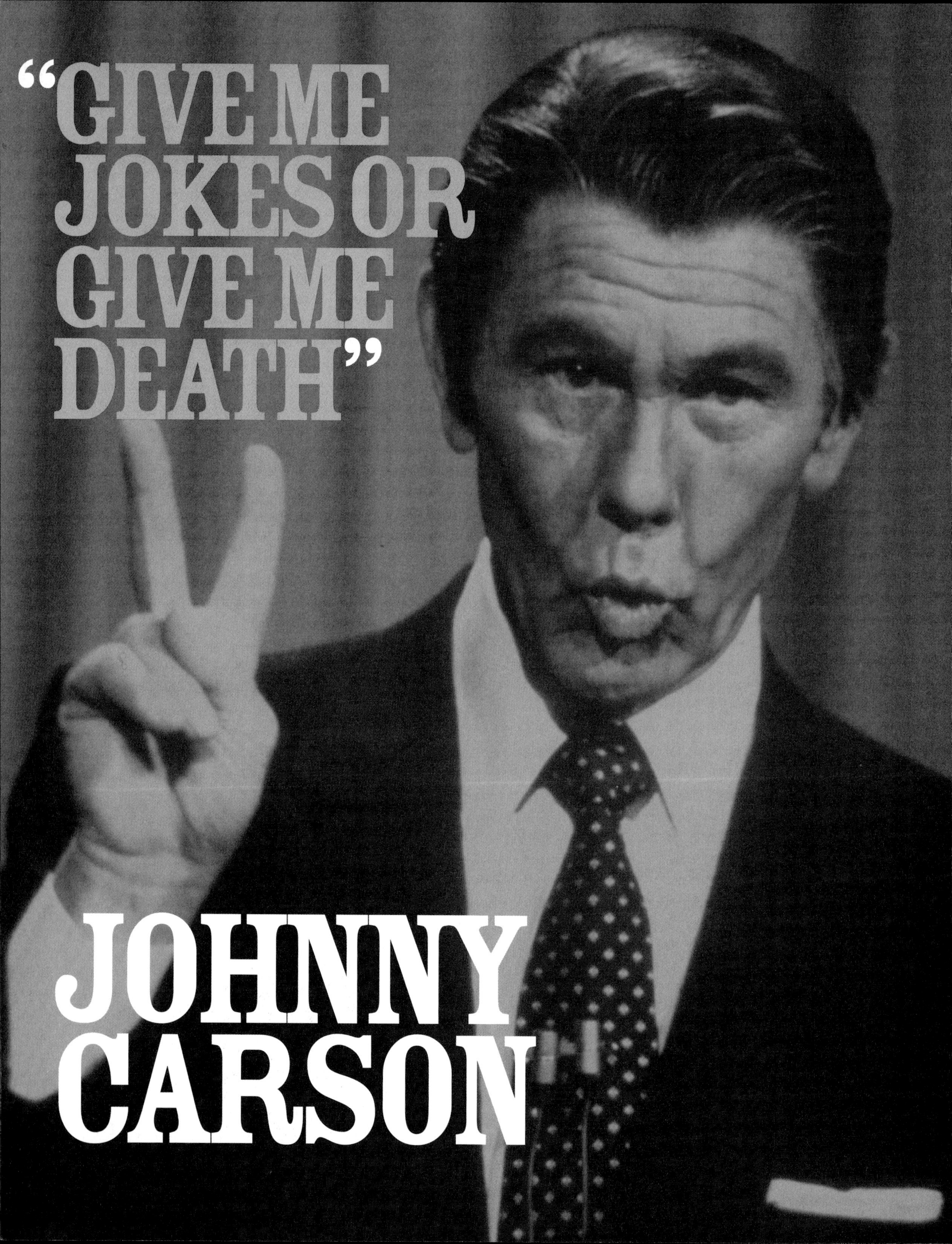

"GIVE ME
JOKES OR
GIVE ME
DEATH"

JOHNNY
CARSON

He ordained the culture. The whole world came to his doorstep. He didn't need comedians to be funny, he just needed information.
–David Steinberg

He seemed to be around forever and, at times, his material seemed to be about two hundred years old.

CARSON, *as colonial comic Shecky Revere:* I didn't know I was a Minute Man until my honeymoon. . . . (*rim shot*) Give me jokes or give me death. . . . George Washington couldn't be here tonight, he's too busy posing for the dollar. (*rim shot*) It was so cold at Valley Forge, he threw his teeth on the fire.

But, for nearly thirty years, millions of Americans went to bed with him every night. And it seemed impossible, rude even, not to refer to him by his first name: "Heeeeeeeeere's Johnny!"

John William Carson was born in 1925, in the very heart of the Midwest heartland, in the small Iowa town of Corning—"No jokes, please," he used to say. His father, a manager for a power company, brought the family to Norfolk, Nebraska. "I just can't say I ever *wanted* to be an entertainer; I already was one, sort of—around the house, at school, doing magic tricks and doing the Popeye imitation," he told *Rolling Stone* in 1979. "People thought I was funny; so I kind of took entertaining for granted." His professional debut came at the age of fourteen when, as The Great Carsoni, he did magic tricks for the Norfolk Rotary Club, wearing a black cape sewn by his mother. He earned three dollars for the gig. He became obsessed with the funnymen whose voices came out of the Philco cathedral radio in the living room. "[I learned joke construction] by observing, by listening, and watching somebody else's work. As a matter of fact, in college I did a thesis on comedy. I taped excerpts from the various radio shows and then tried to break them down and explain what kind of construction they were using."

In 1949, Carson got his first job at fifty dollars a week for doing anything and everything for a local radio station, and when WOW became the first TV station in a five-state area, he was there on the ground floor, learning whatever there was to know about the infant medium of television. Carson—who had no stage, vaudeville, or film background—became the first comedian to create his identity on television at the same time television was trying to create its own. "I've worked ever since I was a kid with a two-bit kit of magic tricks trying to improve my skills at entertaining whatever public I had—and to make myself ready for whenever the breaks came," he said.

I started to watch him when I was eleven or twelve and fell in love with it, I don't think I missed a *Tonight Show* through those years, high school, college, I had to get my Johnny Carson fix on a nightly basis. He was an imp, he said so himself, Peck's Bad Boy, the guy who was standing on the corner watching the parade go by and making sly comments on it. –Bill Maher

Host with the most:
As an up-and-coming comic with Garry Moore; with cohort, Ed McMahon; (right) formal informality.

That break came in 1954 when Carson, who had moved to Los Angeles and was writing for Red Skelton's show, filled in for him one night on live television after Skelton had injured himself in rehearsal that afternoon, CBS was so impressed it gave him his own variety show. It lasted all of thirty-nine weeks. He bounced back in New York as the irreverent host of an afternoon game show called *Who Do You Trust?* on ABC, which ran from 1957 to 1962. All through the 1950s, Carson was perfecting his signature style, borrowing bits and pieces from the comedians he adored. He assimilated Edgar Buchanan's slow burn, Groucho's cantilevered eyebrow, Stan Laurel's guileless shrug, Oliver Hardy's take "after the bucket of paint had fallen onto his head and he removed it," as Dick Cavett said. His great idol was Jack Benny and he incorporated Benny's greatest skill. "In certain instances, I am a reaction comedian," Carson said. "Very often you get more out of it by your *reactions* to things than doing jokes. If you get some nutty dame out there, you can get more out of it by just doing exasperated reactions or takes."

Eventually, Carson absorbed all of those influences into his own style. Where previous generations of comedians might change their names, their faces, their backgrounds to become more American, more acceptable, Carson did the opposite—he folded the styles of various ethnic comedians into his own laid-back Midwestern charm. Mel Brooks called him Supergentile, and Bob Newhart elaborated, "Mel is correct in a certain way. There's a certain quality about being from the Midwest that you don't put on airs and, and you don't act like something you're not, because they're gonna see through it. Yes, John was Supergentile, but maybe he was also Supermidwesterner." For Carson, it was that affability—however it might be characterized—that gave him his superpowers:

> First of all, the most important thing to me in comedy—the greatest thing a performer can have if he is going to be successful, is an empathy with the audience. They *have* to like him. And if they like the performer, then you've got eighty percent of it made—it's amazing what you can get away with and what they will accept from you.

His hard work and essential likability paid off, and in 1962, he was offered one of the prime jobs on television: taking over NBC's late-night *Tonight Show* from its mercurial host, Jack Paar. Paar was contentious, emotional, and politically engaged. He also presided over the most difficult job in television at the time—a nightly live talk show, broadcast for an hour and forty-five minutes, the longest slot on the air. It was too difficult even for the ambitious Carson—he initially turned it down. But after cleverly insisting on a series of interim hosts to provide a "palate cleanser," Carson debuted in Rockefeller Center's Studio 6-B with *The Tonight Show Starring Johnny Carson* on October 1, 1962. Carson had figured a way to make it work. He told himself he wouldn't be a Jack Paar imitation. "I had done nearly everything you could do in the industry," he said. "It all just boiled down to being my natural self and seeing what happened."

What happened was the most successful show of any kind in television history; within three years, it was being watched by twice as many people as had watched Paar, and at its height, it was watched by 10 to 15 million people a night. (He created a seismic shift in the broadcasting industry by moving his program to studios in Burbank, California, in 1972.) Whether Carson was a comedian hosting a talk show or a talk show host doing comedy was an irrelevant distinction—he was the best at both. The show gave him a forum to indulge his favorite indoor sport. "He loved nothing better than to laugh," recalled Carl Reiner. "His soul was happy. He really loved comedians. When he heard something funny, it was good for the comedian and good for him."

Almost immediately after taking over the reins of *The Tonight Show*, Carson brought on more and more comedians. Other television shows, such as *The Ed Sullivan Show* showcased comedians, but Carson's talk show venue could offer comedians something they couldn't get anywhere else: a chance for America to discover who they really were, and frequently the comedians discovered who they were themselves.

> What made Johnny Carson a great host was he was a great listener. He listened and he went where you were going. He didn't have twelve questions in front of him, and you said, "And so I killed my mother-in-law," and he'd go, "You have a new dog, don't you?" He went with you. He was also the best straight man in the world. He knew just when to come in and say, "How fat was she?" And you just wanted to go, "God bless you." —Joan Rivers

HE LOVED NOTHING BETTER THAN TO LAUGH.
—Carl Reiner

SUPERGENTILE

Carson's enthusiasm for comedians and performing ended when his show came down at one in the morning (later on, it came down at twelve-thirty); he protected his privacy fiercely. "From the time I was a little kid, I was always shy," said Carson. "Performing was when I was outgoing." Friends and intimates claimed to see a more outgoing side of Carson when the studio lights were turned off, but Dick Cavett's perceptions appear to be accurate:

> After the show once, three tourists who maybe got out the wrong exit, found themselves face-to-face with Johnny, and they'd say, "Oh, Johnny, I got to tell you a story about—" I would see him just die. That kind of thing was hard for him. And I've always felt sorry for the social pain that he went through. Johnny was the most socially uncomfortable man I think I ever met.

Carson would grow particularly testy when reporters asked about his four marriages, or worse, about his annual salary, which was, at one point, over $5 million, the largest in television history. "I was raised in the Midwest, where it was considered impolite to ask somebody how much they made," he told Mike Wallace on *60 Minutes*. In a moment of candor, Carson admitted, "I'm getting well paid off it, but it's the toughest job on television." And the toughest part of the toughest job was Carson's favorite.

"The monologue truly is the pride and joy of his appearance on the show," said his longtime producer, Fred de Cordova. On every broadcast afternoon, Carson would be presented with six different full-length monologues crafted by his writers; he himself would pick out the best fifteen or twenty gags, often adding his own to create a seven-minute commentary that one critic called "the voice of Middle America." "For thirty years, Johnny's show was the town square of America. It was a familiar place we could all gather. And we came to know and trust and like him," said George Carlin. Carson's monologue wouldn't be entirely political—he'd be clever enough to include some odd bits of trivia and anecdotes from the American scene—but if anything appeared on the radar, he would clock it, or rather, he put it on the radar by clocking it. His own political preferences were carefully guarded. "You never really knew who he voted for," said Bill Maher, an ardent fan.

Carson's neutrality—or appearance of it—was less a matter of privacy than of survival. "When a comic becomes enamored with his own views and foists them off on the public in a polemic way, he not only loses his sense of humor, but his value as a humorist," Carson said. "He becomes declassified as a humorist." It wasn't always easy for him to keep his counsel. Once, in the early 1970s, frequent guest David Steinberg did a long, fairly unprecedented, harangue against Richard Nixon:

> I finished the show and Johnny was saying to me, "I love what you did, but you're ahead of the audience on this." I said, "What do you mean?" He said,

"Well, the audience isn't ready for where you are with Nixon." When he decided to call Nixon a crook, the whole country was with him at that moment. In fact, his point of view was exactly the same as mine, but Johnny had perfect pitch.

Still, for Carson's shrewd sense of the ridiculous, there were some gifts that kept on giving. In May of 1992, when then Vice President Dan Quayle condemned the television character of Murphy Brown as being part of a national "poverty of values" because she was

an unwed mother, Carson went in for the kill:

> Any Brown supporters here? I'm talking *Murphy Brown*. Let's go to the news and see if Dan Quayle has condemned the lifestyle of Urkel on *Family Matters*. You get the feeling that Dan Quayle's golf bag doesn't have a full set of irons? . . . Quayle said illegitimacy is something we should talk about in terms of not having. How about illiteracy?

Needless to say, that was the beginning of the end of Quayle's fragile credibility. Carson's intuitive knack for the right jokes at the right time, elegantly served up, made *The Tonight Show* one of the most fluid and happily predictable shows on television. "We create the show while it's on the air," he once said. And when it was time for that show to close, his impeccable sense of timing shone through once more.

You try doing this with a straight face: Carson—patriotic, mousy, Egyptian, and blabby—*Aunt* Blabby.

"When he leaves [the air] on May 22, 1992, the closest thing we'll have to a national barometer will be the Weather Channel," wrote *TV Guide*. Although Carson made some memorable appearances as host of the Oscars, *The Tonight Show* was first and always his home turf. He never pitched a commercial product, and he consistently resisted hundreds of requests to play roles in sitcoms and movies. Why would he? He had already mastered his greatest role: Johnny Carson. "When he said he was done, he was done. I mean, that guy had ethics like nobody's business," said Roseanne Barr. Indeed, Carson was as good as his word—he resisted every attempt to drag him back into the spotlight. During the thirteen years between his retirement and his death, he told friends he had only one regret: not being on the air during the Monica Lewinsky scandal. "I haven't seen such an abundance of material in my life!" he said. "It's almost funnier than any jokes you could make."

For almost thirty years, Carson vanquished every late-night rival they put on against him, and to the successful comics and future hosts who followed in his footsteps, he

Passing the torch:
David Letterman, Garry Shandling, and Jay Leno
show up for an anniversary tribute.

was a god. "He was just, just phe-nomenal," said Bob Newhart. "At one point, I filled in for him. I did three weeks in New York and I was absolutely destroyed. I mean, at the end of three weeks I was a limp dishrag, I had nothing left. And he did it for thirty years, so." Like mil-lions of Americans, Roseanne feels his absence tangibly:

He always put it together and put it straight for us. And nobody could get politicaly out of line because he didn't let 'em. He took 'em down—right and left. Dem and Repub. If we had Johnny now, if Johnny was still alive and on the air, we'd never have gone to Iraq. He would not have let that happen.

A strong statement, but not improbable, when you think about it. Steve Martin, in a eulogy in the *New York Times*, wrote, "[He] gave each guest the benefit of the doubt, and in this way [he] exemplified an American ideal: you're nuts but you're welcome here."

Carson had a shot at his own epitaph in 1979, while being interviewed on *60 Minutes*:

I'D PREFER NOT TO HAVE ONE AT ALL— WHERE IT NEVER GOT TO THAT POINT. I DON'T KNOW. I THINK SOMETHING LIKE, "I'LL BE RIGHT BACK."

ROWAN & MARTIN'S LAUGH-IN

"THEN YOU KNOW WHAT I'M HERE AFTER"

It lasted three seconds—tops—but it may have ushered in five and a half years of the most controversial presidency in American history.

BET YOUR BIPPY

Fickle Finger of Fate:
Dan Rowan and Dick Martin, front and center, of their goofball cast, which includes Goldie Hawn, Arte Johnson, Henry Gibson, and Ruth Buzzi, inside ladder.

Fickle Finger of Fate: Dan Rowan and Dick Martin, front and center, of their goofball cast, which includes Goldie Hawn, Arte Johnson, Henry Gibson, and Ruth Buzzi, inside ladder.

THEY SAID "BUT IT DOESN'T MAKE ANY SENSE." AND I SAID, "BUT YOU LAUGHED."
—George Schlatter

When Republican presidential candidate Richard M. Nixon made his terse appearance on *Rowan & Martin's Laugh-In* in September of 1968, his bit was but one of the hundreds of cameos, sight gags, one-liners, punch lines, slapstick inanities, and political zingers that made up every episode of the madcap mosaic montage that was the number one television show of the late 1960s. Had Nixon lost the election two months later, no one might have remembered his appearance, but to be part of *Laugh-In*—for three seconds or five seasons—was to be at the center of the pop culture zeitgeist of America.

Dan Rowan and Dick Martin had become a popular comedy team in the late 1950s, achieving a kind of B-level fame in Vegas and on television specials. Their double-act was a refined, three-martini version of Burns and Allen, with Rowan usually trying to explain important things to the attention deficient, jovially randy Martin. Hip and cool in their Botany-500 tuxedoed way, they made the perfect keystone hosts for the insane cocktail party that producer George Schlatter created: a supercollider of unstable eclectic comedy elements without the dreary rigors of a beginning, middle, or end.

Schlatter surrounded his genial hosts with a lunatic repertory company of almost a dozen comedians. All were young, most were unknown; several, such as Goldie Hawn and Lily Tomlin, went on to breakout careers. Most of *Laugh-In*'s humor was on a burlesque level, updated with candy-colored psychedelia: "Do you believe in the hereafter?" murmured Arte Johnson's dirty old man. "Of course I do," responded Ruth Buzzi's frumpy spinster. "Then you know what I'm here after." *Da-da-dum-de-dum.* Of the show's many popular catchphrases, the most popular by far was "Sock it to me!" (It was usually said by the pert comedienne Judy Carne right before being hit with a bucket of water or a giant hammer or something: "It may be Japanese rice wine to you, but it's sake to me!" *Boom*!) These chestnuts were counterbalanced by some political spice—nothing excoriating, just hip enough to grab a couple of handfuls of late sixties preoccupations and toss them into the air, like confetti. Tommy Smothers, taking time out from getting in trouble over at CBS, showed up for a one-liner: "Let's all get behind President Johnson. And push."

One afternoon in 1968, Nixon was in NBC's Burbank studios to do a news appearance. Paul Keyes, another of *Laugh-In*'s producers, had been a Nixon speechwriter and was still friendly with the candidate. It had been part of the show's MO to feature cameos from guest celebrities—Johnny Carson, Bob Hope, Bette Davis—tossing off a quick one-liner or two, and to have Nixon do one would be a memorable coup. Keyes asked; Nixon, who, according to Dick Martin, "loved to be funny," said yes. Schlatter and Keyes sat Nixon down in the studio and asked him to say the four magic words. Schlatter recalls:

> We went over and I said, "Just say 'Sock it to *me*?'" "Okay, right . . . Sock it to me." "No, no, Mr. Nixon, that sounds too intense. If you could just kind of smile and say like it's a surprise: 'Sock it to *me*?'" "Yes, yes, I'm new at this comedy business." And we did six takes until we finally got the one that we used on the air: "Sock it to *me*?" where he was kind of cute. He said the rest of his life that appearing on *Laugh-In* was what got him elected. And I believe that. And I've had to live with that.

Whether or not Nixon's cameo on *Rowan & Martin's Laugh-In* actually got him elected is a matter for political historians to decide, but it certainly went a long way to leavening his dour personality. The appearance did have its ramifications; it led to the FCC instituting an equal time resolution for political candidates on nonpolitical or news shows. And as Schlatter pointed out, "Nixon was the first kind of presidential candidate to ever appear in the midst of anything like that. And now, of course, it's standard operating procedure for presidential candidates to appear. And they all have joke writers."

Oh, and speaking of equal time, what about Hubert Humphrey, Nixon's Democratic rival? The producers of *Laugh-In* chased him all over the country, trying to get him on camera, but his campaign manager nixed the idea, thinking it would be demeaning to have their candidate on a goofy Monday night show. Who had the last laugh?

DA-DA-DUM-DE-DUM.

Ringie Ding-a-ling:
Lily Tomlin as Ernestine; Buzzi, Hawn, and Gibson cooking up some business; "Say goodnight, Dick."

IF YOU DIDN'T LAUGH AT THE FIRST JOKE, THERE WERE THREE MORE COMING.

–Dick Martin

"AND I JUST COULDN'T RESIST IT"
CAROL BURNETT

Carol was so personable, she was like somebody in your family that you trusted and you knew she didn't ever mean harm to anybody and it was just funny for funny's sake.

–Roseanne Barr

If Carol Burnett had accepted the offer from CBS to do a sitcom in the mid-1960s, the world would have been a very different place.

When I had the chance to do a variety show, CBS tried to talk me out of it. They said, "Well, you know, that's Dean Martin and that's Sid Caesar and that's Milton Berle and that's Jackie Gleason. You'd be much better off doing . . ." They had some pilot half-hour sitcom called *Here's Agnes*. And you can imagine what that was. And I said, "No, I really want to do the variety show. I want guest stars, I want to have a rep company. I would be the star of a sketch at one point. We'd all be together as a family."

One of Burnett's great gifts was that she made the audience feel like family, too. In 1978, *TV Guide* wrote, "When she comes out to say good night, you momentarily sense that you're not just looking at an entertainer—you're looking into the face of a human being. People loved Carol Burnett. They felt her comedy spoke to them." Burnett's own family was more difficult.

Born in San Antonio, Texas, in 1933, Burnett spent nearly all of her youth with her maternal grandmother; her parents, both alcoholics, had relocated to Los Angeles, hoping to bring the family back together someday. Her Nana took Carol to Hollywood when she was seven—but the dreams of becoming one big happy family were never to be. She was essentially raised by her grandmother in a tiny apartment on Wilcox and Yucca, while her mother lived down the hall.

Plays well with others:
Burnett with chum Julie Andrews; Harpo;
and Lucy (facing).

We were what you'd call poor. My grandmother would save up what she could and we would go to maybe four movies a week. Double features, so at times I would see eight movies a week. I would come home and playact these movies with the kids on the block. It was a great way for me to be influenced as a child because the bad guys always got it, the good guys succeeded, and they were all beautiful and there was gorgeous music or this or that or funny, slapstick fall-down stuff. I just loved the movies.

She loved the movies so much that, as a teenager, she worked as an usher for the Warner Bros. Theater on Hollywood Boulevard. When she refused to seat a couple toward the climax of an Alfred Hitchcock movie—for fear the ending would be ruined for them—she was fired on the spot. Her mother, in rare moments of lucidity, wanted her to be a journalist, but once Burnett got onstage in college, she found her calling. "When I went to UCLA something drew me into an acting class. They laughed when they were supposed to and that was a big turn-on."

In 1954, thanks to a thousand-dollar check courtesy of an anonymous benefactor, Carol moved to New York and checked into a large showbiz family at the Rehearsal Club, a sprawling dormitory for aspiring actresses made famous in *Stage Door*. It wasn't long before she broke out, with a bit of specialty material—"I Made a Fool of Myself over John Foster Dulles"—in which she professed to be enraptured by the dour, reserved Secretary of State in the Eisenhower administration, the least likely sex symbol in

America, as even he himself admitted. The song made Burnett the hottest nightclub comedienne in New York. Typical of her basic decency, when Burnett heard that Dulles had become ill with cancer in 1959, she dropped the song from her act.

She made a few routine TV appearances, but it wasn't long before she became a regular on a live program that suited her talents. After Burnett filled in for comedienne Martha Raye on *The Garry Moore Show* with only a few hours' notice, Moore put her permanently on his evening variety show. It proved to be the best possible training ground. There was nothing Burnett couldn't do—singing medleys, playing opposite guest stars, parodying the latest TV commercials, jumping out of balsa-wood windows. Burnett quickly became the center of the show, and her popularity soared. Occasionally, in the press, she took the rap for playing the clown too often—something women on television weren't supposed to do. "I'm not afraid to make myself unattractive. Most women are afraid," she told an interviewer in 1963. "Now the sloppier I am, the more comfortable I am, and the better I feel in a comedy sketch."

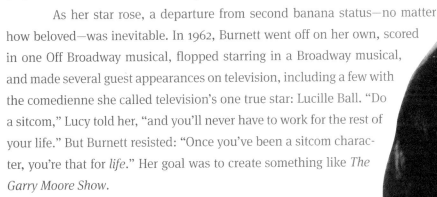

As her star rose, a departure from second banana status—no matter how beloved—was inevitable. In 1962, Burnett went off on her own, scored in one Off Broadway musical, flopped starring in a Broadway musical, and made several guest appearances on television, including a few with the comedienne she called television's one true star: Lucille Ball. "Do a sitcom," Lucy told her, "and you'll never have to work for the rest of your life." But Burnett resisted: "Once you've been a sitcom character, you're that for *life*." Her goal was to create something like *The Garry Moore Show*.

In the fall of 1967, Burnett's wish came true. CBS executives were apprehensive—Dinah Shore had been the only other woman to carry a prime-time variety hour—but *The Carol Burnett Show*, with its felicitous initials, quickly became a big hit. Burnett surrounded herself with a family of brilliant second bananas—Harvey Korman, Lyle Waggoner, Vicki Lawrence, and eventually Tim Conway. Burnett began and ended each episode talking with the audience, and she would usually perform a duet if the guest star was a singer, but it was the sketch comedy, especially the parodies of the movies she loved in the 1940s, that brought her to new heights as a comic artist. Said Buz Kohan, one of her chief writers, "Carol always loved to play those characters which she would never get to play in real life."

"It's a form of growing up, I guess, when you can make fun of those things that you enjoyed in childhood and now, now you're satirizing," said Bob Newhart. Burnett got to be "Mildred Fierce," or strut her stuff along "Sunnyset Boulevard," or borrow a neighbor's pool to film an Esther Williams spoof.

I'M NOT AFRAID TO MAKE MYSELF UNATTRACTIVE. MOST WOMEN ARE AFRAID.

Shot in the temple:
Burnett as Starlett in "Went With the Wind";
Vivien Leigh, in the original; spoofing Shirley
Temple; the real item. (Below) Bob Mackie's
sketch.

I don't think we were mean-spirited when we did the movie takeoffs. We were just trying to give the essence and, and do a parody of it. I wasn't doing Joan Crawford, I was doing Mildred Pierce. I was doing Crawford's character. I think the reason they worked, also, not only were they brilliantly written, but I think people knew we were doing it out of love.

The show's prodigious costumer, Bob Mackie, gets credit from Burnett and the rest of the crew for bringing Burnett's outrageous characters to life. "Carol really doesn't come alive until she gets the costume on," said Kohan. "And Bob Mackie had this wonderful sense of humor that was so in tune with what Carol could do." In 1976, after NBC broke ratings records with a prime-time broadcast of *Gone With The Wind*, *The Carol Burnett Show* knew it was time to turn to the granddaddy of all Hollywood movies. It proved to be their finest quarter of an hour.

"Went With The Wind" is remembered as one of the best collaborations between ensemble, writers, and a costumer ever seen on television comedy. As Burnett remembers it:

The biggest laugh I ever got was when I came on top of the staircase as Starlett O'Hara, with the curtain rod in my dress. I have to say, "Thank God for Bob Mackie." When I went into costume fitting, Bob said, "I have this idea," and brought out that curtain rod. I only showed it to Harvey because I didn't want him to crack up while I'm coming down the stairs. So, when I came down, it was a burst of laughter—the audience and the crew and the band. Then of course to have that great punch line when he says, "Starlett, you're beautiful. That dress is you." And her line is, "Well, I saw it in the window and I just couldn't resist it."

The show kept adding recurring sketches, including "The Family," a particularly vicious look at the domestic battles waged in kitchens all across America that bore more than a passing resemblance to the disappointments that Burnett suffered growing up. As her head writer, Arnie Rosen, said in 1972, "I think a lot of Carol's comedy is survival oriented. You take a woman like that, a girl with the childhood she had—there's going to be that survival instinct or there's going to be nothing. You take a woman who never shows temper, and who knows what outlet there is for it in her work?"

When Burnett started her series in 1967, there were nineteen prime-time variety and game shows on the three networks. When the 1975–1976 Emmys rolled around, there were only two nominees left standing for Outstanding Musical Variety Show: *The Carol Burnett Show* and a newcomer called *Saturday Night Live*. "I think we got better," she said. "When I started out, I was this young girl just going, 'Ahhhhh-a-haaaaahhhh-hhh!!' or whatever, and as we got older and matured, I wasn't quite as loud as I used to be because it wasn't required anymore. And I could delve more into the funny characteristics of a character rather than swinging from a chandelier. Although I did a lot of that, too." Three years later, after 286 episodes—each one of them with the same comfortable format—and twenty-two Emmys, Burnett decided to quit swinging on the chandeliers. Although she has expanded her range as a serious dramatic actress (and a playwright), she never lost her pure enthusiasm for the allure of show business, just like when she was a kid going to double features in Hollywood. "Why do we all go into this business in the first place? To have fun. As a kid, that's why you playact.

I think us people in show business are the luckiest because we chose it. There are no want ads for actors."

Cleaning up: Burnett's second family: Vicki Lawrence, guest Jim Nabors, Burnett, Harvey Korman, and Lyle Waggoner; (above) cheery charwoman.

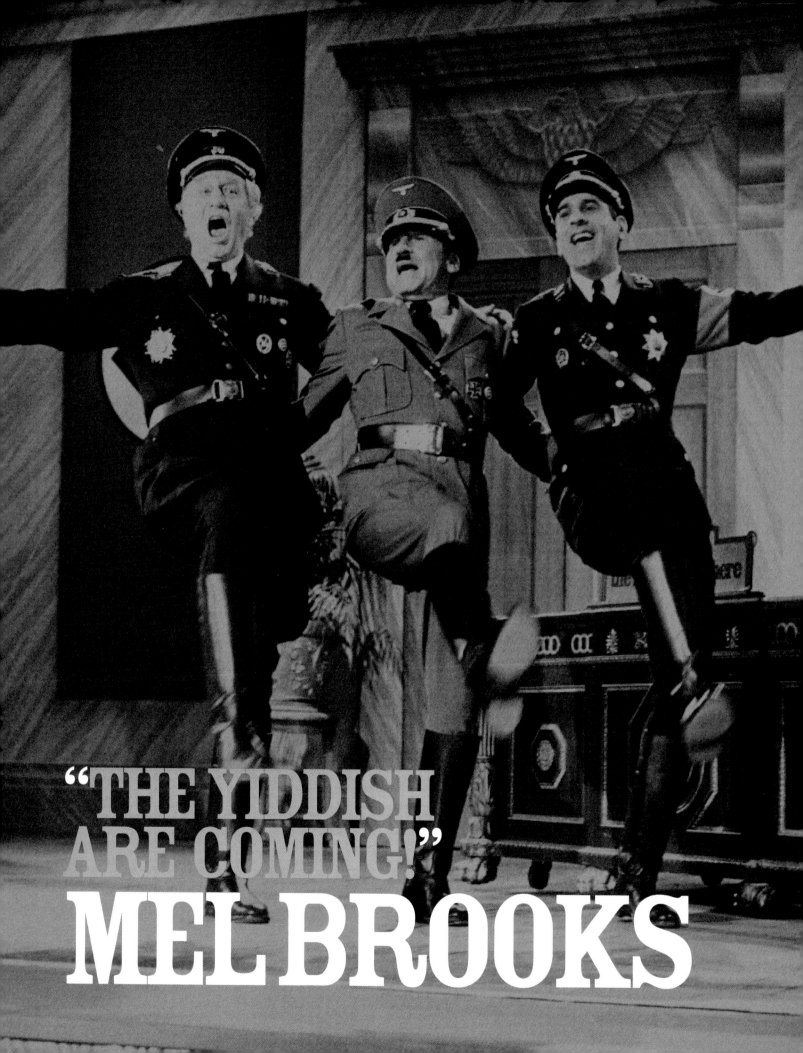

"THE YIDDISH
ARE COMING!"
MEL BROOKS

Carl Reiner: About four days ago, a plane landed at Idlewild Airport. The plane came from the Middle East bearing a man who claims to be 2000 years old. He spent the last six days at the Mayo Clinic. Sir, is it true that you are 2000 years old? **Mel Brooks:** Oh, *boy*, oh, yes....I'll be–I'm not *yet*–I'll be 2000 October 16th....

When Mel Brooks and Carl Reiner brought out their first comedy album, *The 2000 Year Old Man*, in 1960, it became a phenomenon, selling over a million copies at $4.98 apiece. For The 34 Year Old Mel Brooks, it couldn't have happened a moment too soon. Brooks's career as a comedy writer was in a kind of freefall; admired by many, unemployed by more, he was considered too brash, too over-the-top, too meshuga to cooperate with producers, directors, and writing staffs. All of which was true, so Brooks leaped over the typewriter and sold his most original commodity: himself.

In reality, Brooks was born, not 2000 years ago (nor was his real name George M. Cohan, as he liked to joke), but as Melvin Kaminsky on June 28, 1926, in Brooklyn. "We were so poor," Brooks said in a 1975 *Playboy* interview, adding to one of comedy's great opening lines, "my mother couldn't afford to have me; the lady next door gave birth to me." His father died when he was three and he was left in the care of his doting mother, who raised Mel and his three brothers by working in the Garment District. Brooks was admittedly the adored little king of his household—"It's good to be the king!"—but the tedium of his Depression-era existence was relieved only by his reputation as the class clown and by the movies. He loved the Marx Brothers and their more manic B-movie clones, the Ritz Brothers. He wasn't too fond of Boris Karloff: "I was terrified by Frankenstein as a kid—thought he was coming up the fire escape—and I'd see that metal rod in his neck and scream."

Like many other Jewish kids in the 1930s and '40s from Brooklyn or the Bronx, Brooks escaped every summer to the leafy retreats of the Catskills resorts, only he indulged his talent as a teenage tummler. "My first sketch was pretty advanced for the Catsills," he recounted. "The girl and I walked out from the wings and we met at the center of the stage.

HE: I am a masochist.

SHE: I am a sadist.

HE: Hit me. *(She does, very hard in the face.)*

HE: Wait a minute, wait a minute, hold it. I think I'm a sadist.

Melvin got hit even harder after he enlisted as a solider in World War II and was sent to the German front. "It was very noisy, and I thought that I would not want to be in the war very long because of the noise." The war seared itself on his mind, even fueled his comic engine. "When the blond-haired Teutons have been nipping at your heels for thousands of years, you find it enervating to keep wailing," he told *Playboy*. "So you make jokes. If your enemy is laughing, how can he bludgeon you to death?" Actor Lewis J. Stadlen, who appeared in Brooks's Nazi comedy *To Be or Not to Be*, commented, "The way I imagine it, Mel found himself in some foxhole and said, 'If I ever get out of this alive, I'm gonna dedicate the rest of my life to making Adolf Hitler look ridiculous.' "

That would come later; after the war, he found himself as an informal comic sidekick to Sid Caesar, pushing his way onto the writing staff of *Your Show of Shows*. He became famous for showing up late and supplying the most outrageous ideas—many of which were simply unproducable. "One night, we were totally stuck," remembered Larry Gelbart. "Mel said, 'Wait! Wait! Listen to this.' And then he broke into a chorus of 'All of Me.' He just sang it. He didn't have an idea, but it was just so damn entertaining, we just plotzed." One afternoon in the Writers' Room, Brooks and Carl Reiner invented something that was not only damn entertaining, it became legendary. Reiner recounted:

> There was a show on the air called *We the People Speak* and it recreated the news of the day. But I thought it was such a good idea—that somebody was actually someplace they couldn't have been—and Mel was sitting on my right and I go, "Here was a man who was actually at the scene of the crucifixion two

WE WERE SO POOR, MY MOTHER COULDN'T AFFORD TO HAVE ME; THE LADY NEXT DOOR GAVE BIRTH TO ME.

thousand years ago. Isn't that true, sir?" and Mel's first words were "Oh, boy." "You were there?" I continued, "You knew Jesus, yes?" "Sure," he said, "a lovely boy, thin. Wore sandals . . ."

Reiner and Brooks were the hit of the party circuit, and George Burns advised them to record their act, because if they didn't, he was going to steal it from them. After Caesar's various shows were canceled, Brooks was left without a place to come to work in the morning—even late—and he often returned to the *2000 Year Old Man* sketches with Reiner simply as a way of keeping himself going until something more substantial came along. Brooks

was not only throwing off hilarious ad-libbed one-liners about world history, he was reimagining Western civilization from a Jewish immigrant perspective. "My comedy comes from the feeling that, as a Jew, and as a person, you don't fit into the mainstream of American society," he said. "It comes from the realization that even though you're better and smarter, you'll never belong."

REINER: Sir, I read somewhere that you lived in Boston. Did you know Paul Revere?

BROOKS: An anti-Semite bastard. He hated the Jews. He was afraid they were moving into the neighborhood, the fear—"They're coming, they're coming, the Yiddish are coming."

REINER: Sir: it was "The *British* are coming!"

BROOKS: Oy, my God!

Working his way up:
Brooks, with Harry Crane and Danny Simon, as writers for a Jerry Lewis TV show; with Kaye Ballard and Carl Reiner; behind—and in front of—the camera as Rabbi Tuchman in *Robin Hood: Men in Tights.*

Although Brooks had found his comic voice as the 2000 Year Old Man, he still hadn't quite found his audience. Between 1959 and 1965—"that terrible period where I couldn't get anything off the ground"—Brooks had tried writing for various TV shows, Broadway shows, even a screenplay with Jerry Lewis, but aside from creating *Get Smart* with Buck Henry and marrying acclaimed actress Anne Bancroft, the big payoff that Brooks had dreamed of hadn't materialized. He decided to take matters into his own hands by directing his outrageous original screenplay about the Broadway world he grew up idolizing (as well

It's good to be the king:
Brooks in *Blazing Saddles*; *History of the World, Part One*; clowning on the set of *Young Frankenstein*.

I never did any jokes to have other people laugh. For me, there is no audience—there's an "audi-I." If *I* laugh, it's funny.

–Mel Brooks

as the greedy, dysfunctional Broadway world that he had known as a beleagured book writer).

The Producers, as the world now knows, is the story of Max Bialystock, a failed producer, who teams up with a timid accountant, Leo Bloom, to create a guaranteed box office disaster and then pocket the flop's overcapitalized investments. In an era where every inappropriate source or historical event had been musicalized for the Broadway stage, Brooks took the final leap by dragging in his old nemesis as the punch line. The film's musical (and originally the film itself) was called *Springtime for Hitler* (a spoof of an old summer stock chestnut called *Springtime for Henry*). *The Producers* (a compromise title) was made for less than a million, ahead of schedule, and won Brooks a 1968 Academy Award for Best Original Screenplay. It also won him a reputation for an outrageous, tasteless, undisciplined sense of humor, along with many detractors and a hard-core cult following.

Brooks's frequent partner in crime, Gene Wilder, said that "Mel grabs a shotgun, loads it with fifty pellets, and points it in the general direction of one enormous target. Out of fifty, he'll score at least six or seven huge bull's-eyes, and those are what people always remember about his films." His next major project involved several shotguns and a battery of six-shooters; *Blazing Saddles* was the perfect anarchic comedy for the early 1970s. Working with a team of writers, including Richard Pryor, Brooks fashioned the first screen parody that completely deconstructed an entire film genre.

> I decided that this would be a surrealistic epic because the official movie portrait of the West was simply a lie. . . . We used dirty language on the screen for the first time and to me the whole thing was like a big psychoanalytic session. I just got everything out of me—all my furor, my frenzy, my insanity, my love of life and my hatred of death.

The film spewed a cornucopia of jokes in all directions: sex jokes, Jewish jokes, black jokes—and one sequence that studio executives at Warner Bros. begged him to cut. "The farting scene is funny because farts in our world are funny," Brooks said, defending the scene around the campfire where bean-devouring cowpokes express themselves. *Blazing Saddles* appealed to adolescents of all ages and its box office grosses—so to speak—were one hundred times its budget of $2 million. It made Mel Brooks the king of comic parody.

Brooks's follow-up film was based on an idea brought to him by Wilder, and they collaborated on a screenplay that paid homage to the monster movies that had scared the pants off Brooks as a child. Brooks directed *Young Frankenstein* with a loving touch that took the idea of death seriously while making it screamingly funny. "Underneath the comedy in *Young Frankenstein*, the doctor is undertaking the quest to defeat death—to challenge God," Brooks said in an interview at the time. "Our monster lives, therefore he wants love, too. He's really very touching in his lonely misery." The movie, which was turned down by Columbia Pictures because its initial budget of $2 million was too high, wound up making $90 million for Twentieth Century Fox.

The huge crossover appeal of Brooks's parody films attest to the fact that you don't have to be Jewish to love them, but there's a basic anarchic strategy to the copious Jewish references and characters in his movies. Jason Alexander, who played Max in the Los Angeles stage version of *The Producers*, argues:

Mel took the sense of humor that he knew completely, that Jewish, borscht belt, vaudeville sensibility. And in his satires, he laid it on where no Jew has gone before. There's no Jews in the Wild West. There's no Jews in Frankenstein's castle. There's no Jews in the great silent movies. He just put them in places that we don't belong. And that juxtaposition is what was so funny.

Indeed, Brooks's preoccupation with humiliating Hitler by mocking him turned into a near obsession. Hitler, or some version of him, is seen in numerous Brooks films. When he won one of many Tony Awards for the 2001 musical of *The Producers*, he told the audience, "I want to thank Hitler for being such a funny guy on stage." Not everyone thinks Hitler is so funny. Alexander recalls:

> During a performance of *The Producers*, as they were doing the "Springtime for Hitler" number, somebody in the audience got very, very offended and vocally so. And stood up, and was yelling and screaming and walking out of the theater, and Mel happened to be in the house. And he gets to the back of the house and he confronts the guy and he says, "What's your problem!?" And the guy says, "I was in World War Two and this is a sham, this is a disgrace!" And Mel goes, "You were in World War Two? I was in World War Two—I didn't see you!"

But—even though he's unrepentant about shoving it in his audiences' faces—it's myopic to see Brooks's parodic genius as simply inserting Jewishness into other genres, like a cinematic Mad Libs. That a major film studio would have given an untried outsider such as Brooks a full-length picture seems like sheer folly, but ironically, the full canvas of a movie screen allowed Brooks to do what no parodist had been able to do before; Brooks spoofed movies with the full vocabulary of the movies. He could spoof John Ford's mise-en-scène in *Blazing Saddles*, the art direction of the Universal horror films (and to make a successful comedy in black and white in 1975 was heroic beyond belief), or Hitchcock's tracking shots in *High Anxiety*. He went beyond making fun of the material *in* the movies, he made fun of the whole experience *of* the movies; Mel Brooks created the first metaparodies.

Brooks's later parodies in the 1980s and 1990s weren't as keen or as popular as his 1970s blockbusters, and critics took him to task, but his fortunes changed right at the beginning of the twenty-first century, when his stage adaptation of *The Producers* won the most Tony Awards in Broadway history and went on to become an immense financial empire. Then in 2007, Brooks engineered a Broadway musical version of *Young Frankenstein* that played to sold-out houses.

Still, one gets the feeling that Brooks will never be entirely satisfied, or certainly never entirely at rest. It just wouldn't be funny. As he said in his 1975 *Playboy* interview:

> Tragedy is if I cut my finger. . . . Comedy is if you walk into an open sewer and die.
> The greatest comedy plays against the greatest tragedy.

A nice peppering of pessimism on the pastrami of comedy.

> REINER: Do you have any hope for the world?
> BROOKS: No. As long as the world is turning and spinning we're going to get dizzy and make mistakes. If some smart guy can solve it and stop so we're not nauseous, then we'll solve the problems of the world. Thank you, good night.

In Der Fuerher's Face:
Dick Shawn as a singing and dancing Hitler in *The Producers*; the stage version, 2001; dress rehearsal for "Springtime for Hitler."

"THAT'S *TERRIFIC BASS*"
SATURDAY NIGHT LIVE

We came on just after Watergate and questioning authority was just a big part of that time and also of the DNA of the show. We thought that our job was that whoever's in power, you go after them, because they already have the power. —Lorne Michaels

In the fall of 1974, between Richard Nixon's departure from the White House, the continued war in Vietnam, and double-digit inflation, Americans didn't have much to laugh about. Then Johnny Carson took away one of the few things that people *were* laughing at.

"WE'RE WILD AND CRAZY GUYS"

"I DON'T THINK IT'LL EVER WORK," SAID ONE EXECUTIVE, "BECAUSE THE AUDIENCE FOR WHICH IT'S DESIGNED WILL NEVER COME HOME ON SATURDAY NIGHT TO WATCH IT."

We are still not amused:
Lorne Michaels; the second season for
the Not Ready For Prime Time Players
and a facsimile of the Queen.

In the television graveyard of weekend late-night programming, reruns of *The Tonight Show*, called *The Best of Carson*, were one of the few profitable programs for NBC. Carson wanted to move the reruns to the weeknights, to give himself more vacation time. NBC had a year in which to turn the slot over to local affiliates or come up with some evening programming to replace *The Best of Carson*. NBC president Herb Schlosser gave the challenge to producer Dick Ebersol, who had worked in the sports division. Ebersol concluded that the key to success was a younger audience: "Johnny was the most brilliant person in the world, but his show wasn't for teenagers."

For a producer, Ebersol hired Lorne Michaels, a thirty-year-old Canadian who had made a name for himself writing for *Laugh-In* and some Lily Tomlin specials. "Through a process that to this day remains mysterious," said Michaels, "I was chosen to develop this new show." The network wanted a conventional talk show hosted by everyone from Rich Little to Burt Reynolds to Linda Ronstadt, but Michaels was looking for a different sensibility, for viewers "who were of a certain age, we'd grown up on television, and we knew the kind of show we wanted—but there wasn't one on the air then."

Michaels and Ebersol flew to Los Angeles to meet with Carson as a courtesy and to receive his blessing. "Carson was incredibly gracious and nice," recalled Michaels, "and we realized we'd be doing one night a week, ninety minutes, and he was doing five nights a week, ninety minutes, so it didn't seem so scary." Getting talent in Los Angeles was proving difficult, so reversing the course of Carson's move to Burbank, the new show would go back to New York, to NBC's famous Studio 8H in Rockefeller Center. It would be broadcast live—which in those days meant it would be a dangerous thing to do. "This was terrifying because even the technical people in that building hadn't done a live show since *Howdy Doody* in 1952," recalled Robert Klein, one of the hosts during the first season.

There had been several successful comedy variety shows on the air in the early '70s—Sonny and Cher, Dean Martin, Andy Williams—but Michaels consciously threw out every convention that had kept variety shows churning along on TV for a quarter century. The sets for the show would be three-dimensional and realistic—"We wanted the show to look the way New York did, which at that point had the phosphorescence of decay all about it." The musical guests would be honest-to-goodness rock and rollers, not Las Vegas types, and they would be introduced simply, without any of the nauseating obsequiousness found on other shows. There would be a different host every week to change things up, and that host would be chosen to appeal to a younger audience—Lily Tomlin, Richard Pryor, or George Carlin, who hosted the first show. Most significantly, there would be no star and therefore no second bananas—just a talented kamikaze ensemble of seven actors, nearly double the usual number for a typical variety show. That ensemble would become the hallmark of everything the show wanted to achieve.

Michaels didn't want a typical cast of theater or television actors; he brought them from the underground world of improvisational theater, from Chicago's Second City, or the Groundlings from Los Angeles, or New York's own *National Lampoon's Lemmings*. Chevy Chase was hired first as a writer; John Belushi initially refused to even audition. "My television set has spit all over it," he told Michaels. It was exactly the attitude Michaels had been looking for:

> When I began I found the most talented and most interesting people that I could find and I think I attracted a certain like-sensibility. In the six months before we went on the air, sort of rounding people up, I don't think there was ever a moment where I doubted that I could actually get it on in the way that I was hoping I could. I knew other people were out there, looking for the same thing.

Right up to its October 11, 1975, debut, the new show—officially called *NBC's Saturday Night*—was met with skepticism by NBC executives. "I don't think it'll ever work," said one, "because the audience for which it's designed will never come home on Saturday night to watch it." In far-off Aspen, Colorado, Steve Martin was watching, after finishing a concert: "When I saw the show, I won't say what I thought because it involves profanity. But I was elated and disappointed at the same time because I thought I was alone. And suddenly I realized there were others who were on the track of a kind of new comedy."

It wasn't until midway through its first season that *Saturday Night Live* hit its groove. The hosts were more integrated into the comedy, and the Not Ready for Prime Time Players began to step up to the plate and gain a huge following. When Pryor was the host in the late fall of 1975, he was, according to producer Bernie Brillstein, "very influential in taking the show to another place. Because all of a sudden the cast were really rebels." Alan Zweibel, one of the show's writers, defined their style:

Cast of characters:
The Coneheads; Aykroyd and Belushi spoofing *Nixon's Final Days*; Belushi, the eighth samurai; he's Chevy Chase—and Gerald Ford is not.

> With the Catskills types, it was stand-up comedy; these were people with an improv background where they pushed the limits. It was just a totally different sensibility. It was more energized, it was more physical, it came at you from a different direction as opposed to a monologuist just standing there telling jokes.

Saturday Night Live borrowed from previous variety show traditions, to be sure, but every one was taken to new extremes. Commercial parodies were often outrageous and sometimes elaborately produced, costing between $10,000 to $13,000 each. Few will forget Dan Aykroyd dropping a whole bass into a blender during "Bass-o-matic," or the "Royal Deluxe II Circumcision" parody, where a bris is performed in the backseat of a bouncing town car. Anne Beatts, one of the writers, also in charge of putting together the commercial parodies, recalls:

> What distinguished a lot of the stuff that *SNL* did is that it was much closer to *real*. And I found out something interesting in doing the parody commercials, that if you

had a commercial that was a minute long, in order to parody it you kind of needed a minute and twenty seconds, because you needed the minute to set up the reality of the product, whatever it was. And then you needed the extra time for the joke.

A parody on *Saturday Night Live* wasn't just a crazy send-up of a current movie performed by talented comedians; invariably the sketch pointed out the phoniness or inconsistency or the commercial ramifications of the source material—it pulled back the curtain on the wizards of the media. For example, a *Star Trek* parody in the first season brought in Elliott Gould as the villain posing the ultimate threat to Captain Kirk and his crew—he was an NBC executive canceling the show, while pointing out how cheap the sets and costumes looked. (A decade later, *SNL* would bring in William Shatner himself to make fun of *Star Trek*'s cult following.) But *SNL* did have other rigorous standards about what went into a sketch. Anne Beatts recalled that "there was a rule that Lorne had made early on: 'No Walter Crankcase.' By which he meant that we didn't do joke names, we didn't do joke costumes. . . . If Dan Aykroyd was doing Jimmy Carter, then he would be appropriately dressed as Jimmy Carter."

And most notably, it was in those moments when Aykroyd or another cast member took on a president that *Saturday Night Live* went brazenly where no prime-time political satire had gone before. When it came to presidential satire, *SNL* played hardball. Chevy Chase mocked President Ford for his dimwitted clumsiness; Aykroyd took on Carter for his obsequious piety and Nixon for his paranoia and sexual inadequacy—even his wife, Pat, was depicted (by Madeline Kahn) as an alcoholic. Decades later, the show would take on Clinton with even more outrageous vigor, but it's easy to forget how shocking—and refreshing—such mockery was at the time. (When Al Gore's relentless woodenness was parodied during his 2000 presidential campaign by Darrell Hammond, Gore's advisers made him watch, as a kind of aversion therapy.)

Inevitably, the show's popularity began to upset the equilibrium of the ensemble. After the first season, Chevy Chase left for a film career. (Johnny Carson—who was consistently asked to be a guest host and just as consistently refused—was not impressed; "I didn't think Chevy Chase could ad-lib a fart after a baked-bean dinner," he said.) Throughout the show's first five years, the temptations for cast members to break out on their own were enormous. Michaels kept as tight a rein as possible on his ensemble—they never did talk show appearances, for example—but he couldn't keep Aykroyd and Belushi from doing films or Gilda Radner from performing a one-woman show on Broadway. By the time the cast got around to one of their more notorious sketches on May 24, 1980—"Lord and Lady Douchebag"—it would be the last time the original Not

Younger than shwiiingtime:
Mike Myers and Dana Carvey; Aykroyd, Belushi, and Chase face *Star Trek*'s last mission. (Right) Rudy Giuliani joins Tina Fey and Jimmy Fallon; Carvey with his thousand points of light and one dim bulb: George H. W. Bush.

Ready for Prime Time Players (sans Chase, but with Bill Murray) would perform together.

Michaels and the original cast departed after the fifth season; the next season with a brand-new cast was calamitous, and most of them were fired. The season after that, with even more cast replacements, looked grim. The election of Ronald Reagan as president should have brought with it a bounty of satirical humor, but instead the network censor worked overtime to impose a more conservative tone on the show. Soon the press was calling the show *Saturday Night Dead*. It almost ground to a halt until Dick Ebersol, who eventually replaced Michaels, put one of the featured players front and center. Eddie Murphy was barely past voting age when he joined the show, and especially when he teamed up with cast member Joe Piscopo, he proved that rumors of *Saturday Night Dead* were greatly exaggerated.

Yet strangely, what provided the resurrection of *Saturday Night Live* was the sad death of breakout star John Belushi in March of 1982. In many ways, his uncontrollable energy was the best example of the show's iconoclastic arrogance. According to Brillstein:

> Some people give off vibes when they walk down the street, and everyone knows they're there—everyone knew John was around. He was just bigger than life. You come across these guys very rarely, but he had that stuff. It's like a sparkler—on July Fourth, they go out.

Although Belushi had long left the show to become a movie star, his passing changed the tone of *Saturday Night Live*. In a way, the show was now liberated, freed of comparisons with the past. The show would always go back to the tried-and-true elements of parody and satire while bringing along new casts, new generations of comic talent. "New wine in old bottles," as Lorne Michaels, who returned to produce the show in the mid-'80s, put it. Among the major performers who have passed through Studio 8H since 1983 are Julia Louis-Dreyfus, Dana Carvey, Billy Crystal, Will Ferrell, Christopher Guest, Michael McKean, Mike Myers, Chris Rock, Adam Sandler, Martin Short, Sarah Silverman, Ben Stiller, and Damon Wayans.

The inconsistency of the show is as legendary as its longevity. Astonishing to think that a child born on that October night when the show debuted would now be a thirty-three-year-old adult—and perhaps he or she might have outgrown the antics of *Saturday Night Live* long ago. Still, in its day, the show's outlook and output were remarkable. And few shows of any kind had the same relationship with its audience. As Anne Beatts summed it up:

> I think that the big thing that *Saturday Night Live* did was to erase the distinction between the creators and the viewers—there was no "us" and "them": we were "them." So, it was really about what made *us* laugh. And somehow they let us put it on. I think that a lot of the people watching felt that they could've written the show if only they were a little smarter and less stoned. Or more stoned.

Saturday Night Live was like a candy store that's closed from six at night until six in the morning. Come here, you kids, here's the key. NBC figured, oh, well, it's late at night—let them do what they want. Little did they know that they had seven of the funniest people that ever lived who were on the same page at the same time.

–Richard Belzer

"YOU CAN'T COMPLAIN"
BILLY CRYSTAL

The comic has to make people uncomfortable. When I would host the Oscars, I would make them a little uncomfortable. They are uncomfortable anyway because they are in tuxedos and they're nominated and the lights are on them, but you've got to sting a little. We're not just honey gatherers. We gotta sting. –Billy Crystal

The cast was there. George Carlin was there. Even Andy Kaufman was there. But during the 1975 debut episode of *Saturday Night Live*, Billy Crystal was sitting in a lonely train car on the Long Island Rail Road, chugging his way back home to Long Beach.

Crystal, an up-and-coming comic, had been promised a slot on the opening show by Lorne Michaels. His managers had negotiated six minutes of time for Crystal, so that he could perform a fairly elaborate B-movie spoof that involved Victor Mature, a tarantula, and a bowl of crumbled potato chips. When the timing of the final run-through proved tight, Michaels cut Crystal down to two minutes; his managers balked at the about-face, and, to use the lingo of Crystal's beloved baseball, took the ball away from him only hours before the broadcast. (In retrospect, Crystal's bit was probably too square for the emerging *SNL* profile.) The train ride back to Long Beach was about an hour long, but it would take nine years before Crystal would return to make his enduring mark on *Saturday Night Live*.

In the meantime, he would inch up, rung by rung, the career ladder as one of the most varied and genial comedians of his generation. Crystal's delight in the razzle-dazzle of showbiz came naturally; his uncle and his father created and ran Commodore Records, the foremost independent jazz label of the 1950s, and young Billy was immersed in the peculiar idiosyncrasies of jazz musicians—not that far off from those of comedians, actually. He even had Billie Holiday as baby sitter for one afternoon. That same train track on the Long Island Rail Road took Crystal into the wonderland of New York City, where he could catch movies, sneak into Commodore jam sessions, or grab a bleacher seat in Yankee Stadium. He was also heavily influenced by Jonathan Winters, the *2000 Year Old Man* records of Reiner and Brooks, and Bill Cosby. "I could relate to Cosby," he once wrote. "He had brothers. I had brothers. He played ball at Temple. I belonged to a temple. So there was a bond." The Crystal family television console, however, was dominated by Sid Caesar and *Your Show of Shows*; after Caesar did a *King and I* spoof one night, Crystal's dad bought Billy a bald cap wig and Crystal did his version of Caesar doing Yul Brynner in the living room for weeks: "*Your Show of Shows* brought a sense of parody to me because they would do things that were familiar, but they would make fun of them—'Oh, so you can take something and bend it a little and do your own thing with it!'"

After the *Saturday Night Live* disappointment, Crystal continued to do stand-up, often as an opener for rock acts—"The audience would have timed their drugs for the headliner. You would walk out before they were peaking and it was a little rough."—and even opened for Sammy Davis, Jr. He was given the lead in *Rabbit Test*, a film directed by Joan Rivers, and did the obligatory TV rounds, including a small part on *All in the Family*. For four seasons, he played the first openly gay character on network TV, Jodie Dallas, on the outrageous sitcom *Soap*. Still, Crystal felt as if he were treading water. Then, in 1984, Dick Ebersol, who had replaced Lorne Michaels as executive producer of *Saturday Night Live* and was in desperate need of someone to jump-start the show, made a surprising offer: would Crystal come back to *SNL* as a regular, if Ebersol could promise some first-rate costars and a better-than-average salary?

He looks mahhhvelous:
Crystal as Fernando (above) and Sammy, an early hero.

Crystal (Bill) Persuasion:
(top) Roping a steer in *City Slickers* (1991);
(below) as Buddy Young Jr. In *Mr. Saturday Night*
(1992); (opposite) at the 76th annual Academy
Awards show.

BUDDY YOUNG, JR.: I KNOW YOU'RE OUT THERE, I CAN HEAR YOU RELOADING!

Crystal stunned his managers by taking the offer seriously—very seriously. "It was the place I always wanted to be. I'd done *Soap* for four years, I was headlining in Vegas, I was doing concerts all the time, but I had a million characters chained up inside me and they wanted to come out." Those characters exploded onto the stage of Studio 8H for only one season, but, joined by his promised costars—Martin Short, Christopher Guest, and Harry Shearer—Crystal beefed up *SNL*'s bullpen of colorful eccentrics. His phony talk-show host, Fernando, with his oleaginous obsequiousness—"You look mahhhvelous!"—presaged our nation's addiction to celebrity sycophancy. (Crystal always completely improvised the "Fernando's Hideaway" sketches.) He joined with staff writer Larry David to create an elderly, cranky Jewish weatherman, Lew Goldman:

GOLDMAN: Here's the weather in Brooklyn, where I live:

For Monday and Tuesday, the forecast is "You can't complain."

Wednesday: Feh!

Thursday and Friday: Don't be a big shot, take a jacket.

Crystal was also the first white performer since Eddie Cantor to get away with mocking African American celebrities in blackface, spoofing his hero, Sammy Davis, and Muhammad Ali (although his Ali had what looked like a faint tan). Crystal took particular delight in impersonating an imaginary veteran of the old Negro League.

But just when Crystal thought he'd gotten through the spring training of his first season, Michaels returned as producer and plugged in a brand-new cast. Crystal missed the danger and freshness of the show—but he'd have to settle for becoming a movie star instead. He had a string of successful vehicles where he could indulge his inner lunacy but package it up with his considerable charm: *Memories of Me* (1988), where he shared the screen with another idol, comedian Alan King; *When Harry Met Sally* (1989), where he tapped into the Woody Allen romantic side of his personality; *City Slickers* (1991), a fish-out-of-water comedy that he also produced; and *Mr. Saturday Night* (1992), his most personal film, a tribute to the hard-working borscht belt comics he grew up admiring.

"Sometimes," Crystal said, "people who don't know what they're talking about will use the phrase 'borscht belt comic' in a derogatory sense. Well, you know something, you dope, borscht belt comics were some of the greatest comics who ever lived. They're brilliant technicians who can get more laughs out of an audience than someone who is being terribly ironic and seemingly smarter than everybody else."

In 1990, Crystal, who had grown up playing out his Hollywood fantasies in his Long Island living room, was given the ultimate Tinseltown gig: hosting the 62nd

Annual Academy Awards. A formidable task, but Crystal had his own way in: "Everyone was making fun of [the lousy] musical numbers [on previous broadcasts]. So I said, 'Well, why don't we do a musical number, and I'll do it alone and, and instead of the overblown thing, we'll make it look like it's overblown—but it'll just be me.'" Crystal channeled Al Jolson and knocked 'em dead with his inane song parodies, reducing the pretentiousness of Oscardom to daffy little jingles:

> *Lord of the Rings: Return of the King* (to the tune of "My Favorite Things")
> Hobbits with feet big and hairy and smelly
> More epic battles than Gest and Minnelli
> Ian and Viggo, a queen and some kings--
> This is the gang in *The Lord of the Rings*.

Eventually, after using the medley on several additional Oscar-hosting gigs, Crystal tired of that formula and, in collaboration with other writers and special effects editors, found a way to insert himself hilariously into a montage of classic film clips: "It gave me a chance to be funny before I came onstage. I became my own opening act." Crystal's bubbly irreverence became so addictive that he has been asked to host the mega-event eight times—only Bob Hope has controlled the Academy Awards podium more often.

Unlike other comedians of his generation, Crystal never resorted to provocative language, destructive pronouncements, or sexual situations (well, he sometimes becomes preoccupied with his penis). His deep affection for those who toil in the boiler room of show business trying to entertain people—whether it's in a Catskills resort, a tiny jazz club in the Village, a television studio for an afternoon kiddie program, the Dorothy Chandler Pavillion, or your parents' living room—is immediately apparent and hopelessly infectious. Perhaps that's why, for many, Billy Crystal is the ultimate host—he just wants to make sure everyone's having a nice time. "It is better to look good than to feel good," cooed the narcissistic host, Fernando, in his Corinthian-leather tones, but Billy Crystal is a master at making his audiences feel good, too.

Early in his career, Crystal bombed while auditioning material for manager Jack Rollins:

He said, "You didn't leave them a tip." I said, "What do you mean?" He said, "You didn't leave them something extra on the table. You never once said 'I' in your whole thing, you never once said 'I think.' I want to know what you—Billy—thinks, so leave the tip." And that's the greatest advice I've ever been given: Leave the tip. It's a little extra something that lets the audience know who you are.

ANNOUNCER: And here they are, the most inoffensive black men on TV . . . the Brothers Brothers:

My brother's a brother and so am I—
Or so it appears to the casual eye.
The network execs don't want negroes real,
So oreos like us get a hell of a deal.
So, it's prime-time hi-de-ho . . .

THE WAYANS BROTHERS
"TWO SNAPS IN A CIRCLE"

'em 122

For Keenen Ivory Wayans and his brother Damon to play the most inoffensive black men on television was a real stretch, a tribute to their considerable comic talents. With *In Living Color*, a half-hour program that debuted on the fledgling Fox Network in 1990, they, in tandem with their repertory company, completely inverted the racial dynamic of the comedy-variety show, shook up the tenor of television comedy, and bolstered a fourth broadcast network into the bargain. The show was television's first ongoing satire from a black perspective, but in the words of series writer Larry Wilmore, "it was more than black humor. It was kind of a breakthrough show because it really, in my mind, it introduced a kind of hip-hop culture to television."

The series was the brainchild of a comedian and filmmaker named Keenen Ivory Wayans. Wayans, born in 1958, grew up as the oldest sibling in a family of ten, raised in the Fulton House project in New York's Chelsea neighborhood. Around the crowded dinner table, they learned about comedy. "Everything was a joke," he said. "If you got a whuppin', when you got back to the table you heard nine other people doing impressions of your screaming." Wayans paid particular attention to his younger brother, Damon. "We were always the class clowns. Always could play the dozens better than average people and consequently wound up getting chased home a lot for saying the wrong thing to the wrong person," said Keenen.

Keenen tried to make his way out of the projects as a manager at McDonald's but decided to risk the stand-up comedy route. At the age of nineteen, he played a gig at the Improv, when a young black man came backstage to see him. "I thought I was the only funny black guy in New York. Now I see there are two," said the sixteen-year-old. It was Eddie Murphy. Six years later, Wayans was in Los Angeles, working on Murphy's concert film *Raw* and making films with Robert Townsend. In 1988, he tried writing and directing his own film, spoofing a genre that didn't even exist when Mel Brooks made *The Producers*. *I'm Gonna Git You Sucka*, at once a parody and a loving tribute to the blaxploitation era, cost $3 million to make and earned nearly $20 million. Film executives were still unimpressed, but the brand-new Fox Network, which needed signature projects to create an identity, thought Wayans's concept for a satirical variety show was just what the doctor ordered.

"Keenen put the show together like a head coach or the owner of a football team puts together a team," said cast member Tommy Davidson. "He went after the best players who could pull off his sketch show." As executive producer, head writer, and star of the show—the first black person to hold down those roles in a comedy-variety show—Wayans put together eight cast members, and in a complete inversion of *Saturday Night Live*, two of them were white, while six of them were black. (They included Damon, Davidson, David Alan Grier, Jim Carrey, and eventually Jamie Foxx; the writing staff, too, was a mixture of black and white writers.) As he did when he was growing up, he looked after his family—Damon and younger sister Kim joined the show, and after a while, so did three other siblings. "I think there are a total of twenty-three Wayans that worked on the show," said Wilmore. "Some were in utero at the time."

The composition of the cast allowed for a wider and deeper look at American pop culture. Suddenly, black celebrities who were vital to American life but usually unseen and unmocked started being skewered on *In Living Color*: Redd Foxx, Arsenio Hall, Mike Tyson, Oprah Winfrey, Louis Farrakhan, Jesse Jackson. "*In Living Color* shows different sides of black life and black culture," said Wayans at the time. "The more people know about you, the less they have to fear about you. And the more they want to know."

Over to the dark side:
(previous) Keenen Ivory Wayans and David Alan Grier are "Men on Films";
the cast of *In Living Color*; Wayans off-stage and as Homey da Clown.

Although the show took swipes at some time-honored genres—*Star Trek*, say, or a presidential press conference—the racial perspective lifted the spoofs into another level. In one sketch, the second *Star Trek* film, *The Wrath of Khan*, becomes "The Wrath of Farrakhan" as the Nation of Islam leader Louis Farrakhan plays the villain, invading the starship *Enterprise* in order to free the crew's racially diverse members from the subjugation of Captain Kirk. An original character played by Keenen, Homey da Clown (created by Paul Mooney), was a kiddie entertainer who loathed his gigs and, thus, all kiddies—"Homey don't play dat!" was his cry of outraged objection to a request for some demeaning party trick. Said Wilmore:

> We had black characters doing things that were from our point of view, not white writers having one black actor or character represent all of black people. Homey da Clown—at his heart he's not only a black guy which he might've been on another show. He's a guy that hates being a clown, and will make kids pay for that.

The show was a hit with audiences (the sexy backup group Fly Girls—which featured Jennifer Lopez and Rosie Perez at various points—didn't hurt), and *In Living Color* often landed in the Top Ten, a particularly impressive feat for Fox, then the "fourth network."

"Objectively, *In Living Color* is compared to *Saturday Night Live* because they were both sketch shows, but [*SNL*'s] better days had passed by the time we got on TV," said Tommy Davidson. "So the only comparison that I make is that our cast was as good as *Saturday Night Live*'s peak cast and we came into the TV world when *Saturday Night Live* was doo-doo."

Yet despite audience and critical acclaim, some of the show's original sketches caused consternation in several circles. Some leaders of the black community blasted "Homeboy Shopping Network," where Damon and Keenen played ghetto kids selling electronics out of the back of a truck. Another ongoing sketch, called "Men on Films," featured Damon and David Alan Grier as two extremely swishy amateur critics busting on (and outing) their favorite film stars with finger-popping glee ("Two snaps in a circle!"). Rather than necessarily offending two groups at once, according to Wilmore, "back then, we got a lot of letters from gay people, gay groups, who loved it." Still, those sketches were often blue-penciled by Fox at the last minute, along with anything else that might combine the explosive mixture of race and sex. To Tommy Davidson, the provocative critical mass of *In Living Color* made a lot of sense:

> The society around us at the time was a lot more intensified than the society that was around the *Saturday Night Live* inception years. Reagan came along and busted all the unions, so all of a sudden working people didn't have any more rights. A lot of things, crack hit the city, crack hit all the urban sectors and it hurt white America as well.

After two seasons, interference from Fox, along with its insistence on showing reruns of the series, proved too much for Wayans and he left the show, which sputtered on for an additional couple of seasons. Still, *In Living Color* tilted the balance of racial comedy on television and brought a fresh battalion of comedy superstars to the forefront. Wayans trained his satirical sights on wider—and *whiter*—targets; his *Scary Movie* film spoof remains the most commercially successful film directed by an African American. There was also something hopeful about Wayans's vision for television satire: "I was confident that what was funny would be funny and that people would get into it. I don't think that people of America are as race conscious as some of the institutions that control America."

The other side of great comics; spoofing the Marx Brothers (above) and La Wanda Page and Redd Foxx.

"I'M NOT GOING TO BE YOUR MONKEY"

JON STEWART
AND *THE DAILY SHOW*

Here's the way I look at it–President Bush has uranium-tipped bunker busters and I have puns. I think he'll be okay. –Jon Stewart

Partners-in-crime:
Stephen Colbert and Jon Stewart; (right) *The Daily Show* correspondents; John Kerry and Stewart.

HE IS LIKE A FIERCE TEDDY BEAR TO ME.

–Richard Lewis

In 2004, the Television Critics Association bestowed its award for "outstanding achievement in news and information" not on ABC's *Nightline* or PBS's *Frontline* but on the previous year's winner for outstanding achievement for comedy: *The Daily Show*. Instead of accepting in person, the show's host, Jon Stewart, filed a report from the home front: his studio at Comedy Central on New York's West Side. "We're fake," he told the organization. "See this desk? It folds up at the end of the day, and I take it home in my purse." The Television Critics Association was not the first to confuse *The Daily Show* with the real thing. In 2003, Senator John Edwards announced his presidential candidacy on the show, to which Stewart replied, "Senator, I should have probably broken this to you earlier: this is a fake show. It may not count."

But *The Daily Show* counts with cable viewers—some 1.5 million viewers tune in four nights a week, almost a quarter of the audience for a network news broadcast. Since the show debuted in 1996, the bombast and increased entertainment quotient on network news have only increased, making so-called reality a hapless collaborator for the show's satire. "It started off as just a parody show, but in time has come to mean a lot more," said the show's "Senior Black Correspondent," Larry Wilmore. "A lot of people actually get their news from *The Daily Show* now because it's really become more of an insidious satire on the news more than just a fun parody."

The format of *The Daily Show* was to imitate the structure of the network news as closely as possible, with anchormen, special correspondents, and a topical array of sound bites from political figures, many of whom said far more hilarious and contradictory things in real life than if they had been scripted by a bunch of writers. The original host was Craig Kilborn, and other correspondents were Steve Carell and Stephen Colbert. According to Wilmore, "They seemed so authentic, like real news guys. The first time you were tuning in, it was like, 'Oh, my God, is this real?' " Wilmore himself fills a particular niche, one that no network news team would be without:

> I'm the Senior Black Correspondent, so I give my perspective on cultural issues. My job is to "keep it real" with Jon. (I'm using black slang right now, just so you know.) Most of the brothers on the news either do the weather, because we like black people telling us how cold it is or how warm it is, or they are on on the weekend, because that's when football comes on—we're comfortable with that.

It would seem that Jon Stewart has very little trouble keeping it real. Born Jonathan Stewart Liebowitz in suburban New Jersey, where he grew up reading *MAD Magazine* and being bullied at recess, Stewart joined *The Daily Show* in 1999, after the former stand-up comic spent years playing musical chairs on several network and cable programs. The phony anchor chair has proven to be a perfect fit for Stewart's contentious bottom:

> I think of myself as a comedian who has the pleasure of writing jokes about things that I actually care about. I have great respect for people who are in the front lines and the trenches of trying to enact social change. I am far lazier than that. I am a tiny, neurotic man, standing in the back of the room throwing tomatoes at the chalk board. And that's really it.

"Jon Stewart has something that very few have," said Richard Lewis. "He is like a fierce teddy bear to me. He could talk about really tough news stuff, but he can do it in a way that you want to hug the guy anyway."

Like Will Rogers and Johnny Carson before him, Stewart's own politics remain obscure. When asked if he thought the country would be better off run by Republicans or Democrats, he replied, "I have no idea." The only real allegiance Stewart and the show have is to the joke, going after the mistakes that real-life politicians and newscasters make on a daily basis. "That's what it's like to be a comedian," he told Bill Moyers. "You basically stand and stare at the world and hope it craps out 'cause that's a good year for you. So that's not a pleasant feeling."

Coincidentally or not, as the world's news has grown more unpleasant, *The Daily Show* has become more popular—and influential. In 2004, a report revealed that, within the 18- to 35-year-old demographic, more people got their news from *The Daily Show* than any national news broadcasts or journals. Said David Steinberg, "Jon Stewart is invaluable to the younger generation because they get their news from him. And why wouldn't they get their news from him? He's not objective. When you have to watch this phony objectivity acted out by all the newscasters, it just doesn't work." Stewart himself said, "Honestly, we're practicing a new form of desperation, where we just are so inundated with mixed messages from the media and from politicians that we're just trying to sort it out for ourselves."

In October 2003, Stewart had to sort it out for himself when he made headlines taking on the hyperbolic talking heads on CNN's *Crossfire*. His smackdown with conservative host Tucker Carlson drew a line in the sand and made Stewart a hero to many:

> STEWART: It's not honest. What you do is not honest. What you do is partisan hackery. And I will tell you why I know it.
>
> CARLSON: You had John Kerry on your show and you sniff his throne and you're accusing us of partisan hackery?
>
> STEWART: Absolutely.
>
> CARLSON: You've got to be kidding me. He comes on and you . . .
>
> STEWART: You're on CNN. The show that leads into me is puppets making crank phone calls. . . . What is wrong with you?
>
> CARLSON: You need to get a job at a journalism school, I think.
>
> STEWART: You need to *go* to one. The thing that I want to say is, when you have people on for just knee-jerk, reactionary talk . . .
>
> CARLSON: Wait. I thought you were going to be funny. Come on. Be funny.
>
> STEWART: No. No. I'm not going to be your monkey.

Like his former correspondent Stephen Colbert, and Bill Maher on HBO, Stewart has been pushed farther and farther into the belly of the beast. As their notoriety has increased, so does the public's desire for them to comment on the political and cultural life of this country, and it gets harder, and more essential, to maintain their comedic nonobjectivity. Stewart and his show have always maintained their unique roles and First Amendment protections as comedians.

On May 24, 2007, Al Gore appeared on *The Daily Show*:

> AL GORE: [This show] makes a point—that actually if you want to get through a lot of the nonsense and get through the heart of the news, this is the place to get it. Back in the Middle Ages, the court jester was the only person allowed to tell the truth without getting his head cut off; now in the current media environment, the only way to get past all the nonsense is to make a joke.
>
> STEWART: That's a compliment, right?

Right.

CHAPTER THREE

NEVER GIVE A SUCKER AN EVEN BREAK

SMART-ALECKS AND WISEGUYS

When people expect
to get something for
nothing, they are sure
to be cheated and
generally deserve to be.
—P. T. Barnum

THE BIG(GER) PICTURE

Even though *Poor Richard's Almanack* told us that "Early to bed and early to rise, Makes a man healthy, wealthy, and wise," Americans have a special place in their hearts for the characters who can stay out late, sleep in, and still make a buck: the wiseguys, charlatans, con men, flimflam men, fast talkers, and smooth operators.

We may not like being conned, but the con itself can make for a terrific show. The actor Jason Alexander, who spent years on television's *Seinfeld* as George Costanza, a character always haplessly and hopelessly trying to take advantage of someone before they took advantage of him, observed that "Everybody loves a good con man—even in real life. I always say if a guy has pulled a fast one on me and I've fallen for it, God bless him!"

As a comic archetype, the wiseguy or con man has to be capable of putting on a helluva show. P. T. Barnum, the father of American hucksterism, understood this perfectly: "An honest man who arrests public attention will be called a 'humbug,' but he is not a swindler or an impostor. If, however, after attracting crowds of customers by his unique displays, a man foolishly fails to give them a full equivalent for their money, they never patronize him a second time, but they very properly denounce him as a swindler, a cheat, an impostor." Herman Melville, whose 1857 novel *The Confidence-Man* gave both the name and the concept of the con man to American culture, articulated the more existential resonance of being conned: "It is—or seems to be—a wise sort of thing, to realize that all that happens to a man in this life is only by way of joke, especially his misfortunes, if he have them. And it is also worth bearing in mind, that the joke is passed round pretty liberally and impartially, so that not very many are entitled to fancy that they in particular are getting the worst of it."

The wiseguy made his earliest comedic appearance over two centuries ago as the "Yankee peddler" in folktales and in short fiction: a slick, smooth, traveling mountebank who could talk faster—and, out of necessity, run faster—than the country yokels he was pulling one over on. This archetype metamorphosed into the kind of snake-oil salesman and bunkum artist that W. C. Fields embodied in several films set in the nineteenth century, such as *Poppy* or *My Little Chickadee*. In fact, Fields nearly had his chance to impersonate one of the great charlatans in movie history, drawn from that same snake-oil salesman tradition: Professor Marvel (and his fantasy analogue, the Wizard) in *The Wizard of Oz*. Lyricist E. Y. Harburg had always imagined Fields playing the humbugging Wizard, particularly at the end of the 1939 film, where the Wizard's orotund oracular orations were crafted with Fields in mind (in the end, contractual arrangements precluded such felicitous casting). As the world moved into the twentieth century, Fields's Victorian bearing, costumes, and verbal formulations soon gave way to a leaner, meaner form of huckster, trying to contend with the modern world—and with its more urban catalog of obstacles, irritations, and potential suckers: bosses, cars, policemen, society ladies, contracts, insurance policies, tax collectors, celebrities, and so on.

In order to make his way, the modern American wiseguy needed to be aggressive and unsentimental. Perhaps it's the latter characteristic that best defines his comic persona; Fields relinquished some of this Victorian sentimentality when he played more contemporary characters, and there are many aficionados who prefer the unapologetically anarchic Groucho Marx of his earlier Paramount years over the more humane Groucho of the MGM years. Though one can be sure he was sorely tempted, Jack Benny never embraced an Ebenezer Scrooge-like final act of redemption—such sentimentality would have irreparably damaged the decades-long cultivation of his petty persona.

Along with a contempt for sentiment, the wiseguy embodies a concomitant lack of respect for tradition, society, values, and manners. When Groucho tried to crash a society weekend on a Long Island estate (*Animal Crackers*) or tried to insinuate himself into the inner circle of the opera world (*A Night at the Opera*), he was attempting to belong to a club that wouldn't normally accept him as a member. Storming the ramparts of accepted society is part of the game: Eddie Murphy swaggered his way into a Beverly Hills country club wearing only a T-shirt, a football varsity jacket, and an air of fearlessness.

One born ev'ry minute:
P.T. Barnum, granddaddy of 'em all; Frank Morgan as Professor Marvel—bunkum, Kansas-style.

The wiseguy tradition is often passed down from generation to generation; or, perhaps more accurately, the wiseguy of one "outsider" group passes the torch to the next unassimilated group when he or she finally gets inside. Fields was of Scottish-Irish stock; his heir apparent was the Jewish Groucho Marx. "The Kingfish" of *Amos 'n' Andy* claimed the con man mantle for African Americans and passed it to Fred Sanford; Paul Lynde was the standard-bearer for the smart aleck in the gay community. Freddie Prinze, of *Chico and the Man*, not only inherited the name of Chico Marx—one of history's great grifters—but brought the fast-talking wiseguy to the Hispanic community. Joan Rivers proved—at just about the right time—that wiseguys don't even need to be *guys*.

Wiseguys stand on each other's shoulders. If a con man of a previous generation could pull off a perfect scam, why toss it aside, just for the sake of modernity? Jason Alexander describes the stratagems of George Costanza: "George is a guy of very average skills and abilities. He is, in many ways, the perfect fifteen-year-old Long Island kid, who lives on Long Island but thinks he's a New Yorker. There's a little bit of the slickster of Phil Silvers's Bilko in there, you know, always trying to talk your way out of something." When George was having sexual relations with the cleaning woman on the desk of his office and the boss called him out, George's response is:

> GEORGE: Was that wrong? Should I have not done that? I tell you I gotta plead ignorance on this thing because if anyone had said anything to me at all when I first started here that that sort of thing was frowned upon, you know, 'cause I've worked in a lot of offices, and I tell you people do that all the time.

"That," said Alexander, "is pure Bilko."

Such verbal legerdemain is a key part of the huckster arsenal. These wiseguys are easily the most verbal of comic archetypes—they use, abuse, and manipulate language to get what they want; it's no accident that Joan Rivers's mantra was "Can we talk?" The Kingfish could torture the English into such bizarre farragos that his marks never knew when they were being fleeced; likewise, Phil Silvers could simply yammer on at such a velocity that it would make a sucker's head spin. But verbal skill isn't always about talking quickly and confusingly; it can simply be trenchant wit, complex thoughts boiled down to their essential truth. Paul Lynde was a past master at this with his "zingers"—so named for their speed and accuracy—on *The Hollywood Squares*:

> HOST PETER MARSHALL: Paul, it's well known that small amounts of female hormones are found in the male body. Are male hormones ever found in the female body?
>
> LYNDE: Occasionally.

Disguise also figures prominently in the huckster's bag of tricks. Everything from Groucho's mustache to Bilko's horn-rim glasses allows the wiseguy to slip undercover, to navigate in dangerous waters. Jack Benny, by all accounts the most generous guy in show business, made his career out of impersonating the meanest skin-flint in the neighborhood. Redd Foxx's Fred Sanford was never above feigning a heart attack to manipulate the situation. Eddie Murphy was a genius at having some very centered characters pretend to be something else to get what they wanted; his convict in *48 HRS* pretends to be a cop, while his Beverly Hills cop pretends to be a street criminal. Larry David is not above hiring a prostitute to pretend to be a passenger so that he can drive his car in the High Occupancy Vehicle lane.

A fine tootsy-frootsying:
Jason Alexander as George Costanza; Chico Marx pulls one over on his brother.

Yet, as the British playwright William Congreve wrote, "No mask like open truth to cover lies, / As to go naked is the best disguise." Ironically, most of the seeming hucksters were actually telling the truth—or desiring to tell the truth—their whole careers. The flimflam of W. C. Fields only exposed the masks and pretensions of upper-class society. When Groucho says to Margaret Dumont, "You've got beauty, charm, money. . . . You have got money, haven't you? Because if you haven't, we can quit right now," it seems like the height of rudeness, but he's only articulating what millions of gold diggers have thought but have never had the courage to express. Larry David could become enraged when a handicapped man ties up a nonhandicapped bathroom stall; Joan Rivers could point out the hypocrisy behind idolizing a sex goddess such as Elizabeth Taylor when she was well past her prime. (Needless to say, even the victims of such a rant recognize the publicity value; when, in her act, Rivers stopped criticizing Cher's fashion sense and ostensible sexual appetites, Cher called to complain that she had been dropped.) Even our most contemporary verbal wiseguy, Chris Rock, gets his most major laughs by articulating truths that no one else will dare express:

> Everybody is talking about gun control. No, I think we need some bullet control. I think every bullet should cost five thousand dollars. Five thousand dollars for a bullet. Know why? 'Cause if a bullet cost five thousand dollars, there'd be no more innocent bystanders. That'd be it. And people'd think before they shot someone: "Man, I will blow your fucking head off, if I could afford it. I'm gonna get me a second job, start saving up, and you a dead man. You'd better hope I don't get no bullets on layaway!"

Sadly, perhaps, few of these truth tellers achieved much happiness from the opportunity to perorate from their comic soapboxes. Most of the comedians who took up the wiseguy mantle were rather miserable in their professional lives; condemned by nature to tell the truth while fabricating it as outward show, they (Fields, Groucho, Redd Foxx, Paul Lynde, Larry David, in particular) had terrible times with the hypocrisy and foolishness of producers, directors, studio executives, publicists, and so on. "Would you rather do what you want to do or what a network executive wants you to do?" asked David. "What's gonna be funnier? So, of course, if you don't compromise, it'll be funnier because you're doing what you want rather than what somebody else wants." The resistance to compromise created some beautifully aggressive comedy, but it seems to have given the wiseguys little comfort at the end of the day. But then, a wiseguy by nature succeeds by creating fools—why would these comedians want to suffer fools gladly? Perhaps these wiseguys and smart-alecks have succeeded at making us laugh because they realize that the patina of power and respectability is the greatest con of all; by pulling back the curtain, as it were, so that we can discover that the mighty Wizard is actually a befuddled humbug, they actually use their own chicanery to reveal the greater chicanery of American society. As Barnum said, we all like a good trick, but it does have to be a *good* trick. Wiseguy Chris Rock brought it all together nicely when he "pulled back the curtain" on contemporary illusionist David Blaine and his attention-getting, publicity-seeking stunts:

> Are we so desperate for entertainment that we fall for a trickless magician? Saw a lady in half. Pull a rabbit out of a hat. Do *something*. What's his last trick? "I'm in a box and I ain't going to eat." I'm in a box and I ain't going to eat? That ain't no trick. That's called living in the projects.

Truth to power:
Agnew and Nixon "sting" the nation; Chris Rock, shooting straight.

"AND YOU'LL BE CRAZY FOR THE REST OF YOUR LIFE"
W.C. FIELDS

As my dear old grandfather Litvak said, just before they swung the trap, he said, "You can't cheat an honest man. Never give a sucker an even break or smarten up a chump." –W.C. Fields

In 1920, one of the last puritanical vestiges of the Victorian era invaded the modern American scene: Prohibition. From the moment in January when the Eighteenth Amendment was adopted by all forty-eight states, people all over the country were trying to get around it. A former congressman, Fiorello La Guardia, warned that "It would take 200,000 additional police officers to enforce Prohibition in New York City; and it would take another 250,000 to police the police."

On West Forty-second Street, backstage at the New Amsterdam Theatre, thirsty actors could find liquid refreshment in the dressing room of Florenz Ziegfeld's latest star comedian: W. C. Fields. "He didn't always drink," said his grandson, Ronald Fields, "but he was a lonely guy and he used booze as a way of getting people to come to him. It made him popular with his fellow vaudevillians." Fields had worked out a convenient way to procure his stash—he'd get his booze from the stewards who worked on the ocean liners that docked down the block. That was easy. Fields was having a harder time with his boss—the great producer of the *Follies*, Florenz Ziegfeld. Fields had joined the *Follies* five years earlier as an eccentric juggler who performed pantomime routines at a salary of two hundred dollars a week. He was now making four times that, performing in sketches with other comics like Fanny Brice, Eddie Cantor, and Bert Williams, and audiences adored him.

Ziegfeld was another story. Fields himself noted that "Ziegfeld spent fortunes on comedians, but never liked them. Why he tolerated me for so long, I do not know." The comedian and the producer were locked in a struggle over a new sketch for the *Ziegfeld Follies of 1920*. Fields wanted to put in a sketch he had written about a cranky dad, his annoying wife and kids, and their frustrations with the family Ford, a situation that millions of Americans were enduring on a daily basis. Ziegfeld hated this dull, middle-class drudgery stuck in the middle of his glamorous revue, but Fields insisted and persisted; "The Family Ford" became the hit of the 1920 *Follies*. It changed the direction of Fields's career and set it forever after. The sketch allowed him to expand his range, but it also paradigmatically set him in conflict with anyone and everyone who thought they knew better about his brand of comedy. As he told an interviewer in 1926:

> I realized that if I was ever to get the chance I wanted, I would have to work it out for myself. So I began to change my methods. I still did the juggling tricks which were expected of me, but more and more I subordinated these to real human comedy in gesture, expression, and action. I had always made up my own acts; built them out of knowledge and observations of real life. I'd had wonderful opportunities to study people; and every time I went out on the stage I tried to show the audience some bit of true human nature. I tried to deal in ideas, not in mere mechanical stunts.

Balls in the air:
Fields as a vaudeville juggler; demonstrating an artful stunt in his pool routine.

Fields had downed many tankards full of true human nature, often with hardship as a chaser. William Claude Dukenfield was born in 1880, into a working-class neighborhood of Philadelphia, to a volatile British immigrant bartender named James Dukenfield and a tough lady with a sense of humor named Kate whom young "Whitey" rather alarmingly resembled. At the age of eleven, Fields got into a violent argument with his father—something about an unfortunately placed shovel—and walked out on his family. He lived a peripatetic and grubby existence, sleeping in leaky culverts, eating handouts in local bars, but in his words, "It was a glorious adventure and every boy in the neighborhood would have been glad to change places with me." His childhood may or may not have been the Dickensian horror he later made it out to be, but even before he left home, he certainly chafed under the workaday authority of his imperious father and was always looking for a profession that allowed him, as he put it, "not to have to get up early in the morning."

Young Fields discovered a way out by diligently mastering the art of juggling, making his professional debut at the age of seventeen. Along the way, he experienced hard times. He worked for a scam artist who ran a shell game; he was pressed into service where he had to pretend to drown twice a day in Atlantic City to attract crowds for a vaudeville show; he worked for a series of managers to whom, he said, "salaries were only polite fictions." He married a woman named Hattie Hughes, whom he added to his act; she was only slightly more supportive of him onstage than off. During one foreign tour, Hattie went back to America to have and raise their only son; when she refused to rejoin Fields on his juggling tour overseas, he turned his back on her and their son. At the height of a successful German tour in 1902, Fields was fired and replaced with an animal act. "Ever have an experience like that?" he asked. "It's the end of the world, it's hell."

But there was triumph as well; by 1915, Fields had been recognized as "the best comic juggler in the world, bar none." That year, Fields was brought back to America from an Australian tour by producer Charles Dillingham to provide some expert comic manipulation around a billiards table for a new musical, with a ragtime score by Irving Berlin, called *Watch Your Step*. Due to wartime shipping restrictions, it took Fields thirty-nine days to join the company out of town in Syracuse; he and his bit were cut the next night. It was the kind of injustice that would drive Fields mad his entire career.

However, later in 1915, he made his first short film, *Pool Sharks*, and when Ziegfeld hired Fields that same year, it was confirmation of his talent. Fields would perform in nearly a dozen shows for Ziegfeld, and it was in the *Follies* that Fields found his comic voice—literally. He made a breakthrough in "A Game of Golf" (also known as "An Episode on the Links") in 1918 and wound up recycling bits from that sketch for years. Although Fields had been performing his pantomime juggling act for nearly two decades, audiences now split their sides at his baroque neologistic formations and his strange muttered ways of spitting out curses. He also began writing his own sketches—and wound up reviving and revising the same two dozen scenarios throughout his career. Fields still chafed under any kind of authority. When Ziegfeld closed an all-comedy revue starring Fields out of town, the comedian never got over it: "There wasn't a damn thing I could do about it. So now you know why I'm nervous—or crazy and nuts, as some of my friends call it—why I never feel safe in this blankety-blank business I juggled myself into."

Fields came into his own by breaking away from Ziegfeld in 1924 and starring in a stage vehicle called *Poppy*, a sentimental carnival tale that gave him the role of a lifetime—in fact, it gave him a role that he'd play, one way or another, for the *rest* of his lifetime. Professor Eustace McGargle is a master of flimflam flummery who tries to marry off his daughter into a higher social circle. Fields's long-winded shaggy dog stories, rococo turns of phrase, and general chicanery all came together in this show:

JUDGE: Mr. Whiffeen tells me your wife has passed away.

Cheating an honest man: a gallery of flim-flammers: *Poppy* (1936); *Sally of the Sawdust* (1925); *The Old-Fashioned Way* (1934).

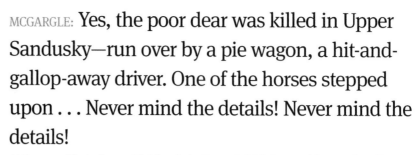

MCGARGLE: Yes, the poor dear was killed in Upper Sandusky—run over by a pie wagon, a hit-and-gallop-away driver. One of the horses stepped upon . . . Never mind the details! Never mind the details!

At the age of forty-four, with his role in *Poppy* (which he would commit to film twice, first in a silent version directed by D. W. Griffith), Fields became fixed in the American popular consciousness as the high-hatted con man with a marked deck in his pocket.

POKER PLAYER: Uh, is this a game of chance?

FIELDS: Not the way I play it, no.

By 1931, Fields had had enough of Broadway producers and went west to make sound pictures (he had mixed results with his silent short subjects). Unlike many other Broadway comedians, he hadn't been hurt by the stock market crash—he saw the Wall Street bubble for the con it was. "If these stocks are so good, why do the presidents of these companies want me in on it?" he asked sensibly. "They don't know me, they don't give a damn about me." He signed a contract with Paramount while making some short films for

Modern times:
As an accidental director in *The Bank Dick* (1940); a disdainful dentist in *The Dentist* (1932).

Mack Sennett that were essentially recycled versions of his stage sketches. Among them were "The Dentist," which displayed Fields at his most curmudgeonly and covertly obscene (one moment where a female patient wraps her legs around him as Fields relentlessly "drills" her is still jaw-dropping) and "The Fatal Glass of Beer," with its blizzard-inducing refrain, "Tain't a fit night out for man nor beast!"

It was a while before Paramount quite knew what to do with their fifty-year-old star; in the early thirties, he was consigned to cameos or inefficiently absurd pictures. "Fields fought a never-ending battle with producers and studio executives and sometimes he won, sometimes he lost," observes film historian Leonard Maltin. "He wanted his characters to be more human, more sympathetic at times, and the studios just wanted the comedy. You'd think he'd be fighting for just his comedic independence, but he was fighting for his own point of view as well as his comedy." The comic persona Fields was trying to develop in Hollywood was full of sympathetic grace notes and emerged slowly, but indelibly, out of its roots in "The Family Ford" and "Sleeping Porch" (another comic sketch he created in his revue days)— the henpecked husband, besieged by life's inconveniences. "He is the surprised and blinking troll entangled in the details of his day," wrote one of his collaborators, J. P. McEvoy, in 1924.

It's a Gift (1934) was, like most of Fields's films, a loosely connected series of set pieces bound together with package string to produce a thin plot, but for many it's his masterpiece. It was the perfect expression of his comic philosophy—"If anything can go wrong, it will"—wedded to his ability to juggle not only objects but also life's unpredictable obstacles. By the end of the film, despite every dream and effort going up in smoke, Fields manages to look on the bright side. "You're drunk!" someone protests to Fields. "And you're crazy," he replies. "But I'll be sober tomorrow and you'll be crazy for the rest of your life."

Between 1933 and 1934, Fields would make eight films and, forever liberated from his pantomime, became one of Hollywood's great verbal comics. But it was Fields's more colorful—and more scandalous—language that he delighted in sneaking past the censors. By the time Fields was enjoying his box office success, he had to contend with a new form of authority, the Hollywood Production Code, which seemed intent on ruining his best material by requesting constant revisions of his screenplays. He fought back the best way he knew how—by ignoring them. "Any clever comedy writer or comedian could find ways to outwit or outsmart the production code," said Leonard Maltin. "He did get to say 'Godfrey Daniel,' which was a lovely euphemism [for 'God damn it']. It didn't escape their notice, they were not happy about it. But he got away with it just the same."

Some of what Fields got away with is still outrageous. In *The Bank Dick*, he tells an auditor who wants to pull down the window shade in a bar, "You can pull anything you want to." Fields seemed obsessed with sneaking the word *pussy* into as many films as possible—the bar in *The Bank Dick* is called the Black Pussy Café, and in *Poppy* he pretends to get the name of another character wrong:

COUNTESS DEPUIZZI: I am the Countesss DePuizzi!

MCGARGLE: The Countess De Pussy?

COUNTESS DEPUIZZI: Monsieur, no. *DePuizzi*—La Comtesse DePuizzi!

MCGARGLE: Oh, quite so, quite so! Pardon my redundancy.

In his last great film, *Never Give a Sucker an Even Break*, in the middle of a scene in an ice-cream parlor, Fields turned to the camera and said, "This scene's supposed to be in a saloon but the censor cut it out. It'll play just as well this way."

What seemed to bother the censors—and certain audiences—more was Fields's seeming antisocial curmudgeonly behavior: despising his wife and mother-in-law, snarling at dogs, kicking little kids in the behind. "I was the first comic in history to pick fights with children," he said. "People didn't know what the unmanageable baby might do to get even—I got sympathy. Maybe you wouldn't call it sympathy. Maybe you'd call it forbearance." Much of it was an act—a good act—but an act. Rose Marie appeared in a bizarre movie with Fields called *International House* when she was ten years old: "He wasn't as mean as they made him. He was very nice to me—a very nice man." Leonard Maltin observed that "Fields was enough of a showman to understand that it was to his benefit that people think he was that guy, but he was not that guy. If you read his correspondence, you see what a sensitive man he was, but there are certainly aspects of his private life that came through in his, in his characterization, most notably drinking, which became more pronounced as years went on."

EGBERT SOUSÉ: Is that gun loaded?

MOTHER IN BANK: Certainly not! But I think you are!

Fields's infatuation with alcohol was part of his enduring persona on camera and off. Someone once asked him if he liked to drink water and he supposedly responded, "Are you kidding? Fish fuck in it." In real life, the gag was less funny. According to writer Hal Kanter, "I would suggest that he did drink from my personal observation. Either that or he used gin as an aftershave lotion or a mouthwash." By 1937, Fields was so ill from drink and overwork that he had to be hospitalized. Friends thought he might not make it back. But he stared down the "Fellow in the Bright Nightgown," as he called Death, and bounced back by appearing on radio—a much less strenuous job than writing and starring in his own films. His comic foil was a ventriloquist's dummy named Charlie McCarthy and it brought him a new legion of fans.

FIELDS: **Tell me, Charles, is it true your father was a gateleg table?**

CHARLIE MCCARTHY: **If it is, your father was *under* it!**

Fields had spent two decades of his professional life squaring off against authority and it was hardening his shell, turning him into an offstage curmudgeon. Someone once foolishly tried to wangle a charitable contribution from him while he was on the set. He told them that he only gave money to one charity, F.E.B.F—Fuck Everybody But Fields. Fields still maintained his contempt for film producers, inept directors, sponsors, and censors—anyone who was trying to get in his way. But when he made his other masterpiece, *The Bank Dick*, in 1941, no other star in Hollywood had above-the-title billing and carried contractual responsibility for writing and directing as well as performing at the age of sixty.

You've heard the old legend that it's the little put-upon guy who gets the laughs, but I'm the most belligerent guy on the screen. I'm going to kill everybody. But at the same time, I'm afraid of everybody—just a great big frightened bully. There's a lot of that in human nature. When people laugh at me, they're laughing at themselves. Or at least the next fellow.

By the time World War II came along, film producers and audiences were looking for new comics, fresher faces. Critics who had championed Fields's idiosyncratic humor since his vaudeville or *Follies* appearances were becoming few and far between as well. Fields, exhausted and without the energy or collaborators to sustain the vehicles he wanted, was losing his touch by the time the war ended. He was never everybody's tumbler of gin, but then Fields never wanted to be. Throughout his career, he carried with him the one trait you need to be a great juggler or a great confidence man: confidence.

On Christmas Day, 1946, the Fellow in the Bright Nightgown caught up with Bill Fields.

"It's a funny ol' world," he once muttered in the film *You're Telling Me*. "Man's lucky if he gets out of it alive."

Anything For a Laugh

By W.C. Fields

American Magazine— September, 1934

I have spent years working out gags to make people laugh. With the patience of an old mariner making a ship in a bottle, I have been able to build situations that have turned out to be funny. But—to show you what a crazy way this is to make a living—the biggest laugh on stage I ever got was an almost exact reproduction of an occurrence one evening when I was visiting a friend, and it took no thinking-up whatsoever.

At my friend's home it didn't even get a snicker, but in the theater, it caused the audience to yell for a full minute.

On the stage I was a pompous nobody. The telephone rang. I told my wife I would answer it, in a manner that showed I doubted she was capable of handing an affair of such importance.

I said, "Hello, Elmer. . . Yes, Elmer. . . Is that so, Elmer?. . . Of course, Elmer... Good-bye, Elmer."

I hung up the receiver and said to my wife, as though I were disclosing a state secret, "That was Elmer."

It was a roar. It took ten or twelve performances to find that "Elmer" is the funniest name for a man. I tried them all—Charley, Clarence, Oscar, Archibald, Luke, and dozens of others—but Elmer was tops. That was several years ago. Elmer is still funny—unless your name happens to be Elmer. In that case you will probably vote for Clarence.

I don't know why the scene turned out to be so terribly funny. The funniest thing about comedy is that you never know why people laugh. I know what makes them laugh, but trying to get your hands on the *why* of it is like trying to pick an eel out of a tub of water.

"Charley Bogle," spoken slowly and solemnly with a very long "o," is a laugh. "George Beebe" is not funny, but "Doctor Beebe" is. The expression "You big Swede" is not good for a laugh, but "You big Polack" goes big. But if you say "You big Polack" in a show you'll be visited by indignant delegations of protesting Poles. The Swedes don't seem to mind.

I don't know the why of all this—any more than I know why a man gets sore if he slips and falls, while if a woman falls, she laughs. Nor why it is harder to put over comedy in Kansas City than in any other city in the United States, and easier in New York.

Flo Ziegfeld never thought a comedy act was any good unless there was a beautiful girl in it, and he picked on me when I was doing my golf game in the *Follies*.

It was a scene in which I came on the golf course with a caddy and had troubles for eighteen minutes without ever hitting the ball. Lionel Barrymore told me it was the funniest gag he ever saw—and you can't laugh off a testimonial like that!

One day Ziegfeld saw a picture in a paper showing a society girl with a Russian wolfhound. He dropped the paper, ran out, bought a wolfhound, and told me he was going to have Dolores, one of his glorified girls, walk across the stage leading the hound, in the middle of my act!

I squawked, but it didn't do any good, and at the next performance, just as I was building up some laughs by stepping in a pie that somebody had left on the golf course, out of the wings—for no reason except that Ziegfeld had told her to do it—comes Dolores, with slow, stately tread, leading the Russian wolfhound.

I lost my audience instantly. They didn't know what it was all about. I wasn't going to give up my scene without a fight, so I looked at Dolores in amazement, and then at the audience as if I, too, were shocked at this strange sight on the golf course. When she was halfway across the stage I said, "That's a very beautiful horse."

It got a big laugh.

Dolores was so indignant because I had spoiled her parade that she grabbed the hound around the shoulders and ran off the stage with him in her arms—and that was another laugh.

Ziegfeld and Dolores raised the very devil. I maintained that I had improved the scene. Finally we compromised. I was to let her have her moment and was not to speak the line until she was one step from her exit. It turned out that the suspense made it all the better.

I experimented night after night to find out what animal was the funniest. I finally settled upon "That's a very beautiful camel."

You usually can't get a laugh out of damaging anything valuable. When you kick a silk hat, it must be dilapidated; when you wreck a car, bang it up a little before you bring it on the scene.

It is funnier to bend things than to break them—bend the fenders on a car in a comedy wreck, don't tear them off. In my golf game, which I have been doing for years, at first I swung at the ball and broke the club. Now I bend it at a right angle. If one comedian hits another over the head with a crowbar, the crowbar should bend, not break. In legitimate drama, the hero breaks his sword, and it is dramatic. In comedy, the sword bends, and stays bent.

Professors of Humor will tell you the audience must not be allowed to guess what is coming, that humor is always based upon surprise. The theory is often true, but in *You're Telling Me!*, my most recent moving picture, I have a scene in which the laugh depends upon the fact that the audience knows in advance exactly what is going to happen.

I play a stupid and self-important inventor and I explain the details of my new burglar trap. According to my plan, I shall become friendly with the burglar, invite him to sit down and talk things over, and, when he sits in a chair, a lever will automatically release an immense iron ball which will hit him, *Socko!* on the head and kill him instantly.

From that moment the audience knows what's coming—that pretty soon I'll forget about the iron ball and will sit in the chair myself. The laughter begins when I start toward the chair. It reaches its peak *before* the ball whams me on the bean.

If I sat in a chair and the ball fell on my head, and *then* it was explained that it was a burglar alarm, the scene would fall flat. The success of the scene depends upon the absence of surprise.

I know we laugh at the troubles of others, provided those troubles are not too serious. Out of that observation I have reached a conclusion which may be of some comfort to those accused of "having no sense of humor." These folks are charming, lovable, philanthropic people, and invariably I like them—as long as they keep out of the theaters where I am playing, which they usually do. If they get in by mistake, they leave early.

The reason they don't laugh at most gags is that their first emotional reaction is to feel sorry for people instead of to laugh at them.

I like, in an audience, the fellow who roars continuously at the troubles of the character I am portraying on the stage, but he probably has a mean streak in him and, if I needed ten dollars, he'd be the last person I'd call upon. I'd go first to the old lady and old gentleman back in Row S who keep wondering what there is to laugh at.

"WHATEVER IT IS, I'M AGAINST IT"
GROUCHO MARX

In the topsy-turvy world of vaudeville, the "top of the bill" was the last and best spot in the show. By the fall of 1914, W. C. Fields, "Eccentric Juggler," had earned the top of the bill, but one night, at Keith's Vaudeville Theater in Columbus, Ohio, there was one act he couldn't follow. It was called "Fun in Hi-Skule," and it featured four boys from New York, the "4 Marx Bros" as they were billed, for those who couldn't count:

Now our act had grown and we had about twenty-four people in the act. Fields was to close the bill and follow us, but one day Fields went to see the manager of the theater and told him he had to leave for New York. He said, "You see this hand? I can't juggle anymore because I've got noxis on the conoxis and I have to see a specialist right away." I met him fifteen years later and I said, "We knew there wasn't a goddamn thing wrong with you!" And Fields said, "You didn't think I was going to follow you cocksuckers with that act you had. Twenty-four people plus a harp *and* a piano! And I was up there fucking a lot of boxes!"
—Groucho Marx

CHICO: Okay, now I got one for you: what is it gotta a big-a black cigar, a big-a black mustache, and is a big-a pain in the neck?

GROUCHO: Hmm. Let me see. Does he wear glasses?
CHICO: Aha! You catch-a on quick!

Groucho and His Brothers:
Offstage, left to right, Harpo, Zeppo, Chico, c. 1929.

The Four Marx Brothers were a four-ring circus of chaos, but even they had their ringleader. Groucho Marx was one of the most enduring comedians of the twentieth century, with a career that lasted for seven decades, but his journey to fame was one of the most ridiculous things anyone ever heard.

Julius Henry Marx was born in October of 1890 to German Jewish immigrant parents; "My father was the worst tailor in New York," he often said. His mother, Minnie Marx, was another story altogether; she came from a family of entertainers and her brother was Al Shean, a successful vaudevillian. Her determination to get her boys out of their Yorkville poverty and into showbiz would be the key factor in their eventual success. As actor Lewis J. Stadlen, who played the young Groucho in a 1969 musical of their lives, *Minnie's Boys*, pointed out, "I think to understand Groucho one has to know his placement in the Marx family. The first Marx child was born dead and the family was obviously bereft. And then Chico (Leonard) came along, and so he received the love of the dead child and he was his mother's favorite. Two years later Harpo (Adolph) came along and he was the father's favorite. And then Groucho came along two years later and he was nobody's favorite."

Minnie was determined to get her boys onstage in vaudeville. "Where else," she reasoned sensibly, "can people who don't know anything make money?" It was young Julius, at age fourteen, who was pushed out onstage first, when his mother made him answer an advertisement for a boy singer to become one third of the Le Roy Trio. Alas, Le Roy and his partner (and lover) stole Groucho's pay and abandoned him on the road, but Minnie saw it as a good start—at least the boy proved he could be an earner. She kept sending one boy after another out on the road, despite their meager talents—the fourth son, Milton (Gummo), was recruited to be a human ventriloquist dummy, then Harpo was passed off as a singer—on the theory that three salaries were better than one. Plenty of young boys at the turn of the century would have loved to have run away to join the circus, but not young Groucho; he was miserable. "I was sorry I never went to college—I wanted to be a writer," he complained decades later.

Minnie Marx pushed her boys up the ladder of success with a mixture of determination, effrontery, and sheer chicanery. For nearly two decades, through a series of trials and errors, the Four Marx Brothers—Gummo had left showbiz and been replaced by the youngest brother, Zeppo, while the eldest, piano-playing Chico, joined late in the game—developed into the craziest, hardest working, most successful act in vaudeville. It was a tough, long grind, and the Marx Brothers simply outlasted failure by reinventing their act a thousand times.

Why, outside the necessity of sheer survival did we do this? We all wanted to be the best, the most perfect, the most flawless, the funniest that we could possibly be. Nobody else could be funny for you. It takes many years on the stage, in front of a live audience, to learn this art, to learn how to deliver those carefully chosen words in the most casual, artless way. –Groucho Marx

By 1922, with the "boys" nearing forty, playing the Palace, and breaking every record in vaudeville, it was time for the next step. Typical of their anarchic (or exhausted) spirit, they had Chico, an inveterate gambler, take over the managerial reins from their mother. He bet their money on a vehicle for Broadway, assembling a second-rate revue from bits and pieces of rejected shows, but *I'll Say She Is* took the town by storm when it opened in New York in 1924. It also allowed Groucho to break out of the pack. Alexander Woollcott cooed in the *New York Sun*: "Not since sin laid its heavy hand on our spirit have we laughed so loud and so offensively. One might note, too, how fluent and fresh is the humor of Mr. Julius Marx, who rewrites his part every night and essentially is as much a topical commentator as Will Rogers."

Even Ziegfeld offered them a spot in his *Follies*, but Chico, no longer content to rely on borrowed goods, held out for a first-class Broadway musical vehicle. In 1925, they got it—from two of the best, songwriter Irving Berlin and "the gloomy dean of American comedy," playwright George S. Kaufman. For *The Cocoanuts*, Kaufman structured the Marx Brothers' routines into something with an unobtrusive narrative, refined their personas, and tailored Groucho's antic dialogue to fit his anarchic spirit perfectly:

> Florida, folks—sunshine, perpetual sunshine, all the year around. Let's get the auction started before we get a tornado. . . . This is the heart of the residential district. Every lot is a stone's throw from the station. As soon as they throw enough stones, we're going to build a station. . . . You can get any kind of home you want to. You can even get stucco—oh, how you can get stucco.

Kaufman's collaboration brought the team to a new level. According to Dick Cavett, "Kaufman was Groucho's god. The only thing he ever repeated in the old folks sense to me was, 'You know the greatest compliment I ever had? George Kaufman said, "Groucho, you're the only actor I'd allow to ad-ib in something I wrote." ' And he'd get a little teary when he said that thing."

A second Broadway vehicle, *Animal Crackers*, written by Kaufman with Morrie Ryskind in 1928, also became a hit and introduced Groucho's most indelible character, Captain Jeffrey T. Spaulding, the African explorer. While the Marxes were performing *Animal Crackers* at night, they were committing *The Cocoanuts* to film in Astoria, Queens, during the day. It would be Groucho's first encounter with the absurdity of the Hollywood studios:

> In the film of *Cocoanuts*, I was called into conference and informed I would have to discard the black painted moustache. When I asked why, they explained, "Well, nobody's ever worn a black painted moustache on the screen. The audience isn't accustomed to anything as phony as that and just won't believe it." "The audience doesn't believe us anyhow," I answered. "All they do is laugh at us, and after all, isn't that what we're getting paid for?"

When October of 1929 began, Groucho Marx, a deeply pessimistic human being, was at his happiest. He was married, the father of two children, a star of stage and now the screen, living in an expansive house in Long Island, and with a substantial life savings—nearly a quarter of a million dollars—in the bank. Or, more accurately, invested in the stock market. By the end of the month, he was wiped out. The prodigal brother, Chico, remarked that Groucho had saved every nickel "and look what happened. I had fun, and he didn't, and now he's starting from scratch with me." To repair their fortunes, the Marx Brothers had no choice but to "Go West," as it were, and they arrived at the same studio as their old

On your Marx, get set, go!
A pensive Groucho; success on Broadway in *The Cocoanuts* (1925); *Animal Crackers* on film (1930).

vaudeville colleague W. C. Fields, Paramount, at the same time, the spring of 1931. "It was very easy to become acclimated to California, we all felt five years younger," wrote Groucho. "That's how many years the studio took off our ages in publicity stories."

The brothers made three films for Paramount, the first two written by, among others, S. J. Perelman. They did much to cement the image of Groucho as a conniving anarchist; *Horse Feathers* cast him as a college president without a shred of academic discipline, even gave him his own anthem:

Dismay for Hollywood:
On the backlot with his brothers (including Gummo, left of Groucho); at MGM in *A Night at the Opera* (1935); *A Night in Casablanca* (1946)—too much work.

Your proposition may be good,

But let's have one thing understood:

Whatever it is, I'm against it.

But for Groucho, the on-screen larks took a lot of effort; as he commented about his own publicity photos, "Groucho didn't have as good a time working on films as he seemed to be having." His dissatisfaction, which was a deep personality trait, largely came out of arguments with producers, directors, and scriptwriters who presented him with inferior material. That would all change—briefly—when Chico played bridge one day with MGM's boy wonder, Irving Thalberg, and the producer put them under contract for the prestige studio in 1935.

Thalberg was probably the only film producer that Groucho ever respected. He thought the Marx Brothers needed to create sympathy for their characters, rather than simply create anarchy, and brought in George S. Kaufman to create some first-class material for them. *A Night at the Opera* and *A Day at the Races* were their biggest commercial successes and featured some of their choicest bits. *A Night at the Opera*, Groucho's personal favorite, contained the legendary stateroom scene, the "sanity clause" contract scene, and the best repartee between Groucho and his favorite paramour, the imperious (and often clueless) dowager Margaret Dumont:

MRS. CLAYPOOL: Otis, do you have everything?

GROUCHO: I've never had any complaints yet.

"That line," recalled Groucho, "was cut by censors in thirty-seven states." Although, as in his earlier films, Groucho frequently tried to flimflam other characters, most often Dumont, he could always be beaten at his own game by his older brother Chico. It was a reflection of their real-life "tootsie-frootsying." Stadlen recalled, "When Chico died, they said, 'How much money did Chico make in his life?' and Groucho, who paid for the funeral, said, 'Well, find out how much I have, and that's how much Chico lost.'"

When Thalberg died before *A Day at the Races* was completed, Groucho lost most of his interest in the brothers' MGM contract. He would have been happy to give up the studio grind and stop acting in inferior movies, but throughout the 1940s he was forced to slap on the greasepaint again, usually to help Chico pay off his gambling debts. *A Night in Casablanca* (1946) was the last film to be fully built around all three brothers and it had its moments, but for Groucho, a fifty-six-year-old man forced to twist himself into some tedious slapstick pretzel while hanging from an airplane, the handwriting was on the wall. "As I hung there like a plucked turkey, I said to myself, 'Groucho, old boy—and believe me, you are an old boy—don't you think this is rather a ridiculous way for you to be spending your few remaining years?' " His offscreen skepticism was beginning to overwhelm the magic of his on-screen skepticism. Stadlen observed, "He was a man who was pretty much always looking up to God and saying, 'Why is life so inequitable?' Groucho would say all the things that all the rest of us would like to say. So the inability to dissemble in a world in which everybody is lying about everything has a lot to do with the appreciation that people feel about him."

After the *Casablanca* picture, Groucho vowed, "I'm never going to get behind that phony mustache again. I'm through with the whole racket." He tried to go into retirement and even tried his hand at playwriting, but an episode of spontaneous ad-libbing with Bob Hope on a radio show in 1947 proved the beginning of a whole new career. Groucho was soon offered a spot hosting his own radio quiz show. "I've flopped four times on radio before," he responded, "I'm interested in anything. I might as well compete with refrigerators. I'll give it a try." After a slow start, *You Bet Your Life* became a hit, and when the show made its transition to television in 1950, Groucho, who was now supporting two ex-wives, leapt at the chance. "I must say I find television very educational," he wrote in a magazine article. "The minute somebody turns it on, I go into the library and read a good book."

For his appearance on television, network executives, in a complete reversal of *The Cocoanuts* days, insisted that Groucho put on his old greasepaint mustache. Once again, Groucho told the executives where to go and simply grew his own. He also changed his personality, becoming more generous, more accessible; he seemed to do his best to insure the contestants would walk home with a few hundred dollars. The program was taped in advance and edited down, providing the best showcase for Groucho's witticisms. It also gave the producers a way to temper Groucho's more provocative lines:

CONTESTANT: My husband works a twenty-four-hour shift.

GROUCHO: He works a twenty-four-hour shift and you have ten children? Imagine if he worked at home. He's probably scared to come home. He'd walk in the door and ask what's new and you'd tell him.

For many viewers in the 1950s, especially the younger generation without access to revival houses or VCRs, the Groucho of *You Bet Your Life* was the one they knew—not so

A little-a snoop more:
Once Groucho gave up pictures in the late 1940s and grew his real mustache, he became a media star all over again.

much the frenetic huckster of the Hollywood days but a witty compere who was more concerned with putting money *into* people's pockets. David Steinberg observed that the show

"gave him a whole other life; America got to see this guy—not with the fake mustache, not walking the Groucho walk and all of that—just being calm and witty, and sort of charming. And of course his timing was impeccable."

The quiz show ran for eleven years, but by the mid-sixties, Groucho had outlived Chico and Harpo and a third marriage had run aground. Although in his eighties, he kept his career alive by attending screenings and appearing in concerts and television, particularly a triumph at Carnegie Hall in 1972. He didn't exactly mellow with age; he missed his brothers, he missed simpler times, he missed the sedate life of letters he never got to enjoy. "Times have changed," he told his great acolyte and friend, Dick Cavett. "I'm an incongruity." According to Lewis Stadlen, "He realized at this time in his life that he was a social icon, and he knew that people felt gratified when he insulted them, so that was his means of communication." Cavett recounted that

> I always was afraid I was never going to see him again. When we'd say good-bye at the hotel and the door would shut, I would think that last glimpse might be it. And happily it wasn't for a long time. I called him once after a trip back east and he sounded like a dead man over the phone. "Hello." I said, "Groucho?" "Yeah." "Are you okay?" "No." He then went on to describe a nightmare airport trip he'd had from New York—an eleven-hour flight: "And I went over to the luggage area and there's an old Jewish woman standing there. And she says, 'You're Groucho Marx, aren't you?' And I said, 'Yeah.' And she said, 'You know, you weren't very funny on the plane.' And I said, 'Go fuck yourself.'"

Groucho's last years were not peaceful; he was in ill health and embroiled in legal wrangling over his family's objections to a young woman named Erin Fleming who had become his companion. He never got the epitaph he craved: "Here lies Groucho Marx. And lies. And Lies. PS: He never kissed an ugly girl," but when he died, in 1977, the world mourned a comedy legend recognized around the world. Even his glasses and mustache—the mustache that had been such a cross to bear—could be bought by any kid at a five-and-dime store, creating an instant connection to comedic immorality.

Say the secret word:
Game show host extraordinaire; with Marilyn
Monroe in *Love Happy* (1949).

GROUCHO: I met a priest in Montreal and he told me his mother loved me. I didn't know those fellows had mothers. And he said, "I just want to thank you for all the joy you brought to the world." And I said, "And I want to thank you for all the joy you've taken out of it."

The Cocoanuts (1925)

(In this scene, written for the Broadway production by George S. Kaufman, Groucho, as Mr. Schlemmer, tries to sell Willie—Chico—some Florida property.)

SCHLEMMER: You wired me about some property. I've thought it over. Now I can let you have three lots watering the front, or I can let you have three lots fronting the water. Now these lots cost me nine thousand dollars and I'm going to let you have them for fifteen because I like you.

WILLIE: I no buy nothing. I gotta no money.

SCHLEMMER: You got no money?

WILLIE: I no gotta one cent.

SCHLEMMER: How're you going to pay for your room?

WILLIE: Thatsa your lookout.

SCHLEMMER: Oh, so you're just an idle rumor.

WILLIE: Well, you see, we come-a here to make-a money. I read-a in de paper, and it say "Big Boom in Florida." So we come. We're a coupla of big booms, too.

SCHLEMMER: Well. I'll show you how you can make some real money. I'm going to hold an auction in a little while in Cocoanut Manor. You—you know what an auction is, eh?

WILLIE: I come-a from Italy on the Atlantic Auction.

SCHLEMMER: Well, let's go ahead as if nothing happened. I say, I'm holding an auction at Cocoanut Manor. And when the crowd gathers around, I want you to mingle with them. Don't pick their pockets, just mingle with them, and—

WILLIE: I'll find time for both.

SCHLEMMER: Well, maybe we can cut out the auction. Here's what I mean, if someone says a hundred dollars, you say two—if someone says two hundred dollars, you say three—

WILLIE: Speaka up?

SCHLEMMER: Now, if nobody says anything, then you start it off.

WILLIE: How am I going to know when to no say nuthin'?

SCHLEMMER: Well, they'll probably notify you. You fool, if you don't say anything, you'll hear 'em, won't you?

WILLIE: Well, mebbe I no listen.

SCHLEMMER: Well, don't tell them. Now then, if we're successful in disposing of these lots, I'll see to it you get a nice commission.

WILLIE: How about some money?

SCHLEMMER: Well, you can have your choice. Now, in arranging for these lots, of course, we use blueprints. You know what a blueprint is, huh?

WILLIE: Sure, I had 'em for dinner last night. Blueprint oysters.

SCHLEMMER: Boy, give you an inch and you take a mollusk.

WILLIE: Yeah, I'm shellfish that way.

SCHLEMMER: Well, I walked right into that one. It's going to be a cinch explaining the rest of this thing to you, I can see that.

WILLIE: I catch on quick.

SCHLEMMER: Look, Einstein, do you know what a lot is?

WILLIE: Yeah, it's-a too much.

SCHLEMMER: I don't mean a whole lot. Just a little lot with nothing on it.

WILLIE: Any time you gotta too much, you gotta whole lot. Look, I'll explain it to you. Sometimes you no gotta much: sometimes you gotta whole lot. You know what, it's a lot. Somebody else maybe thinks it's too much: that's a whole lot, too. Now, a whole lot is too much, too much is a whole lot: same thing.

SCHLEMMER: How is it you never got double pneumonia?

WILLIE: I go around by myself.

SCHLEMMER: Come here, Rand McNally and I'll explain this thing to you. Now here is a map and a diagram of the entire Cocoanut section. Here's Cocoanut Manor and over there is Cocoanut Heights. That's the swamp. Down here, where the road forks, is Cocoanut Junction.

WILLIE: Where you got Cocoanut Custard?

SCHLEMMER: That's on one of the forks. You probably eat with your knife, so you won't have to worry about that. Now here's the main road leading out of Cocoanut Manor. That's the road I wish you were on. Now over here, on this site we're going to build an Eye and Ear Hospital. That's going to be a sight for sore eyes.

WILLIE: I see.

SCHLEMMER: Over here is the old coffee factory. I grew up playing on the grounds. You understand?

WILLIE: That's where you bean.

SCHLEMMER: Here is the riverfront. All along there, those are the levees.

WILLIE: That's the Jewish neighborhood.

SCHLEMMER: Well, we'll pass over that. You're a peach, boy. Now, here is a little peninsula, and here is a viaduct leading to the mainland.

WILLIE: Why a duck?

SCHLEMMER: I'm all right, how are you? I say, here is a little peninsula, and here is a viaduct leading to the mainland.

WILLIE: All right. Why a duck?

SCHLEMMER: I'm not playing Ask-Me-Another. I say, that's a viaduct.

WILLIE: All right, all right. Why a duck? Why-a-no-chicken?

SCHLEMMER: I don't know why-a-no-chicken. I'm a stranger here myself. All I know is that it's a viaduct. You try to cross over there a-chicken and you'll find out why a duck. It's deeper water, that's viaduct.

WILLIE: That's-a why-a-duck?

SCHLEMMER: Look—suppose you were out horseback riding and you came to that stream and wanted to ford over there, you couldn't make it. Too deep.

WILLIE: But what do you want with a Ford when you gotta horse?

SCHLEMMER: Well, I'm sorry the whole matter ever came up. All I know is that it's a viaduct.

WILLIE: Now, look—I catch-a on to why-a-horse, why-a-chicken, why-a-this, why-a-that. I no catch on to why-a-duck.

SCHLEMMER: I was only fooling. I was only fooling. They're going to build a tunnel there in the morning. Now, is that clear?

WILLIE: Yes. Everything—excepta why-a-duck.

SCHLEMMER: Well, that's fine. Now I can go ahead. I'm going to take you down and show you our cemetery. I have a waiting list of fifty people, just dying to get in. But I like you—

WILLIE: Ah, you're my friend.

SCHLEMMER: I like you and I'm going to shove you in ahead of all of them. I'm going to see that you get a steady position.

WILLIE: That's-a good.

SCHLEMMER: And if I can arrange it, it will be horizontal.

"IF I CAN'T TAKE IT WITH ME, I'M NOT GOING" JACK BENNY

Jack Benny: Rochester, I'll hold the phone, but I want you to get out my birth certificate.

Rochester: Got it, boss.

Benny: What's written in the spot that says "Date of Birth"?

Rochester: A hole.

Benny: A hole?

Rochester: Yeah, boss, we erased it once too often!

Although he spent the second half of his career protesting that he was perennially 39 years old, Jack Benny was born in 1894, on Valentine's Day in Chicago. He wasn't born Jack Benny, but Benjamin Kubelsky, the son of a strict, sober Jewish couple. Benny's life story was rather different than his peers: "I did not triumph over adversity. I did not go through struggles and hardship. I always had shoes and warm clothes. My only handicap is golf."

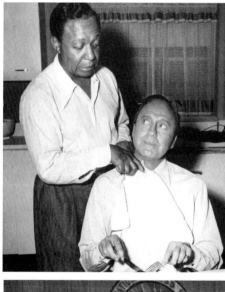

Well...!
Benny as a vaudeville wiseguy and MC; with Eddie (Rochester) Anderson; fiddling away with Richard Nixon at the piano.

The Kubelskys moved to Waukegan, along Lake Michigan, and according to Jack's daughter, Joan, "He would stare out over the lake instead of practicing his violin or doing homework, and think of foreign places and faraway lands. He was a daydreamer and he wanted to go into vaudeville, he wanted to leave home."

Benny nearly got his chance at fifteen, while he was playing violin in the pit orchestra of the vaudeville theater in Waukegan—it was his first job. During one performance, he was noticed by the mother of the four boys clowning onstage that night and Minnie Marx offered Benny a chance to tour with the Marx Brothers. Emma Kubelsky was horrified that her son would throw his life away in vaudeville, and the Kubelskys kept young Benjamin at home. But after a stint in the navy, safeguarding the shores of Lake Michigan, there was no stopping Benny. He went back to vaudeville, playing violin in the orchestra, and was given a few comedy lines onstage; soon, the balance shifted, with Benny telling more jokes and playing less violin.

Eventually, Benny Kubelsky became Ben K. Benny, then Jack Benny, and he settled into a respectable vaudeville career as a wisecracking comic. His persona evolved over twenty years on the circuit. "He would play Peoria and he got a laugh about being cheap, and so he did two jokes about being cheap during the next gig in Chicago," recounted Joan Benny. His musicianship, his *timing*, gave Benny an edge over his somewhat mediocre material. In 1927, Benny added a female comic sidekick and a wife, both in the person of Sadye Marks, who was introduced to him by Zeppo Marx years earlier; she became better known as Mary Livingstone. But by the late 1920s, Benny was only slightly more distinguishable than a dozen other smart-aleck comics.

Hollywood found some brief use for him as an amiable master of ceremonies in films such as *Hollywood Revue of 1929*, but good scripts were not forthcoming and Benny intuited that vaudeville was soon going to be on its way out. So, on March 29, 1932, he ventured into a new medium for the first time: radio. Appearing on a fifteen-minute radio program hosted by a Broadway columnist named Ed Sullivan, his first line was, "This is Jack Benny talking. There will now be a slight pause while everyone says, 'Who cares?'" Canada Dry ginger ale cared—they signed Benny to host his first radio program. "He started off as kind of a wiseguy comedian and as the years went on, the wiseguy image was subdued and the other characteristics of the Jack Benny we know and love—the vain, sometimes childish, always cheap comedian—came to the fore," said film historian Leonard Maltin.

Benny added a stock company. His wife, Mary, played an amorphous combination of girlfriend, secretary, and gal Friday. There was his portly announcer, Don Wilson; his narcissistic band leader, Phil Harris, who had a fondness for the booze; eventually, Dennis Day, a cross between a boy tenor and puppy dog. In 1937, Benny added perhaps his most unforgettable comic sidekick. Eddie Anderson started as a one-shot character, a Pullman porter, but due to popular demand, he joined the show as Benny's valet/butler/chauffeur, Rochester. Maltin observes that "it was a wonderful troupe. If you tried to invent it overnight, I guess it wouldn't have happened. It evolved, week by week, season by season. They kept refining and perfecting what they were doing and, and that's the reason why it was the funniest show on radio."

But the greatest comic creation of *The Jack Benny Program* was the character called

Jack Benny. "He was always put upon," observed Joan Benny. "He was always kind of the patsy. He didn't tell jokes—he was the butt of the joke." Benny himself understood perfectly that his persona was, appropriately, money in the bank:

> My kind of comedy lasts because the Jack Benny character includes a composite of all the faults people may have, all the human frailities. He's stingy and vain and insecure—insecurity is based on stinginess, which is fear of the future. Who isn't afraid of the future? So—we exaggerate, we make a joke of it, and people recognize something in themselves. There's a lot of everybody in Jack Benny.

Comedian David Steinberg observed that with his characterization, "Jack Benny did something that's amazing. He's Jewish and he played cheap, miserly, but he did it so charmingly and so effortlessly that no one noticed that he was in what others might consider anti-Semitic territory." To his basic vanity and stinginess, Benny added pettiness, jealousy, a host of phobias, and a wonderful epicene quality, where he was both entranced and terrified by glamorous women:

BENNY: I'd like to buy some lingerie.

CLERK: What size are you?

By the mid-1930s, there was no more popular comedian on the radio. As Johnny Carson would say, "That character was so well identified and well established that if you had followed that show at all and you could write, you could almost write it yourself." Benny's writers, whom he always admired and treated well, dropped him down in a million different variations of the same basic scenario. Once Benny played Faust, but canceled the deal on Satan, saying, "If I can't take it with me, I'm not going." As a phony contestant on Groucho's *You Bet Your Life*, Benny forfeited $3,000 by refusing to answer the final question: what is Jack Benny's real age? The greatest payoff came one Sunday night in 1948 at seven o'clock—perhaps the most famous exchange in radio history:

ROBBER: Your money or your life. (*pause*)

ROBBER: I said, "Your money or your life!"

BENNY: I'm thinking it over!

Comedian Richard Belzer astutely assessed the brilliance of that response: "That joke took twenty years to write, you know what I mean?"

Benny's timing was legendary in the business. Actress Kaye Ballard said, "You laughed at what he was thinking, not just at what he said." Benny himself said, "My timing is right for me. It wouldn't be right for Bob Hope, it wouldn't be right for George Burns—my timing is right for me." Benny used his personal timing to slow down the rat-a-tat-tat world of radio comedy and, in doing so, revolutionized the medium. Another radio comedian put it best:

> Practically all comedy shows on the radio owe their structure to Benny. He was the first to realize that the listener is not in a theater with a thousand other people, but in a smaller circle at home. The Benny show is like tuning into someone else's home.

That comedian was Benny's mythical archenemy, Fred Allen.

Allen was a former juggler who hosted and wrote most of his own show, *Town Hall Tonight*. One night at the end of 1936, a ten-year-old violinist named Stuart Canin came on

HE DIDN'T TELL JOKES —HE WAS THE BUTT OF THE JOKE.

Allen's show to play a tricky bit of virtuosity called "The Bee."

ALLEN: A little fella in the fifth grade at school and already he plays better than Jack Benny. After hearing you play, Stuart, I think Jack Benny should hang his head in shame. . . . Benny is the only violinist who makes you feel the strings would sound better back in the cat's intestines.

Two weeks later, it was Benny's turn.

BENNY: Fred Allen is a broken-down juggler who was made tone-deaf as a result of being hit in the head by some falling Indian clubs he's failed to catch during his many years as a failure and small-time vaudeville act.

And the feud was on. Entirely bogus, it was a ratings boost for both comedians. When a tree planted in Benny's honor in Waukegan died, Allen said, "Of course it died—the sap is in Hollywood." The feud continued, lasting, off and on, for nearly two decades—even taking itself into the new medium of television. According to Joan Benny, actually they were "very close friends. They adored each other—the only reason they weren't closer is because Fred Allen lived in New York and we lived in Los Angeles."

Benny was raided by CBS from his long-standing radio network NBC in 1950 and quickly became the cornerstone of their Sunday night television programming. He was adamant about not appearing every week on television, for fear of overexposure—for nearly a decade he appeared monthly or every other week. It was part of his genius for timing. As he wrote in *Collier's* magazine:

Only time will tell, but it is my personal opinion that a comedian can go on year after year in television and still hold his audience. To me, the essential quality of a great comedian is humility and sincerity, and I don't feel that this performer will ever tire his audience.

Whether audiences noticed it or not, *The Jack Benny Program* was a hybrid of two different shows: a comedy-variety show where Jack Benny chatted with the audience and a sitcom featuring a character called Jack Benny. Whatever it was, the program was a surreal funhouse inhabited by the peculiar idiosyncrasies of Jack Benny and his pals. Several shows were retreads of radio material—the "Your money or your life!" exchange was restaged for the cameras in 1956—but viewers were also treated to Benny's talent as an impersonator and his generosity to up-and-coming comedians. Dick Van Dyke recalled:

When I was on the show, we did a Sherlock Holmes sketch. Jack was Holmes and I was everyone else in the cast: all the suspects, the maid, the butler, and I don't know who all. And I had to keep quick changing and coming back dressed as different people. And toward the end, I started messing up, coming in as the maid with a mustache. I worked really hard, but I got not one laugh. I would come in in

Straight man:
Benny, nose-to-nose with Fred Allen; old friend Groucho Marx.

my stupid outfit, the audience would just stare at me. And then Jack would go and look at the audience and they would fall on the floor. All he had to do was that wonderful take of his. I think maybe, over the years, he trained people.

"He loved other comedians," said Joan Benny. "He didn't want others to fail so that he would be better *than*. That didn't work for him. He had this feeling that if other comedians did well, it was good for everybody." Nowhere was that more apparent than in Benny's relationship to Eddie Anderson. Someone once asked Benny if he was afraid that Rochester would steal the show: "Let him!" he replied. "He'd *better* steal the show—it needs it!"

Benny was always very sensitive to audiences' responses to Rochester onstage and off. During a USO tour during the Second World War, he bawled out a GI for making racist remarks about Rochester and humiliated many a hotel clerk into letting Anderson stay at the same hotel with the rest of the company. Historian Gerald Nachman remarked that after World War II, "Benny decided that he would take away all the stereotypical parts of the Rochester character and concentrate on the one brilliant stroke—which is that Benny was really a servant to Rochester."

By 1962, *The Jack Benny Program* was faced by strong competition from the Western *Bonanza*. Benny watched it one week—"If I myself get so absorbed in *Bonanza* that I forget my own program," said Benny, "what chance have I got with the millions of other viewers?" The fall of 1965 was the first season in thirty-three years without a Jack Benny program on the air. He spent his last decade doing TV specials and devoted himself to playing the violin for charities all over the world. After receiving one humanitarian award, he said, "I don't deserve this award. But I have arthritis, and I don't deserve that, either." He was, next to Bob Hope, probably the most charitable comedian in history. He was beloved by millions, many of whom couldn't believe—or didn't want to believe—that he wasn't a self-serving skinflint in real life. Once, during a routine physical, he told the nurse he was unable to provide a urine sample. "Boy," she replied, "you never give *anything* away, do you!"

But Benny had no one to blame but himself for the endurance of his persona. Larry Gelbart felt that "he would look at the audience with a look of a calf that had just found out where veal came from. And so you felt you knew him, and you felt that you can make fun of yourself and not be a fool, because he's being a fool for you and we know that's a play, anyway."

In the fall of 1974, Benny made plans to act opposite Walter Matthau in the film version of Neil Simon's vaudeville valentine *The Sunshine Boys*, but he became suddenly ill and was diagnosed with pancreatic cancer. He passed away quickly, the day after Christmas, and his part in the movie was filled by his best friend, neighbor, and vaudeville comrade in arms, George Burns.

In his eulogy for Benny, Bob Hope said, "For a man who was the undisputed master of comedy timing, he left us much too soon. He was stingy to the end. He gave us eighty years and it wasn't enough."

39 and counting...
Reprising vaudeville with Bob Hope; Jack's favorite hobby.

ROCHESTER: I'd like to buy something for my boss.
CLERK: Is he the executive type?
ROCHESTER: No-o-oooo . . .
CLERK: Is he the sportsman type?
ROCHESTER: No-o-oooo . . .
CLERK: Is he the playboy type?
ROCHESTER: No-o-oooo . . .
CLERK: There's not much left.
ROCHESTER: *That's* it!!

Vaudeville and Broadway

They appear as brightly colored ghosts to a certain generation raised on the last vestiges of the variety show on 1970s television: Bob Hope, Jack Benny, Milton Berle, maybe even Jimmy Durante, gussied up in striped blazers with straw hats and canes, doing the old soft shoe in front of some studio-created backdrop. These were headliners of vaudeville, strutting their stuff and reprising material more than a half-century old for the benefit of those in the television audience old enough to remember—and enjoy—their triumphs in what was, in its day, the most popular form of entertainment in America.

Vaudeville was the next logical extension of the music hall, a popular form of urban entertainment in the mid-nineteenth century, a venue for a variety of acts, performed in front of an all-male audience while it enjoyed a beer or two. It would take a great visionary to turn vaudeville into an accessible, acceptable commodity for the middle class, and he appeared in the guise of producer Tony Pastor. He opened his eponymous theater off New York's Union Square in 1881, with the provision that there be no liquor in the audience and that the material onstage be fit for family audiences, and vaudeville soon achieved massive, nationwide popularity. The roots of its name are shrouded in legend (*voix de ville*, French for "voice of the city," sounds pretty reasonable), but Americans in nearly every city understood that vaudeville meant the best, or at least the most energetic, form of live entertainment—by 1900, there were 2,000 vaudeville houses, half of all the theaters in the country.

Vaudeville shows featured almost a dozen different artists, or acts, at a time, performing all kinds of material—songs, comedy routines, magic, acrobatics, novelty acts, dramatic readings—on what were called "bills." The performers repeated their acts (which lasted around ten minutes) at least twice a day for a week, and then the bill moved on to the next town (or in big cities, the next theaters). By the turn of the century, E. F. Albee and B. F. Keith joined forces to create the largest network (or circuit) of theaters and artists in the country, the United Booking Office. Their management of family-friendly acts, railway logistics, and "continuous" vaudeville (nonstop shows from lunchtime to after dinner) created an inequitable but efficient system that inspired thousands of performers to devote their whole lives to breaking into the "big time"—the best theaters on the best circuits—a vaudeville phrase that, like many others, has entered the American lexicon.

To develop one's act in vaudeville was often a career-long endeavor. A performer had to define and refine his or her skills in a hotly competitive world and come up with something that no one else could do—or at least no one could do as well. For a comedian, this was a particular challenge. A dog act or a magician required little from an audience other than sheer amazement; a comedian had to land a gag whether he or she was in Sheboygan or Brooklyn or Fort Worth, Texas. It was in the latter town that a young Bob Hope flopped with his audience, using material that had scored elsewhere. A vaudeville manager came backstage and told him, "Why don't you slow down and give them a chance? These people aren't going anywhere. They came in here to be happy. It's summertime. It's hot. This is Texas. Relax and you'll be all right." Hope took the advice—grudgingly—and within the week he *was* all right.

Comedians also had to suffer through the easy currency of their material. Fred Allen, who stumbled up the ladder as a comic juggler, recalled:

Comedy acts were always the target of pirates. . . . There was a young comedian whose father regularly attended the opening show at the Palace. If any of the acts had new lines, jokes, or song titles, the father copied them down and wired them to his son. The act continued convulsing the Palace audience in New York, little dreaming that its best jokes were being told in Omaha, San Francisco, or wherever the son happened to be playing.

There was little remedy for such deviousness. Some comedians even made it part of their act; Milton Berle was so open about his larceny that he was dubbed by Walter Winchell "The Thief of Bad Gags."

Vaudeville was more a matter of style than of material. It was not so much what the two- and three-a-day favorites said and did as how they said it and how they did it. For fifty years, vaudeville's minstrels found their way into all lands, preaching their gospel of merriment and song, and rousing the rest of the world to laughter and to tears. –Fred Allen

Vaudeville was tough on anyone working their way up the ladder; the pay was poor, the conditions were terrible, the billing was never big enough. Still, performers kept at it—what, and leave show business?—even if they had little to offer. The young George Burns, né Nathan Birnbaum, was so lousy that "after playing a theater, I would have to change my name. The booker who booked me would never give me another job if he knew who I was. It never crossed my mind that there was any reason to change the act, so I changed my name instead." Among Burns's more than two dozen noms de guerre were Jimmy Ferguson, Jimmy Delight, even a member of the team of Links and Burns—although he was Links. Go figure.

Vaudeville also gave rise to a variety of performance styles that still exist to this day: genial hosts with witty banter (Frank Fay, Milton Berle), double-acts (Smith and Dale, Burns and Allen), triple acts (Durante, Clayton, and Jackson; the Three Stooges), even quadruple acts (the Marx Brothers). Even the impressionist act—extremely popular up until the early 1980s—was created in vaudeville. What comedians really had to learn was economy, speed, personality, and variety—it often helped if, like Eddie Cantor or Jimmy Durante, you could tell jokes, sing, dance, and play a musical instrument. "I got a million of 'em!" rasped Durante about his jokes—and he wasn't exaggerating, either.

Much has been made about the sudden death of vaudeville after 1927. It wasn't all that sudden. The Broadway revue siphoned off stars, as did radio, by the mid-1920s. Once vaudeville turned into a stepping-stone for other, more lucrative and more relaxing professions, its days were numbered. Sound film provided the final resting place for vaudeville; many historians claim May 7, 1932, as the funeral date, when the Palace, New York's most prestigious vaudeville house, switched from two-a-day shows to the lower rent four-a-day shows, interspersed with short films. A

few months later, they began to screen feature films exclusively; ironically, the first one was *The Kid from Spain*, starring Eddie Cantor, one of the Palace's greatest headliners.

Perhaps, at least at the beginning of vaudeville's demise, Broadway inflicted more wounds than did motion pictures. Broadway revues were becoming increasingly sophisticated after World War I, and more competitive with each other. One way for a revue producer, such as Florenz Ziegfeld, to rise above the crowd was to import a vaudeville superstar or, even better (and cheaper), to create a Broadway superstar from the rank and file. But tastes changed somewhat in the mid-1920s, and audiences demanded narrative shows, and thus, the musical comedy was born: a trifle, to be sure, but at least a trifle with the pretensions of a plot. This proved to be a boon for

a successful comedian—the first "crossover" in popular entertainment. A comedian could now go from touring in vaudeville, to being one of several bananas in a Broadway revue, to holding down an entire musical comedy vehicle that showcased his talents exclusively. Eddie Cantor was the most successful of these

crossover comedians, but Fanny Brice, the Marx Brothers, Jimmy Durante, Willie and Eugene Howard, Ed Wynn, Clark and McCullough, Bert Lahr, and Bob Hope eventually followed suit and created brand-new audiences for themselves along the Great White Way.

At the same time, nonmusical Broadway comedies were beginning to find their own unique voices, with or without crossover comedians. Before the 1920s, native comedies were skimpy and formulaic: scrappy boy meets scrappy girl, he loses her, he gets her, and they live scrappily ever after. That soon changed with the emergence of playwright George S. Kaufman who, along with collaborators such as Marc Connelly and Edna Ferber, created the first full-fledged American satires, such as the silent-film spoof *Merton of the Movies* and the show business comedy of manners *The Royal Family*. With the Gershwin brothers, Kaufman and Morrie Ryskind were the first playwrights to poke fun at American government and the presidency in book musicals like *Of Thee I Sing*. Following in Kaufman's rat-a-tat-tat, wisecracking satirical style were other gifted playwrights like Moss Hart (a frequent Kaufman collaborator), George Abbott, Mae West, Philip Barry (more genteel), and Ben Hecht and Charles MacArthur, whose blissfully anarchic *The Front Page* and *Twentieth Century* would both go on to have major Hollywood legacies.

This golden age of American stage comedy would be eventually diluted by the advent of sound film as many idiosyncratic stage comedians and Broadway writers went west to Hollywood. With the exception of the zany, freewheeling *Hellzapoppin'* in 1938 and a few classics, such as Kaufman and Hart's *The Man Who Came to Dinner*, the take no prisoners style of 1930s comic anarchy no longer seemed appropriate as America entered the Second World War; the successful comedies of the 1940s, such as *Harvey* and *Arsenic and Old Lace*, were comparatively benign. In the 1950s,

Into the limelight: (Previous pages) Comic trio Eddie Jackson, Jimmy Durante, and Lou Clayton; genial host Frank Fay; (below) a quartet of old-timers: John Carradine, Jack Gilford, David Burns, and Zero Mostel in *A Funny Thing Happened on the Way to the Forum*.

stage comedies were forced to compete with television and did so with the most effective weapon available to them: mild doses of suggestive sexuality. Typical were George Axelrod's *The Seven Year Itch* (a more interesting play than movie, despite the appearance of Marilyn Monroe), and *Never Too Late* by Sumner Arthur Long, in which a man in his fifties discovers that he has impregnated his wife.

Ironically, just as sound films gave vaudeville stars a new immortality by capturing their work forever, a generation of talent forged by television reinvigorated Broadway comedy in the 1960s, especially musical comedy. Five veterans of the writing staff of *Your Show of Shows* turned their hands to writing successful musical comedy librettos: Larry Gelbart (*A Funny Thing Happened on the Way to the*

Forum), Neil Simon (*Little Me*; *Promises, Promises*), Michael Stewart (*Bye Bye Birdie*; *Hello, Dolly!*), Joseph Stein (*Fiddler on the Roof*), and Mel Brooks (actually, his 1960s musicals were flops—but wait until *The Producers*). They were joined by such veterans as Abe Burrows and Betty Comden and Adolph Green in creating a new era of joyously silly musical comedies—shows for the proverbial tired businessman. Simon was practically a one-man cottage industry for successful comedies—*Barefoot in the Park*, *The Odd Couple*, *Plaza Suite*, and more, many of which were turned into movies.

Invigorating the proceedings was almost a new generation of Broadway clowns all of whom originally started on the stage but had developed into television stars eager to spread their wings, bring their comic talents to

a starring role in a narrative musical, and, not coincidentally, grab a huge percentage of the weekly gross. They included Phil Silvers, Jackie Gleason, Sid Caesar, Lucille Ball, and Carol Burnett. Among the buoyant musical comedies of the time, pride of place must be given to *A Funny Thing Happened on the Way to the Forum* (1962), written by Gelbart, Burt Shevelove, and Stephen Sondheim, a homage to burlesque reset in ancient Rome. *Forum* maintains its low comic genius and, over the years, in revivals, tours, and a film version, has provided a happy home for such varied comics as Zero Mostel, Phil Silvers, Dick Shawn, Mickey Rooney, Buster Keaton, Nathan Lane, and Whoopi Goldberg.

The last three decades have not been kind to stage comedy, a victim of television and movies, but Broadway has recently seen a rebirth of the musical comedy, after about a two-decade preponderance of ponderous pop-operas. Led largely by Mel Brooks's *The Producers* in 2001, there has been a march of shows conceived almost exclusively to tickle the funny bone in song and dance: *Hairspray*, *Avenue Q*, *Monty Python's Spamalot*, *Xanadu*, and *Young Frankenstein*. The theater has always embraced certain stars as their own, comedians who both ennoble and energize a live event with their presence: Beatrice Lillie, Bert Lahr, Carol Channing, Sam Levene, Robert Morse, Zero Mostel, and Nathan Lane. Alas, these comedians were not always able to make successful transitions into film or television— something about them being larger-than-life.

But larger-than-life is exactly what a theatrical audience demands, whether it knows it or not. Vaudeville and Broadway have given center stage to a special kind of performer who can connect with a spectator across the footlights all the way to the back row in the balcony. When you bought a ticket to see them in person, cavorting around a stage, playing to that night's crowd, it was a once-in-a-lifetime event; it was the stuff of legend.

Kingfish: Would you believe me if I told you I'm trying to keep Andy outta jail?

Amos: No.

Kingfish: Well, when I want your opinion, I'll ask for it.

"EXCUSE ME FOR PERTRUDIN"
TIM (THE KINGFISH) MOORE

On the immensely popular radio show *Amos 'n' Andy*, the Kingfish was always trying to bamboozle the title characters. The actor playing the Kingfish, Freeman Gosden, was already putting one over on the radio audience—he was playing both Andy and the Kingfish, two black characters; even more audaciously, Gosden was white.

Freeman Gosden and Charles Correll were white musicians and comedians who began a brief radio serial, *Sam 'n' Henry*, about a pair of small-time black pals, in 1926. Borrowing liberally from the minstrel tradition, the show moved to Chicago's WMAQ in 1928 and was transformed into *Amos 'n' Andy*. By 1930, the fifteen-minute daily radio serial was expanded to a weekly half-hour program, and the antics of Amos and Andy enthralled the country. The great composer Eubie Blake recalled that "no matter what movie house you attended, the show would come to a sudden stop at seven o'clock and loudspeakers would bring to the audience the fifteen-minute *Amos 'n' Andy* spot."

Amos Jones and Andy Brown represented the entire package of management and labor at the Fresh Air Cab Company in Harlem (so-called because there was no windshield). As the show expanded, so did their universe. New characters filled out the stories, often performed by black actors, but none caught the audience's fancy more than George Stevens—"the Kingfish" of the local lodge, the Mystic Knights of the Sea. According to cultural historian Mel Watkins, "Through the voice of Freeman Gosden, the Kingfish would emerge as one of the electronic media's more memorable and outlandish rogues. He was an unscrupulous, conniving dandy, larger than life, more obstreperous, more indefatigable and unrepentant than any con artist (black or white) who had emerged in a radio or TV sitcom."

About face:
Freeman Gosden and Charles Correll, the original Amos and Andy; with Alvin Childress, Spencer Williams, and Tim Moore for the TV incarnation.

Amos 'n' Andy stayed popular long enough to be attractive to broadcasters in the television age. Gosden and Correll initially thought they might black up for the TV screen, but wiser minds prevailed. A national talent search produced a new ensemble of gifted black comic actors to play the beloved characters in a series that debuted in 1951 on CBS. Stepping into the neatly polished shoes of the Kingfish was Tim Moore, a chitlin circuit veteran of retirement age—in fact, he had just retired to his hometown of Rock Island, Illinois. Throughout his stage career in segregated vaudeville, Moore would demonstrate some of the ingenious survival tactics that the fictional Kingfish flaunted in a more larcenous vein. He had been a boxer, a carnival geek, a medicine show huckster, an alumnus of the *Blackbirds* revue on Broadway, and a broad comedian in race movies. It was a challenge to become the physical (and racially specific) embodiment of a character that had thrived only in the imaginations of millions of Americans, but Moore pulled off the scam—unlike the Kingfish, whose plans usually crashed and burned by the final credits.

As the adventures of *Amos 'n' Andy* evolved from the radio shows of the 1930s to the sitcoms of the 1950s, the Kingfish took over more and more of the weekly plot, which most often centered around one outlandish scheme after the other, usually at the expense of the trusting Andy. Once, he tried to sell Andy a house—only it was a fake front from an abandoned movie set. Cheech Marin remembers watching the Kingfish hatch some harebrained scheme to sell Andy a set of binoculars: "Kingfish looks through them and says, 'Hmm, there's an ant crawling up that building. Hmm. Got something in his mouth. Hmm, a crumb of bread. Let's see—whole wheat.' Just cracked me up. They just had the most absurd humor, and black humor can be real surreal. Sometimes very abstract. And I had caught on to that early because, you know, I was so hammered by it."

The Kingfish had a recurring expression—"Holy Mackrel!"—an overbearing wife named Sapphire, and a deep loathing for manual labor:

SAPPHIRE: Well, George, you don't have to look for a job no more. I got a job for ya at the Superfine Brush Company as a door-to-door salesman.

KINGFISH: You done what! Now look here, Sapphire, you can't do that. It's a violation of the Atlantic Charter, the Constitution, the Monroe Doctrine, and not only dat, it's a violation of one dah four freedoms, de freedom of speech!

SAPPHIRE: Freedom of speech?

KINGFISH: Yeah, you didn't give me a chance to say no.

From the moment the show debuted on television, the NAACP vehemently protested the image of blacks showcased by *Amos 'n' Andy*. With his mangling of the English language and his combination of shiftlessness and shiftiness, the Kingfish was exhibit A. Larry Wilmore recalls that "actually, on *Amos 'n' Andy* you didn't just have those guys—you saw black lawyers on the show, black doctors, a lot of middle-class people that *didn't* talk like the Kingfish. But at the time, those characters were so broad and there was a history behind them from the radio. And there was nothing else representing blacks on television." Ultimately, it was the sponsors' lack of enthusiasm for a program with a cast of African American characters that spelled the end of *Amos 'n' Andy* on network broadcasting in 1953, after more than seventy episodes. The network was about to showcase Moore in a spinoff called *The Adventures of the Kingfish*, but that went by the wayside as well.

Since its banishment, *Amos 'n' Andy* has had its admirers and detractors, but no one could gainsay the vibrancy of Moore's characterization. Redd Foxx said, "I worked with Tim Moore at the Apollo and that man was a true professional, an unforgettable actor. It was comedy, man, it was laughs. Some people would say, 'Hey, they shouldn't be doing that,' but if they look at their mothers and fathers around the house, they'd see the same things happening." Unlike the outcome of the series itself, the Kingfish triumphed in the end, surviving as a vibrant American prototype, the first transcendent beloved scoundrel from the black tradition.

By the time the 1950s came to a close, Americans were embracing their con men from a more comfortable place, but Tim Moore and the Kingfish had their moment in the limelight. "Excuse me for pertrudin'," as the Kingfish would often say, but he brought audiences a lot of laughs by pertrudin' as long as he did.

Eternal struggle:
Moore with Ernestine Wade, as his wife, Sapphire.

IN THE WORDS OF THAT GREAT AMERICAN POET RALPH WALNUT EMERSON, YOU ALL HAS MY INFERNAL GRATITUDE!

—The Kingfish

My ancestors go all the way back. There was Major Horatio Bilko, who sold extra tickets on the boat to Washington's crossing of the Delaware. That's why the general couldn't sit down. —Phil Silvers as Sgt. Ernie Bilko

PHIL SILVERS
"GLADDASEEYA

During the out-of-town tryout of *Top Banana*, his 1951 Broadway vehicle, Phil Silvers was checking into his Philadelphia hotel. "Now, my wife will be joining me between eight and ten tonight," he confided to the desk clerk, in his inimitably ingratiating hi-how-are-ya style. "But she works in disguise for the FBI, so she might check in as a blond or a brunette—ya never know."

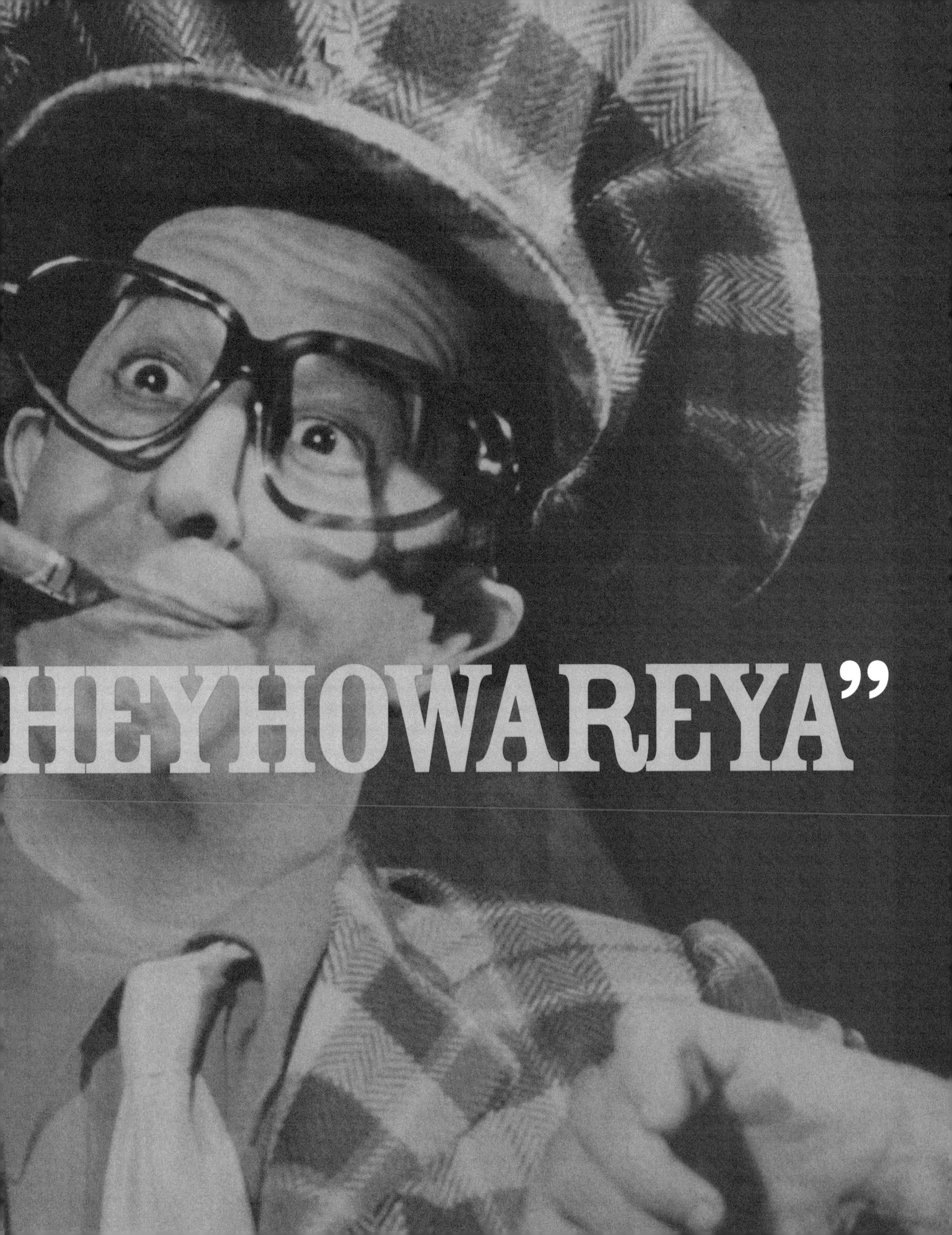
HEYHOWAREYA”

"All ya need is an angle," Silvers sang in another show, *Do Re Mi*, and he spent much of his life trying to work an angle onstage and off. His fast-paced geometry began on the edge of Brownsville, a poor Jewish immigrant section of Brooklyn, where Fischl Silverstein was born in 1911. "Since my parents were immigrants, I didn't have much to talk about with them," he later wrote. "The only way I could get together with people was by singing. Anywhere. Any time." He had a pure tenor voice that brought him straight to vaudeville.

Like the Marx Brothers before him, Silvers skipped high school to become a star attraction on the circuit and by the time he was bar mitzvahed, he had wowed them at the Palace. When his voice cracked, it spelled curtains for his career as a boy singer, so instead he became a tummler in the Catskills, learning how to do anything for a laugh. It was good training for Silvers's next career move: burlesque.

For five years, Silvers worked his way up to be a top banana at Minsky's, where he mastered eight hundred separate bits and sketches. "Burlesque was about the only steady work in 1932," Silvers said. "The only chance you had for individuality or freshness was your own improvisation. [My innovation] was a recognizable human being in black horn-rim glasses." A bit part in a Broadway musical called *Yokel Boy* brought Silvers to the legitimate stage in 1939; when the lead comic left the show out of town, the part was rewritten for Silvers and he was a smash—an MGM contract and a trip to California followed. Ultimately, Silvers's film career during the war was a big disappointment to him and he chafed under the limitations of his casting, usually playing the hero's best friend (often Gene Kelly—*Cover Girl*, *Summer Stock*), thankless roles so undistinguished and indistinguishable that Silvers referred to them all as "Blinky." Silvers split his time in Hollywood between gagsters and gangsters. He was a pal of Bugsy Siegel's—who borrowed gas ration coupons from Silvers—and began a lifelong addiction to gambling.

Cheer up, pal:
Silvers (bottom) looks glum in Broadway's *Yokel Boy* (1939); perhaps because they cut his scene, above, from *Strike Up the Band* (1940).

In 1948, he jumped at the chance to go East and legit again, this time in a period musical called *High Button Shoes*. Silvers played the supporting part of a bald—and balding—con man named Harrison J. Floy, and the public was beginning to recognize his unique talent. Jason Alexander, who played the character years later in a revival, said, "Phil Silvers built his whole persona on a version of the con man. It was always slick. It was always double-talk, it was always the ability to do one thing and say another or sell it as something else." Broadway opened new doors for him. Silvers told a reporter, "Sometimes, when I take time out to be grateful, I am grateful for three things—first, I don't have to go to school today; second, I don't have to fly today; third, I don't have to play the Copa."

SILVERS: ## WHAT'S TELEVISION? BURLESQUE WITH AN ANTENNA—THAT'S TELEVISION.

***Top Banana* followed. It was a star vehicle** about a megalomaniacal TV comedy star that allowed Silvers to parody Milton Berle. Even Silvers, who offstage was a self-doubting neurotic, had to admit it was a hit—and it inspired him to heights of generosity. Costar Rose

Marie recalled that the supporting company was filled with great second and third bananas: "He got every burlesque comic he could think of. And I said to him, 'Phil, these guys can steal this show right under your nose. You know that?' He says, 'No. It'll only help me. It'll make it better.' " Silvers operated on all cylinders and drafted in his best burlesque bits and won a Tony Award for his troubles.

In 1951, a comedy success on Broadway meant that a television sitcom would not be far behind. "Jack Benny said TV would be calling but don't take a sitcom; it's too much hard work," recalled Silvers, but CBS wanted Silvers to work with writer Nat Hiken, who had previously done shows for Fred Allen and Martha Raye. They started with the idea of an army sergeant, dismissed it, then went through nearly forty ideas for a sitcom—Silvers as a racetrack tout, larcenous theater agent, bellboy. He hated them all. Then one day, the army sergeant made sense to Silvers. "I would be a scamp again, this time protected by the uniform of the U.S. Army." And so, on September 20, 1955, Sgt. Ernie Bilko first saw the light of prime time. Bilko was an Army lifer during peacetime, a con man who ran the motor pool at the small-town Fort Baxter during the day and, out of boredom and larceny, ran every scheme in the book at night. In the pilot episode, he's discovered running a poker game in his quarters; while fleecing some poor private, he tells him, "When you play with me, you don't lose money, you're learning a trade." Growing up, it was Larry David's favorite show: "Bilko did a lot of selfish things all the time, he would con people, he would do anything to get his way—and he was funny as he was doing it."

Unlike most network sitcoms, *You'll Never Get Rich* was filmed in New York and rehearsed in a hall above Lindy's Delicatessen. (Two months after its premiere, it was renamed *The Phil Silvers Show*—it was only called *Bilko* informally.) The Manhattan location allowed Hiken to enlist a wonderful ensemble of ex-burlesque comics and aspiring New York actors to play the hapless victims in Bilko's platoon (including Dick Van Dyke, Dick Cavett, Paul Lynde, and Alan Alda). In a realistic reflection of the 1948 act that desegregated the U.S. Army, Silvers's show featured black actors in the platoon—making it one of the few racially integrated telecasts of the 1950s.

Ya gotta start from the bottom of the bunch: With burlesque pals in *Top Banana*; TV star as Sgt. Bilko with Phil Ford, right.

What audiences also weren't seeing elsewhere on television was Silvers's megawatt energy. According to Garry Marshall, all the situation comedies that preceded *The Phil Silvers Show* "were like the hum of the air conditioner—*hmmmmm*—they were nice, smooth. Then in came Phil Silvers like gangbusters and really turned it around. He would get the audience's attention and make them pay attention and he was quick and fast." Silvers and Bilko were perhaps the first, best match of a comic actor and character in a situation comedy in television history.

CHAPLAIN: I don't know why I like you, Bilko. You're everything I was put on earth to fight: you're a cheater, a liar, a con man.

BILKO: Maybe it's my personality?

"Phil's personality was very close to Sergeant Bilko's," remembered Dick Van Dyke. "He knew what he was doing, and there was a lot of poker playing between takes." To

Silvers, Bilko "was the eternal dreamer, the con man who dreamed up elaborate strategies to bamboozle the system. His high-flying plots collapsed because, like the hero of Greek tragedy, he had a fatal flaw. He was a softy. You had to like Bilko because inside everyone, even the straightest pillar of the community, there is a con man wiggling to get out." Jason Alexander said, "Silvers was the comedic version of the rogue that we love—the bad guy that we root for." Audiences never rooted for Bilko more than when he tried to prevent a chimpanzee from being accidentally inducted into the army in a classic episode called "The Case of Harry Speakup." If any comedian could ad-lib with a monkey, it was Phil Silvers, who according to one critic, "had to fight for his life, a quarter of a century ago, before audiences enthralled by the striptease."

For its debut season, *The Phil Silvers Show* won five Emmys, including two for Silvers. His competition as Best Actor? George Gobel, Milton Berle, Sid Caesar, and Jack Benny. In fact, ever since Berle's show had debuted six years earlier, Silvers's show was the first program to beat him in the ratings. A year later, the show was an even bigger success in England, perhaps because, as one critic wrote, "it must have represented what the British liked to believe were real Americans." The show was abruptly canceled after four seasons. According to television historian Gerard Jones, "Phil Silvers was infuriated—he never got much of an explanation from CBS. My own hunch is that it was disturbing to the network executives that, at the height of the Cold War, Americans would or should really like to see a con man in the armed forces as a hero. For years after that, there was nothing at all so anti-authoritarian in American comedy."

Silvers brought his talents back to Broadway in 1961 playing a big-shot wannabe in *Do Re Mi*, where now he was singing his scams to music. Typically of Silvers, he was intimidated by the big Broadway names who put the show together: "All great. All proven. So, if this show is a failure, I will not have any excuses. Who can I blame but myself?" He had nothing to worry about; he was a hit once again. But trust did not come easier to Phil Silvers. He was, according to Dick Cavett, "a very depressed man, with horrible, awful bouts of depression." He was a compulsive gambler who carried wads of cash on him despite being deeply in debt, in case a sure thing might come along. He finally achieved a happy family—a successful second marriage and, just like Eddie Cantor, five daughters (he once said, "There was never a toilet seat up in my house")—but he was never able to find a new character to replace Bilko. His luck, career-wise, ran out on him in the 1970s; he had a huge success in a Broadway revival of *A Funny Thing Happened on the Way to the Forum* in 1972, and even won a second Tony for it, but Silvers suffered a stroke early in the show's run, and it closed prematurely. He recovered, but he was never at full tilt again; his characteristic energy finally gave out in 1985.

Not the reflective type:
Silvers backstage; reviving *A Funny Thing Happened on the Way to the Forum* (1972).

Still, despite how untrustworthy Silvers made Bilko appear, the television audience trusted him to deliver week after week. Bilko became so integral to the American scene that, half a century after his first appearance, in a poll asking which TV character would make the best U.S. president, Bilko came in fourth, following Homer Simpson, President Bartlett (*The West Wing*), and Dr. Frasier Crane.

The con man with song in his heart had fooled 'em once again.

"CHIFFON WRINKLES TOO EASILY"
PAUL LYNDE

By the mid-sixties, comic actor Paul Lynde was in despair about his relentless typecasting; producers kept putting him in a box. In 1966, that's just what a new game show did–literally–and *The Hollywood Squares* turned him into a national phenomenon.

Lynde was born in the quintessential midwestern town of Mount Vernon, Ohio, in 1926, the last and—as far as his parents were concerned—least of their five children. His upbringing was almost a parody of a conventional upbringing. "During lunch we'd talk about what we'd have for dinner," he said. Clearly food was important in the Lynde household; when he arrived at Northwestern University toward the end of the war, his mother's cooking had ballooned him to 260 pounds. Lynde quickly became the comic star of the renowned drama department. "I wanted to do Shakespeare," he said, "but whenever I read a part, people laughed. Finally, my professors started suggesting I read to them privately. So I'd go to a professor's office and read, and then *he'd* laugh at me."

New face in town:
With Robert Clary and Eartha Kitt in *New Faces of 1952*.

In 1948, Lynde left the Midwest behind for a career in New York, along with his classmates Alice Ghostley and Charlotte Rae. He struck comic gold as one of the most memorable performers in *New Faces of 1952*, probably the last, best example of the revue form that had cultivated comedy stars for three decades on Broadway. Lynde had written his own signature sketch, that of a bandaged, injured lecturer who attempted, in vain, to put a positive spin on his recent trip to Africa: "My late wife and I enjoyed Africa . . . here's a piece of the skirt that was left. I don't recommend it for the kids—there's not much to do unless they hunt." With his trademark snarky delivery, nervous laugh, and chin waggle, which gave every punch line just the right flourish, Lynde created the perfect off-center character; one got the feeling that he wasn't really all that broken up to discover his wife had been eaten by a lion.

But even though audiences were eating *him* up, Lynde was growing anxious about becoming a second banana, onstage and in life. When he was first starting out in New York, he received news that the remains of his other brother, a soldier who had been missing in action overseas, had been discovered. His mother died weeks later, and his father died a few weeks after that. It left a chasm of loneliness in Lynde that he could never fill—certainly not with his sporadic TV appearances on *Sgt. Bilko* and *The Jack Benny Program*. Things looked up when Lynde landed the part of the harried dad, Harry MacAfee, in the 1960 Broadway smash *Bye Bye Birdie*. His rendition of "Kids"—"What's the matter with kids today?"— allowed his unapologetic misanthropy to shine through, set to the tune of a Charleston. Dick Van Dyke, who played the leading role in the show, remembered what Lynde brought to the role, which included some of his own ad-libs: "They [originally] wrote MacAfee as a poor husband who was supposed to be a kind of a Caspar Milquetoast. But as done by Paul he took on a lot more. He was speaking for society as a whole—'I didn't know what puberty was till I was past it!'"

PETER MARSHALL: Paul, true or false? Bob Hope and Jackie Gleason were recently seen in Central Park dressed as women.

PAUL LYNDE (*nervously*): **Was anyone else identified?**

Lynde was frustrated when the big-screen version drastically cut his material to build up its new star: "*Bye Bye Birdie* should have been retitled *Hello, Ann-Margret*," he carped. Colleague Rose Marie recognized that the frustration ran deeper. "Paul was somebody absolutely special. Paul wanted to be a dramatic actor. And he couldn't do it, because every time he would open his mouth, people would start to laugh. But he loved acting and he loved being in show business, so he had to use that to do what he wanted to do." So, it was back to guest appearances on TV variety shows and series. According to one critic, "He made more rounds than a milkman," and at his height in the mid-1960s, Lynde logged in nearly two hundred prime-time programming hours a season. Viewers loved his special appearances as the mischievous, epicene Uncle Arthur on *Bewitched*, and talk show hosts like Mike Douglas could always count on Lynde for a good laugh. Once Lynde brought a huge book to the set of Douglas's afternoon show. "That's a big book, Paul, is it a Bible?" asked Douglas. "No," Lynde responded, "those are my fears. . . ."

Offstage, Lynde dealt with those fears by self-medicating. Lynde also wrestled with his homosexuality, worried that any public outing would spell the end of his ambitions. Newspaper interviews invariably referred to him as a bachelor, although it was doubtful that his open-collar wardrobe with its gold chains or his way with a zinger would have fooled any sophisticated viewer. When the daytime celebrity-based game show *The Hollywood Squares* came along in 1966, it provided the perfect showcase for Lynde's gift with a slightly salacious quip, eventually featuring him as the "center square." There was nothing square about Lynde's knowing retorts to countless dumb questions—back then, in a gentler age, they were the hippest thing on daytime television.

PETER MARSHALL [host]: Paul, why do Hells Angels wear leather?

LYNDE: Because chiffon wrinkles too easily.

MARSHALL: Eddie Fisher recently said, "I am sorry. I am sorry for them both." Who was he referring to?

LYNDE: His fans.

MARSHALL: Billy Graham said he would like to urge people to reserve sex for the only place it belongs. Where is that?

LYNDE: A state prison.

And while we're on the subject . . .
Lynde, out of Africa, in *New Faces*; in the closet, as the dad in *Bye Bye Birdie* on Broadway.

The game show, which featured him for a decade and a half, was a mixed blessing for Lynde. On the one hand, it gave him the popularity he craved and made him a very rich man, but his beloved bitchy zingers (crafted for him expertly by a cadre of writers) only typecast him further. "He was not a happy person, Paul," said Dick Van Dyke. "I think that he felt that his career should have gone further than it did. As a supporting actor he was hysterical. But you try to make someone like that a star and for some reason it doesn't work." Lynde's major professional heartbreak was a pilot called *Sedgewick Hawk-Styles, Prince of*

Danger, in 1966, where he played a Victorian detective—"If you didn't get Sherlock Holmes, you got me"—and its period flavor put some distance between him and his contemporary persona. Sadly, just as the pilot was about to be picked up, a companion of Lynde's fell to his death while clowning around, drunk, in the actor's hotel room. Lynde always suspected it was the bad publicity that put an end to the potential series, but it was just one more destructive note in a life that was self-destructive enough on its own.

Center of attention:
The Hollywood Squares.

Comedian Richard Lewis, who knew Lynde briefly when their *Hollywood Squares* chores overlapped, said, "He just had this really amazing authentic voice and timing, but maybe he was not the kind of guy you want to drive cross-country with." Drunken bouts with waitresses, stewardesses, and traffic cops were frequent occurrences, according to Rose Marie. None of this behavior, or his sexuality, seems to have been leaked to the public. In 1971, Lynde placed fourth on a national survey of favorite TV comedians, behind Flip Wilson, Carol Burnett, and Bob Hope. ABC offered him his seventh series—six previous pilots showcasing Lynde never made it to the starting gate—once again playing a cranky dad with an annoying family. In the age of *All in the Family* and *Maude*, *The Paul Lynde Show* was unconvincing, especially in the scenes featuring Lynde with the wife and kids. It failed after one season. He went back to *Squares*, known by show business fans and ordinary folk as a guy so funny he could get a laugh reading the phone book; in fact, in West Hollywood, there was a nightclub act where someone imitated Lynde reading the phone book.

The times conspired against Lynde; a decade later he might have thrived in a more open, accepting environment of entertainment. As Joy Behar said, "He was in the closet, in this industry, which means you can't be yourself. You have to come out if you're going to be a great comedian." But although Lynde was no Burt Reynolds, neither was he a pathetic caricature of an unhappy homosexual. He was immensely successful, beloved by his loyal audience (which included a huge number of middle-aged women who wrote him love letters), and a pioneer in spite of himself, "getting away with being gay on TV on an almost daily basis" decades before it became the thing to do, according to his biographers, Steve Wilson and Joe Florenski. When he died alone in his Beverly Hills home in 1982 of a heart attack, Lynde was on the verge of a changing world. He understood his own unique style. "A lot of people don't find Paul Lynde funny," he once said, "but that's good, because if we all laughed at the same thing, we'd let Bob Hope do it, and there wouldn't be any jobs for the rest of us." All Lynde really wanted was the attention afforded other great comic misanthropes without any of the attendant complications of his lifestyle.

MARSHALL: In *The Wizard of Oz*, the Tin Man wanted a heart, and the Lion wanted courage. What did the Straw Man want?

LYNDE: He wanted the Tin Man to notice him.

Paul Lynde on *The Hollywood Squares*

Peter Marshall: The great writer George Bernard Shaw once wrote, "It's such a wonderful thing, what a crime to waste it on children." What is it?

Paul Lynde: A whipping.

Peter Marshall: Paul, how many fingers in the Girl Scout salute?

Paul Lynde: Gee, I don't remember. The last time I saw it was when I didn't buy their cookies.

Peter Marshall: According to the great poem by Edgar Allan Poe, "We loved with a love that was more than love, I and my..." I and my what?

Paul Lynde: Gym teacher.

Peter Marshall: If the right part comes along, will George C. Scott do a nude scene?

Paul Lynde: You mean he doesn't have the right part?

Peter Marshall: In *Alice in Wonderland*, who kept crying "I'm late, I'm late?"

Paul Lynde: Alice—and her mother is sick about it.

Peter Marshall: According to Tony Randall, "Every woman I've been intimate with in my life has been..." What?

Paul Lynde: Bitterly disappointed.

Peter Marshall: Paul, Snow White... Was she a blonde or a brunette?

Paul Lynde: Only Walt Disney knows for sure...

Peter Marshall: Prometheus was tied to the top of a mountain by the gods because he had given something to man. What did he give us?

Paul Lynde: I don't know what you got, but I got a sports shirt.

Peter Marshall: According to the French Chef, Julia Child, how much is a pinch?

Paul Lynde: Just enough to turn her on...

Peter Marshall: It is considered in bad taste to discuss two subjects at nudist camps. One is politics. What is the other?

Paul Lynde: Tape measures.

Peter Marshall: Paul, in the early days of Hollywood, who was usually found atop Tony, the Wonder Horse?

Paul Lynde: My Friend Flicka.

Peter Marshall: During the War of 1812, Captain Oliver Perry made the famous statement, "We have met the enemy and..." And what?

Paul Lynde: They are cute.

Peter Marshall: What is the name of the instrument with the light on the end that the doctor sticks in your ear?

Paul Lynde: Oh, a cigarette.

Peter Marshall: In one state, you can deduct five dollars from a traffic ticket if you show the officer . . . what?

Paul Lynde: A ten dollar bill.

Peter Marshall: It is the most abused and neglected part of your body—what is it?

Paul Lynde: Mine may be abused but it certainly isn't neglected!

Peter Marshall: Elizabeth Taylor calls it "the Big One." What is it?

Paul Lynde: They both look the same to me!

"I RANG THE BELL DIDN'T I?"
REDD FOXX

Guy goes every day to the same diner, looks over the menu, and always orders the same thing: ham and eggs. Every day, the same thing: ham and eggs. Waitress decides to play a trick on him and scratches it from the menu. He comes in, she says, "You know that thing you like so much? I scratched it." "Well, wash off your hand and get me some ham and eggs."
–Redd Foxx

Redd Foxx was the most successful underground comic in history: "Redd Foxx sold millions of records before he even knew how to count to a million," said Dick Gregory. In fact, he sold more than 10 million LPs–party records as they were called–to legions of fans who had never even seen him in person, his gruff, scotch-soaked voice beguiling them in the after-hours.

Comic Reynaldo Rey, a colleague of Foxx's, was more charitable than Gregory: "You have a party, you had to play a Redd Foxx record—that was a part of the party. After the dancing and singing and right before getting *totally* drunk you played Redd Foxx." Foxx's own life was anything but a party.

He was born in 1922 as John Sanford in the ghetto of East St. Louis. His father walked out on the family, and his mother, who couldn't contend with John and his brother,

Laff of the party:
Foxx at the Playboy Club; party album.

WHEN YOU WERE A KID, YOU HAD TO SNEAK HIS ALBUMS, BECAUSE YOUR FOLKS HID THEM. HE WAS VERY DANGEROUS IF YOU WANTED NOT TO GET A LICKIN'.

–Whoopi Goldberg

Fred Sanford, sent them out to a Catholic boys' home in Chicago. He had little affection for anyone other than his brother and never forgave his mother for sending them away; according to Rey, years later, "when he made it big on television, she pops up and says, 'Son!' And he tells her, 'Hey, get this bitch out of here.'" Sanford found himself playing in a washtub band on street corners and, while a teenager, ran away to Harlem, where he had trouble in mind. In Harlem, John Sanford got the nickname Red because of his hair color and light skin, and he later added another d. Sometimes he was called Chicago Red to differentiate him from his pal Detroit Red—Malcolm Little, the young Malcolm X. "They busted suds together, they worked in the chicken shack together," said Rey. "They were the best of friends. Redd and Malcolm whored together, stole things, robbed and stole. They did all sorts of little things, but they never got caught."

The fringes of showbiz beckoned. Redd cut a few rhythm and blues singles with Kenny Watts and his Jumpin' Buddies and eventually got his comedy start introducing strippers at a Baltimore nightclub, throwing salty jokes in between his appearances. He changed his name, saying, "I'm a fox. I want to be named after the fox, the red fox," and made his new name on the chitlin circuit and by recording his early party records—there would be fifty-two in all. By the late 1950s, he had built a following, an arsenal of jokes, and a point of view. "I work basic," he said. "All I do is talk about what you do. If you don't do it, I don't talk about it." Rey observed that "Redd took pride in using double entendres. When Redd first started in comedy he didn't use profanity. He let your mind see the dirt, but he never cursed":

A guy asks another guy, "How's your love life?" Guy says, "Not so good, my wife cut me down to once a week." The other guy says, "Well, it could be worse—there's three other guys she cut out completely."

Fellow goes to a house of ill repute. Got both legs in a cast, both arms in a cast. Madam opens the door, takes one look at him: "What *you* want?" Man says, "I rang the bell, didn't I?"

What's got five hundred legs and a cherry? Two hundred fifty strippers and a Tom Collins.

Foxx didn't crack the mainstream barrier until the mid-1960s with some television appearances on *The Today Show* and *The Tonight Show*, but his exposure was minimal compared with his popularity in the black community. He could keep up with the racial tensions of the time—"I don't know why they say all negroes carry knives. We don't all carry knives; I carry an ice pick"—but it was his language that kept him from crossing over. Foxx claimed the objections were overreactions: "I just say what people really say. People pretend they never say 'shit'—when I slam your hand in my car door, you will."

By 1970, Foxx had broken into Vegas, which was the right kind of venue for him, and became a favorite of the wee small hours crowd. He was also gaining a reputation for being as aggressive as his material. "I don't have to be up here entertaining you. I could be in an alley with a blackjack waiting for one of you suckers," he'd tell the crowd; he wasn't kidding. "Redd carried a razor blade and a switchblade, and you better give him his money," recalled writer and comedian Paul Mooney. "And he would always want you to put his money in a brown paper bag." According to Reynaldo Rey:

> [Comedian] Slappy White and Redd were buddies. And so Slappy borrows five hundred dollars from Redd, and Redd said, "Okay now, Slappy, I want my money," and Slappy cut out and didn't pay Redd. So next week, Redd says, "Slappy, what about my money, man?" He says, "I'll take care of you tonight, man." But Slappy's gone, he done, period. So, next week, we're sitting in Redd's dressing room. Redd always carried a gun, he had a pocket sewn into all of his pants and he kept a little derringer right there. So Slappy was seated across from Redd, and Redd took out his derringer, and he removed the bullet from the derringer, and he leaned over, popped Slappy in the forehead with that bullet. And he picked it up and reloaded it. And Slappy said, "What's that all about, man?" And Redd said, "If you don't pay me my money, the next one will be coming much faster."

You dummy!
Foxx and Demond Wilson in *Sanford and Son*; the BBC's *Steptoe and Son* with Harry H. Corbett and Wilfrid Brambell.

Foxx might have ended his days in a Vegas show room at two a.m.—or in the morgue at five a.m.—if fate hadn't intervened in the person of *All in the Family*'s producer, Bud Yorkin, who had purchased the rights to a British sitcom about an ornery junk man and his son called *Steptoe and Son*. He and his partner, Norman Lear, were looking to transpose the show to an American venue, featuring an ethnic family; NBC was fine with that—just as long as the family wasn't black. But Yorkin caught Foxx in the small role of a janitor in the film *Cotton Comes to Harlem* and brought him from Vegas to Hollywood to work on the pilot. According to Yorkin, Foxx was so eager to try a sitcom that he offered to remove his false teeth to play the part. In the end, all that was required was Foxx's talent. When an NBC executive saw the live run-through of a pilot of the newly dubbed *Sanford and Son*, with Demond Wilson joining the cast as Foxx's son, he ordered the show on the spot, even though the production staff had only weeks to complete the series before it aired.

After its debut at the beginning of 1972, *Sanford and Son* was a hit in the ratings, moving almost immediately to number two, right behind *All in the Family*, and just as it had for Phil Silvers, the sitcom form gave Foxx the perfect showcase for his crusty chicanery. Foxx didn't have to reach far to play the cantankerous junk man—he even went back to his beloved brother to give *Sanford and Son*'s title character his family name. His colleagues from the old days were happy to see him triumph in the mainstream as Fred Sanford; said

Reynaldo Rey, "That was Redd. A hankety ol' man. But he would raise hell with you one minute and give you a hug the next minute." To a younger generation of comedians, such as Tommy Davidson, the sight of Foxx on prime time in their living room was a revelation: "Fred Sanford represented every old black man that I know, who were the funniest people on earth. Redd showed that even though you come from a blue-collar background or you are an older African American person that you are just as endearing, as trustworthy, just as vulnerable, as any other human being."

> AUNT ESTHER: Fred Sanford, why is it every time I come over to your house you call me ugly?
> FOXX: Because I'm not the type to lie.

Foxx proved less than endearing on the set. The troubles began before the taping of each episode. "He'd warm up the audience with all these jokes that were really for a stag party," recalled Yorkin. "So I finally said, 'That's it, pal, you did your four warmups, no more. How are we gonna top one of your dirty jokes?'" Like W. C. Fields and Groucho Marx, Foxx had a deep distrust of his producers and tried to level the playing field the best way he knew how. Just when *Sanford and Son* was getting its highest ratings, Yorkin got a call from the stage manager:

> "You better come down, Bud, because Redd wants to talk to you." I went down to his dressing room and Redd said, "I don't think I can go work today." "What's the problem, Redd?" He said, "Well, I think I'm getting an ulcer in my stomach." I said, "Oh, really? What did the doctor say?" "The doctor said if I was making fifteen thousand dollars a week, I wouldn't have to worry about eating the way I do, I wouldn't have these ulcers. I need fifteen thousand dollars to make these ulcers go way." Redd figured when he was ready to make a move, he'd make a move.

Foxy grandpa:
With acolytes Eddie Murphy and Richard Pryor in *Harlem Nights* (1989).

Production was shut down for five weeks while Yorkin and Foxx negotiated a new salary. Occasionally, Foxx and the producers could work together to a positive end. The show's writers had all been white until, during the second season, at Foxx's insistence, the producers called in two black stand-up comics, Richard Pryor and Paul Mooney. Foxx was also instrumental in bringing classic African American performers onto the show, including Slappy White and La Wanda Page, a notoriously ribald nightclub peformer, as his foil, Aunt Esther. Even Lena Horne made a guest appearance.

> HORNE: You paid to see *Stormy Weather* thirty-eight times?
> FOXX: Naw, I only paid once. I went in on a Saturday matinee and came out on Wednesday.

Foxx also insisted on a more realistic depiction of the black community—especially in the use of the word *nigger*. Yorkin swallowed hard and allowed Foxx to say it to another character on the show. The next day, a phone call came from Stokely Carmichael, the former honorary prime minister of the Black Panthers. According to Yorkin, "Carmichael said, 'That's the best show I ever saw. We don't call each other Afro-Americans, we call each other *nigger*—you said it there, and that's exactly right.' "

By the time *Sanford and Son* wound down after five seasons, Foxx had achieved the kind of stardom afforded to only a precious few television personalities. However, for him it was a day late and $15,000 short: "I should have had this career twenty years ago—I'm the funniest man in show business." Foxx made up for lost time, living in Las Vegas and Los Angeles and living large. "If he got a check for ten thousand dollars, he owed eleven thousand of it to somebody," recalled one of his producers. By the time Eddie Murphy hired Foxx (and his other idol, Richard Pryor) to star with him in the 1989 film *Harlem Nights*, he was drowning in debt. The high-profile movie didn't stop the Nevada branch of the IRS from calling him into their offices. When they asked him to account for the half-million-dollar salary he had earned from the picture, Foxx responded, "I gambled and drunk it all up." Within the week, the FBI cleaned Foxx out, taking his house, his cars, his dogs, and according to Reynaldo Rey, "his soul, his heart. He was never the same after that." Foxx joked to friends that he wanted to pay the government, "but I just wasn't going to pay any more taxes to a white president— I'll pay taxes when they have a black president."

Eddie Murphy came to the rescue again, by offering a starring role to Foxx in a TV show that he produced called *The Royal Family*. Slowly, Foxx was climbing out of debt. "The last time I saw him, he was playing dollar poker with a bunch of retired old ladies in Vegas," recalled comedian Robert Klein. "He had a gorgeous Asian wife who was rubbing his shoulders and bringing him Kahlúa." One afternoon in 1991, on the set of *The Royal Family*, Foxx clutched his heart, as he had in nearly every episode of *Sanford and Son* when he threatened to join his beloved wife, Elizabeth, in heaven. The cast and crew thought it was a gag. It wasn't. Redd Foxx was dead of a heart attack at age sixty-eight.

Redd Foxx has his own epitath; he said it at the end of every club date and it summed him up better than anything:

FOXX: **Hope you had some fun. If anyone has been offended by any thing I said, I want you to know from the bottom of my heart— I don't give a shit.**

"LAST GIRL BEFORE FREEWAY"
JOAN RIVERS

I'm Jewish. I don't work out. If God had wanted us to bend over, he would have put diamonds on the floor. —Joan Rivers

As the Second World War was winding down, little Joan Molinsky was spending her summer at Camp Kinni Kinnic in the woods of Vermont. The camp director sent a letter home to her parents: "Joan is a born leader, but you have got to watch her. She could become either another Truman—or a Hitler." All Joanie wanted was to play Snow White in the camp play. She got cast as Dopey. Something inside her swore she would never be dopey again.

The road from Joan Molinsky, Dopey, to Joan Rivers, one of the savviest, sharpest, and most successful comedians in showbiz, began in 1933, in Larchmont, New York, a largely Jewish town in suburban Westchester. Her upper-middle-class parents had her whole future mapped out for her: respectable Jewish summer camp, respectable Jewish values, and, God willing, a respectable Jewish husband. Joan had other ideas: "I didn't start out to be a comedian. I wanted to be an actress and I fell into the comedy because I was funny at the office and I found that was a way to make a little money, waiting to be an actress." The straitlaced Molinskys were horrified at Joan's decision and told their daughter that showbiz was filled with prostitutes and drug peddlers—certainly not the place for their nice Barnard-educated daughter.

A struggling acting career was all that seemed in the cards for Joan in the late 1950s. "I had no woman that I grew up watching saying, 'I'd like to do that,'" she said about her comedy aspirations. "But very early on, while I was still in college, someone brought me to see Lenny Bruce. And it was absolutely an epiphany for me, because he absolutely said what everyone thought." Despite her parents' protestations and embarrassment, Rivers persisted as a comedian. No matter how crummy the joint she played, she still saw herself as a nice Ivy League graduate: black dress, a string of pearls, nicely done hairdo. "It was a very tough road in those days, especially for women, because if you were at all attractive, you weren't supposed to be funny. I had to come onstage and look like a nice girl but still do jokes, and I didn't know where to go."

In the beginning, she went wherever her "sleazo" agent sent her—often to the Catskills, because she owned a beat-up Buick and could drive the talent back and forth to the city. Her driving skills may have been better than her discretion at that point; one night, after playing a gig on the borscht belt, she recounted, "I came out after one of these black singers and they had applauded him so amazingly, I said, 'I'm so glad you loved my husband.' Well, I could have just gone home right there."

But home in Larchmont, where she was still living with her parents, was no bargain, either. As a change of pace, she took a gig in Chicago in 1962 with Second City, the groundbreaking improvisation troupe that was the darling of the city's intelligentsia. Still, Rivers felt that the company's high level of literary and cultural allusions had little to do with her own experience and personality. "So I told the truth about my life and I spoke things that they gasped at," she said. When she returned to New York, she tapped into her own frustrating past and projected a disappointing future:

MY MOTHER IS DESPERATE FOR ME TO GET MARRIED. OUTSIDE OUR HOUSE SHE PUT A SIGN: "LAST GIRL BEFORE FREEWAY."

Can we talk?
Rivers as a great conversationalist: on her show, and on others' (Johnny Carson).

Rivers said, "People would just go, 'What, is that true?'" They didn't know what to think of me." Maybe not, but they still enjoyed her as she worked her way up the ladder from appearances with Jack Paar to *The Ed Sullivan Show* to a long-awaited debut on the New York–based *Tonight Show* in 1965. "They brought me on the Carson show as a girl writer—they couldn't say I was a comedian—and at the very end of the evening he said to me on camera, 'You're gonna be a star.' And that changed my whole life." She began appealing to a cadre of women in the audience who understood the contemporary anxiety of trying to make themselves and their families or husbands both happy at the same time. "I was very lucky because I was the only woman at that time coming up. [The other comedians of my generation] had our own voices and our own things to say. None of us wanted to say, 'My mother-in-law,' because we didn't have a mother-in-law."

When Rivers *did* get a mother-in-law in 1967, after marrying producer Edgar Rosenberg (she had a brief, unsuccessful first marriage in the late 1950s), she could no longer pretend she couldn't get a date, so she approached her act from a new angle. Visibly pregnant, she would remark, "My husband is mentally dressing me." And although it was unheard of to say "pregnant" on national television, Rivers turned her nine months of gestation into some of her best material. When describing what she would say to the delivery nurse: "Knock me out with the first pain, and wake me up when the hairdresser arrives."

Audiences ate her up, because, like all good comedy, her remarks—however hysterically rendered—were the articulated thoughts of what her fans knew to be so. "I truly am the one that stands up and goes, 'No, wrong way.' How we say, 'Oh, beauty doesn't count.' Go tell that to a girl who hasn't been asked to dance. It's all such lies. So why don't we say to everybody, 'Beauty does count, so make yourself look good'?" As Rivers moved into the 1970s and '80s, her comedy got edgier, her wisecracks more acerbic, her language saltier. She was a huge attraction on the Vegas and resort circuits, where she could work uncensored, while at the same time developing a wide fan base appearing on *The Tonight Show Starring Johnny Carson*, where Carson made her the permanent guest host in the mid-1980s. By then, Rivers was training her sights on targets other than Joan Rivers.

She turned a corner and began taking on the major celebrities of her day; it was a winning, if vitriolic, addition to her act, and she adopted her catchphrase—"Can we talk?"—as a way of connecting directly with her audience. It seemed like a natural evolution: "It was stupid to worship a fat lady like Elizabeth Taylor when she was fat. If I heard one more person say, 'She's the most beautiful woman in the world'—she's the most beautiful three women in the world at this point." Taylor was, shall we say, a wide target for Rivers—"Liz has more chins than a Chinese phone book"—and some of her other observations could cut pretty deep:

> Katharine Hepburn beat me out of a Shake 'n Bake commercial. Why couldn't she just say she had Parkinson's? She made *us* feel bad.

As America kept indulging its appetite for celebrity antics, Rivers rode the wave to even greater fame. She suffered some major setbacks, such as the failure of her own talk show, the suicide of her husband, Edgar, and in many ways—launching her own line of products, becoming a red carpet commentator, indulging in the glories of plastic surgery—she has embraced the perquisites of the celebrities she disparages. But beneath Rivers's admittedly phony exterior lurks a wit that will always target the truth, like a heat-seeking missile. After 9/11, she addressed her remarks to the widows of that tragedy, and by extension, the rest of us:

> Nobody would rather have a check than the husband? Anyone married over ten years? Go home tonight, and when he's lying in bed, and he's kind of drooling, and the hair is coming out of his ears and those ugly feet with the broken toes and the white guck on the bottom are sticking out—look at him and think, "Harry or a check? Harry or Tiffany's?" And see what you come back with.

It all hits home with Joan Rivers because, in the end, her home in Larchmont, with its misguided values, was where it all started. "Hypocrisy will eventually turn into lies," she wrote in her memoir, "until you become my mother and my sister, who always had to be the Molinskys of Larchmont and never found a way based on reality. That is what my act is all about."

Do you know what these are, boys and girls? They're drums! Do you know where *these* drums come from? From Africa! Do you know where *these* drums come from? Smokey Robinson was at the Apollo Theater and left his van open in the back of the place. I ripped him off! I wonder how Smokey gonna sound wit' no percussion!

–Eddie Murphy on *Mister Robinson's Neighborhood*

"THERE'S A NEW SHERIFF IN TOWN" EDDIE MURPHY

By the time he had reached his twenty-first birthday, Eddie Murphy had become the comic equivalent of a sweater from an L.L.Bean catalog; he came in a variety of colors. As the hottest new member of *Saturday Night Live*, Eddie could do it in green—"I'm Gumby, dammit!"; he could do it in white—playing a black man disguised in white-face to see how the other half really lived: "What a silly Negro!" But black suited him best. Whether he was inhabiting the

ghetto version of *Mister Rogers' Neighborhood*, or parodying James Brown getting into a hot tub, or creating Velvet Jones, the author of *How to Be a Ho*, or serving an uncanny Stevie Wonder imitation straight up, Murphy brought the 1970s preoccupation with African American culture to its comedic climax in the early 1980s.

Murphy's breakout success on *Saturday Night Live* was won the hard way. He had to audition six times before being hired, initially as a limited featured performer and then slotted into a few token black segments. "I was a nineteen-year-old kid," he said. "The only thing I had *done* was be black." Murphy, born in 1961, grew up in Roosevelt, Long Island, a working-class black neighborhood just over the border from Queens. He'd spend hours honing his impressions of Stevie Wonder and Bill Cosby in the family basement. He told his mother he was rehearsing, but—since Roosevelt High didn't have a drama program—she didn't know what he was talking about. When he hosted a local youth center concert at age fifteen, she found out; he blew the roof off the joint.

Murphy had idolized Richard Pryor since he was a teenager: "Anyone who tells you he's into comedy and doesn't think Richard is the best comedian who ever existed doesn't know what he's talking about," he later said. He began performing stand-up in local nightclubs while still in high school, and at an age when his former classmates were deciding on a college major, in 1980 Murphy had earned his spot on TV's hottest variety show. "If a sitcom flops, you're never heard from again," he told a reporter early on. "I don't want people to say a few years from now, 'Whatever happened to Eddie Murphy?'" But in the early 1980s, all anybody wanted to talk about was Murphy and the arsenal of characters he brought to late-night television.

WELL, TELL BILL I SAID HAVE A COKE AND A SMILE AND SHUT THE FUCK UP, JELL-O PUDDING-EATING MOTHER-FUCKER.

Murphy paid homage to the singers and comedians whose records he devoured in the basement of his Roosevelt home; it was the first time many Americans had seen black performers—Cosby, James Brown, Michael Jackson—imitated at all, let alone so brilliantly (to be fair, he did a mean Art Carney and Jerry Lewis, too). When he had time off from *Saturday Night Live*, Murphy returned to the stand-up stage, and although he earned huge audiences he also got some flack for his aggressive street language, especially from one of his idols, Bill Cosby. According to Murphy, in his filmed concert, *Raw*, Richard Pryor advised him on how to handle the criticism: " 'Whatever the fuck makes the people laugh, say that shit. Do the people laugh when you say what you say?' I said, 'Yes.' He said, 'Do you get paid?' I said, 'Yes.' He said, 'Well, tell Bill I said have a Coke and a smile and shut the fuck up, Jell-O-pudding-eating motherfucker.' " Murphy's own answer to his critics was, "Richard Pryor was dirty before me and Redd Foxx was dirty before him. . . . To go to some club and listen to somebody tell jokes and get offended if they say the word *fuck* makes no sense. If you don't want to hear fuck, stay home and watch TV." In 1982, audiences were enjoying Murphy far from the living room TV.

48 HRS was the first buddy-cop film of the 1980s and was originally slated to star Mickey Rourke and Richard Pryor. Murphy got his shot at movie stardom when his idol—and four other actors—turned down the part of a black convict given a forty-eight-hour leave to help find a criminal. One scene where Murphy, as Reggie Hammond, fronted his way into a redneck bar was unforgettable:

> REGGIE: You start running a respectable business and I won't have to come in here and hassle you every night. You know what I mean? And I want the rest of you cowboys to know something, there's a new sheriff in town. And his name is Reggie Hammond. So y'all be cool. Right on.

When Murphy saw an early screening, it hit him how huge his career was going to be: "I'll never get that reaction from an audience again. They went, 'Oh, this guy's going to be doing movies for a while.' You can get born only once in this business, but you can die over and over again."

Although costar Nick Nolte earned ten times Murphy's salary, the twenty-one-year-old walked away with the movie, which went on to make nearly a hundred million dollars. With one film, Murphy had crossed over into stardom. His film persona was ideally suited for the 1980s. Larry Wilmore, "Senior Black Correspondent" on *The Daily Show*, described the difference between the Richard Pryor of the 1970s and the next generation:

> Pryor's thing was still kind of "the man might do this, and fuck you! But I'm gonna still run." The man can't hear me say, "Fuck the man," you know? Eddie, on the other hand, was in control of his destiny. Eddie was like, "Fuck you, motherfucker!" Eddie was a man who wasn't confined by those old rules of society. He could be judged just like anybody else. He was confident, he was direct, and people loved that brashness.

The rest of the 1980s gave Murphy one perfectly suited film role after another—*Beverly Hills Cop*, *Trading Places*, *Beverly Hills Cop II*, *Coming to America*, *Raw*—and he returned the favor by giving Paramount Studios their greatest comic moneymaker since Mae West back in the Depression.

Murphy's talent for creating multiple identities led to him often playing more than one part in his films, usually enfolded in latex, exploiting the genius of the makeup department. But nearly every Murphy role in the 1980s asked him to use his own genius at disguise— playing someone adept at playing someone else, in order to perpetrate a con of some kind. His transplanted Detroit detective, Axel Foley, in *Beverly Hills Cop*, was a master at it:

> AXEL: Don't you think I realize what's going on here, miss? Who do you think I am, huh? . . . But I'm not some hotshot from out of town, I'm a small

Hercules! Hercules! Hercules!
Box office strongman: *48 HRS* (1982); *The Nutty Professor* (1996).

reporter from *Rolling Stone* magazine that's in town to do an exclusive interview with Michael Jackson that's gonna be picked up by every major magazine in the country. I was gonna call the article "Michael Jackson Is Sitting on Top of the World," but now I think I might as well just call it "Michael Jackson Can Sit on Top of the World Just As Long As He Doesn't Sit in the Beverly Palm Hotel 'Cause There's No Niggers Allowed in There"!

And just the way Murphy was inspired by Pryor, Murphy was inspiring a new generation of hip black street performers. Tommy Davidson recalls, "I was attracted to everything Eddie Murphy did. Eddie represented the African American wiseass dude—an intelligent, smart-ass, will whoop your ass, hero, on-screen. Sexy, too. There had been nothing seen like that on-screen—it's the first time we were seen for what we really are, which is all those things." As one critic wrote, "Not since Richard Pryor has a black comic played so dauntlessly—and so adroitly—with racial, and racist, stereotypes." Murphy crossed over spectacularly with white audiences, while at the same time honoring the heroes of his own black comic tradition. One such homage, *Harlem Nights*, featuring Pryor and Redd Foxx, closed out the 1980s on a rare sour note, as Murphy's vanity project as director, writer, and star flopped at the box office. It was nearly a decade before Murphy bounced back to superstar status.

Jerry Lewis had been another of Murphy's comic idols, and the 1996 remake of *The Nutty Professor* gave Murphy a natural role as the lead character's fast-talking, slick alter ego, Buddy Love. But where Murphy triumphed was with the shy, self-effacing, chubby hero (and all the members of his immediate family). By getting in touch with his original ingratiating charm, Murphy was back on top, adding his vocal talent to creating memorable characters in animated features like *Mulan* and the various Shrek movies. His films in the twenty-first century have remained of varying quality, but Murphy has proved an accessible figure to the next generation, the children, perhaps, of those who experienced the electricity of watching him bust up a redneck bar two decades earlier.

Eddie Murphy remains the most successful comedian in American movies; also, not coincidentally, the most successful black performer in American movies. Perhaps his appeal lies in his regard for the past, while he unapologetically busts down the doors to the future. Audiences simply ate it up when Eddie Murphy gave them the finger—and no one ever had more fun doing it. As he once told *Playboy* magazine:

Bill Cosby was influenced by Groucho Marx: the cigar, he never stands straight onstage when he's walking, and he mumbles. You can draw a line from me to Richard and from Richard to Bill, and from Bill to Groucho. And I guess Groucho never thought it was gonna go from

"LAST NIGHT I SHOT AN ELEPHANT IN MY PAJAMAS" TO "SUCK MY DICK!"

Filth flarn filth:
The lighter side as Axel Foley, Beverly Hills cop; and as idol Bill Cosby.

DAVID: It was a near-death experience. It's made me rethink everything.

SUSIE: Well, maybe you could be a nicer person now.

DAVID: What do you mean, "nicer person"? I'm a nice person.

SUSIE: Ehhh . . .

DAVID: "Ehhh"? What's with the "ehhh"?

SUSIE: Never mind, Larry.

"I COUNTED YOUR SHRIMP"
LARRY DAVID

In the classic film *It's a Wonderful Life*, George Bailey survives a near-death experience, only to rediscover the importance of friends, family, and a moral, ethical, and generous life. He is the paradigm of American values. Larry David, on the other hand, is not. The character David plays at the center of *Curb Your Enthusiasm* is the anti-George Bailey, a craven, disgruntled, impolitic comedy writer who finds most American values simply too tedious to uphold. One feels that David is responding not just to George Bailey but to the aspirations of humanity when his character says, "It must be hard to be nice to people twenty-four hours a day." The real Larry David expounds:

> We don't feel like being nice, it goes against our instincts, our real instincts. We're all so dishonest all the time, nobody can really ever express how they feel about anything because we're gonna hurt people's feelings. And this character isn't really that aware of how people feel. He's more aware of what the truth is and expresses it.

David was born in 1947 in Sheepshead Bay, Brooklyn, growing up in an apartment "with my mother, my aunts and cousins and the screaming and the yelling and the neighbors and the lack of privacy. Those are my comedic influences." He later became a history major in college because he thought "it would be the easiest way to get through it." Moving to New York City in the early seventies, he was reduced to aimless soul-sucking odd jobs: chauffeur, taxi driver, paralegal. "When I was living in New York and didn't have a penny to my name," David said, "I'd walk by an alcove or something and think, that would be a good place for me when I'm homeless." Comedian Richard Lewis was a friend of David's at the time (and attended basketball camp with him in their teens, but that's another story): "His place was really a hellhole. He had a piano and he tortured people, he played one song over and over. I was, like, 'You gotta stop. People are gonna murder you.' He said, 'Well, this is all I know.' He tortured people, he was an annoying guy. A great guy who could annoy on a dime."

Realizing that he would never be a lawyer or a doctor—and thus denied an impressive credential for picking up girls—David eventually turned to stand-up comedy, where he could annoy people professionally. It usually worked the other way around. Recalled Lewis, "He wanted undivided attention from a nightclub audience! That's insane, man! I mean, people would say, 'Can I have another scotch?' and then he'd storm off." But, still, David learned something: "Audiences are there to be feared; that's pretty much what I learned. Avoid them at all possible costs, yeah." But in the rare gigs when he did tough it out, David's bizarre, uncompromising routines—pretending to be so comfortable with the audience that he wanted to address them in the familiar French *tu* form—made him, in writer Alan Zweibel's words, "a comic's comic." "Which," according to David, "means I sucked." At one point, he was a staff writer on *Saturday Night Live* (he can be glimpsed as an extra in several episodes); after toiling all season, he got only one of his sketches on the air, just before closing. Frustrated, he quit one day, and then slunk back to work the next; no one even noticed he'd been gone.

In 1988, a fellow stand-up comedian named Jerry Seinfeld asked David to work with him on pitching a comedy to NBC. It became *Seinfeld*. Even in front of a network president, David behaved as if he were still doing stand-up. According to cast member Jason Alexander:

> Larry went into the NBC office with Brandon Tartikoff—before there was any notion of this being a show—and said, "You can't change it. You can take it off the air, but

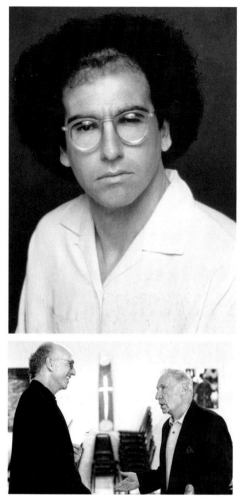

Any club that would accept me as member: Larry David as a disaffected TV writer; with Mel Brooks.

DAVID: Can't you just look at my back?

DOCTOR: What do you do for a living?

DAVID: I'm a writer.

DOCTOR: So, I'll come to you and ask you to write a bunch of shit for free.

you can't change it—this is the show." Just kind of laying down the law to Brandon Tartikoff, who's going, "I don't even know what the show's about yet. Why are you yelling at me?"

David stayed on as a producer and writer for seven seasons before moving on, and the series became one of the great phenomena of popular culture. According to Zweibel, "You talk about timing—here was a guy who waited for the rest of the world to catch up to him. Larry was unyielding in his comedy. He wanted to do it his way. He wouldn't compromise. And then all of a sudden he had the opportunity to do everything he always wanted to do. He waited until the time was right for him." David became a millionaire many, many times over from the syndication sale of *Seinfeld*, but it didn't seem to make him any happier.

In 1999, David produced, wrote, and starred in a one-shot "mockumentary" for HBO about a successful comedy writer named Larry David who was about to tackle the stand-up stage once again. It evolved into the 2000 series *Curb Your Enthusiasm*. *Curb Your Enthusiasm* allowed David to access his inner antisocial curmudgeon and place him center stage in a loose-limbed situation comedy. David Steinberg, who has directed several episodes, points to the show's tradition:

> Larry is a Jewish W. C. Fields in a way. Also, the Larry David show is very similar in a way to *The Jack Benny Show*, because Jack Benny played Jack Benny! He had a family around him that was made up but like his own. If you pitched this to the network, that you were going to play a wealthy writer who had a series on television, they'd say, "No one's going to identify with you." But the most personal comedy finds the widest audience.

Larry David's character, like Fields's or Groucho's, is always negotiating with the basic inequity of life. According to Jason Alexander:

> Larry doesn't walk into the world going, "What mischief can I make today?" He just asks the questions no one would ever ask, out of curiosity. He sees a car-pool lane and goes, "I don't have anybody in the car—what would be wrong about having a prostitute come in the car just so I can use the car-pool lane?"

David's litany of woes come from a historical tradition of comedic obstacles: wives, dogs, children, shopkeepers—even blind men (although probably no other comedian has attempted to scalp tickets for High Holiday services). But like other curmudgeons in the past, David has his own unique ethical center. Richard Lewis, no slouch at irritation himself, sums up the human connection of the David character: "He comes off as this kind of guy who is irritating and is bugged by everything—hardly the truth. This is a guy who has such ethics, but who just wants to do his thing." David defends his character's ethics, arguing, "What, picking up a hooker and taking her in the car-pool lane? That's not unethical. It would be unethical to go in the car-pool lane *without* the hooker! So there! I've proven that the character is ethical!"

The real-life Larry David has no difficulties separating himself from his irritating, petty, and passive-aggressive persona:

> [The character] says what's on his mind, he's completely honest about everything and all the little social things that come up on a daily basis in his life, all these little stupid rules that people have to follow, he's able to break. I think he's pretty happy. He's a lot happier than I am, I could tell you that. He doesn't work as much as I do, I know that. I'm working for him, you know?

DAVID: I saw how many shrimp you took at dinner; I counted your shrimp.

ALAN WASSERMAN: Larry, why don't you take your 475 million dollars and buy yourself a fucking shrimp boat?

Was that wrong?
With Jerry Seinfeld and alter-ego Jason Alexander; playing bingo with Shelley Berman as his dad.

CHAPTER FOUR

"WOULD YA HIT A GUY WITH GLASSES?"
NERDS, JERKS, ODDBALLS, AND SLACKERS

You gotta be a football hero
To get along with the beautiful girls.
— "You Gotta Be a Football Hero" (1933)

THE BIG(GER) PICTURE

The American Dream has always been about success. You can be the hero, win fame on the battlefield or the football field, and get the girl in the end. If you look like a million bucks, you can make a million bucks. Our history is full of golden boys and girls whose social ease, material and romantic success, and effortless charm make them the idols of everyone in their circle. They've got it all.

Except they are not particularly funny.

As far back as the Victorian era, conformity has been a strong American trait. In the middle of the 19th century, there were implicit rules about normative behavior, but there were also explicit codes—books about proper conduct, proper dress, proper hygiene. The Gibson Girl—the subject of a series of illustrations by Charles Dana Gibson—provided the first standard for feminine beauty in America. It almost goes without saying that these standards upheld white, Christian, responsible, well-mannered, and often rural values. These cultural values constructed a powerful edifice, and in creating them, the guardians of society automatically created another category: the outsiders. Now, *they* could be funny.

As the twentieth century began, conservative society came under numerous threats to its hegemony. There had been an overwhelming wave of immigrants from the less exalted countries in Europe—Ireland, Italy, Eastern Europe, with its large contingent of Jews; African Americans migrating from the Deep South to cities in the Midwest and northeast; and in 1917, a new threat called communism. It was proving difficult to keep outsiders outside, where they belonged, so various nativist trends flamed into the public and political consciousness: the Ku Klux Klan, various anti-immigration laws (1917 and 1924), the Palmer Raids of 1919. Along with the patriotism invoked by World War I, these movements presented a clear dividing line between those who belonged and those who didn't.

Such tensions soon burrowed their way into the world of comedy, most noticeably in Chaplin's 1917 short, *The Immigrant*. Those who looked down at the recent arrivals could laugh at the Little Tramp's predicaments, while actual recent arrivals laughed with him. (Decades later, Chaplin was cited as being "anti-American" for a brief moment in the film where he kicks a government inspector in the pants.) The "Dutch" comic duo of Weber and Fields poked fun at the malapropisms and misunderstandings of these new ethnic citizens. When Eddie Cantor made his debut at the *Ziegfeld Follies*, he played his Yiddish card for laughs, as did Fanny Brice, while colleague Bert Williams, as an African American, was trapped behind the blackface mask of the ultimate outsider. The characters that these three played in various sketches and skits were invariably figures of fun, confusion, incompetence, and marginalization. Yet mainstream Broadway audiences of the time would have rarely encountered Jews or blacks in social situations outside a theater. These characterizations were amusing to mainstream audiences because they were so alien, and the footlights provided a protective barrier against any real engagement with these outsiders.

Sand in your face:
The transformation that transformed America.

After the First World War, another marginalized group—women—was given the right to vote, and one more barrier was trampled. The emancipated role of women invigorated the newest social trend of the Roaring Twenties, the youth movement. The collegiate craze invaded nearly every aspect of American culture: the way people dressed, drank, danced, and looked forward to the future. Football, especially college football, suddenly became a national religion. The athletic, chiseled, wholesome, comradely football hero became a national icon, abetted by such newly minted personalities as Charles Lindbergh, Red Grange, and Babe Ruth (although no one but John Belushi would have actually emulated Babe Ruth). This is what makes Harold Lloyd's *The Freshman* (1925) so poignant and so persuasive; he transformed the idea of "making the team" from a literal desire to play football to a grander, more mythic desire to be included in the mainstream of American society. Lloyd's granddaughter, Suzanne, pointed out that Harold was "the regular fellow who wore glasses, like Clark Kent, but he was also a kind of superperson, who was not going to be defeated."

As the 1930s wore on, the immigrant outcasts of the earlier decades had gradually woven their way into the fabric of society. When Eddie Cantor started to become a nationwide superstar in talking pictures, he realized he had to downplay the Yiddishisms that went over so well on Broadway; he was now an American comedian, not merely a Jewish one. Cantor banked on the image that Lloyd had created, the scrawny but plucky little squirt who screwed his courage to the sticking place. This iconic image of the "97-pound weakling" was further promoted by Charles Atlas's 1929 body-building advertisements, in which Mac, the weakling who had sand kicked in his face, was transformed into a hero. The year 1938 gave the world the ultimate transformation of a cowardly weakling into a hero when Superman appeared for the first time. The most engaging joke (and it was a good one) was that Superman was never the disguise—it was Clark Kent who was the disguise, the pretend coward who allowed the mighty Superman to bestride the planet undetected. That provided an excellent comic tension, as anyone who has seen Christopher Reeve in the 1970s film versions can attest, and its essential inversion was borrowed by generations of comic actors.

Underneath, there's something there: Christopher Reeve as Superman as Clark Kent.

Physical cowardice became a great stockpile for comic gags all the way through the end of World War II. While our best and brightest were fighting around the world, comics such as Jack Benny and Bob Hope, with their vain cowardice, provided a release valve for a nation struggling to keep up its stiff upper lip. One of the great ironies of outsider comedians is that their exterior personas—again, like Superman's—belie their real-life internal character. Hope and Benny gave more concerts to servicemen, in more dangerous places, than any other performers in the Second World War. Likewise, however, they embodied the "little man" or the rejected suitor in their film comedies. Cantor and Hope were among the most successful, adored, and powerful men in show business. The audience knew that, too, which only added to the fun.

There is also a subtle form of social Darwinism in this sort of outsider comedy. The outsider of one generation becomes the insider of the next; why shouldn't assimilation, so prevalent in American society, extend itself to the world of comedy? The role of outsider gets passed on to the most recent arrival at the nation's doorstep. In Bob Hope's 1940 film *The Ghost Breakers*, he plays the most cowardly of men—of white men, that is. The black comedian Willie Best played Hope's valet, and in one scene they entered a haunted house together:

BEST: Hey, boss, you ain't goin' upstairs, are ya? Where those ghosts is?

HOPE: Listen, you stay there, and if a couple a fellas come runnin' down the stairs in a few minutes, let the first one go. That'll be me.

BEST: If somebody passes you, that'll be me.

After World War II, the monolithic edifice of accepted behavior began to crumble. Women and African Americans had earned more respected places in society, and fighting men of all races and creeds had fought together overseas. It became apparent, with the publication of Kinsey's *Sexual Behavior in the Human Male* in 1948, that the normative ideal was not so normative after all. Americans began to understand psychological deviation; men and women with neuroses and compulsions not only lived among us but could make us laugh, because we were neurotic, too. Jonathan Winters, whose career burgeoned during this Age of Anxiety (and who also suffered from psychological stress) caught the tenor of the times: "Now the freaks are on television, the freaks are in the movies. And it's no longer the sideshow, it's the whole show. The colorful circus and the clowns and the elephants, for all intents and purposes, are gone, and we're dealing only with the freaks."

Suddenly, doors of possibility were being flung open and more outsiders were being invited to the party. Several months after Kinsey's second major volume, *Sexual Behavior in the Human Female*, was released in 1954, Phyllis Diller made her nightclub debut in San Francisco. At the same time that the Freedom Riders set out from Washington to Alabama in 1961, black comedian Dick Gregory became the first stand-up artist to cross the color line, at the Playboy Club in Chicago. The television airwaves were filled with strange people who suddenly moved next door; clearly, they were some kind of analogue for this new wave of cultural outsiders. It was easier to tolerate hillbillies, sexy genies, Martians, monsters, and Munsters, perhaps, than blacks or homosexuals—but if you could laugh at those weirdos, maybe you were on the way to accepting the rest.

Kooky, but kool:
The Addams Family.

At about the same time—the mid-fifties to the early sixties—two new concepts entered the country's consciousness. First came the idea of "hip." The football heroes that Harold Lloyd idolized were now too square; it would be far more "in" to be "out." To be outside the mainstream—think Brando, Kerouac, Miles Davis—became much more interesting than to be in the mainstream, and it was a far more exclusive club. Also, a new word entered the language of American slang—*nerd*—supposedly derived from a line in Dr. Seuss's *If I Ran the Zoo*. It was initially hard to explain exactly what the word meant—a drip, a drag—but nerds certainly weren't hip, although both nerds and hipsters were outside the mainstream. Perhaps the best way to differentiate between the two would be to say the eccentric Addams Family was certainly hip; it was unlikely, however, that they would have the Munsters over for hemlock tea—*they* were too just nerdy.

It wasn't long before the counterculture of the late 1960s mashed the two concepts together. Perhaps this can be dated from the moment Dustin Hoffman became the leading man in *The Graduate* in 1967. Soon the glamorous leading man and the glamorous comedian—Cary Grant, Joel McCrea, Tony Curtis, Jack Lemmon—vanished from the scene and Woody Allen ascended the throne. Allen was the perfect conflation of nerd and hip; you had to know something about, say, forties movies, Greenwich Village, and Jewish culture to get his jokes, but he was still skinny and getting beaten up in his films. "I have, I think, an appropriate amount of self-loathing and I think that's important for everybody," he said. "I don't trust people who are too confident about themselves." Yet even as Allen's unconfident characters made audiences laugh, they knew he was confi-

Nothing's rougher than high school: Jaleel White as Urkel; Christopher Mintz-Plasse as Fogell, aka McLovin in *Superbad* (2007).

NERDS OPENLY LIKE WHAT THEY LIKE. THEY'RE SO PASSIONATE— JUST NOT ABOUT POPULAR SUBJECTS.
—Jaleel White

dent enough to become a sex symbol for an entire subsection of society. Like Cantor and Hope, Allen was an inside joke—he was getting far more action in real life than his characters did; he could play both sides of a character simultaneously. It was a calculated sleight of hand, a juxtaposition of inside and outside mastered by another magic aficionado, Steve Martin, a decade later. "Preening under the guise of being gawky, one-upping while appearing dim, planning meticulously while seeming to improvise," wrote critic Laurie Stone about Martin. He made being unhip so hip that guys everywhere aped his style, taking on characteristics that would have horrified them (and their prospective dates) only years earlier.

All the outsider characters up through the mid-1970s desired to get into American society, to somehow raise their lot and achieve their aspirations by, at very least, getting the pretty girl in the end. But in the middle of the decade, a new breed of disaffected outsiders emerged who had no interest in fitting in, achieving status, or even in showing up for work. They were slackers, thrilled that no one wanted them at the party or on the team, because that would have required some effort on their part. The seminal comedy to promote this way of life was 1978's *National Lampoon's Animal House*. It is the complete antithesis of Lloyd's *The Freshman*; who would want to join the football team when one could get smashed at the toga party?

While "Boys Behaving Badly" became the dominant film genre of the 1980s and 1990s (*Stripes*, *The Jerk*, *Ghostbusters*, *The Blues Brothers*, *Up in Smoke*, and so on), the ranks of nerddom opened up, allowing new kinds of outsiders to join the club—or be rejected from the club, as the case may be. Nerds from all walks of life were enshrined in the 1984 film *Revenge of the Nerds*, a kind of hall of fame of geekdom, and the first black nerd appeared on television in 1989 when Jaleel White, in the person of Steve Urkel, hiked his pants way too high for nine seasons on the sitcom *Family Matters*. A black nerd was a watershed figure (although, to be fair, Larry B. Scott's Lamar Latrell in *Revenge of the Nerds* was black *and* gay); the very hipness of black culture made such a character nearly unimaginable. In fact, Mary Bucholtz, a linguist at the University of California, Santa Barbara, coined a term in 2007, *hyperwhite*, for describing nerds, implying that every choice of clothing, music, demeanor, or leisure activity embraced by nerds was the technical opposite of everything embraced by black culture. It's an interesting point; nothing gets a cheap laugh faster than a white geek—sorry, hyperwhite geek—pathetically trying to copy the moves or jargon of black hipsters.

Such mind-bending cultural inversions effectively blur the distinctions of insiders and outsiders. Who would have thought, a century ago, that to be hyperwhite would be so uncool, while black culture would be the very essence of "in"? (In Eddie Murphy's version of *The Nutty Professor*, the audience loves his fat, nerdy professor and loathes his hip, flashy, alter ego, Buddy Love.) In the late 1980s, comedian Ellen DeGeneres brought a genial edge to the time-honored comic female dilemma of being self-conscious, unattractive, and awkward. Soon she had her own sitcom, modeled on her gawky persona, obsessed with fitting in, unable to get a date on Saturday night. When DeGeneres eventually outed both her character and herself on national television (surely a first—both at once), it was a daring move and not without its consequences. In one fell swoop, she completely inverted the female nerd role: it's no longer that guys don't find Ellen attractive—it's that Ellen isn't attracted to guys. She incorporated her outing as one of the many vexing problems of trying to fit in anywhere in the world. Famously, she hosted the Emmy Awards ceremony several months after the 9/11 attacks and told the enthusiastic audience: "We're told to go on living our lives as usual, because to do otherwise is to let the terrorists win, and really, what would upset the Taliban more than a gay woman wearing a suit in front of a room full of Jews?"

Still, even with an engaging lesbian nerd on the scene, there was plenty for boy nerds to do as the twenty-first century began. Comedians such as Jim Carrey, Chris Farley, Jack Black, Ben Stiller, Rainn Wilson, Adam Sandler, and Will Ferrell have made cottage industries out of the inability to function gracefully in civilized society, and audiences have embraced their antics heartily. In 2007, producer/director/writer Judd Apatow has become the Florenz Ziegfeld of geekdom. His losers are big winners. Within four years, his string of film comedies (*The 40-Year-Old Virgin*, *Knocked Up*, *Superbad*)—equal parts charmingly sympathetic and hilariously filthy—have grossed over a billion dollars. One can't get much more "in" than that. "I can't write about a character that Cary Grant would play," said Apatow. "I don't know how that person talks. I do know that there are people who smoke pot with fishbowls over their heads. That I understand. You have these kids and they're underdogs and they're goofy, but in a way they know that they're cool, also—that's how I always felt as a kid: 'There's something about me that I think is special, but no one seems to be noticing. And I hope that one day they will.' "

That day, a century in the making, may have finally arrived. When the twentieth century began, America knew where its heroes were coming from. As the twenty-first century begins, we're not so sure. Perhaps the dweebs, misfits, oddballs, and slackers were American heroes all along:

Living well is the best revenge: Robert Carradine triumphant in *Revenge of the Nerds* (1984).

LEWIS: Hi, Gilbert. I'm a nerd too. We have news for the beautiful people. There's a lot more of us then there are of you. Any of you that have ever felt stepped on, left out, picked on, put down, whether you think you're a nerd or not, why don't you just come down here and join us. Okay? Come on.

GILBERT: Just join us, because no one's gonna really be free until nerd persecution ends.

—*Revenge of the Nerds*

"STEP RIGHT UP AND HAROLD LLOYD

Harold Lloyd was not a comedian, but the best actor to play a comedian I ever saw.
–Hal Roach

CALL ME SPEEDY!"

"Lonesome Luke" was not going to cut it; that much Harold Lloyd knew in his gut. Luke was a comic character that Lloyd had played in nearly seventy silent shorts since 1915. Luke's persona was borrowed from Chaplin, only his clothes were too tight, whereas Chaplin's were too baggy. There was another not insignificant difference—Luke wasn't nearly as funny.

> I never used my glasses to draw special attention to them. They were like my nose, my mouth, my eyes. They were something that was a part of me. I never took them off. In *The Freshman*, where people were stepping on my face, the audience didn't stop to think, "Oh, his glasses will be broken!" They just didn't think of my glasses as separate from my own personality. —Harold Lloyd

This fact was confirmed for Lloyd one night when he and his comic foil, Bebe Daniels, were sitting in a movie theater and a Luke short appeared on the screen. A boy sitting next to them said, a bit too loudly, "Oh, here's the fellow that tries to do like Chaplin." That was it. Lloyd, an inveterate tinkerer—with both gizmos and human psychology—decided that a change was in order.

It was a natural extension of Lloyd's constant search for perfection. He was born in a small Nebraska town in 1892, the son of a squabbling mother and father who traveled all over the country before breaking up their marriage. Lloyd went to school, studied acting, and even barnstormed a bit in Nebraska. One day, a large insurance settlement landed in his father's lap. A flip of the coin determined that Lloyd and his dad would put down their newfound stakes on the West Coast. By 1914, Lloyd was trying to break through in Hollywood by playing an unconvincing range of small character parts for five dollars a day. Getting nowhere fast, he teamed up with a young comedy pioneer named Hal Roach, who was making one-reelers. As Lloyd recounted, Roach had a fight on the set one day with his leading comic and the comic quit on him. "So [Roach] came over to me and said, 'Lloyd, you can do it just as well as he can. I think we'll make you the comic.' So I did it, and that's the way I started in."

He and Roach cranked out the Luke comedies for Pathé and achieved a small success, but when Lloyd decided to toss out the ludicrous grotesqueries of Luke's physical appearance, he went completely in the other direction. The simple addition of a pair of lensless tortoiseshell glasses reframed Lloyd's career from a whole new perspective. Now the comic possibilities stretched into the distance. He said:

> Glasses give you a studious expression, serious, but you don't have to do that, you can belie that appearance. They make you studious, then you do something entirely to dispel that idea. You become a funny character because you don't act the way a normal person would act. My character with the glasses and clothes was just a funny young man—but after a number of pictures, he becomes a funny character.

As Lloyd's granddaughter Suzanne Lloyd pointed out, the choice of glasses was not a facile one: "In the early teens, if you wore glasses, they weren't fashionable like they are now. It was a stigma, it was a handicap, it implied there was something wrong with you. Harold felt that putting on the glasses would make him more of a real person."

Lloyd's new persona—he was never given a permanent name—made its debut with the one-reeler, *On the Fence*, in 1917. If Lloyd's trademark glasses made him seem more of a coward or a milquetoast, it was all the more reason to put him into dangerous scrapes, the likes of which had never been seen in silent film. He would undergo a (literally) hair-raising experience on a building ledge in *High and Dizzy*, balance on the girder of an unfinished skyscraper in *Never Weaken*, plan a prison break with a toothache-suffering giant in *Why Worry?* and hide out in a harem two decades before Hope and Crosby in *A Sailor-Made Man*. The paramount achievement of his thrill pictures was *Safety Last*, a 1923 feature, where Lloyd played a department store manager who hires a "human fly" for publicity purposes and gets stuck filling in for him. Lloyd did most of his own stunts and set up the complicated camera angles that captured the danger high above a Los Angeles business district. It would be Lloyd's most iconic picture—his desperate clinging to the minute hand of a huge clock, suspended a dozen stories over a busy street, is one of American comedy's signature images.

While such "thrill pictures" enthralled audiences, Lloyd himself was underwhelmed by their influence. "The funny thing is they always pegged me as a stunt come-

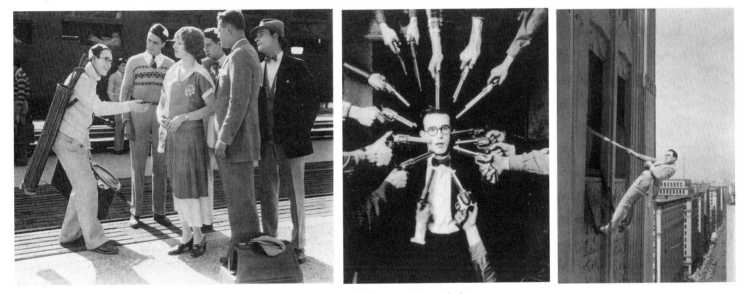

Eager beaver:
Lloyd in *The Freshman*, introducing himself as Speedy; in trouble, both in *An Eastern Westerner* (1920) and *Feet First* (1930).

dian, when actually out of nearly two hundred fifty to three hundred films, I only made five that had thrills like that," he said in 1968 of *Safety Last*. But his innovative spirit connected with audiences anyway. "I call him more of an adventurer than anything," said Suzanne Lloyd. "He was always on the *edge* of trying to get ahead and finding a new adventure." And although Lloyd often played the craven coward, he was braver than the audience knew; he accomplished all of his famous stunts with the practical use of only one hand.

In 1919, Lloyd had filmed one of the very first of the much-imitated haunted house comedies, *Haunted Spooks*. While he was clowning around with some stage props for a publicity shoot on the picture, he decided to put a cigarette in his mouth and light the fuse of a papier-mâché bomb. Unfortunately the bomb was all too real—it went off, and Lloyd lost his right thumb, his index finger, and half of his right palm. The accident set his career back nearly a year while he recovered, but adventurer that he was, Lloyd took the advice of film producer Sam Goldwyn (whose initial career was glove maker) and had a prosthetic glove built for his right hand. Lloyd kept his handicap and its solution a secret from the public for the rest of his career—a smart move, as it was nearly impossible to spot his gloved hand during his daring antics.

Lloyd did something even more courageous after the accident than pratfalls and stunts; he defied the two-dimensional slapstick of silent comedy. In the 1921 feature *Grandma's Boy*, he created a character-centered drama about a young man whose childhood cowardice is redeemed by his grandmother's faith in him—and the faith he discovers in himself. Chaplin was so moved that he wrote Lloyd a letter saying, "I can't believe what you've done with this movie." By 1925, Lloyd was rivaling Chaplin at the box office and producing far more comedies than either the Little Tramp or Buster Keaton. He had also established himself as an entirely different type of comedian. Where Chaplin's Little

FEW COMEDIANS WORKED AS AGGRESSIVELY —AND AS BRAVELY— FOR A LAUGH AS HAROLD LLOYD.

Tramp existed on the fringes of society and Keaton inhabited his own hermetically absurd world, Lloyd's characters got dressed every morning and headed out into the fast-paced, aggressive, urban world of the 1920s, eager to make a living—as a soda jerk or shoe salesman—and hopeful to find the woman of his dreams. It was that winning eagerness to fit in that provided the comic engine of his masterpiece, *The Freshman*.

In *The Freshman*, Lloyd not only tapped into the twenties craze for college and youth, he created the ultimate valentine to the underdog. He plays Harold Lamb, a youngster so eager to become the Big Man on Campus that he learns all the college fight songs in his bedroom at home. Aping what he believes to be the irresistible affability of a campus hero, he introduces himself to everyone by dancing a jolly jig, proffering a hand, and exclaiming, "Step right up and call me Speedy!" Lloyd is met with jeers rather than cheers although, honoring his own comic sweetness, he never seems to accept that he is being mocked. In several sequences that would be imitated for the next eighty years, Lloyd attempts to make the football team but is drubbed into the ground in a series of ritual humiliations.

Chum in a scrum:
Lloyd triumphant in *The Freshman*.

Usually, Lloyd worked with his writers to create the big knockout gags and then worked backward to create the setup. With *The Freshman*, it was different. "I came in and said it isn't going to work, boys," Lloyd recounted decades later. "I haven't got the spirit into it. I've got to know what's going to happen before this in order to catch the quality and the spirit of this character wanting to win the game." Of course, by the final fade-out, he has won the big game, the girl, and the hearts of the audience. *The Freshman* would be this blueprint for one of the great comic formulas: The Nerd Triumphant.

When *The Freshman* was released, it made nearly three million dollars—almost ten times its cost. Paramount was able to lure Lloyd away from Pathé, the company he had worked with since he entered pictures, by offering him a deal that gave him 77 percent of the domestic gross on his pictures and 90 percent of the foreign gross. Talk about a hero.

His grit and determination were admirable, but they were not enough to allow him to survive the transition to sound. Lloyd was a canny producer of his work during the silent era, but his managerial gifts escaped him when he moved into talkies, and he never found the right vehicle or the right deal to restore his former glory. He owned most of his films and held on to the rights as tenaciously as he had held on to to a clock hand; because he didn't trust the technology of the medium, Lloyd never allowed his films to be shown on television, and it cost him a new generation of comedy fans. He finished out his years traveling the globe to lecture about silent movies and tinkering with hi-fi systems and 3-D technology in his California estate. Lloyd passed away in 1971. In his seminal book *The Silent Clowns*, Walter Kerr wrote about Lloyd that "the glasses were, after all, the saving grace. They masked and justified the nakedness of the aggression." Few comedians worked as aggressively—and as bravely—for a laugh as Harold Lloyd.

What was great about Harold Lloyd was that he was the misfit in the wrong social situation. But he was there intentionally. There's nothing funnier than a completely uncool guy saying "I do fit in—I'm fooling 'em!" No, you're not. That's why we're laughing.

–Michael McKean

"I CAN'T EAT HAM SANDWICHES"
EDDIE CANTOR

Cantor: I think I'm more the type for these swashbuckling roles. Only last night I had a dream that I was the star of *The Three Musketeers*. There I was alone on a desert island with my two other musketeers, Betty Grable and Virginia Mayo.

Cesar Romero: Now, wait a minute—the three musketeers are all men.

Cantor: Listen, when I dream, I do my own casting!

—*The Eddie Cantor Show* (1947)

If Eddie Cantor's rags-to-riches biography sounds like the worst kind of cliché, that's okay; he came by it honestly. As far as the "rags" part goes, Edward Israel Iskowitz entered the world in 1892, born into the shabby tenement life of New York's Lower East Side. It wasn't an easy existence—both parents died by the time he was three, and he was raised by his beloved grandmother Esther, who eked out a living selling candles. Like many a skinny Jewish boy before and after him, young Izzy survived by his wits—and his jokes:

> I grew up lean, big-eyed, eager, singing in backyards, playing in gutters. I was not introspective—whatever that is. I simply took to life. In short, I was a typical New York street boy who, by a peculiar and deft twist of fortune, eventually lands in the Bowery Mission or in a bower of roses.

Making people laugh was a way out of the slums, and the teenage Eddie found work in knockabout vaudeville, making funny voices and funny faces in small-time venues around the city. He had no definite persona back then, except that he was very good at being "fresh," as it used to be called—talking back in an insolent manner. Like many a comic of the early twentieth century, he turned to a conceit that was less than fresh—in the other use of the word—the blackface mask. Yet even within this stale tradition Cantor made a clever adjustment:

> I decided to add a pair of white-rimmed spectacles, which gave me a look of intelligence without straining my face. Unwittingly, I had added an intellectual touch to the old-fashioned minstrel. By putting on glasses, the sooty spirit of the cotton fields was brought up to the twentieth century.

Cantor's hyperkinetic energy was a pure expression of the new century and it brought him to the attention of Florenz Ziegfeld, who, after trying him out in his after-hours nightspot, put him front and center in his prestigious Broadway *Follies* in 1917. Cantor was equally adept at singing and dancing and, in the annual show's various revues sketches, he cornered the market on what he called "ludicrous weaklings." In a famous sketch in an osteopath's office, a burly nurse manhandled Cantor into a pretzel; audiences were twisted around with laughter themselves. As critic Gilbert Seldes put it, "Cantor is at his best when he chooses to play the timid, Ghetto-bred, pale-faced Jewish lad, seduced by glory or the prospects of pay into competing with athletes and bruisers—the lamb led to slaughter."

Steady Eddie:
Cantor, in blackface, with trademark glasses; onstage in *Kid Boots* (1923).

For Cantor, the *Follies* provided the family structure he never knew growing up. He joined two of the other great talents of the *Follies*, Will Rogers and W. C. Fields, onstage and on tour—Ziegfeld called them his Three Musketeers—and Rogers was a respected father figure to Cantor. One night, after Cantor had scored a knockout with the *Follies* audience, he was disconsolate in his dressing room; his grandmother had just died, and Cantor was bereft that she had missed his triumph. "Why, Eddie," drawled Rogers when he poked his head in, "how do you know she *wasn't* watching—and from the best seat there is?" Cantor also reserved a special place for the man he said taught him everything he knew about comedy: the black Ziegfeld star Bert Williams. Cantor became the first white comic to appear on Broadway opposite a black comedian.

Cantor's friendship with Williams and his own upbringing gave him a healthy respect for the underdog. When Ziegfeld defied the unionizing of poorly paid chorines during the Actors Equity strike of 1919, Cantor broke with him completely. (The incident also brought out Cantor's wicked sense of justice; when theatrical giant George M. Cohan also resisted Equity and vowed that, if the union won, he would quit the theater and run an elevator, Cantor retorted that "Somebody better tell Mr. Cohan that to run an elevator he'd *have* to join a union.") By 1927, Cantor made his peace—and his contract—with Ziegfeld and became the first comedian to have a *Follies* built around him. Onstage for two hours of the show's two-and-a-half-hour length, he clowned, sang, danced, and impersonated Mayor Jimmy Walker. But by the late 1920s, tastes were changing and Cantor could no longer be contained in revues, no matter how much stage time he had; he wanted his own musical comedy vehicle. Cantor made Ziegfeld buy the musical rights to a play called *The Nervous Wreck*—it was perfect for him, he said, because he had already suffered a nervous breakdown working on the *Follies*. It became *Whoopee!* and made him a superstar.

Whoopee! (1928) was typical of the disjointed comic mishmash of early musical comedies. Cantor played Henry Williams, a Jewish hypochondriac who winds up on an Indian reservation and helps to resolve the romantic plot. It allowed the bespectacled Cantor to serve up his "ludicrous weakling" to a fare-thee-well, especially when pursued by his besotted nurse:

> MARY CUSTER: Oh, poor Henry. Let me hold your hand.
>
> HENRY WILLIAMS: It's not heavy. I can manage. Hold your own hand. . . . Why do you make overtures to me when I need intermissions so badly?

Cantor also introduced the hit song "Makin' Whoopee" in the show and indulged in some of his expected ethnic self-deprecation; referring to Charles Lindbergh's extraordinary transatlantic feat the year before—and the sustenance that kept the aviator alert—Cantor's character explains, "I'll never be an aviator. You know why? I can't eat ham sandwiches." When *Whoopee!* was produced as a film by Sam Goldwyn in 1930, it inexplicably lost its exclamation point but gained Cantor a new audience across the country (although he always did better—surprise—in urban centers). He traded in Ziegfeld for Goldwyn as a new father figure, and the film producer built several successful vehicles around Cantor, including what is probably his most engaging film, *Roman Scandals*, originally written for him by two Pulitzer Prize-winning playwrights, Robert E. Sherwood and George S. Kaufman. In *Roman Scandals*, Cantor played a janitor in a museum of classical antiquities who is transported back to the salacious days of ancient Rome, a kind of *Hester Street Sharpie in Emperor Augustus's Court*. According to film historian Leonard Maltin, "He inherited Harold Lloyd's mantle of playing that kind of young, innocent fool out on some errand or other."

By 1933, the country was eating up Cantor's antics—it desperately needed his relentless optimism. He was called "the Apostle of Pep," and according to Joe Franklin, "Eddie Cantor was the antidote that we needed at that time and he really got this country

"PROSPERITY MIGHT BE AROUND THE CORNER," HE WROTE, "BUT NOBODY KNEW THE NAME OF THE STREET."

Toga party:
Roman Scandals (1933).

through some very hard times." Cantor had suffered along with the rest of the populace. He had been wiped out by the stock market crash in 1929, but he climbed out of the hole the best way he knew how. "Prosperity might be around the corner," he wrote, "but nobody knew the name of the street. Laughter and lightheartedness in times like these is the only remedy." Beginning in 1931, Cantor dispensed that remedy on radio, becoming the first established comedy star to host his own radio show, *The Chase and Sanborn Hour* (later *The Eddie Cantor Show*). It became an overnight smash (or as Cantor once said, "It takes twenty years to become an overnight success") and ran for the next two decades. Cantor's aggressive amiability was perfect for the radio, although fans were often perplexed by the studio audiences' persistent laughter throughout the program—Cantor could never restrain his slapstick tendencies and frequently clowned around, did dance steps, or goosed his costars, antics that were, of course, invisible to listeners at home. "People tend to forget that in the early thirties Eddie Cantor was number one," said Franklin. "He was number one in the movies—not number two or three, number one—and far and away number one every Sunday night from eight to nine."

If Cantor reached the top by playing an anemic milquetoast in the movies, frightened to death of women, in real life it was another story. He had literally married the girl in the tenement next door in 1914, and he and Ida were the happy parents of five daughters—and thanks to Cantor's chattiness on the radio, everyone in America knew all about them.

Even as he conquered new fields, Cantor never forgot his roots. Whether it was as an entertainer or as a humanitarian, he was always looking out for the little guy. Like his role model Will Rogers, Cantor used his celebrity to make the world a better place. He created the March of Dimes, rescued Jewish families from Nazi Germany, campaigned for the State of Israel, and denounced an anti-Semitic radio host named Father Coughlin, even through he was temporarily dropped by his sponsors because of it. When television came along, he conquered that, too. He agreed to host NBC's *Colgate Comedy Hour* in 1950 only if he could serve as one of four rotating hosts; the network agreed, and even while alternating the program with Fred Allen, Martin and Lewis, and Abbott and Costello, Cantor's shows were still the most popular. The increased exposure of television did not dampen his sense of ethics, either; he was bombarded with hate mail for using his handkerchief to mop the brow of Sammy Davis Jr. during one *Colgate* broadcast. In response, he brought Davis back the next week—and mopped his brow again.

The wind was taken out of Cantor's sails when his beloved Ida died in 1962, and as a result of persistent heart problems, Cantor died two years later. Cantor's "look at me" energy has not transcended the decades well, but Cantor was devoted to giving the audience everything it wanted, and then a little extra on top. He was, without a doubt, the first comic celebrity to succeed in every medium of the twentieth century: stage, vaudeville, movies, radio, and television. In the 1920s and '30s, nobody embodied the "little guy" better than Eddie Cantor, and his reward—as well as the reward for millions of Americans—was to become the biggest man in show business.

Makin' whoopee:
Cantor returned to Broadway in 1941 in *Banjo Eyes*; *Whoopee* was based on his great stage triumph in 1928.

The Comic Side of Trouble

by Bert Williams

originally published *The American Magazine*, January 1918

(Bert Williams was the first mainstream African American comedian. He was engaged by impresario Florenz Ziegfeld to star in his *Follies* in 1910; it was an unprecedented move, but Ziegfeld had brought other "outsider" comics into the mainstream, including Eddie Cantor and Fanny Brice.)

One of the funniest sights in the world is a man whose hat has been knocked in or ruined by being blown off—provided, of course, it be the other fellow's hat! All the jokes in the world are based on a few elemental ideas, and this is one of them. The sight of other people in trouble is nearly always funny. This is human nature. The man with the real sense of humor is the man who can put himself in the spectator's place and laugh at his own misfortunes.

That is what I am called upon to do every day. Nearly all of my successful songs have been based on the idea that I am getting the worst of it. I am the "Jonah Man," the man who, even if it rained soup, would be found with a fork in his hand and no spoon in sight, the man whose fighting relatives come to visit him and whose head is always dented by the furniture they throw at each other. There are endless variations of this idea, fortunately; but if you sift them, you will find the principle of human nature at the bottom of them all.

Troubles are funny only when you pin them to one particular individual. And that individual, the fellow who is the goat, must be the man who is singing the song or telling the misfortunes, fielding flatirons with his head, carrying large bulldogs by the seat of his pants, and picking the bare bones of the chicken while his wife's relations eat the breast, and so forth.

I find much material by knocking around in out of the way places and just listening. For among the American colored men and negroes there is the greatest source of simple amusement you can find anywhere in the world. But Americans for the most part know little about the unconscious humor of the colored people and negroes, because they do not come in contact with them. A short while ago I heard an argument between two men. One of them was pretty cocky and tried to bulldoze the other, who was trying his best to be peaceable, and kept saying, "I don't want no trouble with you now."

Presently it got too warm for him, and the peaceable man turned to the other and said, "Looka hyah, nigga, you better get away fum me, 'cause I'm jes' going to take this bottle an' bathe your head with it." Of course I put that line into the *Follies* the next day.

I hope nothing I have said will be mistaken to mean that I think I have found a recipe for making people laugh, or anything of that sort. Humor is the one thing in the world that it is impossible to argue about, because it is all a matter of taste. If I could turn myself into a human boomerang: if I could jump from the stage, fly out over the audience, turn a couple of somersaults in the air, snatch the toupee from the head of the bald man in the front row of the balcony, and light back on the stage in the spot I jumped from, I could have the world at my feet—for a while. But even then I would always have to be finding something new.

People sometimes ask me if I would not give anything to be white. I answer, in the words of the song, most emphatically, "No." How do I know what I might be if I were a white man? I might be a sand-hog, burrowing away and losing my health for eight dollars a day. I might be a street-car conductor at twelve or fifteen dollars a week. There is many a white man less fortunate and less well equipped than I am. In truth, I have never been able to discover that there was anything disgraceful in being a colored man. But I have often found it inconvenient—in America.

When Mr. Ziegfeld first proposed to engage me for the *Follies* there was a tremendous storm in a teacup. Everybody threatened to leave; they proposed to get up a boycott if he persisted; they said all sorts of things against my personal character. But Mr. Ziegfeld stuck to his guns and was quite undisturbed by everything that was said. Which is one reason why I am with him now, although I could make twice the salary in vaudeville. And I have acquired enough philosophy to protect me against the things which would cause me humiliation and grief if I had not learned independence.

Meanwhile, I have no grievance whatsoever against the world or the people in it: I'm having a grand time. I am what I am, not because of what I am but in spite of it.

I feel very humble, but I think I have the strength of character to fight it.

—Bob Hope to President Kennedy, on receiving a Congressional Gold Medal, 1963

"NOT ME. I USED TO BE IN VAUDEVILLE"
BOB HOPE

When Bob Hope moved to Hollywood in 1937, he needed all the strength of character he could muster. He had been there before, but the short subjects he made in the early 1930s failed to make much of an impression; in fact, Hope had been having trouble making an impression for years.

Born Leslie Townes Hope in England in 1903, Hope was four when his family came to America, and his father languished as a stonemason, unable to make much of a living in Cleveland. Young Hope turned to a variety of vocations as he made his way to adulthood. It wasn't all roses—"We'd have been called juvenile delinquents, only our neighborhood couldn't afford a sociologist," he once said—and he tried to click as a boxer, a dance instructor, a hoofer, and half of a vaudeville team, toiling in the Midwest.

Slippery slope:
Hope worked his way up the ladder; *The Ziegfeld Follies of 1936* with the Nicholas Brothers; with vaudeville partner George Byrne; celluloid fame with Jane Russell (1948).

Hope made it to the Broadway stage in the early 1930s, as the supporting comic in casts for musical comedies headlined by stars like Jimmy Durante and Ethel Merman. It was indicative of Hope's early indifferent luck that, even though he introduced major songs by Jerome Kern, Ira Gershwin, and Cole Porter ("It's De-Lovely"), the Broadway cognoscenti greeted him with a shrug. When he shuffled off to the West Coast, as a replacement for Jack Benny in a comic omnibus called *The Big Broadcast of 1938*, it seemed like his last, best chance for the big time. Thanks to a wistful, whimsical duet (with Shirley Ross) called "Thanks for the Memory," Hope's ease and charm caught fire. Now, there was no stopping him.

He proved to be the perfect kind of comedian to hold down a series of comedies with a horror or mystery framework. Hope could play at bravery, or more interestingly, play a coward pretending to be brave—"I'm so scared, even my goose pimples have goose pimples," he cracked in his first haunted house comedy, *The Cat and the Canary* (1939)—all the while letting the audience in on the joke, without destroying the spooky framework of the picture. It was a tricky balancing act, but one that Hope performed to elegant perfection. "With Bob Hope, you're not laughing at the jokes, but at a guy who's vain and cowardly and says to some guy who's menacing him, 'You're looking good—what do you hear from your embalmer?' You're laughing at the character all the time," said his acolyte, Woody Allen. "He was vain, a coward's coward, a womanizer, but always brilliant. A superschnook."

CICILY: Don't big empty houses scare you?

HOPE: Not me. I used to be in vaudeville.

—The Cat and the Canary

Hope was also attractive enough to be a credible romantic lead. Even with his famous ski-jump nose, lantern jaw, and effeminate swagger, he could wear a double-breasted suit like nobody's business—but he added a delightful dash of inadequacy, just enough to endear him to audiences, if not to the heroine. "The girls call me Pilgrim, because every time I dance with one I make a little progress," went one of his lines in *The Ghost Breakers*. John Lahr, in his perceptive 1998 *New Yorker* profile of Hope, called this character "a sheep in wolf's clothing." His delivery, "soufflé-light," as Woody Allen called it and perfected after facing years of hostile crowds in vaudeville, allowed Hope to get in and out of the most improbable situations—a radio actor posing as a private detective, say, or an eighteenth-century barber pretending to be a French king.

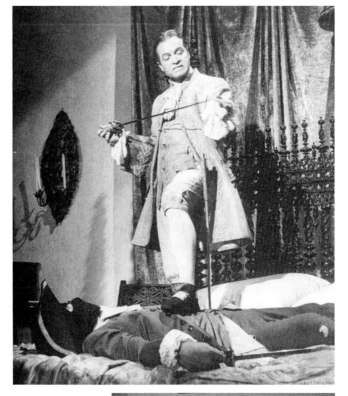

Comic foil:
Pretending to be the hero in *Monsieur Beaucaire* (1946); Bob "Pepsodent" Hope, radio star.

Hope's film persona was no accident. "We never told Bob this," said Mel Shavelson, one of his many writers, "but we took his own characteristics and exaggerated them. The woman chaser. The coward. The cheap guy. We just put them in. He thought he was playing a character. He was playing, really, the real Bob Hope." Hope's genius for mocking self-deprecation allowed him to replace aging solo artists such as Eddie Cantor and W. C. Fields to become one of the comic linchpins of the early 1940s; he made an astonishing twenty comedies between 1938 and the end of World War II. But in the late 1930s, you couldn't be a comedy superstar without conquering one other medium:

(*Hope switches on the radio.*)

BOB HOPE (*on radio*): How d'ya do, ladies and gentlemen, this is Bob Hope, the Pepsodent Kid, still hanging on by your teeth. And I'm here to tell you that I—(*Hope switches off radio.*)

HOPE: I can't stand that guy.

–My Favorite Blonde

Hope had done surprisingly little radio before hosting the *Pepsodent Show* in 1938, but as soon as he was given this prime-time platform, he realized that he needed a hook. Unlike radio's two biggest comic stars, he couldn't impersonate an ongoing character like Jack Benny or come up with a unique gimmick like Edgar Bergen and his ventriloquist act with Charlie McCarthy. "True to vaudeville formula," he said about his radio style, "I attempt to make my topics newsy and seasonal." So he threw out any attempt at narrative or structure and put the emphasis on the jokes—twenty-three of them, in his first seven-minute opening monologue. Larry Gelbart, who served as yet another one of Hope's writers in the late 1940s, recalled:

> A Hope show would contain various elements. There was the monologue, first and foremost, which is just a string of jokes, about four or five different subjects.
> Usually politicians, stuff about his life and about the larger life that the American people were living, what we call one-liners, just quick jokes. It was kind of a bulletin board of current events.

According to his protégée, Phyllis Diller, Hope's laugh machine was pure mathematics: "Everything was set up, pay off. He went for six laughs a minute." But it took a lot of work to come up with an hour's worth of six laughs a minute, and Hope relied on a battalion of writers to fill the artillery of his rapid-fire delivery. "Bob appreciated what his writers gave to him and he paid them handsomely for their contributions," recalled another writer, Hal Kanter. "If he was a glutton he wasn't a selfish glutton. He was able to spread his gluttony among his writers." Hope kept his writing staff on a very tight leash, phoning them at all hours for all kinds of favors, but he was honest about how much he needed them. "I think I was also the first [comedian] to admit that openly that I employed writers," he once wrote.

"In the early days of radio, comedians fostered the illusion that all of those funny sayings came right out of their own skulls." Soon, Hope's personable style and mastery of the one-liner made the *Pepsodent Show* the number three comedy show in the ratings, right behind Benny and Bergen. By 1943, Hope's program would be number one. And still, Hope sought another high profile role.

HOPE: I can't go on! No food, no water. It's all my fault. We're done for! It's got me. I can't stand it! No food, nothing! No food, no water! No food!

CROSBY: What's the matter with you, anyway? There's New York. We'll be picked up in a few minutes.

HOPE: You had to open your big mouth and ruin the only good scene I got in the picture. I might have won the Academy Award!

—*The Road to Morocco*

Boning up:
Hope, trapped in a harem, in *The Road to Morocco* (1942); with Bing in *Variety Girl* (1946). Far right: hero to servicemen for four decades.

In 1940, the Academy of Motion Picture Arts and Sciences made Hope their first single host for the Oscars. He was perfect as the sardonic, yet personable, host, and his mock display of seething envy was a new addition to his self-deprecating character. "Welcome to the Academy Awards—or as it's known in my house, Passover," went his most famous remark, and Hope wound up as the Oscars' host for eighteen separate legendary occasions. Not content to be a solo player, he teamed up with his genial pal from the golf links, Bing Crosby, that same year, for an unforgettable series of comedies. Their loosey-goosey buddy films would initiate a movie genre that continues—although rarely as effortlessly—to this day.

Supposedly turned down by the team of Burns and Allen, *The Road to Singapore* proved to be the perfect vehicle for both Crosby's laid-back romanticism and Hope's dubious heroism; the "whole" of each of the seven *Road* pictures was immensely greater than the sum of its disparate parts. Largely, this was the result of the Hope-Crosby banter, and the Pirandellian in-jokery that made each picture feel like an invitation to a round of golf with your best pals. Film historian Leonard Maltin observes that "As audiences in the mid-forties became more show-business savvy, the idea of being on the inside of a joking relationship between two stars was very appealing. Bing Crosby and Bob Hope break the fourth wall and refer to inside stuff that assumes you get what's going on, that makes an audience feel good."

HOPE: A fine thing. First, you sell me for two hundred bucks. Then I'm gonna marry the Princess; then you cut in on me. Then we're carried off by a desert sheik. Now, we're gonna have our heads chopped off.

CROSBY: I know all that.

HOPE: Yeah, but the people who came in the middle of the picture don't.

CROSBY: You mean they missed my song?

—*The Road to Morocco*

Such cornball antics were most welcome, because as Hal Kanter was the first to admit, "the stories themselves would not hold up under any serious consideration as drama." The casualness—one might even say contempt—with which Hope and Crosby made the pictures was an immense part of their charm. Comic Dick Martin remembers watching the duo film *The Road to Utopia*: "The studio was right next to Wilshire Country Club. And in the middle of a scene, Crosby would say, 'I think I hear the links calling, Robert.' So, they told the director that they were off to play eighteen holes."

The next stage in Hope's climb to legendary fame was far from casual. On May 6, 1941, he hosted a live broadcast of the *Pepsodent Show* from March Army Air Force Field in Riverside, California. The GIs proved to be such an enthusiastic audience that he continued to perform his show at various stateside army bases. When the Japanese bombed Pearl Harbor six months later, Hope told his radio audience, "To most Americans, morale is taken for granted. There is no need to tell a nation to keep smiling when it's never stopped. It's our ability to laugh that has made us the great people that we are." Hope began the greatest road show of his career—perhaps of anyone's career. From May of 1941 until June of 1948, Hope performed almost all of his four hundred radio programs at navy, army, or air force bases, including six separate tours for the USO, traveling to his native England and as far afield as the most remote islands in the South Pacific. "He has caught the soldier's imagination," wrote John Steinbeck. "He gets laughter wherever he goes from men who need laughter. It is interesting to see how he has become a symbol."

The USO tours turned Hope into a national hero. He had only one cardinal rule: when visiting army hospitals, no one in his troupe was ever allowed to cry while meeting with injured vets. For America's number one coward, that was a brave thing to do. When the war ended, Hope commented, "In common with the GIs, I kept thinking of a nice long rest. The only difference was that the GIs really wanted one and I was afraid I'd be given one." As *Time* magazine perceptively wrote at the time, "While he hugs the limelight with a show-

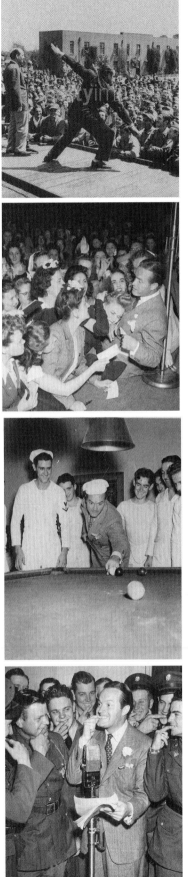

HE HAS CAUGHT THE SOLDIER'S IMAGINATION.

man's depthless ego, in Hope himself there is a hunger, perhaps a final vanity, to reach people as a human being." Reach people he certainly did; in the seven years since he first warbled "Thanks for the Memory," he had become the most famous American comedian in the world.

The USO tours kicked off his lifelong addiction to being on the go. His four adopted children used to joke that they spent more time with their peripatetic dad at Burbank Airport than at home. Perhaps it was his unresolved vaudeville roots that kept him moving.

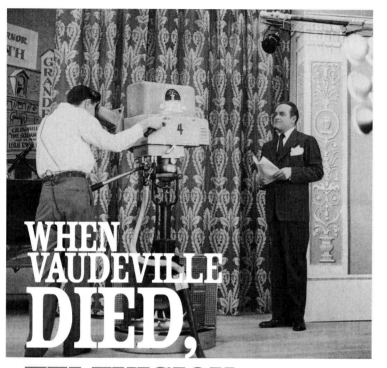

Stock in NBC: Hope began a sixty-one-year contract in 1950.

Recalled Hal Kanter, "He used his radio show to slough off his movie work. He used his movie work to slough off his radio show. He used the both of them to slough off his golf game, and he used his golf game to slough off his family. He was always, always in action, doing something somewhere. And he would travel anywhere to get laughs. And to pick up a few bucks too, incidentally." The bucks were not exactly few, either. Through a combination of shrewd business contracts and a knack for real estate, Hope's fortune was valued at the low *nine* figures.

Much of that was earned when Hope made the inevitable move to television in 1950 and negotiated a sixty-one-year contract with NBC. "When vaudeville died, television was the box they put it in," Hope once joked, but he was a success there, too; his televised USO tours during the Vietnam War were among the most watched programs of all time. Over the decades, Hope became a national institution, performing for eleven presidents, while idling his comic engine into a well-crafted, sometimes soulless, cue-card driven machine. His conservative politics dismayed many, and his conservative manner in private was frustrating, too, even to his own family. Dick Cavett, a childhood fan, interviewed Hope in the 1970s on his talk show:

WHEN VAUDEVILLE DIED, TELEVISION WAS THE BOX THEY PUT IT IN.

I wondered—as many people have wondered—was there anyone underneath the Hope facade, the great comic picture that he was covered with? And during this one show, at one point I got so conversational with him—without his doing any gags—that he stated some fact about himself. When he was a kid, he got a scar, a little scar: "I got that from protecting my dog. Some guys were throwing rocks at my dog and I went up—" And he didn't have a punch line for it. And then he said, "Hey, would you rather have a gag on that one?" And I said, "No. That's just fine." Amazing man.

Despite his signature tune, Hope had little use for memories. He kept moving through the decades with the same drive, the same preoccupations. Although he would protest during the Academy Award ceremonies that no one ever took him seriously as an actor, Hope never had any real interest in breaking a winning formula. Even old age became useful fodder for a gag. "Is there sex after sixty?" he was asked in *Playboy* magazine. "You bet. And awfully good, too. Especially the one in the fall." Hope lived two months past his hundredth birthday, just like his old pal George Burns, who costarred with him in his second feature, *College Swing*, in 1938. The day he turned one hundred, Hope delivered his final one-liner: "I'm so old, they've canceled my blood type."

Bob Hope One-Liners

(The complete Bob Hope Joke File—more than 85,000 pages—has been digitally scanned and indexed according to the categories used by Bob Hope for presentation in the Bob Hope Gallery of American Entertainment at the Library of Congress. Here are bu a few selections, by topic.)

BOXING

I used to be a professional fighter, but I had to give it up; the resin on the canvas almost blinded me.

In my whole boxing career, I was never knocked out. I used to faint.

I was a little too confident. But in the third round, I decided to take my bathrobe off.

I hurt my hand in the first round. The referee stepped on it.

GIRLS

Spring . . . that's when a young man's thoughts turn to something fancy, and I have to take what's left.

Every spring, I find myself fighting girls off. 'Course they're usually just nurses trying to give me my hay fever shots.

But I'm really an expert on romance. When I was a boy, my father told me all about the birds and the bees . . . but I still can't figure what a bird sees in a bee.

I'm a girl watcher. All men are girl watchers. I knew a fellow who used to drive his wife crazy because he slept with a smile on his face all the time.

But spring is a wonderful thing. Last night at Grauman's Chinese Theater, my footprints sneaked all the way over to Jane Russell's.

HOPE: You do get my heart beating a little faster. Can you hear that pitter-pat?
GIRL: I do hear the pitter.
HOPE: Well, the pat'll be along any minute now.

When I'm alone with a girl at her home, I read Shakespeare to her. It's over my head and it's over her head, but it's better than going out and spending money!

I've been studying chicks longer than Colonel Sanders.

I think this country is well prepared for a woman president. We've already had our share of boobs in the White House.

AMERICA

America . . . the land of the free and the home of the brave and Bob Hope.

But I'm really proud to be an American . . . Yessir, this country is really the land of opportunity. Just look at Sinatra and Crosby. Where else could a piece of spaghetti and a meatball wind up with so much gravy?

Yessir, this is the land of opportunity where everyone has an even chance to grow up, be a movie star, and get investigated.

ACADEMY AWARDS
(Hope and Losers)

I can just imagine how nervous some of the performers are out there tonight, wondering whether or not they won an Oscar . . . I never have to worry about that . . . Every time it comes to voting, the Academy crosses my name off the list and starts voting.

There are two acting awards I never got, the Oscar and the presidency of the United States.

But I think it's shameful what some people will do just to get an Oscar. Besides, I've tried every one of them and they don't work.

In a way, it's a distinction not to receive an award. That's the way I feel about it, and my psychiatrist agrees with me.

But, after all, what is an Oscar? It's a beautiful thing, but you can't take it with you . . . Of course, I'd like a chance to try.

I called up Charlie Brackett, the president of the Academy, and told him, "It isn't fair . . . you never give awards to comedians." He said, "Quit worrying about other people."

I may have to call Martin Luther King. The Academy and I still aren't integrated.

I've given up trying to win an Oscar. I think I'll just have Mickey Rooney bronzed.

If you were to ask me the funniest twenty-five people I've ever known, I'd say, "Here they are–Jonathan Winters." —Jack Paar

"JUST THIS SIDE OF MARS" JONATHAN WINTERS

In 1954, the Department of the Air Force released Regulation 2002, which established "procedures for information and evidence pertaining to unidentified flying objects." It was the first comprehensive response to the large number of UFO sightings in the country. They missed one: a nightclub comic plying his trade in Greenwich Village, while sending checks back home to his wife and two kids in Ohio–Jonathan Winters.

Well, I definitely come from outer space. I can't discuss it at this time because the Pentagon has pleaded with me not to say anything further. We've been here for a while but I think we're gonna get out now because of the war and everything. But you can always come to see us. We're just this side of Mars.

Winters was born in 1925, into a wealthy banking family from Dayton. His parents divorced when he was seven and, by all accounts, he had a depressing childhood. According to Robert Klein, a great admirer of Winters, "He was an only child, lonely, he would go into his room and interview himself. And his mother would go, 'Jonathan! Who's in there with you?' " Winters went on to a three-year stint in the South Pacific and returned to Ohio, where he settled down with his new wife, while both attended the Dayton Art Institute. One night, toward the end of the 1940s, Winters's wife, Eileen, noticed there was a local talent contest and first prize was a wristwatch. Winters didn't own one, so she encouraged him to compete, since he was always "the life of the party." He won the contest, the watch, and a shot as a local disc jockey on a very early morning show.

It was there that Winters's career—and troubles—began. Winters realized that no one would come on the show at six a.m., so he developed an inventive solution:

> About the fourth or fifth day I said, "We have wing commander Emory Lugbody here, just flown a secret aircraft over, think it was a Spitfire. Anyway, he's here with us and landed at right field. "Nice to have you here, sir . . ." Then we went to some music, and then the switchboard lit up. The manager of the station came up and he said, "Where'd you get this guy?" And I said, "I did the guy." He goes, "Don't do this anymore. Time and temperature. Do the commercials, play the music. Okay?"

By 1953, Winters opted to pursue his comedy career in New York, leaving his wife and two kids back home. Initially his act was full of impressions of obvious movie stars like Boris Karloff, Clark Gable, and Gary Cooper. One night while performing at Le Ruban Bleu, he was offered some good advice from an anonymous backstage visitor.

> He said, "You do great impressions, but remember they're all stars, and all you're doing is shining their shoes. The minute you do them, they know who you're doing, they don't know you. Where'd you come from?" I said, "I come from Ohio." "What about doing characters from Ohio? Making up some characters?" So then I made up, not only characters from Ohio, but I went really far out and did flying saucer landings, Custer's Last Stand, gasoline attendants . . .

His vast omnibus of comic characters—all derived from the recesses of his baroque imagination—caught the attention of Jack Paar, who launched Winters's career through a series of appearances on his talk show. In the mid-1950s, there was no one like Winters—all twenty-five of him. While he performed a broad range of characters, they were all original. While he created banter, he was a solo performer. While other comedians did jokes, Winters sketched verbal portraits. While he was working in hip, urban venues, his characters were small-town midwestern eccentrics. And much of his comedy was improvisational, nearly unheard of in that era. He was like a deranged human radio receiver, channeling bizarre transmissions that emanated only from the farthest reaches of his brain. As Klein put it, "He's a one-man show, pure and simple."

DON'T DO THIS ANYMORE. TIME AND TEMPERATURE. DO THE COMMERCIALS, PLAY THE MUSIC. OK?

Winters and his discontent:
Brought in by San Francisco police in 1959; his many faces; Maude Frickert (opposite, top); hunting lions, tigers, and bears, no doubt.

But while Winters's talent was pure, his career was rarely simple. "I was in really a little bit of trouble in the beginning," he recounted. "It wasn't my material, but I was asked to work in a tuxedo, and I said, 'I'm not a maître d'. I'm not in the orchestra. My characters are not tuxedo people. If I do a baseball player, what am I doing in this black tie? I can't do it.'" He was frustrated by the time restrictions of his own fifteen-minute TV show in 1957 (one of his guests was Lenny Bruce); he felt exploited by the low pay on television talk shows; he was too expansive for brief guest shots, and no film seemed capable of containing his multitude of voices. The stress was showing; between an intense series of nightclub appearances, separation from his family, and a dependence on alcohol, he snapped in 1959 and withdrew from the performance scene to get his act together.

When he returned, Winters moved more methodically and less maniacally into the world of LP recordings, variety shows, and film cameos. In historian Gerald Nachman's words, "A lot of people really respected him, because he was out there on a high wire. And he often fell off. But very often, he made it to the other side brilliantly." Commentators often found the madcap, manic intensity of some of eccentric characters to be "sick" or in poor taste, but audiences loved the literal-mindedness of rural rube Elwood P. Suggins, the egotism of jungle potentate King Kwasi of Kwasiland, and most of all, the midwestern grit of little old lady Maude Frickert. Frickert, who embodied the determination of an earlier generation (and the sexual appetite of a later one), always had a host of eccentric relatives and boyfriends, including one who tried to fly by "Scotch-taping 142 pigeons to his arms."

> Maude was based on an aunt I had, Aunt Lou Perks. And she was a crippled lady, bedridden most of her life. But she was a hip old lady. You think of a lot of older people as kind of square and ready to go and take their dirt naps and stuff. But through Maude, you could say a lot of things without going too far out.

It may have been his unwillingness to follow someone else's script that prevented him from a bigger presence in films and on television sitcoms in the 1960s and 1970s, but there is no question that Winters's improvisational skills inspired a generation of comedians; among them, only Robin Williams came close to his gearshift genius. When Winters joined his acolyte to play another alien in the TV sitcom *Mork and Mindy* in 1981, it was a poignant meeting of two freewheeling comic geniuses and introduced Winters to the largest audience he'd had in years. He was the 2000 winner of the Kennedy Center Mark Twain Prize for Humor. It was a great honor for Winters—his chief influences are Mark Twain and "fellow Buckeye" James Thurber—but even there he got himself in trouble. "In the rehearsal, the producer came out with the [bust of Mark Twain] statue. The head was about that big. So I said to the producer with a straight face, 'Did Mister Twain die in the Congo?' He said, 'No, why?' 'Well, his head has been shrunk. You must have stiffed them at the foundry.' That did it. They wouldn't give me the award on the air."

Such blandishments of celebrity have rarely mattered to Winters, anyway. Trained as an artist, he'd much prefer to see his subjects as comedy than subject them to judgment:

> I like to sit in any city in the world, or in the countryside, and just look at the people—you draw on these people, it's like art. My characters have a point of view. They believe in what they're saying and what they're doing they know to be pretty true. And when they voice their opinions, they feel that they're not alone in their thoughts.

I think Jonathan really tiptoed along the edge and he looked over the edge more than once. He used to live out here in Malibu where I live and I'd see him at the market and he'd be walking up and down the aisles doing these characters. "Okay, Jonathan, it's time to buy your groceries and go now." —Cheech Marin

Think of me as a sex symbol for the men who don't give a damn. —Phyllis Diller

"EITHER I'M TALKING OR THEY'RE LAUGHING"
PHYLLIS DILLER

In the middle of the Eisenhower era, you couldn't be more out of the mainstream than to be a female comic. It took a lot of guts for a 37-year-old housewife named Phyllis Diller to work up enough material to hold down a set at San Francisco's Purple Onion in 1955. It wasn't a lark—with five kids to feed and a deadbeat husband, Diller made her nightclub debut in order to pay the bills. Even then, it wasn't easy.

Female comics were few and far between; Belle Barth and Rusty Warren had cult followings, but their hard-core raunchy material could only be found on party records or clubs with a mostly male clientele. Jean Carroll could command stylish venues and had her own television show (briefly), but she came from a longtime vaudeville background, helped up the ladder by her husband and manager. The only major showbiz experience Diller had before her debut at the Purple Onion was an appearance as a contestant on Groucho Marx's *You Bet Your Life*, where she bombed, big time.

My cooking is so bad my kids thought Thanksgiving was to commemorate Pearl Harbor.

Still, Diller had three things going for her: she had been a clever copywriter for an advertising firm, she had a gold mine of material, and she was desperate. Her scrambling existence trying to make ends meet in a San Francisco suburb proved to be her comic lifeline. "My material came from my own life, my real life of having a lot of kids, a lot of housework, a lot of cooking. I had in-laws. I had neighbors. I had stuff to hate," she said.

Housework can't kill you, but why take a chance?

For more than a decade before she hit it big, Diller was the family breadwinner, dragging her kids around the country trying to raise them in hotels, while she perfected her act. Her husband pretended he was her manager, but basically he just spent her paycheck. Then one night in a Washington nightclub, Bob Hope happened to catch her act. Diller thought she had bombed and tried to sneak out of the club, but Hope cornered her and told her she had something special. His approval boosted her confidence and changed her fortunes. "I copied Robert, because I felt he was a great role model. He knew when to go into a place and when to leave a place. Some people never learn that. But you know the shortest distance between two laughs is a one-liner."

My mother got me a hope chest. She hopes there's a chest.

Soon Diller became Hope's unofficial protégée, adopting his rapid-fire delivery for her own devices. "Hecklers would have had to make an appointment, because there's no dead air in my act," she said about her style. "Either I'm talking, or they're laughing." In return, Hope eventually hired her to costar in three films, twenty-three television specials, and six USO tours, giving her a national platform.

The TV screen in our home is so filthy, for years the kids thought they were listening to the radio.

Diller realized that if she told the story of her life—boiled down into lean, mean one-liners—she would automatically draw at least one half of the audience to her side. "I was talking about the things that women were dealing with in those days, like ironing," said Diller. "They had never heard the other side of the story. It was always the man's mother-in-law. Now it's *my* mother-in-law." Joan Rivers points out how radical Diller actually was: "She was the first one that there was such rage and such anger in her comedy. She had the anger that is now in all of us. And that's what made it so funny, because she spoke for all these women that were sitting home with five children and a husband that didn't work."

Giving comedy a lift: Diller in daffy mode; with idol, Bob Hope, on USO tour; in more elegant days, circa 1960.

I just bought a new peekaboo blouse. Men peek, then boo.

As the sixties went on and as Diller became a ubiquitous presence in nightclubs, talk shows, and on variety shows, her physical appearance became more extreme and outrageous. It was all part of the plan:

I started out looking like the girl next door. And you don't have to pay to look at that mess, you know. So, little by little, I got showbiz. I always wore the gloves. All clowns wear gloves. Mickey Mouse. I remember a lot of the male guys had a cigar. It's something to do with your hands. And I went for this 1929 flapper look. And they always had a cigarette holder. And it also gave me a reason to hold up my right hand. And I used it to show hostility.

I've been asked to say a couple of words about my husband, Fang. How about short and cheap?

Diller had a few good reasons to be hostile. She divorced her first husband in the mid-sixties, after decades of supporting him. Her second husband turned out to be gay, having affairs with other men in Diller's hotel suite while she was onstage performing. "Fang"—originally derived from "Fang-face"—became the catchall name for the men who had disappointed her and for underachieving husbands everywhere.

Fang knows nothing about sex. On our wedding night he brought a book to bed. And colored.

As the decades marched on, Diller toned down the grotesquerie of her stage appearance and joyously embraced the perks of plastic surgery. Her act, however, changed very little—a barrage of one-liners about the frustrations of being female in a domestically demanding culture, punctuated by a cackle that sounds like a combination of a wicked witch and a duck undergoing a colonoscopy. Not everyone was amused. "It was right in the beginning of women's lib and burn your bra," said Diller. "And of course, some of those pushy babes tried to make a loud noise. But screw 'em. I was doing what I do, and I was doing it well. I *was* women's lib. I told 'em to go to hell—I don't know where they went."

Diller performed stand-up at the best clubs in America for nearly half a century, all the way to a farewell concert in 2005. She outlived two husbands, but Fang still hung in there, even as her career slowed down. Her jokes may have been old, but in her gloved hands, they were younger than springtime.

You know you're old if your walker has an airbag.

I was thrown out of NYU for cheating on my metaphysics exam; I looked within the soul of the boy sitting next to me. —Woody Allen

"NOT EVEN IF IT WOULD HELP THE SPACE PROGRAM"
WOODY ALLEN

Getting a Woody: as writer and Broadway star of
Play It Again, Sam (1969), with Diane Keaton and
Jerry Lacy; confronting the classics.

I won second prize in
the contest: two weeks
at an Interfaith camp
where I was sadistically
beaten by boys of all
races and creeds.

Woody Allen still learned enough metaphysics to become a human comic version of Cartesian dualism. Influenced by both Bob Hope and Ingmar Bergman, Allen is a celebrity and a recluse, a writer-director made famous by his performances, a skinny schnook who has been romantically involved with some of the world's most glorious women, a seeming technological incompetent who has made more than three dozen pictures, a bumbler and a serious thinker, equally enthralled and terrified by those great opposing forces, sex and death.

There are even, literally, two Woody Allens: Allen Stewart Konigsberg, born in 1935 and raised in the Midwood section of Brooklyn, and Woody Allen, the nom de plume that Allen adopted when he was sixteen so that his high school friends wouldn't recognize the attributions for the jokes he was getting published by Manhattan gossip columnists at two dollars a pop. Allen grew up enamored of the plays of George S. Kaufman and the glamour of Hollywood movies. By his own admission, he was never a great student—"I wasn't literate, but my references were witty"—but that didn't stop him from writing for television shows like *The Colgate Comedy Hour* while still in his teens. He gradually worked his way up the comedy ladder, writing material for Sid Caesar's last major show, *Caesar's Hour*, sketches at the fabled Camp Tamiment, material for *The Garry Moore Show* and wound up making $1600 a week by the age of twenty-four. In 1960, he was inspired by the casual ease of Mort Sahl to perform his own material as a stand-up comedian.

Over the next eight years, Allen established himself as one of the most original, whimsical, thoughtful, and modern of the new breed of stand-up comics, and he played every venue and program, from the Village to Vegas, from *The Kraft Music Hall* to *The Tonight Show*. With his oversize glasses, gray suit, and abstracted stammer, Allen was anything but polished onstage—and that was precisely the point. The girders of his nightclub routines were the one-liners about his own ineffectuality, as both a sexual being and a human being:

> I asked my wife's best friend if she would consider committing adultery with me and she said, "Not even if it would help the space program."

But Allen could also go on wild fantastical farragoes; one famous saga involved bringing a live moose to a costume party, where it locked antlers with the Berkowitzes, a Jewish couple dressed as a moose. The sheer inventiveness of Allen's outlook was breathtaking. Comedy writer Alan Zweibel observed that "it was all tongue-in-cheek, but you went along for this ride, so he was able to go in and out of this fictitious world and the world that you're sure he did, in fact, live in." In the early sixties, Dick Cavett was working for *The Tonight Show* and was sent to scout Allen in a nightclub appearance. "He was bombing with the most brilliant material line for line I had ever heard. I remember realizing this is not the average comedy writer when he described an unpleasant-looking young woman as, facially, resembling Louis Armstrong's voice. Now you knew this was not a gag writer of the cheapest kind."

As the 1960s ended, Allen's stand-up career was doing very well; he wasn't. The grind was simply too much. As he told biographer Eric Lax, "When I was in a nightclub, I couldn't eat breakfast, knowing I was going to perform at ten o'clock at night. . . . The simple difference between being alone or not is all the difference in the world." Allen had had some success contributing to (and making supporting appearances in) the screenplays of some wacky comedies (and even more success as a Broadway playwright), but it was time to take center stage in, and control of, his own work. Allen originally offered his screenplay of *Take the Money and Run* to Jerry Lewis, but when Lewis begged off, the 1969 release became the first of nearly forty films written, directed, and (often) starring Woody Allen. The crime story "mockumentary" performed well enough, but more importantly it gave Allen a chance to retrofit the comic persona of his idol for his own purposes.

"Right up until my teens, I tried to act like Bob Hope and make the jokes and snap off the one-liners effortlessly," he said. He also told interviewer Richard Schickel, "To me, probably, Hope is the biggest comic influence on my performing. . . . I think that I do Bob Hope all the time. I'm just nowhere as good, but he's all over my work in a shameless way." (Another comedian was a different story, according to Allen: "Because I wore these glasses, people used to make the Harold Lloyd comparisons, and the ones that didn't like me would say, 'Glasses do not make him a Harold Lloyd.' Now, the truth of the matter is I never liked Harold Lloyd. He's never been an influence on me or someone that I've really appreciated.")

Because of the increased sexual openness of the neurotic 1970s, Allen's attempts to get the girl in his movies were more fraught with tension, anxiety, and frankness. "He touched a nerve," said Mort Sahl, the man who inspired Allen to start performing. "Instead of being a friend of the leading man, he was the leading man. And the dilemma of him was reflected by the audience saying it's the dilemma of all of us: 'I want to meet that girl.' 'You can't meet that girl, Woody. I'm telling you she's trouble.' And the only thing that's interesting about her to Woody is that she *is* trouble."

What allowed Allen to transcend his nebbishy persona—which might have gotten simply irritating over the years—was the fact that, implicitly, audiences knew he wasn't really that incompetent. He might say, as he did in *Crimes and Misdemeanors*, that "My love life is terrible. The last time I was inside a woman was when I visited the Statue of Liberty," but anyone who read a newspaper knew it wasn't true. At the age of nineteen, Allen got married, but it was a painful five-year experience. True to the comedian's form, Allen recycled his frustrations, at one point, telling the audience of *The Dick Cavett Show*, "My ex-wife is suing me for a million dollars, because I made an amusing remark about her. She came home late at night, and was violated. Knowing my ex-wife, it was not a moving violation." He went on to have highly publicized affairs (and working relationships) with Louise Lasser (whom he also married), Diane Keaton, and Mia Farrow. Still, he couldn't let the old gags go. When asked how fame affected him, Allen responded, "I get rejected by a higher class of women." His witty self-deprecation made him the hero of an entire generation. "A lot of people got laid in college because Woody Allen was this skinny, bespectacled guy who could be a role model for them," said writer Anne Beatts.

As Allen's career achieved monumental proportions in the late 1970s and early 1980s (he remains the most nominated screenwriter in Academy Award history and has won three Oscars), he also expanded into a literary career, becoming the first real "come-

WOODY: That's quite a lovely Jackson Pollock, isn't it?

MUSEUM GIRL: Yes, it is.

WOODY: What does it say to you?

MUSEUM GIRL: It restates the negativeness of the universe. The hideous lonely emptiness of existence. Nothingness. The predicament of Man forced to live in a barren, Godless eternity like a tiny flame flickering in an immense void with nothing but waste, horror and degradation, forming a useless bleak straitjacket in a black absurd cosmos.

WOODY: What are you doing Saturday night?

MUSEUM GIRL: Committing suicide.

WOODY: What about Friday night? —*Play It Again, Sam*

Early, funny ones:
Woody, about to lose his head in *Everything You Always Wanted to Know About Sex* (1972); time traveler in *Sleeper* (1973); Russian around in *Love and Death* (1975).

dian of letters" since Will Rogers, writing short stories for *The New Yorker*, book reviews, and plays. His general comic persona (and his glasses) remained the same over the years—as historian Gerald Nachman put it, "He played to our own self-consciousness about everything, a guy we could really identify with, because he was ill at ease in almost every situation"—but his very deftness belied that persona. Dick Cavett pointed out, "Much of his comedy is based on his life, as almost everyone's is. But it wasn't a duplicate of his life. If he were the character that he played, he wouldn't have been able to write that stuff. That's sort of ironic, isn't it?" The dichotomy is plainly apparent to Allen, as he told Eric Lax:

> I play a guy who lives in New York—or who sounds like he lives in New York—who's believable in a certain amount of things, and has a certain limited range . . . and I can do that decently well, but I can't go beyond that. And so I wear my own clothes, and I sound like me, and I wear these glasses and I look like me, and people think that there's either very little similarity or no similarity between me onstage and off.

His more serious endeavors have sometimes alienated fans and critics—even actual aliens:

> WOODY: But shouldn't I stop making movies and do something that counts, like, like helping blind people or becoming a missionary or something?
> ALIEN: Let me tell you, you're not the missionary type. You'd never last. And, and incidentally, you're also not Superman; you're a comedian. You want to do mankind a real service? Tell funnier jokes. We love your films, especially the early, funny ones.
>
> *–Stardust Memories*

Allen contends that it was not the audience that left him—rather, *he* left *them* and moved on to other avenues that provoked his inquiring mind. But to his eternal credit, Allen continues to plug along, making, on average, one intensely personal film a year (interestingly, the films he admires most are not his fans' favorites, and vice versa). He has inspired several generations of comedians, including Jason Alexander, who frankly admits that his first audition for the character of George Costanza was a rip-off of Allen: "To me he's one of the great innovators in my lifetime. He has spawned a whole bunch of guys . . . the nebbish comics, the Will Ferrells, the Steve Carells, Adam Sandler, Ben Stiller. It all goes directly to Woody Allen."

"His one regret in life is that he is not someone else," concluded the bio on the dust jacket on his first collection of short stories. As a kid, he was fascinated by magic (as were Johnny Carson, Dick Cavett, and Steve Martin), and he considers his career to be "a brilliant illusion that has lasted now over fifty years and includes scores of movies." There's something wistful about the childhood conjurer who still believes in the power—and the relief—of transformation. Mort Sahl summed it up:

> Woody Allen had said that when he saw me it changed his life. The perception of what you could do. So then I go to thank him, and I isolate him at a party, and I say, "Thank you for saying I changed your life." And he says, "Mort, can you change it back?"

Psychological Warfare

By Woody Allen
(Originally produced at Camp Tamiment, 1958)

(SCENE: IN ONE. A BARREN BATTLEFIELD WITH PERHAPS A BARBED WIRE POST. FROM SR A GROUP OF MEN ENTER. THEY ARE DRESSED EXACTLY LIKE AMERICAN G.I.S. THEY CARRY NO WEAPONS. ONE IS A SGT. WHILE THE OTHERS ARE PVTS. THE AUTHENTICITY OF REAL WAR MUST BE ACHIEVED.)

SGT.
Company–halt! Men, in a minute we're going to meet the enemy. We've got to take this island. They've got it well fortified. They're brutal, clever, and extremely dangerous. Get ready for a savage battle. Are there any questions?

PVT.
(RAISING HIS HAND LIKE A SCHOOLBOY)
May I leave the war!?

SGT.
I know how you feel, Private, but try to have courage.

PVT.
I'd feel so much better, sir, if we were using guns.

SGT.
I'm surprised at you men. You know guns went out of style after the last war. Times change. Right now we use a much greater weapon than mere firearms. Psychological warfare. Hit them in the ego—hit them in the id—hit them in their inferiority complexes—and if that doesn't work, hit them below the belt and we'll go back to the old way! ...Okay now men—get ready. We're going to charge. And remember—we may be using psychological warfare but this is still war. Now let's go!
(THEY CHARGE, PERHAPS TO THE OMINOUS BEATING OF A KETTLE DRUM. THE PRIVATES CHARGE RIGHT OFF STAGE. THE SGT. ADVANCES AND AN ENEMY SOLDIER ENTERS FROM SL. THEY NOTICE ONE ANOTHER, CIRCLE ONE ANOTHER, STALKING THEIR GAME. SUDDENLY THEY BEGIN THEIR BATTLE.)

SGT. (CONT'D)
You're too short! You're too short and your mother never loved you!

ENEMY
You're a nail biter and you still have to sleep with a light on in the room!

SGT.
You're a failure in life! You buy all your clothes at Klein's!

ENEMY
I'M a failure? –You live in Westport with your own wife!

SGT.
Now just a minute! Leave my sex life out of this!

ENEMY
Aha – a weak spot! Sure it's a weak spot. You don't need saltpeter in your food!

SGT.
That's not true! Women love me, I'd bet my wife on it! Uh!

ENEMY
You'd bet your wife on it—there's an interesting slip!

SGT.
What I meant by that was—!

ENEMY
I know exactly what you meant. You big, fat, neurotic! You know, I don't think you could surrender even if you wanted to!

SGT.
Ooooh! I can too surrender!

ENEMY
Oh, you can surrender!

SGT.
Now wait a minute, you're getting me confused...!

ENEMY
(PUTTING HIS ARM ON SGT.'S SHOULDER GRAVELY)
You're a very sick boy, you know that.

SGT.
Please, give me a chance to think...!

ENEMY
Everybody's staring at you! Unloved, rejected, crazy!

SGT.
(BEGINS TO STAGGER WILDLY AS HE AMBLES TOWARD WINGS)
It's no use —I'm hit! Medic! Stretcherbearer! Stretcher! I'm wounded!
(TWO MEDICS RUN OUT HOLDING INSTEAD OF A STRETCHER, A COUCH. THE WOUNDED SGT. HOPS ON IT LIKE A MAN MOUNTING A STRETCHER AND THE TWO MEDICS RUN OFF WITH HIM LIKE THEY WERE TAKING OFF A WOUNDED MAN. HE LIES IN THE CLASSIC ANALYSIS POSITION.)
It all began when I was a little boy– my father hit me!

BLACKOUT

Comedy Albums

Recordings have revolved around comedy as long as there have been recordings. Monologuist Cal Stewart recorded several jokes as the rustic "Uncle Josh" as far back as 1897. The first recorded comedy sensation was probably a comedian named Joe Hayman, who put out a series of routines about a Jewish immigrant besieged by technology, most famously "Cohen on the Telephone," which came out in 1913. Comedy songs were particularly popular; every vaudeville or musical comedy star worth his or her salt, such as Eddie Cantor or Fanny Brice, waxed their choice bits. By the time these celebrities moved to radio in the early 1930s, there was so much comedy on the airwaves to be had for free that few people bought comedy recordings. In the late 1940s, bandleader Spike Jones had some big successes with his novelty numbers like "Der Führer's Face" and his frenetic desecrations of pop standards such as "Cocktails for Two."

But unlike popular songs, which were routinely crafted in three-minute segments, comedy was a victim of 78 rpm technology; the listener might get a "bit" from a comedian, but rarely a routine and never an entire performance. When the long-playing record came along in 1948, it provided around forty-five minutes of playing time, but even then comedy took awhile to catch fire. Listeners could purchase repackaged episodes of old radio comedy shows, but among the few pioneers to lay down tracks of original comedy in the 1950s were the eccentric hipster guru Lord Buckley, the radio parodist Stan Freberg (who had a hit single with his spoof of TV crime shows, "St. George and the Dragonet"), and Tom Lehrer, whose first album came out on a ten-inch LP.

The first comedy album of the modern age was Mort Sahl's *The Future Lies Ahead*, released on Verve in 1958. Norman Granz was a pioneering jazz record producer and signed Sahl to record his routines in front of a live audience (an unauthorized recording of a Sahl concert had been taped in 1955). Sahl's records did very well and his largesse extended to his colleague Shelley Berman, who was making a name for himself performing comic monologues in nightclubs in Chicago and on the West Coast. Berman recalls how Sahl changed his career with a simple suggestion:

Mort said, "Hey, I've made a record with Verve. Why don't you do the same thing?" I said, "Oh, my God, put all of my material on a record? Forget about it! I'll never be able to do it. Because the surprise will be gone and everybody will know my stuff." And Mort said, "Go on, try it." So the technicians came for two nights, or something like that, at the hungry i and just went to town recording me. And one day I saw my record in a window. An LP. With a picture of me. And they picked a title, *Inside Shelley Berman*. I was pretty thrilled about that. And then somebody told me I was on the charts. I said, "What the hell is that?" I didn't know a thing. And suddenly I was handed a tremendous check for my royalties. And there, now, I realized, "My God, I'm a star." I had no idea it would be so successful. I had no idea that it would make such a big difference in our industry.

Inside Shelley Berman is generally regarded as the first hit comedy album and was the first full album to win a Grammy in the Spoken Word Comedy category in 1959 (The only other previous Grammy for comedy went to—eek!—the single "The Chipmunk Song"). It now occurred to producers (and listeners) that they could recreate the best forty-five minutes of a comedian's live set; it also occurred to the comedians that they could reach a much larger audience. This innovation changed the life of a former accountant from Chicago who had been playing around with a tape deck, expounding on some funny phone calls he had made with another pal at work. His name was Bob Newhart:

I had three routines, I had the "Driving Instructor," the "Submarine Commander," and "Abe Lincoln." So, a disc jockey friend of mine, Dan Sorkin, in Chicago, said that the Warner Brothers record executives were coming through town, calling on Dan and some of the other top disc jockeys. Dan called me up. He said, "Put what you have on tape and I'll play it for them." So I put them on tape, brought it down there, they listened to it. And they said, "Okay, okay, we'll give you a recording contract, and we'll record your next nightclub." And I said, "Well, we have kind of a problem there, I've never played a nightclub." So they said, "Well, we'll have to get you into a nightclub." So my first date was at Tidelands in Houston, Texas. It was the first time I ever walked out on a nightclub floor.

The resulting thirty-two-minute album, *The Button-Down Mind of Bob Newhart*, was released early in 1960; it zoomed to the top of the charts—not the comedy charts but the Billboard charts for *all* of popular music. "It just went crazy," said Newhart. Later that year, Warner Bros. put out a sequel, *The Button-Down Mind Strikes Back!*—and that album shot to number one. In fact, both of Newhart's albums occupied the top two spots for nearly thirty weeks, a record not surpassed until 1991 when Guns N' Roses took the top two spots. Newhart is a good loser: "And I always say, 'Well, you hate to lose a record but at least it went to a friend.'"

The comedy album phenomenon of the 1960s brought comics into living

rooms around the country in a variety of ways. Albums of mainstream artists like Berman, Newhart, Nichols and May, the Smothers Brothers, or Jonathan Winters were a way for fans to remember favorite routines that they had seen on *Ed Sullivan* or a television talk show. For comedians under the radar, such as Dick Gregory, Carl Reiner and Mel Brooks, or Tom Lehrer, it was a way to attract a cult following. For an artist like Bill Cosby, his albums—he had three top ten records between 1966 and 1968—were a way of keeping his persona in the public imagination while waiting for better television or film projects to percolate. Albums also were the only way that raunchier comedians like Lenny Bruce could reach a larger audience; Redd Foxx had a cottage industry with "party records"—records of blue material that cultivated a huge underground nationwide audience. The comedy album also exploded at an odd confluence of technology and society; it allowed a sophisticated audience, for the first time, to have unfiltered access to extended passages of mature comedy. Newhart sees the phenomenon as a matter of shifting consumer demographics: "Nightclubs had kind of priced themselves out as far as a young family was concerned; they became quite expensive. So my understanding was that a lot of the college kids and the young marrieds would get together at somebody's house and they'd have pizza and beer and they'd play a comedy album."

College radio stations and inventive FM disc jockeys were eager to promote their cult favorites (and as Cheech Marin said, playing an entire side of a comedy album allowed a DJ to go out for a smoke) and provided huge exposure. For the right kind of performer, many college students and young marrieds would be willing to shell out the $4.99 for an album. Singer-parodist Allan Sherman sold millions of records from 1962 to 1964. The most bizarre success in comedy album history occurred when a young comedian named Vaughn Meader released a studio album parodying the Kennedys called *The First Family*. From the get-go, the album was a rarity; it was conceived and recorded in a studio, rather than being a memento of a live club date. Stations around the country refused to play it, but in the more sophisticated New York area, it got some air play. Soon, orders for *The First Family* turned into a deluge; released on October 22, 1962, the album became the fastest-selling album of any kind in history and eventually sold an unprecedented 7.5 million copies. Exactly one year and one month after its release, *The First Family* was transformed into a cruel jest and copies were pulled off the shelves. On the evening after Kennedy's assassination, Lenny Bruce was playing a club date, and the audience eagerly anticipated how Bruce would comment on the national tragedy. He did not disappoint; his first words were "Vaughn Meader is *screwed*." And, indeed, he was.

Comedy recordings turned a major corner in 1972 with two releases each by George Carlin (*FM & AM* and *Class Clown*) and Cheech and Chong (*Cheech and Chong* and *Big Bambú*). These were albums geared primarily to college students and best listened to in semidarkness with a bong close

at hand, preferably while there was a term paper that needed to be written. Most importantly, these albums presented routines that were not recoverable by other means—they would never have been performed intact on network television (indeed, all of Cheech and Chong's albums were produced in the studio). When Richard Pryor hit the scene with *That Nigger's Crazy* in 1974, it firmly established the comedy album as the lingua franca of the counterculture. These records could not be listened to in the company of your Aunt Sue, like Cosby's Fat Albert fables, but nor were they the fringe albums of Lord Buckley and Moms Mabley. They were huge, huge commercial hits, and all of the albums listed above went gold (selling over $1 million), as did practically every other album by Carlin, Cheech and Chong, and Pryor in the 1970s. (Albums by Robert Klein, David Steinberg, Lily Tomlin, and various crews from *National Lampoon* deserve a nod as well.)

A hit album was so integral to a comedian's fortunes in the mid-1970s that Steve Martin went through the tortures of the damned trying to get his routines on vinyl. When he finally succeeded with *Let's Get Small* in 1977, Martin not only won the Grammy (beating Pryor's three-in-a-row streak), he became the first comedian with a platinum album (over $2 million in sales). He was such an immense figure at the time that his next album, *A Wild and Crazy Guy*, went platinum before it was even shipped to stores. It was a magical time for recorded comedy; comedians had become the popular equivalent of rock stars.

Yet all magical things must come to an end. Two new trends converged to curtail the glory days of the comedy album. When Richard Pryor filmed *Richard Pryor—Live in Concert* in 1978 (and, four years later, *Richard Pryor Live on the Sunset Strip*), he brought the full effect of a sold-out concert experience to a national audience (provided they were over seventeen years old). By the mid-1980s, home video and cable television were so ubiquitous that they obviated the voice-only appeal of the comedy album. (It must be admitted that it *was* often irritating not knowing what visual gag some idiot in the audience was cackling at.) Oddly enough, the CD, which did damage to other aspects of the recording industry, has been a boon to comedy, with elegant and encyclopedic boxed sets of the albums of Lenny Bruce, George Carlin, and Reiner and Brooks, among many others. And contemporary acts such as Chris Rock, Adam Sandler, and Jeff Foxworthy have done very well with CD releases of their work; Foxworthy has sold over four million copies of *You Might Be a Redneck If . . .*, making it the biggest-selling comedy album of all time.

Still, for a twenty-year stretch, there was something special—an unrepeatable confluence of social habits and technology—about listening to a comedy LP on your turntable. As David Steinberg put it, "Just one person giving you a barrage of ideas that was how you thought and how you talked amongst yourselves—that had never happened before. So the albums were huge—they made sense in comedy because it's all about your ear, what you're hearing, what you try and repeat."

"I HOPE YOU'RE NOT PLANNING ON DOING ANYTHING FOR—THE NEXT COUPLE OF MONTHS"

CHEECH & CHONG

There was an entire generation of youngsters who spent their after-school revelry in front of a black-and-white television set watching reruns of old Three Stooges shorts. When they grew up and shuffled off to college, many of them desired the same kind of sublime, simple silliness, only better attuned to the preoccupations of those who preferred to turn on, tune in, and drop out. For that gang, the twin gods were the child of an East L.A. Mexican-American family and the son of a Chinese truck driver and his Scotch-Irish wife, raised in the Canadian Rockies: Cheech and Chong.

In 1969, Tommy Chong, a former Motown musician, was running a rough-hewn strip club in Alberta, Canada, when Richard "Cheech" Marin stopped by looking for work.

The club's clientele were a hard-to-please bunch of hippies and obstreperous bikers. Chong thought Marin would be helpful in keeping the audience entertained between strippers; Cheech was pleased: "I got five dollars more for hanging out with naked chicks than I did delivering carpets. It wasn't much of a choice." Cheech and Chong alternated between playing music and coming up with outrageous skits—anything to help in the arduous task of getting this particular crowd's attention. "Basically, we were doing hippie burlesque," recalled Marin. "We had tons of skits and the girls would come out and they would take off their clothes. And to this day it was the best time I ever had in my life, you know?"

They eventually moved down to Los Angeles, where they had a better chance of finding an audience that would embrace their counterculture philosophy and Marin's ethnic background. Cheech and Chong developed a series of non sequitur routines that embraced the experiences of the hippies, hangers-on, slackers, and potheads basking in the temperate climate and purple haze of Southern California. Cheech, the more volatile of the two, took on the exaggerated characters with insane voices, like the substitute Catholic schoolteacher, Sister Mary Elephant, who bellowed out "SHUT UUUPPP!!" like a deranged air raid siren. Chong could always be counted on to grasp the last remnant of sanity in his imperturbable, blissed-out way. Even the Three Stooges aspired to some form of employment in the pictures—bakers, plumbers, and so on—and Abbott and Costello tried to become part of the social fabric, but Cheech and Chong had no such exalted goals. "Cheech and Chong were cosmic characters who lived in the here and now," said Marin. "Basically the problem when we woke up in the morning was how to find a joint. But the search of them finding the joint led us throughout the counterculture and all the characters we encountered."

A lot of characters out there encountered Cheech and Chong through their first two record albums, *Cheech and Chong* and *Big Bambú* (whose jacket resembled a package for rolling paper), both released in 1972. They went gold within months, as would their next two albums. The team found their core audience among the millions of misfits and stoners who not only got every reference, but were living them. Other comedians had made booze

CHEECH: That's some heavy shit, man. Hey man, am I driving ok?

CHONG: I think we're parked, man.

CHEECH: Shit. What was in that shit, man? I ain't never had no dope like that before in my life. Man, that's the heaviest shit I ever smoked, man, I smoked a lot of shit before, man, but that's heavy shit.

CHONG: You OK?

CHEECH: I can't breathe, I can't breathe, man.

CHONG: Hey, I got something that will mellow you out.

CHEECH: I ain't never—

CHONG: Take these.

CHEECH: What is that, man?

CHONG: Just take them. Hey, don't take those. I almost gave you the wrong shit, man.

CHEECH: I just took them.

CHONG: Hey, wooooah. You just took the most acid I ever seen anybody take in my life. I hope you're not planning on doing anything for—the next couple of months.

a part of their act—Dean Martin, Jackie Gleason—but the fans of Cheech and Chong had little interest and no ready cash for Jack Daniels. Acapulco Gold was another story, and if Cheech and Chong met their audiences in a low-profile manner that resembled a drug deal, that was just fine.

"We didn't do a lot of TV ever and that was every comedian's goal at the time—'I'm gonna get to be on TV, be on *Ed Sullivan*.' And we had no interest in that at all. We made records in the days when they were black and they were about this big and, and we did concerts, you know? We were on FM radio and we went to the people," said Marin.

Eventually, their fans demanded a larger arena, and in 1978, Cheech and Chong made a film, *Up in Smoke*, which cost a modest $2 million and wound up grossing $47.5 million domestically, making it both the highest grossing comedy and the most profitable film released that year. Though they were essentially creating the "dumb and dumber" genre, their characters remained true to their own backgrounds. Cheech played a Chicano lowrider named Pedro de Pacas and Chong, not to overtax himself, played "Man."

As the 1980s began, Cheech and Chong turned more to movies than to albums, but it was hard to recapture the magic. The Reagan era had made "Just Say No" its motto, and an increasing number of former fans grew up, got real jobs, and just said no to the antics of Cheech and Chong. Still, they were immensely formative, not only as a brilliantly matched comedy team—"We had the same kind of point of view, we were a lot like Laurel and Hardy in that we had two brains sharing one thought," said Marin—but as the first slacker comedy team. "Cheech and Chong was, like, the first dumb guys I heard doing comedy," observes comedian Jeffrey Ross. "They were a little bit slower paced—almost like two Gracie Allens. I was too young at the time to really appreciate it as stoner humor. But I did understand there was plenty of dirtbags hanging out at the 7-Eleven. And for me, Cheech and Chong gave voice to these idiots that I knew around the neighborhood."

Ironically, for all their chatter and blather about drug use and drug paraphernalia, Cheech and Chong were consummate professionals who, literally, played it straight. And if they lit up—as it were—millions of smiles across America, it was because, underneath their weird hairdos, tie-dyed shirts, and do-rags, they were kind of adorable. As Cheech Marin put it:

Contrary to popular belief, we never worked high, ever. It just interfered with our timing and our process. We were popular because we were not threatening. We were the guys who said that the emperor has no clothes on and in a very funny way. My philosophy's always been to slip it in the coffee, you know, and you get the exact same thing but it goes down easier and everybody's fine. . . .

Reefer gladness:
(previous page) In *Up in Smoke* (1978); taking a break; hit album.

I have decided to give the greatest performance of my life! Oh, wait, sorry, that's tomorrow night.
—Steve Martin

"I'M JUST A WILD AND CRAZY GUY"
STEVE MARTIN

WE ARE TWO SWINGING GUYS WHO ENJOY DOING MANY THINGS AND CAN COME ON TO YOU NOW. LOOK AT OUR SLACKS—IT IS BECAUSE OF YOU FOXES THAT OUR POUCHES ARE STRETCHING.

Lunar looney:
Martin mocking a showbiz entrance and (below) as a Festrunk brother on *SNL* with Dan Aykroyd. Right: Starring in *The Jerk* (1979).

For a long time, it seemed to Steve Martin that the greatest performance of his life was always going to happen some other night. In *Born Standing Up*, his 2007 memoir about his early years as a comedian, he began by writing, "I did stand-up comedy for eighteen years. Ten of those years were spent learning, four years were spent refining, and four were spent in wild success."

Shortly after Disneyland opened in Anaheim in 1955, a quiet, stagestruck ten-year-old kid named Steve Martin biked over from his home less than two miles away and applied for a job selling guidebooks to the amusement park. He got the job, making two cents on the quarter, but better than that, Martin was free to roam the most magical kingdom in America. He became entranced with the card tricks, joke books, and silly props at the park's Merlin's Magic Shop, and within five years he had mastered sleight of hand and was performing behind the counter eight hours a day. To Martin, the make-believe world of magic appeared a lot more real than the dreary reality of high school. By the time he left Disneyland at eighteen to perform at another nearby amusement park, Martin had acquired a bag of magic tricks, a banjo, juggling balls, some very old jokes, and a nice sense of the absurd. As he began his career as a performer, this last would come in very handy.

"I moved to Knott's Berry Farm, where I did my act four times a day," Martin told *The New Yorker*. "I bought all these props which I saw as ironic. I thought they were dumb, really dumb, and I was trying to be pointless. In lots of my early shows, people would just look at each other." Martin would juggle all these elements—sometimes literally—hoping, through trial and error, to find a style that would make an audience happy; soon, he realized it was better to make himself happy. "I took out everything from my act that didn't seem original. I didn't want anyone in the audience to say, 'Oh, *that*.'"

In between low-paying gigs at coffeehouses and folk clubs, Martin had to make a living. He got his first big career break in 1967, when, through the intervention of an old girlfriend, he was hired as a staff writer for *The Smothers Brothers Comedy Hour*. The satirical recklessness of that program inspired Martin to pursue his own vision, and in between writing assignments he plied his unique stand-up trade, eventually getting high-profile gigs on the talk show circuit. More often than not, middlebrow audiences were bewildered by his non sequitur inversions of show-biz clichés. Martin pressed forward anyway. Once during an appearance on *The Tonight Show*, he offered a calculation that every second, hundreds of thousands of new viewers across the country were switching on the program; if the studio audience played along with Martin by guffawing at some senseless joke that he cracked, entire swatches of the population would be scratching their heads, going, "Huh?" That was just fine with Martin, as he related in his memoir:

What if there were no punch lines? What if there were no indicators? What if I created tension and never released it? What if I headed for a climax, but all I delivered was an anticlimax? . . . The audience would eventually pick their own place to laugh, essentially out of desperation. This type of laugh seemed stronger to me.

Martin's brand of comedy was helped by a generational shift as the 1970s began. A new group of young people were dismayed by the phoniness they saw all around them, but unlike the disaffected youth of the 1960s, they didn't think angry political stances held much of an answer, either. These youngsters were repelled by the cornball platitudes of their parents' generation yet were still drawn to the television set. It was the perfect audience for Martin's blend of showbiz pomposity and a carefully contrived obliviousness to its artificiality. One Martin routine went:

> Hi, I am the world's greatest comedian. Thank you. Thank you very much. This is too much. I didn't expect this. Thank you. I'd like to start off with an old gag, I haven't really perfected it, yet it's always funny no matter how many times you've seen it. It's the old "forgetting your own name" gag. This is where I start to say my own name and then suddenly I pretend I forgot it. I haven't perfected this yet, but it's something that's really funny. The old "forgetting your own name" gag: "Hi, folks, I'm Steve Martin!"—oh, I blew it!

When Martin saw the television debut of *Saturday Night Live* in October of 1975, he reacted with a simple, "Fuck!" As he later clarified, "I thought I was usurped, but it worked to my advantage." *Saturday Night Live* became Martin's second home. Not only did he appear on the show twenty-three times, hosting it a record fourteen times, but he proved to be the best sport they ever had. One of his greatest creations there (with Dan Aykroyd) was one of the "wild-and-crazy" Festrunk Brothers, whose mismatched plaid outfits were as obstreperous as their pathetic pickup lines: "We are two swinging guys who enjoy doing many things and can come on to you now. Look at our slacks—it is because of you foxes that our pouches are stretching."

Saturday Night Live also allowed Martin direct access to his core audience—millions of young misfits who were engaged, rather than bewildered, by a comedian who twisted balloons into unrecognizable shapes and played the banjo while wearing an arrow through his head as if it were the most natural thing in the world. "If you're opening for a rock act, you can't come out and say, 'So, these two guys walk into a bar, and one guy says to the other guy'—You have to have an arrow through your head to get their attention," said Bob Newhart. "That's how Steve got their attention. They'd say, 'Who is that, who is that crazy man up there acting like that?'" His fans provided Martin with the happiest transformation imaginable: instead of opening for rock stars, Martin now *was* a rock star.

He brilliantly juxtaposed the totally not cool and the cool. While performing near-spastic antics—the kind that would get you beaten up in the school lunchroom—Martin's appearance was attractive, even elegant. "He's a misfit. He looks like an insurance salesman, but he has crazy feet," said Carl Reiner, who would direct him in four films. "A handsome man doing funny things is funnier to me than a funny-looking man doing funny things. You get the best of two worlds." Martin adopted a three-piece white suit in order to be better seen in the larger and larger concert venues he was playing (and so that his shirt wouldn't stick out of his pants); it wound up enhancing his comic persona. "[The suit] picked up on something conventional in the best sense," he said. "Conservative. And it was going nicely against the material I was doing."

By 1977, Martin was making history by playing outdoor amphitheaters and hockey stadiums; audiences were nearing 50,000 a concert. It was unprecedented and, for Martin, it was increasingly wearisome. Said Martin:

He was a breed apart. Somebody different. And when we did *The Jerk* I realized how very very funny and subtly funny he is. And what a weird bent mind he has. It's a good bent mind. Bent well. Angular, we call it.

—Carl Reiner

In a huge concert, there is no individuality. There is nothing that happens that you can take advantage of because ninety percent of the audience isn't aware of it so you're really doing comedy and conducting at the same time. When I was in the smaller clubs, they didn't know what they were going to see, but here they already knew what they were going to see so it was another kind of agreement; it was, "I don't care if I've seen it before, I'm going to now demonstrate how funny I think this is."

Although Martin had become, in his words, "the biggest concert comedian in show business, ever," it was time to branch out. He had an idea for a movie that exploded out of a line in his act. "He comes out and this white-faced, white-haired man says, 'I was born a poor black child.' That's his line, and that was the basis of the whole movie," remembered Carl Reiner, who directed the film, called *The Jerk*. In *The Jerk*, Martin played Navin Johnson who was, indeed, born and raised as a poor black child, and the film chronicles his Candide-like adventures from rags to riches. Navin is a complete misfit, a trusting Baby Huey (one of Martin's favorite comic book characters growing up) squeezed into the frame of Martin's good-looking naïf. The film, released at Christmastime 1979, exploded into a $43 million hit, and Martin's appreciation of the film set led to a new direction; he walked away from stand-up completely. "The movies were very social: you saw people, you worked together on a bit; you were doing something different every day rather than the same thing every day. I just knew I couldn't keep going at it. It was time to try and change."

Toast of the town:
With Michael Caine in *Dirty Rotten Scoundrels* (1988); balloonatic.

Martin filled the movie screens of the 1980s with a gallery of bumptious outsiders: an ineffectual mad scientist (*The Man with Two Brains*); an urban lonely guy (*The Lonely Guy*); a lawyer possessed by the spirit of Lily Tomlin (*All of Me*); a sadistic dentist (*Little Shop of Horrors*); a cretinous con man (*Dirty Rotten Scoundrels*). Most of them were hits, and with *Roxanne*, a modern update of *Cyrano de Bergerac*, which he also wrote, Martin segued into becoming a credible and charming leading man. Twenty years later, Martin has evolved into an elder statesman of American comedy (he hosted the Academy Awards twice) as well as a sophisticated art collector and acclaimed fiction writer and playwright. His career seems to be all about transitions, and Martin is clever enough to embrace change in the right spirit: "In my movie career I played outsiders—*The Jerk*—and insiders—*Father of the Bride*—but there's a certain point where, as you get older, you just cannot be so silly as you were when you were younger because it starts to look pathetic," he said.

There is nothing pathetic about the achievements of American comedy's first rock star. How could anyone who seemed to be having so much fun seem pathetic? The rest of us—well, as Martin used to sing in his act, accompanied by his banjo—that's another story:

> I see people going to college
> For fourteen years
> Studying to be doctors and lawyers
> And I see people going to work
> At the drugstore at 7:30 every morning
> To sell Flair pens
>
> But the most amazing thing to me is
> I get paid
> For doing
> This.

"We're young, we're gifted, and we're Nerds. It's our turn to be popular," wheezed Gilda Radner's septum-challenged, concave-chested Lisa Loopner during her debut on the January, 28, 1978, broadcast of *Saturday Night Live*.

"**THAT'S SO FUNNY I FORGOT TO LAUGH**"
GILDA RADNER

Among the eight talented performers of *Saturday Night Live*'s first five seasons, Radner took her turn to be popular as well; certainly no other performer on the show was embraced in the hearts of so many members of the audience. "She just had this amazing persona because she had this desire to be loved," said her friend and *SNL* writer Anne Beatts. "She was, like, 'Love me love me love me love me.' And people really responded to that. And she would do anything, I mean, she would bang into the wall. And did."

Radner was born in Detroit, nine months after the end of World War II, to a Russian Jewish family. Her father ran a successful hotel in town, and many famous nightclub entertainers performed there. Gilda, already named after a Rita Hayworth heroine, was starstruck at an early age. The first wall she banged into was her father's death, when she was a teenager, and it hit her hard. "She was also heavy," recounted Alan Zweibel, another close friend and *SNL* writer. "So, the death of a Dad and being fat, that was a little bit of a combo platter there, that certainly is a really good recipe to be funny. How else do you survive?"

Gilda went across the border to follow a boyfriend to Canada, worked briefly on a children's television show, and then did improv at Toronto's Second City. She came to New York to perform in the *National Lampoon Show*, where producer Lorne Michaels saw her: she was the first of the Not Ready for Prime Time Players to be hired for *Saturday Night Live*. Through the first five seasons of the program, Radner became the show's heart, winning the audience over with her gallery of misguided misfits. There seemed to be few risks she was not willing to take, whether it was gluing fake armpit hair on to parody Patti Smith, or slamming full throttle into a bedroom door as the hyperactive little girl, Judy Miller:

> And now it's time for the Judy Miller Show!!!!!! Yea!!! And now presenting the beautiful star of our show—here she is, folks, Miss Judy Miller! I am the most beautiful bride in the whole wide world!!!!!

"Part of the charm of Gilda was the child inside of her, that she was not afraid to access," said Zweibel. "She felt comfortable in the world that's in the head of children."

Perhaps her greatest risk-taking revolved around her ability to endow each of her unforgettable characters with a humiliating flaw that would have, in less sensitive hands, consigned them to social marginalization. Her version of Barbara Walters combined a speech impediment with a gargantuan ego: "I mean, wewwy, who does deserve to be Fiwst Wady? Me, Baba Wawa, Fiwst Wady of tewevision." Emily Litella, the "Weekend Update" contributor, incapable of getting the simplest facts straight, was continually railing against "Violins on Television" or "Soviet Jewelry." There was "always something" over-the-top about newscaster Roseanne Rosannadanna, who never seemed to understand the most basic rules of taste or etiquette:

> Sometimes I look at myself and I say, "I'm OK, you're OK," "I'm my own best friend," "Yes, I can," "My erogenous zones," "I am woman, hear me roar"—ROAR!!

No matter how egregious the faux pas of her characters, no matter how goofy they seemed to be, *they* always thought they were perfectly fine; that's because Radner did, too. Anne Beatts remembered that "She once said that she thought comedy originated for her when you're little and you fall down on the ice? And people might laugh at you so you try and make it seem like you fell on purpose? That was the root of her comedy." Nowhere was that more apparent than with Lisa Loopner, the girl nerd who, despite the fact that her breasts were, in her words, "miserable maraschino cherries," still radiated an immense sexual attrac-

It's always something: Lisa Loopner at the piano; with Steve Martin and David Brenner; (opposite) backstage; as Judy Miller, juvenile impresario.

tion to her pizza-faced classmate, Todd, played by Bill Murray. There was a good reason for the healthy, if fumbling, hormonal relationship between Lisa and Todd; unlike the sketches, where Todd was "a boy and a friend, but not my boyfriend," in real life, Radner and Murray were romantically involved. "They were having a relationship that was on and off again," recalled Beatts, "and we always knew when it was on, because at the read-through, Gilda would laugh louder when she heard Bill's stuff."

As Gilda's star ascended, there were the inevitable rungs in the ladder of crossover success—movies, a one-woman Broadway show—but she always turned down the repeated, fervent requests for her to star in her own sitcom. She was happy where she was, on *SNL*, but in 1980, when the original cast left after five seasons, it was time to move on. Her huge fame at the time filled her more with ambivalence than anything else; she told a television reporter that "it happens a lot in comedy that when you get success and celebrity, it changes. There's something about being an underdog, a voyeur, that makes comedy possible." Her movie roles in the early 1980s were surprisingly strident disappointments. Her manager, Bernie Brillstein, observed that "Gilda was a television being. I tried to really make her a movie star— she wasn't right for movies."

If Radner banged into a wall as far as her film career was concerned, that was nothing compared to her next collision. In 1986, she was diagnosed with ovarian cancer. Her life had been on an upswing, largely a result of her 1984 marriage to actor Gene Wilder. True to form, Radner tackled the disease with a fierce command of sunny optimism.

Zweibel recalled her saying, "Jokes are the only weapons that I have; my comedy is the only way that I can combat this fucker." Zweibel arranged for her final television appearance, a guest spot on Showtime's *It's Garry Shandling's Show* in 1988. Radner had been nervous about appearing, between her illness and her long absence from the TV screen, but her fears were for naught. When Shandling asked Gilda, "I haven't seen you in a while. Where have you been?" she answered, "Oh, I've had cancer. What's your excuse?" To which Shandling countered, "Well, I've been stuck on this show, just a series of bad career moves for which there's no cure whatsoever." The audience howled with laughter and tears; even one of the hardened cameramen started crying.

The day Gilda passed away, May 20, 1989, was a Saturday, and Steve Martin was the host for *Saturday Night Live* that evening. The staff, stunned at the news, cut one sketch and substituted it with a clip from 1979 of Martin and Radner performing a daffy dance to "Dancing in the Dark," which began in a club but broke through the fourth wall, spinning both of them—obviously entranced with each other as characters and performers—through the entire studio. It was a magic moment and the best memory possible; Martin was visibly moved introducing the clip. As he remembered twenty-five years later:

> We couldn't wait to rehearse it. Gilda was absolutely delightful. She was so sunny, and I wasn't used to sunny people—I was kind of alone on the road—but you just walked on the set and she was laughing. . . . She also had no inhibitions. She'd be on camera and milk would come out of her nose and, you know, she was just delightful.

"HE WENT BY SO FAST!"

'Tis a bleak night my lord,
Look, the clouds like boogers hang from the
   nostril of the moon.
Aye, 'tis foul these things I say,
I know not what my mind does.
Oh, I once again to walk among you, 'tis foul, late.
Does anyone have drugs to ease my pain?
My kingdom for a Quaalude, I jive you not.

— Robin Williams

ROBIN WILLIAMS

Robin Williams came by his gift for iambic pentameter the honest way. He was an acting student in the early 1970s at New York's prestigious Juilliard School, where his classmates were Christopher Reeve and William Hurt. As producer George Schlatter recalls, "He didn't graduate because they asked him to leave after his junior year. They said, 'No, Robin, there's just nothing more we can teach you. So you should go out and work.'" Williams himself remembers the conversation with the school's founder, the esteemed director and actor John Houseman, a bit differently: "Mr. Williams, the theater needs you. I'm going off to sell Volvos."

An ensemble of actors jumping around in tights would have been redundant for Williams, anyway ("There was a dance teacher, Anna Sokolow, who would grab you where a drill sergeant wouldn't go."). Robin Williams was born in Chicago in 1952 and was raised in a well-to-do suburb outside of Detroit, Michigan, where his father was a busy senior executive with the Ford Motor Company. Neglected by his family, Williams grew up in a thirty-room mansion, where he had the entire third floor to himself. To entertain himself, he created an array of imaginary playmates. Back in the days of the Depression, another youngster from a privileged family sat alone in his room, channeling the recesses of his imagination for companionship. That was Jonathan Winters, and Robin Williams remembered seeing him on Jack Paar's show when he was a kid: "It looked like [Winters] was having such a wonderful time. It looked like anything was possible."

Alien Nation:
According to his producer, Williams was an "actual" alien; keeping his stand-up career on its feet, circa 1979; on *Mork and Mindy*, with Pam Dawber and Jonathan Winters.

When Williams turned sixteen, his father took early retirement and moved the family to Marin County, just north of San Francisco. "It was mellow times," he recalled. "That's where I found out about drugs and happiness. I saw the best brains of my time turned to mud." Williams returned there after leaving Juilliard and soon ventured to Los Angeles, where he did the stand-up rounds. Budd Friedman recalls, "I put him on every time he'd walk in and people would say, 'Why are you putting him on? He ain't got no act.' Trust me, he's got an act. And Robin became a favorite so quickly." One gig at the Comedy Club was caught by George Schlatter, who was revving up a new version of *Laugh-In* in 1977. "He came out in overalls, with a straw hat on, barefoot—it was Jonny Winters squared, you know? And he had a pole, and he put it out over the audience, and he says, 'I'm fishing for assholes.' The moment you saw him, you said, 'This is gonna be an important force. Not just a talent, but an important force in show business.'" Williams made his featured debut on the show in late 1977; his first line was "Ladies and gentlemen, tonight I'm here to talk to you about the very serious problem of schizophrenia—No, he isn't!—SHUT UP, LET HIM SPEAK!"

The *Laugh-In* revival was a flop on NBC. Over at the soundstages at ABC, there was a hit number one sitcom called *Happy Days*. Producer Garry Marshall, on a whim suggested by his seven-year-old son, decided to drop an alien from space down on Fonzie and his friends. Finding the right actor would be crucial, and Marshall called on his sister, Ronnie, who was his casting director. Marshall recalled:

> "Get me Jonathan Winters, get me John Byner, get me one of those crazy guys—Don Knotts, I'll take." "No, we got a guy, Robin Williams," my sister Ronnie said. "What he's done, Robin Williams?" "He stands on a street corner and he does funny things and mimes and he passes the hat. That's his credit." This is who I'm gonna see over the people I want to see? "Yes, you gotta see him." And I said, "But why?" And I remember my sister said very clearly, "You should see him—it's an awful full hat."

Williams's debut as Mork from Ork whipped the studio audience into pandemonium; in the days of sitcom spin-offs, a vehicle was not far behind. *Mork and Mindy* was hastily arranged for the following fall.

There had been aliens on television before—in fact, *Mork and Mindy* was a distaff rip-off of *My Favorite Martian*—but, as Marshall was fond of pointing out, *their* show had an actual alien. On the first day of shooting, Marshall had to contend with the fact that his star was out of orbit:

> He was all set to go, I said, "All right, Robin, we have three cameramen." Three cameras for *Mork and Mindy*, and the average age of the cameramen is seventy-nine, eighty. And so I said, "Okay, Robin, ready, action." And he ran around, he did a very funny thing, he ad-libbed a little, he said the lines, he was all over the place, and I yell, "Cut! Great!" And to Sam, my oldest cameraman, I said, "Did you get that, Sam?" And Sam said, "Never came by here." I said, "You gotta move the camera, Sam. The man's a genius." And Sam said, "If he's such a genius, he could hit that mark right over there and he'll be on camera." So we hired a fourth camera, just to follow Robin.

The four seasons on *Mork and Mindy* turned Williams into a superstar, and he still exercised his comedic skills by working comedy clubs and other venues when the cameras were off:

> [I just started] to incorporate my stand-up into the stuff on the air. And when we started off, people didn't know what it was. They finally had to find a Philippine censor who spoke Yiddish, because I was throwing in a lot of stuff— the censors were going, "I don't know what he is saying, he's saying things which are obscene, I just don't know what they are."

As the ratings wound down for *Mork and Mindy*, the producers came up with one of the greatest stunts in sitcom history: Mork and Mindy gave birth to a baby, and that allowed Williams to be the big daddy of his bigger mentor, the original man from outer space, Jonathan Winters.

Acting chops:
Good Morning, Vietnam (1987) and *Mrs. Doubtfire* (1993).

When Winters arrived to play Baby Mearth, the two got along well, praised each other, and began an ongoing friendship. Apart from the fact that Williams had a tendency to "recycle" Winters's material, the elder spaceman had only one criticism. "Robin started being interviewed about what's it like to work with Jonathan Winters, and he said time and again, 'Jonathan is my mentor.' And I turned to him and I said one day, 'Don't say "mentor" anymore. I tell you why—in Ohio they think that's a salve. Say "idol," we all know that.'"

When Williams left the sitcom in 1982, he exploded on all fronts; for a comedian who fired a full range of synapses in his act, it was no surprise. He made his film debut as Popeye, quickly ventured in dramatic roles, zig-zagged into several successful HBO concerts (including one from the Metropolitan Opera, right across the plaza from Julliard), cut a best-selling album or two. Through sheer determination and talent, he became, arguably, the first comedian to cross over and sustain a dramatic acting career. He was able to bring his improvisatory chops to films like *Good Morning, Vietnam*, where his rants as military disk jockey Adrian Cronauer were firmly in keeping with his eight-cylinder brain:

> Hey, we're back. That last two seconds of silence was Marcel Marceau's newest hit, single, "Walkin' in the Wind." And now, here are the headlines. Here they come right now. Pope actually found to be Jewish. Liberace is Anastasia, and Ethel Merman jams Russian radar. The East Germans, today, claimed the Berlin Wall was a fraternity prank. Also, the Pope decided today to release Vatican-related bath products. An incredible thing, yes, it's the new Pope on a Rope. That's right. Pope on a Rope. Wash with it, go straight to heaven. Thank you.

Although Williams won an Academy Award for a serious performance in *Good Will Hunting*, his most effective screen appearance may have been one where he didn't appear at all: as the voice of the Genie in Disney's *Aladdin*. Only animation could give full vent to Williams's full transformational powers (and that didn't keep him from busting on Disney publicly when they ignored the promotional details of his contract).

Williams's high-octane persona has occasionally gotten him into trouble with substance abuse (he once said that "cocaine is God's way of telling you you are making too much money"), but audiences and film studios have been forgiving. A Robin Williams visit to a talk show or interview gives an audience a pretty big bang for its buck—one usually gets about a dozen personalities. In a visit to *Inside the Actors Studio*, within the span of about forty-five seconds, Williams manipulated a scarf to become a Bollywood film director, an Iranian refugee, a gay Orthodox rabbi, a television chef, a matador, an Amish police detective (don't ask), and a car-washing machine.

Mere words alone cannot describe Robin Williams's manic accelerations—he's an oddball who ricochets around the pool table of comedy—but perhaps the most effective account comes from his mentor, er, idol, Jonathan Winters.

> Robin's like a good air show, he's like a Sopwith Camel, he's a Gatling gun, he's a machine gun, he's a rocket, whatever they're firing in Lebanon today, and here comes Robin. Wings swept this way, he smiles—*whooosh!*—he's gone just like that. And a kid with a little yellow box camera says, "I didn't get a picture—was that Mr. Williams? He went by so fast!" And boy, he does, he does. Whoa! This guy, he goes past the moon and around and back and in for a landing at Andrews Air Force Base.

"HERE I COME TO SAVE THE DAY!"
ANDY KAUFMAN

Even in person Andy Kaufman was eccentric. He was very hard to communicate with. Very quiet and really didn't have much to say. And he got quite a following. He was very strange. Very strange young man. —Dick Van Dyke

Even the oddest of oddball comedians were in it to get laughs. When Steve Martin threw away the rule book and deconstructed his act, he at least had enough consideration to reconstruct it for his audience. Andy Kaufman had none of those commonplace concerns; he was into destruction, pure and simple. James Burrows, who directed Kaufman in scores of episodes of television's *Taxi*, said, "He was the only comic I had ever seen who didn't care if the audience laughed. He would go out and do a routine and he would do it until you laughed."

Kaufman was born in 1949 in the Long Island suburb of Great Neck. Whereas other comics like Jonathan Winters or Robin Williams were on their own wavelength, Kaufman was on his own transmitter. He once told an interviewer, "Ever since I was a little boy, while all the other kids were out playing ball, I'd stay in my room and imagine that there was a camera in the wall. I used to really believe that I was putting on a television show, and that it was going out to somewhere in the country or in the world, and that it was seen by people. I used to have four hours of programming every day."

It was a good thing that he had material to spare. He started out in the stand-up scene, and his brand of humor was trying for the managers trying to book him. "The audience liked [what I did], but the nightclub people didn't," he said. He told Budd Friedman, the owner of the Improv, that he was "from an island in the Caspian Sea"—there aren't any, by the way—and proceeded to perform the routine he called "Foreign Man," a meek, deferential immigrant from some unknown country, devoid of any showbiz savvy whatsoever. "I do imitations," Kaufman would begin, and then go through the usual litany of 1970s icons, each with the same nasal foreign accent: "Archie Bunker—Hello, I'm Archie Bunker. Hello, I'm President Carter, President of the United States. Tank you veddy much. Now I do the Elvis Presley." While everyone in the audience groaned to themselves, Kaufman broke out into the best Elvis imitation anyone ever heard, even Elvis himself, who admired Kaufman's version above everybody else's. Then, as the capper, back to the "Foreign Man": "Tank you veddy much." For the right kind of audience—which could be few and far between—Kaufman was comic nirvana.

His eventual manager, George Shapiro, recalled his initial concerns about Kaufman: "I had a couple of dinners with him because I wanted to make sure he wasn't too crazy, you know, because I have to have good feelings about whoever I would work with. But he was really nice, and he loved his grandma, used to visit her on the way home." Slowly but surely Kaufman was getting placed in higher-profile venues, including the debut episode of *Saturday Night Live*. For a full five minutes, all Kaufman did was lip-sync the refrain to the Mighty Mouse theme song—"Here I come to save the day!"—while patiently waiting his turn for the refrain to pop up again in the song. George Carlin, who was the host on that show, remembered, "I just thought, 'Oh. Well, of course.' It was just another sign that free spirits and oddballs can be rewarded."

Kaufman was rewarded with a recurring spot on Dick Van Dyke's 1976 variety series, several talk show guest shots, and, in 1978, a supporting part in a new sitcom, *Taxi*, where he played a more specific characterization of "Foreign Man," Latka Gravas. But before Kaufman would sign his contract, he held out for an unprecedented concession; the network would have to guarantee four episodes to a nightclub singer named Tony Clifton, who opened for Kaufman's act. "I want to help him in his career," said Kaufman, and Paramount, who produced the series, relented. The joke, of course, was that there was no Tony Clifton—he was a

Wrestling with success:
(previous page) Kaufman with his "Mighty Mouse" act; playing the bongos on *SNL*; as *Taxi*'s Latka; (opposite) world's greatest Elvis imitation; being wrung out in the ring.

put-on act, created and impersonated by Kaufman himself.

The joke backfired on "Clifton's" first day of shooting. "Andy was a big hit right off the bat," recalled Burrows. "Everyone loved Latka right away. And then it came time for Tony." Accompanied by two hookers and making unreasonable demands, Clifton alienated everyone on the set. The producers wanted Clifton fired, but they needed Kaufman's permission first; somehow, he gave them permission to fire his own alter ego. "A couple of actors in the cast were really pissed at this self-indulgent moment," said Burrows, "and I took them back there and I said, 'Guys, just enjoy the theater. You'll never see this again in your life.' " Security guards grabbed Clifton and threw him off the set, and it made the front page of the *Los Angeles Times*. Kaufman said afterward, "This is one of the greatest days of my life. This is theater of the street." When he showed up for the next week's shooting—as Andy Kaufman—he never said a word about the incident.

Whether it was theater of the street, comedy, performance art, or, in fact, self-indulgent chaos is almost beside the point; it was all a part of the incredibly disciplined surrealist set-ups that emerged from Kaufman's unique brain. It all certainly made sense to him: "Pure entertainment is not an egotistical lady singing boring songs onstage for two hours and people in tuxes clapping whether they like it or not. It's the real performers on the street who can hold people's attention and keep them from walking away." Kaufman was able to hold the attention of legions of tolerant fans through his pranks. After his 1979 concert at Carnegie Hall, he arranged for twenty buses to transport the entire audience to a nearby school cafeteria to join him for milk and cookies. Kaufman became obsessed with getting into a ring and wrestling with women as part of his performance. To him, it was a gutsy, "pure" thing to do; the women in the audience, whom he taunted with the most retrograde insults, thought otherwise, and so did many of his old supporters. Fewer and fewer programs would invite him on.

Any other comedian would have given his or her eyeteeth for the exposure that Kaufman was given over five seasons on *Taxi*, and most would have tried to parlay that into wide-screen success. But Kaufman was, clearly, not any other comedian; he would sit down and, with a straight face, read aloud from *The Great Gatsby* until audiences had enough—usually by the second page of the first chapter. George Shapiro said that "one of the most important things in Andy's creative life was getting reactions from the audience. He just wanted to do things that would move an audience."

Sadly, Kaufman was running out of audiences. In December of 1983, he was diagnosed with a rare form of lung cancer, although he hadn't smoked since high school. Apparently, he told a number of friends that he looked forward to faking his own death. The real thing happened in May 1984, but many of his biggest fans still believe that Kaufman is alive and has perpetrated the greatest hoax of all time. Twenty-five years later, it seems that is the only incomprehensible stunt that Andy Kaufman never pulled off. "I've never told a joke in my life, really, in all the years I've been performing," Kaufman once said—and he seemed damn proud of it.

CHAPTER FIVE

HONEY, I'M HOME!

BREADWINNERS AND HOMEMAKERS

Everybody's family is crazy, you gotta love 'em anyway. I think every night at ten o'clock the people are sittin' around the coffee table goin', "Our family's nuts. My brother's insane, granddad's out of his mind," and I think if you walked out that house and walked next door and went in the other house, they're sittin' around the coffee table goin', "Uncle Fred needs to go in an institution and Mama's out of her mind and if my sister thinks I'm gonna loan her money . . ." I'm not alone! Hallelujah!

—Jeff Foxworthy

THE BIG(GER) PICTURE

"All happy families resemble one another, but each unhappy family is unhappy in its own way," wrote Tolstoy in *Anna Karenina*, but then again, he never watched a television situation comedy. The development of the domestic comedy in America, first on stage, then on radio, then finally, ultimately, on television is the evolution of a unique form, one that defines us and is, in turn, defined by us. The domestic comedy can be an imperfect mirror of times—whether it accurately reflects who we are in the moment or portrays a version of how we'd like to think we are is a matter of question—but there's no doubt of its deep and resonant place in American comedy. If Tolstoy had been gazing at a television set in his living room for the past sixty years, as millions of Americans have, he'd have seen thousands of different families—sober families, wacky families, kooky families, ooky families—and all of them were happy, at least by the time the credits rolled that week.

The family unit, so integral to these types of comedies, was actually a long time arriving on the scene. Most American stage comedy in the early part of the twentieth century had to do with rugged individualism: a scrappy hero who fights the forces of oppressive authority so he can get the girl in the end. Other than a few attempts by W. C. Fields in the *Ziegfeld Follies*, the Broadway revue sketch had no time to develop the various members of a nuclear family. Imported British comedies, exemplified by Noël Coward and Somerset Maugham, exalted the badinage of a pair of highly charged, highly intelligent lovers.

When sound was introduced to movies in 1927, that kind of verbal romantic comedy proved exhilarating on the screen; witty dialogue could now finally be exported to audiences everywhere. Beginning in 1934, with the film version of Hecht and MacArthur's stage play *Twentieth Century*, a new genre of movies appeared in movies, eventually called "screwball comedies." They dominated Depression-era screen humor, and the ideas and words (and sometimes the actors) of these screwball comedies often came from the sophisticated Broadway crowd; scores of first-rate comedies featured the idiosyncratic bickering of a romantic couple trying to work through the impossibility of spending eternity with each other, usually with a Manhattan penthouse or an East Coast mansion in the background. As excellent as these films are, children are not only not heard but not seen, either. If affection is bestowed by the leading couple on anything younger or smaller than they, it's usually a pet of some kind: think Asta, the terrier in *The Thin Man* comedies, who also appeared as Mr. Smith, the bone of contention (sorry) in the divorce between Cary Grant and Irene Dunne in *The Awful Truth*. Even the titular character of *Bringing Up Baby* is a leopard.

Family matters:
Kaufman and Hart's Broadway classic, *You Can't Take It with You* (1936).

It's difficult to say exactly why the domestic unit is so conspicuously absent on the screen during the Depression. Perhaps children would have cluttered the elegant escapist landscape of these comedies. Perhaps they were a reflection of hard times; during the Depression, the number of couples who felt they could afford to raise a family dropped precipitously. Perhaps the screwball comedy was simply following the biological math found in the tradition of Shakespeare, Wilde, and the Restoration comedies: before you have a family, you've got to get two people together. That alone provided enough conflict for two and a half hours.

When George S. Kaufman and Moss Hart wrote *You Can't Take It with You* in 1936, they were at the height of their powers. The Broadway giants could have taken on any topic, but they took on a relatively plotless, character-driven story of a "slightly mad family," as Kaufman put it in a letter to his wife. *You Can't Take It with You* is the quintessential domestic comedy; the Vanderhofs, a wacky, devil-may-care, left-leaning extended family of eccentrics, have a daughter who falls in love with the son of the Kirbys, a well-heeled patrician exemplar of disciplined self-government. The play was Kaufman and Hart's greatest hit, won the Pulitzer, was transformed into a much different film by Frank Capra, and exemplified the comic sparks that can fly when a traditional and a nontraditional family crash against each other. *You Can't Take It with You* also challenges, as all great domestic comedies do, the notion that there is such a thing as a conventional American family upbringing.

But at the time that Kaufman and Hart's play was delighting audiences the radio airwaves were beginning to fill up with eccentric families of their own: *The Goldbergs, Fibber McGee and Molly, Vic and Sade*. It's important to remember that domestic comedy supported the wilder, more theatrical variety programs; popular though they were, they did not dominate radio programming. In fact, many of the domestic comedies were only separated by a thin line from more soap-opera-oriented radio serials, such as *The Aldrich Family* or *One Man's Family*, and hadn't yet accessed their inner lunacy. But serials they were, and sponsors and network executives saw how potent it was to create a group of characters whose lives and trials were of constant and repeated interest to listeners.

Bringing up without baby:
Irene Dunne, Cary Grant, and Mr. Smith in *The Awful Truth* (1937).

As the threat of world war began to obscure the fears of the Depression, more and more family stories appeared on the American scene, in both comedic and serious forms. (Thornton Wilder's *Our Town* appeared on Broadway in 1938, and two of wartime's greatest stage hits were the nostalgic *Life with Father* and *I Remember Mama*; both, incidentally, were adapted as television shows in the 1950s.) Americans bonded together with family members, even fictional ones. On *The Goldbergs*, son Sammy went to war and listeners heard his letters home and joyfully welcomed his return. Such supportive relationships were unlikely to be rent asunder when the war was over, and the return of real GIs to the home front from 1945 on created a battalion of new families across the country; by 1947, the U.S. birthrate had zoomed to nearly a third more births than during wartime and nearly five million bouncing baby consumers had entered the world. These burgeoning families were eager to move out of their parents' apartments and contributed to one of the great social shifts in American history, the middle-class suburban exodus; by the mid-1950s, more families owned homes than rented them, something that hadn't happened since the eighteenth century.

Into those homes, along with new washer-dryers, toasters, and barbecue grills, was a new piece of furniture: the television set. In the late 1940s, it would seem obvious to put domestic comedies on this most domestic of devices, but it took awhile for programmers to figure out an efficient way of recreating this kind of comedy given the technical inefficiencies of the video age. But soon transmission quality improved and *The Goldbergs* became, in 1949, the first radio domestic comedy to make the great electronic leap. Soon other shows followed, such as *The Life of Riley*, *The Aldrich Family*, *The Burns and Allen Show*, and *Amos 'n' Andy*. But in keeping with the freewheeling nature of television's early days, Burns and Allen and Jack Benny blurred the lines between variety programs and domestic comedy, Jackie Gleason and Sid Caesar each came up with a mini-domestic comedy in the middle of their variety shows, and in October of 1951, a domestic comedy debuted whose passionate heart beat not in the living room but on the bandstand of the Club Tropicana.

I Love Lucy quickly became a seminal event in television history, and it redefined what the domestic comedy was capable of doing. Lucille Ball was a movie star and a gifted clown, but on *Lucy* she had a vehicle built around her particular gifts and even around her life with husband Desi Arnaz. She would be but the first of legions of idiosyncratic performers who would be liberated (or constricted) by having a domestic comedy built around their skills and personality. She let the reality of her own personal situation dictate much of the proceedings; when she became pregnant in the second season, it was decided to let her character, Lucy Ricardo, have a baby, too (only you couldn't say "pregnant"). When the fictional birth coincided with the real one, 71 percent of all television sets in the country tuned in. Ball, Arnaz, and their writers also solidified the most basic domestic comedy structure of all. According to Max Mutchnick, the cocreator of *Will & Grace*:

> You had a married couple and their best friends. And the married couple carried the "A" story, the serious story that spoke how far they would go to keep their relationship intact. And you had the neighbors, which were just a funhouse mirror of the leads. And that's as straightforward as it gets.

Lucy was gloriously calculated to tickle the funny bone, but it had something even more essential: a spine. Yes, Lucy was wacky and zany and Ricky was explosive and forgiving, but what viewers really bought into was her quest, her hardwired desire to get onstage at the Club Tropicana at any and all costs. Lucy's obsession would prove to be a more addictive narcotic than hearing Molly Goldberg confer her chicken-soup wisdom upon her family.

I Love Lucy provided most of the sheer lunacy in 1950s domestic comedy; viewers, on the whole, preferred to invite families into their homes that they would invite in real life; in fact, they often preferred the kind of families that they aspired to become. White-bread, nicely bred families such as the Cleavers in *Leave It to Beaver*, the Nelsons in *The Adventures of Ozzie and Harriet* (also a radio transfer), and the Andersons in *Father Knows Best* became icons of the decade, and a clip from any one of their shows can still conjure up the conformist ethos of the era. They were the first comedies to present themselves (or have executives present them) as sterling examples of domestic virtues, such as hugging and learning.

The Odd Couple?
No, it's Fred and Ricky, the men's team of *I Love Lucy.*

Not all serial comedies in the 1950s and 1960s had domestic settings; there were also several good vocational, or workplace, comedies on the air. *Our Miss Brooks*, featuring the gloriously astringent Eve Arden as a high school English teacher, debuted in 1950 (talk about a pioneer single career woman), and Sgt. Bilko's relationship with his platoon at Fort Baxter was probably the first extended nondomestic family on television. *The Dick Van Dyke Show* was the most expert pioneer at bringing biological and surrogate families under the same video roof, as it were. By the early 1960s, when *The Dick Van Dyke Show* went on the air, there were enough variations on the domestic comedy theme to coin a new term: the situation comedy.

As the 1960s went on, there were certainly a lot of situations on the air. Perhaps because the real world was so complicated and confusing, the situation comedy ventured out into some very odd territory. The weirdest fringes of pop culture moved into the neighborhood and borrowed the basic conceit of *You Can't Take It with You*. There were Martians who lived next door, talking horses who lived next door, vampires and monsters who lived next door, genies who lived next door, witches who lived next door (and these were the hits)—one wonders how the series' creators managed to find any normal people next door left in town. Perhaps the most identifiable (and the most popular) of these mortgage-owning misfits were *The Beverly Hillbillies*, whose fish-out-of-water adventures came from the imagination of writer Paul Henning. Henning also struck oil by creating two more successful cornpone spin-offs for CBS: *Petticoat Junction* and *Green Acres*.

Whatever one's opinion of these country cousins (critics loathed them, audiences loved them), they were instrumental in pushing television's pendulum firmly to the right. By the time the 1960s ended, sitcoms had become so ubiquitous and so persuasive that they dominated the prime-time schedule (and reruns of them dominated the daytime) and provided common ground for millions of citizens across the country. They now not only reflected trends, they started trends—and sometimes those trends went on too long. The sitcom lineup for CBS was so fossilized and calcified by shows like *The Beverly Hillbillies* that its new network president, Robert Wood, swept them all off the front porch in 1970. Luckily for television history, Norman Lear had been waiting in the wings with *All in the Family*; that show was exactly what Wood needed to swing the pendulum to the left (he thought it was very funny, too), and a new cycle of domestic sitcoms—aggressive, reflecting reality, taking on political themes and challenging taboos—was ushered in and buoyed by the pre- and post-Watergate era.

Since the family unit consecrated in the 1950s seemed to make less sense in the antiauthoritarian, profeminist generational clash of the early 1970s, more and more situation comedies eschewed the time-honored traditions of the past. The workplace comedy evolved into something more complex with shows like *M*A*S*H*, *The Bob Newhart Show*, and *The Mary Tyler Moore Show*, programs where the workplace didn't just substitute for the family; it was a *preferable* family. *The Mary Tyler Moore Show* (created by Allan Burns and James T. Brooks) not only provided an expert ensemble of likable characters, its center was held down by Moore herself, as the first truly modern woman in sitcom history, a single woman who dealt with disappointments at work and in love by actually suffering and triumphing—she couldn't make her problems disappear by wriggling her nose.

By the middle of the 1970s, these issue-oriented comedies had become ubiquitous (and for some, extremely strident, especially Lear's portfolio of programs) and the pendulum needed to swing again. Garry Marshall thought it was time to return to the golden days of yesteryear—the "nice, sweet shows"—and brought a stable of beloved shows to ABC, such as *Happy Days*, *Laverne and Shirley*, and *Mork and Mindy*, uniting kids and parents in their living rooms around the console once again. The first two shows were so issue-free that, although they were set in the 1950s, they seemed indistinguishable from the 1970s. But the pendulum didn't swing back completely; once the gate of sexual frankness had flown open with the Norman Lear shows, it allowed coarser minds to blanket the airwaves in the 1970s and 1980s with sitcoms whose purpose seemed to be pure titillation: *Three's Company*, *Soap*, *Who's the Boss*, *Married . . . with Children*. They certainly didn't advance the cause of television comedy and succeeded at rousing the ire of moralists who tried (and

Playing possum:
The Beverly Hillbillies, a massive success for CBS.

failed) in 1975 to invoke a Family Hour to keep such programming out of the early hours of prime time.

As viewers became able to tape their favorite sitcoms at home on the VCR, the profound audience identification factor with sitcoms only increased, and more and more extended families appeared on the air. James Burrows, one of television's most esteemed program creators and directors, said that "Sitcoms are families. They are families that we introduce the American public to, hopefully they like them. There are some different circumstances. *Taxi* was a family of people trying to get out of a job. *Cheers* was a family of people trying to come to a place. Different kinds of bents, but basically it is a family."

And eventually, there was even a bent family; September of 1988 saw the debut of the first network sitcom to feature two homosexuals, *Will & Grace*, one of whom was the titular hero. Will is involved in a hopelessly platonic relationship with a woman who adores him, and if the sitcom never pretended to be a realistic portrait of gay culture, *Will & Grace* perfectly understood the culture of entertainment—and what mainstream America could absorb. As Max Mutchnick, who created the series with David Kohan, observed: "I always got a lot of heat [from the gay community] that we didn't sexualize Will enough. My thinking was always let's just keep the guy on television. Let's just show people that this man can exist and that he can be your neighbor, he can be your doctor, or he can be your son, and we can learn to live with that."

Situation comedies have rarely changed their form over of the years—something like *The Simpsons* or *Arrested Development* are two shows that have given it a shot; they prefer to change their content, making small tweaks or adjustments within a range of comfortability. Mutchnick puts into context why we invite sitcoms into our living room and what keeps them going: "Sitcoms are comfort food. A sitcom's doing its job if you're watching it and you're thinking to yourself I either wanna be those people or I wanna hang out with those people."

Although the Great Slagheap of Sitcom History is littered with rip-offs composed by corporate executives by committee, the bland leading the blind, the most impressive and unforgettable sitcoms have come from the depths of personal experience. Gertrude Berg, Jackie Gleason, Carl Reiner, Norman Lear, and Roseanne all went deep inside and tapped into their own family experiences to create their sitcoms. (Mutchnick drew upon his experience with a high-school girlfriend, who was brokenhearted to discover he was gay.) Sometimes they portrayed the family they wished they had, sometimes the family they were stuck with, but they didn't need to borrow ideas from the guy across the street to come up with something enduring. Even though these comedies performed globally, they thought locally.

Where does the sitcom go in the twenty-first century? In the words of James Brooks, it goes wherever the American public wants it to go—even into hibernation:

> Sitcoms should provide enjoyment for the audience, through people either empathizing with or thinking they're above these characters and the problems that they go through. I'm not sure that's what the public wants to see anymore. America would rather see real people fall and hurt themselves and suffer consequences and become the biggest loser and be voted off and be able to laugh at real people rather then fictional people.

You're gonna make it, after all:
Pioneering career woman Mary Tyler Moore as Mary Richards; Eric McCormack and Debra Messing breaking barriers on *Will & Grace*.

"YOO-HOO, MRS. BLOOM!"
THE GOLDBERGS

One gets the feeling that if Gertrude Berg could have personally delivered a pot of *tsimmis* and a plate of gefilte fish to every household in America, she would have. Actually, she came pretty close. As Molly Goldberg, for many the quintessential Jewish mama in American culture, Berg brought her charm, her taste, and her wide-open heart to the kitchen tables of millions from the beginning of the Depression all the way through the second Eisenhower administration.

MOLLY: Take your raincoat. It's threatening!

JAKE: It's not threatening *me*.

JAKE: **Molly, your soup is feet for a kink.**

MOLLY: **You mean a president. Ve're in Amerike, not in Europe.**

JAKE: **Oy, Molly, Molly, soon ve'll be eating from gold plates.**

MOLLY: **Jake, d'you tink it'll taste any better?**

A chicken soup in every pot:
Gertrude Berg and her TV clan; (opposite) a movie one-off; and Berg as radio performer and prodigious author.

Berg was born in East Harlem, New York, a year before the twentieth century began, as Gertrude Edelstein, the daughter of a Catskills resort owner. In her late teens, she indulged her talent for writing and mimicry by creating skits for the patrons of her father's hotel. At one point, in the mid-1920s, it looked as though her life would take a very different course; she and her husband, Lew Berg, relocated to Louisiana where he ran a sugar refinery. When it burned down a few years later, Berg, her husband, and two children moved back to New York, to the Grand Concourse in the Bronx, to wait out the rebuilding. While they were waiting, the stock market crashed and Berg had to turn to her inner resources to bring in some much-needed cash for the family.

She went back to writing and created a few appealing scenarios about two generations of Jewish families very much like her own. She thought it would make a compelling serial for the new medium of radio, and she used some family connections to submit the episodes—which she called *The Rise of the Goldbergs*—to broadcast executives at NBC. While she was waiting for their verdict, she did some dialect voice-over work on a Con Edison commercial, as she put it, "reading a Christmas cookie recipe in Yiddish for a public utility in America." Berg's endearing portrait of a typical Jewish family seemed a good possibility to hook listeners, and NBC offered her a contract to write and star in five fifteen-minute episodes per week. *The Rise of the Goldbergs*, debuting in November of 1929, was not only the first radio situation comedy of the Depression; it was, for all intents and purposes, the first situation comedy ever.

Gertrude Berg set promptly to work, going to the public library every day to craft her scripts—until her vigorous acting-out of her characters annoyed innocent readers nearby. She turned her kitchen table into a desk, which was all for the best anyhow, since everything about *The Goldbergs* was centered around the kitchen table. Berg's formula never varied. In her fictional family, Molly was the bighearted mother who dispensed wise advice and mild admonishment, nearly always shouting, "Yoo-hoo, Mrs. Bloom!" up the airshaft of her Bronx apartment to borrow some pots or share some gossip with her neighbor. Her husband, Jake, was in the garment business, and he could occasionally blow his top or make a boneheaded mistake, but Molly was always there to steer him safely back to harbor. This Yiddish-inflected Old World couple had two children, Sammy and Rosalie, first-generation Americans, as well as their Uncle David, an amusing but timid soul who lived with them. The rhythms of their daily lives and the small incidents that seemed momentarily to upset the equilibrium of the household at Apartment 3B at 1030 East Tremont Avenue in the Bronx were the sole dramatic repertory of *The Goldbergs*.

Gertrude Berg knew the Goldbergs well, because there was something of her in each of them. "They're a composite of real people, yes," she told Edward R. Murrow in the 1950s. "You meet people—it's like with your child, you gaze into its face and say he's got his father's eyes, his mother's nose—they're a composite of everyone you've ever known." If there was anything as profound as a dialectic on the show, it was the difference between generations, something that, although it was specifically rooted in the Jewish family, proved appealing to listeners all over the country. "Molly became a person who lived in the world of today but kept many of the values of yesterday," Berg wrote in her memoir, *Molly and Me*. "She could change with the times, as did my grandmother and my mother, but she had some basic ideas that she wanted to pass on to her children. The children, Sammy and Rosie, were myself, my cousins, my own children . . . the first-generation Americans who were trying . . . to help teach their immigrant parents how to become Americans."

Although the radio show, known after 1936 as simply *The Goldbergs*, had a brief hiatus in the mid-1930s, it was one of the most popular shows on the air until 1945. Berg became a heroine in print, in cartoons, in interviews, on the street whenever she visited the Lower East Side—and she still banged out a week's worth of scripts, in addition to playing the lead and supervising the show. There were some minor changes in the show from year to year—the family moved from the Lower East Side to the Bronx to some anodyne suburb in Connecticut, then back to the Bronx—but the range of events that befell the Goldbergs was not terribly wide or adventurous: a report card, a misplaced set of wedding invitations, a raise in the rent, an unannounced relative, a no-goodnik boyfriend for Rosalie—that kind of thing. And no matter what the conflict, it always ended with Molly putting the pieces back together with a heavy dollop of Yiddish wisdom. If there was ever a "learning and hugging" show, it was *The Goldbergs*.

On one pillar of uniqueness, however, Berg stood firm; the show always presented Jewish customs and rituals without any cheapening or whitewashing. Yom Kippur, bar mitzvahs, Passover—they were all celebrated on the show. In a famous episode from 1938, following *Kristallnacht* in Germany, a brick was tossed through the Goldbergs' window during a seder. Such racial specificity only added to the show's appeal, and Berg (as well as the various sponsors and network executives) was always gratified by the many ringing endorsements from clergymen of all faiths and audiences of all creeds during the program's existence.

The only unpleasant patch on the Goldberg landscape came after its inevitable move to television in 1949. During the years between its radio and television incarnations, Berg wrote a successful Broadway play called *Me and Molly*. For the stage version, her husband, Jake, was played by Philip Loeb, and Berg brought him along to play the same role on television. Loeb was also a person of left-leaning political convictions and was named in the blacklist journal *Red Channels* as a communist. Berg leapt to his defense, fighting the sponsors on his behalf. It was no use; the show was canceled in 1951, and to get it back on the air, Berg had to fire Loeb (but she gave him two years' salary). The last five years of *The Goldbergs* on television were nothing to write home about. By the final season, in 1955, they had moved to some characterless suburb called Haverville, with neighbors like everyone else on the dial; it was like serving pastrami on white bread with mayonnaise.

Berg survived for another decade, with her customary bustling energy, starring in Broadway shows, making record albums, even returning in another sitcom. She gets—and deserves—much credit for writing thousands of scripts over her thirty-five-year tenure, but she was undervalued as an actress. Her immense charm, her ability to mix gravity with a few dashes of daffiness, her mischievous eyes, her off-center but welcoming smile—these are what endeared her to America. When she started in radio, she was intimidated by the microphone, but soon, as she wrote, "I began to feel differently about the microphone. It wasn't just an electrical gadget anymore, it became a telephone into which I could tell stories to people I knew were there listening."

Gertrude Berg stayed on the phone for more than a quarter-of-a-century with millions of Americans who could hardly wait until she called again.

"IF SHE MADE SENSE, I'D STILL BE SELLING TIES"
GEORGE BURNS AND GRACIE ALLEN

ALLEN: My father was held up.

BURNS: He was, was he?

ALLEN: Yes, by two men.

BURNS: He was held up by two men . . .

ALLEN: Yes, they held him up all the way home.

Fans of murder mysteries claim that Arthur Conan Doyle's greatest creation was not Sherlock Holmes but rather Doctor Watson, because Holmes would have simply been too brilliant and too forbidding without a character to intercede on behalf of the reader. In terms of sheer intelligence, Gracie Allen would have to be placed at the opposite end of any kind of scale from Sherlock Holmes, but her own "illogic logic" was so immense and so specialized that it, too, needed an intermediary between her and the audience. His name was George Burns, and a great creation he was, too. The team of Burns and Allen achieved the same kind of mythical popularity as Holmes and Watson.

BURNS: Grace, let me ask you something. Did the nurse ever happen to drop you on your head when you were a baby?

ALLEN: Oh, no, we couldn't afford a nurse, my mother had to do it.

Nathan Birnbaum came first, in 1896, one of twelve children crowded into a Lower East Side tenement. He found street corners more enticing than the local public school and as a kid developed a talent for doing soft-shoe dances in saloons for a hatful of coins. He soon turned to vaudeville, undeterred by the fact that he had no unique act and even less talent. Young Nate resorted to anything that would keep him in show business, including playing the unnamed half of a seal act called Flipper and Friend: "The seal smelled better than I did." By 1922, he had acquired little more than two dozen separate stage names and a trunkful of stale gags, ditties, and dance steps.

Gracie Allen was born nearly a decade later, in 1905 in San Francisco, into a showbiz family, joining her dad's vaudeville act at the age of three. She was a lively dancer, with a winning personality and a gift for Irish songs and dialect—a good combination back in those days. By the early 1920s, she had settled in New York and was looking for a stage partner; so was Nate, who had now settled on the stage name George Burns. In 1923, they made their debut together at Newark's Hill Street Theater, with George wearing a loud baggy-pants costume and Gracie supplying the straight "feed" lines. It was a disaster. As Burns recalled:

> When we first started, I had all the funny jokes and Gracie had the straight stuff, but even her straight stuff got laughs. If she asked me a question, they would laugh. While I was answering her, I talked in on her laugh so nobody heard what I had to say. I knew right away that the audience loved Gracie and so, not being a fool and wanting to smoke cigars for the rest of my life, I gave her the jokes.

Once the switch was made, their careers in vaudeville took off with a routine that involved some simple soft-shoe interspersed with the nonsensical patter that made audiences fall in love with Gracie. After a few years on the road, George fell in love with her, too, and proposed. After thinking it over for a week or two (she had another boyfriend), Gracie said yes and the two were married in 1926.

Burns and Allen made their way up to the big time in vaudeville, made a few short subjects, and performed cameos in some Hollywood films. Their economical patter made them a natural for radio, and they debuted as regulars

on *The Robert Burns Panatela Program* in 1932. Allen's simpleminded absurdity appealed to listeners; she was somehow never irritating, but there was a unique form of common sense to her nonsense. Allen herself said that "Gracie's the kind of girl who shortens the cord on the electric iron to save electricity." Lily Tomlin, who adored Allen's comedy, said that "she was never put off by anything, never oppressed by anything, because she could turn it to her own sense of reality." Indeed, Gracie was never actually stupid, but rather frighteningly literal-minded; she was the least ironic comedian ever, and audiences would seemingly do anything to protect her from embarrassment or insult.

> GRACIE: I don't want a husband with money and good looks and personality. I'd rather have George. And I'm not the only woman who feels that way. Plenty of women have told me how relieved they are that he's with me.

Burns, in many ways, had a harder job. As comedian David Steinberg put it, "He was a very funny person, but, at the time, most people thought of George Burns as 'the unfunny one.' He would set Gracie up, never get angry, always sort of dealing with it. George Burns chuckled, then sort of moved on. That's not an easy thing to come by." Dick Martin, who adopted some of Gracie's ding-a-ling imperturbability, called Burns "patience personified." And since Allen had little or no interest in the business part of show business, Burns effectively stepped in, recruiting writers, producing their programs, managing their affairs. He did a darn good job of it, as Burns and Allen evolved into one of the most popular radio teams of the 1930s. By the end of the decade, however, Burns began noticing an alarming change:

> Our ratings kept dropping. . . . I'm in bed one night, two in the morning, and it finally hit me: I said, "We are too old for the jokes we're doing." We were married and on the air we were single. . . . So I woke up Gracie. I says, "Kid, I got it." The next week I went on the air, I said, "Ladies and gentlemen, Gracie and I have been married for a lot of years; we've got two children, and so from now on we're Burns and Allen, a married couple." And you tell different jokes when you're married. . . . When you are thirty-five, you tell jokes about cooking, about roast beef in the oven.

The evolution of Burns and Allen into an acknowledged married couple boosted their ratings once again until 1949, when they made the transition into television. *The George Burns and Gracie Allen Show* debuted the next year on CBS and involved some innovative concepts. Burns came up with the idea of leaning up against the proscenium arch at the beginning of each program, puffing on his cigar, and talking to the audience as if he were a kind of Greek chorus. "You know," he might say, "George S. Kaufman is responsible for tonight's plot. I asked him to write it and he said no." Burns would drawl on about his thoughts on comedy or married life and then there'd be a noise upstage. "Here we go," he'd tell the audience, hop over the tiny line of bricks that separated him from the living room set, and he'd enter the action. Such Pirandellian antics delighted both audiences and critics, but Burns himself thought little of them. As he said at the time,

> BURNS: I'll bet that I'm the first fellow that ever kissed you.
>
> ALLEN: Oh, you are.
>
> BURNS: I believe it, too.
>
> ALLEN: Yeah, and you're the first fellow that ever believed it, too.

Mars and Venus:
(Opposite) Promotional shot, circa 1936; one of several comic omnibus films for George and Gracie; (top) on the radio and on the TV console.

"Television was so new that if an actor burped, everyone agreed it was an innovative concept and nothing like it had ever been done on television before."

But the gag would never have worked on radio, and it helped extend the program's rather thin domestic plotlines—and for that matter, the "What now, Gracie?" banter that had been going on for a quarter of a century. Allen's frail health and general lack of ambition curtailed her involvement in the series by 1958, and Burns ambled on in some ineffectual variations without her. Truth to tell, as a comedian he was lost without her, and when she passed away in 1964, his personal sense of loss was devastating. It seemed as if Burns might pass from the scene as well, except that he was so affectionately regarded in the show business community. His best friend was Jack Benny, and the practical jokes that Burns played on Benny kept them both eternally young; Burns would call Benny at home, ask him to hold the phone for a moment, get in his car and drive over to Benny's house, while Benny held the phone in his hand the whole time. Nothing made Benny laugh harder than being tweaked by Burns.

BURNS: You're not going to burn the roast beef, are you?

ALLEN: Oh, no, I use two roast beefs.

BURNS: Two roast beefs?

ALLEN: Yes, a big one and a small one.

BURNS: A big one and a small one.

ALLEN: Yes, when the small one burns, I know the big one is ready.

Burns had the chance to make it up to his beloved friend when he took over the part of an aging vaudevillian in the 1976 film version of *The Sunshine Boys* after Benny unexpectedly passed away. It opened an entirely new career for Burns, who had been considered not much more than a footnote to showbiz. He went on to play God in a series of films directed by Carl Reiner, who called him "the least perspiring comedian I've ever seen. He was economy at its best." He played gigs on television and stage until the age of one hundred. Dick Smothers remembers seeing him backstage at Caesar's Palace: "He'd be ready to go on, he'd have a martini straight up in one hand and a cigar in the other one. 'Show business is great, Dick,' he said. 'Sing a few songs. Tell a few jokes. Fifty thousand dollars. I love it.' He'd put down the drink, go out, and do his thing. They'd applaud him for being alive."

Burns's second act was indeed an impressive one, but even he knew—actually, he knew better than anyone—that after saying good night to Gracie, he was only making jokes on borrowed timing. As he reported to the audience one night on their television program:

I am George Burns, Gracie Allen's husband. For the benefit of those who have never seen me before, I am the straight man. After the comedian gets done with a joke, I look at the comedian, and I look at the audience. That is known as a pause.... And there's another thing a straight man must know. He must repeat everything the comedian says. For instance, if Gracie should say, "A funny thing happened on the streetcar today," I say, "A funny thing happened on the streetcar today?" and naturally, her answer gets a scream. You know, I've been a straight man so long that, by force of habit, I repeat everything. I went out fishing with a fellow once and he fell overboard and he yelled, "Help, help, help!" I said, "Help, help, help?" While I was waiting for him to get his laugh, he drowned. See, to be a straight man, you have to have a talent, you've got to develop this talent, and you've got to marry her. Like I did.

Radio

Four of the greatest comedy bits in radio were sight gags: the avalanche of junk cascading out of Fibber McGee and Molly's closet; Jack Benny's beaten-up old jalopy, the Maxwell; the ventriloquist act of Edgar Bergen and his saucy, raffish dummy Charlie McCarthy; even the antics of two black Harlem cab owners, Amos and Andy, voiced by two white men.

From one perspective, *all* of radio comedy was a sight gag. Each individual listener had to see the comic event in his or her mind's eye—which meant there were millions of different imaginings of one comic's gag from coast to coast. Within its first decade of broadcast programming, radio rewrote the rules of comedy in America. In fact, radio created so many of the ways that Americans receive and perceive comedy that it is arguably the most influential medium for comedy in our history.

Comedy took awhile to find its potent niche on the airwaves. After the first commercially licensed station broadcast the results of the 1920 presidential election, most of the programming to be heard on the nascent technology consisted of music, news reports, and chat. Comedians ventured skeptically into the new medium; first, it seemed counterintuitive for a comic who had spent years, if not decades, making funny faces and funny gestures to have to rely solely on his voice, and second, the poor transmission quality made it difficult for any comedian to land his material successfully. Eddie Cantor and Ed Wynn were two of the few name vaudevillians who briefly tried their hands at radio comedy in the very early 1920s, but the pioneers of the genre are generally considered to be Freeman Gosden and Charles Correll, two obscure entertainers from the Midwest. They were initially asked by a Chicago radio station to do some cross-promotion with a local newspaper by dramatizing a popular comic strip, *The Gumps*, but they stuck to what they knew better—the minstrel tradition—and created the first comic serial. The daily fifteen-minute adventures of *Sam 'n' Henry*, a pair of black ne'er-do-wells, was broadcast for the first time in January of 1926. A contractual dispute led to their move to another station in 1928 and to the adoption of new names for, essentially, the same characters: Amos and Andy. *Amos 'n' Andy* would grow to become one of the most popular and enduring programs on radio, continuing for four decades.

That the roots of *Amos 'n' Andy* began with the funny papers seems entirely appropriate, because the radio serial was the performance equivalent of a daily (or weekly) comic strip; it was the first time Americans could follow the ongoing adventures of live characters. The desire to keep up with characters who had endeared themselves to the audience proved to be a potent one, and it required immense energy and considerable imagination to fill the insatiable maw of a half-hour

episode every week (in an era when there were no summer reruns). Vaudeville comedians could dine out on the same gags for years as long as they moved from town to town; in radio, they became sitting (or standing) ducks—one broadcast could send a year's worth of gags to every town in America and vaporize your best material in half an hour. Even if you were a comedian in a Broadway comedy or revue, you still had only to play the same two hours of material every night, and then for a thousand people, at the most. There was no way to succeed with a strictly regional joke anymore, and goodness knows you had to stick with your clean material, no matter how well the risqué stuff played. But radio was clearly the wave of the future, and it would be a huge chal-

lenge for ordinary comedians to ride that wave. Small wonder, then, that when Eddie Cantor and Ed Wynn both attempted radio again in the early 1930s (Cantor debuted on *The Chase and Sanborn Hour* in 1931; Wynn as *The Fire Chief*), they used as much of their vaudeville-revue apparatus as they could comfortably drag into a broadcast studio.

A comedy variety show like Cantor's, allying radio's two early mainstays, comedy and music, would seem to be what we'd now call a no-brainer. But even here, the rules were unclear. In Cantor's initial broadcasts, audiences were asked to try to stay completely silent during the proceedings, which were performed behind a glass wall, for fear their laughter would distract the home audience. Well, given Cantor's outrageous antics, that wasn't going to last long; during one of Cantor's ad-lib gags, the audience fell apart and, quickly, so did the glass wall, metaphorically speaking. Cantor liked it better that way and so did the home listeners, who sent in sacks of mail in support of such live spontaneity. Variety comedians had to try new ways to keep both the studio and the home audience engaged. The radio announcer was soon drafted as a comic foil; ensembles of dis-

Those old radio shows—boy, what nostalgia to be right back there in that. Those sounds, they cut through all the other layers of the psyche and put you right back there. They just eliminate everything else and you're there again. —George Carlin

tinct comic personalities became common, as did guest stars; even the sponsor's commercial product was turned into comic fodder. (Sponsors initially disliked the idea, until they realized that humor helped to sell their products better than earnestness.)

By 1935, 70 percent of all American households had radios. Depression economics encouraged the growth of the medium, as radios grew cheaper in cost and as people had less money to spend on traditional entertainment forms like theater or nightclubs. "First of all, it was the only source of home entertainment, unless you had some kind of silly uncle or something," recalled Larry Gelbart. "Radio was a vital part of everybody's life. At night, the comics came on and you shared it with the family. Nobody had a radio in their room. I didn't think I had a room. It was a family affair, and of course, all the comedy was squeaky clean." The audience for comedy developed at a rapid rate, and many comedians now saw radio less as a terror than as a refuge—a necessary evil.

Life was made easier for the variety comedian once the technical rules were sorted out and they discovered those aspects of radio that could actually add to the fun. Although Jack Benny and Bob Hope employed scores of hard-working writers on their respective staffs, they never had to memorize scripts or rehearse them at great length. The loosey-goosey nature of a show like Hope's or Cantor's meant that characters and guests could come and go without much motivation or conventional setup. Unlike a movie or a play, radio could be immediately topical—and it required no sets, props, or real estate other than a broadcast studio. Even a rare unscripted moment could be immediately wrangled from becoming a calamity to a classic. When an errant eagle broke loose from his trainer on a 1940 episode of NBC's *The Fred Allen Show*, flew around the studio, and eventually made a natural deposit on the floor, Allen seized on the joke for weeks, referring to the "ghost's beret" left on Mr. Rockefeller's carpet. (Less amusing, perhaps, to Pepsodent, the show's sponsor, was Bob Hope's ad-libbed rejoinder to Dorothy Lamour when she told him one evening on *The Bob Hope Show* to "meet her in front of the pawn shop": "Okay—you can kiss me under the balls.")

A clever comedian could wring enough subtle changes in the variety format to create something enduring that worked off his personality. Fred Allen created, essentially, a Broadway revue by alternating sketches, parodies, and recurring characters and segments. Jack Benny created an appealing hybrid between a variety show, which he hosted, and a situation comedy, where he played variety-show host Jack Benny. Hope, a product of the slicker 1940s, eschewed sense and sensibility for speed and wisecracks. It was hard to judge what kind of comedian would appeal to a radio audience. Edgar Bergen, an unprepossessing ventriloquist, became a superstar jousting with Charlie McCarthy, and Abbott and Costello were able to use radio as a stepping-stone from burlesque to film. On the other hand, Groucho Marx, that most vocally idiosyncratic of comedians, suffered mightily on radio before scoring as host of a quiz show as late as 1947. W. C. Fields was, at best, a marginal figure on radio; Milton Berle bombed on it; Laurel and Hardy never even tried it.

Perhaps audiences were more particular because radio was the first medium that allowed comedians into their homes. That may also explain why radio was so conducive to the form of the serial domestic comedy. While Bob Hope and his friends could be as outrageous and showbizzy as they wanted to be, there was also a significant place for just plain folks on the radio. In addition to *Amos 'n' Andy*, there were scores of situation comedies that burrowed their way into the hearts of Americans. "These shows had a family of people," said Jonathan Winters. "And you looked forward to listening to them." Some early comedies were broadcast daily for fifteen minutes; later on, most adopted a half-hour weekly format, the better for audiences to grow accustomed to them. *Fibber McGee and Molly* was the quintessential domestic comedy, a slice of small-town midwestern American life, centered by the eponymous married couple, played by a real-life married couple of former vaudevillians, Jim and Marian Jordan. McGee was a genial dope who always bluffed his way through some harebrained scheme, only to be gently upbraided by his long-suffering wife. They filled out their domestic quarrels at 79 Wistful Vista with a

Ethereal laughs:
(Previous page) Bob Elliott and Ray Goulding; (opposite) Jim and
Marian Jordan, *Fibber McGee and Molly*; lonely Charlie McCarthy.

parade of offbeat neighbors, relatives, and servants. (Two of these, neighbor Throckmorton Gildersleeve and maid Beulah, were given their own spin-off series; this, decades before *The Jeffersons*.) The McGees' overstuffed closet became almost as famous as the characters themselves, and the show was on the air, in one format or another, for twenty-two years.

An odder but equally beloved series was *Vic and Sade*, about another midwestern couple, the Gooks, who lived in mythical Crooper, Illinois. The extraordinary conceit of this fifteen-minute daily comedy was that its on-air characters essentially consisted of only four people, the Gook family, who constantly referred to a legion of offstage kooks and eccentrics who resided in their hometown. Somehow, the sole writer, Paul Rhymer, and his talented ensemble kept this absurdist haiku of a comedy going for a dozen years, five times a week.

Of course, as listeners and entertainers alike were to discover, it was the very regularity of domestic comedy that made it so appealing. It was a tricky balance to encourage repetition without incurring predictability, but the best shows could pull it off. These radio shows created something previously unexplored—the running gag, an idea so potent and so welcome that, like the McGees' closet or Gracie Allen's search for her long-lost brother, its very anticipation could engender waves of laughter. Radio comedies created national catchphrases, some of which survive to this day, even if their provenance is known to only a handful of nostalgia buffs: "It's a joke, son!" or " 'Tain't funny, McGee" or "Vas you dere, Sharlie?" Nearly all of radio's serial comedy was domestic in nature (*Duffy's Tavern*, a forerunner of television's *Cheers*, was a rare exception), and its basic vocabulary was bequeathed to television when the time came: marital spats, nosy neighbors, ethnic characters, the surprise guest star, the theme song.

But after World War II, radio was on its last legs. Very few new shows of any interest sprouted up, except perhaps for a domestic comedy called *My Favorite Wife*, starring a fading movie star named Lucille Ball. A pair of whimsical geniuses named Bob Elliott and Ray Goulding broadcast their hilarious burlesques of radio's pomposity out of a local Boston affiliate in the early 1950s and became cult figures. Bob and Ray's ensemble of characters included a cowboy who did rope tricks on the radio; the spokesman for Slow . . . Talkers . . . of . . . America; and obnoxious sportscaster Biff Burns, who always signed off, "This is Biff Burns saying this is Biff Burns saying good night." They paved the way for a legion of goofy broadcasters who dominated

the rush-hour airwaves with their anarchic antics, most notably Howard Stern (although whether he is a pure comedian or a broadcast host or just an agent provocateur is open to question).

But though there is much on the radio in the twenty-first century that is amusing, the comic engine that primed the pump of its golden age is long gone (the only stations dedicated purely to comedy are on the satellite networks). Once television came along, Americans could continue to enjoy the funny faces and funny gestures that radio comedians had given up decades earlier. CBS executive William Tankersley recalled an evening in 1950, after the network had adopted television, in addition to radio, broadcasting:

I remember walking onstage at our studios on Sunset Boulevard when Edgar Bergen and Charlie McCarthy had been on some radio show and the cast had gone out for dinner. And the stage was empty and the lights were kind of dim. And over in a corner there was a suitcase with some wooden pieces on it. Then I saw they were the arms and legs of Charlie McCarthy, whom we all considered to be a smart–aleck, a very urbane, very funny character—and a live person. And there he was—just a pile of wood. And I thought that was a metaphor for the state of radio. And I'm getting the hell outta here.

"I AM THE KING IN MY CASTLE"

THE HONEYMOONERS

If any comedian ever flew by the seat of his pants, it was Jackie Gleason, and as his television wife, Alice Kramden, was always willing to remind us,

RALPH: This is probably the biggest thing I ever got into.

ALICE: The biggest thing you ever got into were your pants.

Gleason was born in Bensonhurst in 1916 and grew up at 238 Chauncey Street, not coincidentally the home of his mythical creation, Ralph Kramden. According to Joyce Randolph, the most memorable of the actresses who played Ralph's neighbor Trixie Norton, "Jackie came up from a poor section in Brooklyn and had a rather difficult upbringing; his father had absconded rather early on. And his mother worked as a change maker in the subway. She passed away when Jackie was a teenager, so he was kind of on his own. He had a diffi-

Calling Bellevue:
A by-the-seat-of-their-pants rehearsal for *The Honeymooners*; Gleason and Art Carney address the script.

IF WE DO IT, WE'LL DO IT MY WAY. IF I FALL ON MY FACE, I WANT IT TO BE MY FAULT AND NOBODY ELSE'S. IF WE'RE A SUCCESS, I WANT THE CREDIT.

cult time. He hung out in the pool halls. I don't suppose he finished school, but he didn't need to; he was a brilliant guy anyhow." Gleason developed a talent early on for passing himself off as a big shot; it proved useful in an early career as an emcee and burlesque comic. By the time World War II was over, he had already scored in some minor Broadway revues and had signed a Hollywood contract as a third banana.

In 1950, Gleason was enjoying a lucrative career as a nightclub comic in Hollywood when a request came for him to come back to New York to be the host for a new variety show produced by the somewhat down-at-the-heels DuMont Network called *Cavalcade of Stars*. He was initially hesitant—a starring role in a sitcom called *The Life of Riley* a year earlier was a bust—but agreed to be yet another comic working like a dog to prop up a variety show. Gleason would only commit to four episodes, yet he soon found that the television spotlight suited his temperament, and in a moment of characteristic bluster, he told the sponsors, "If we do it, we'll do it my way. If I fall on my face, I want it to be my fault and nobody else's. If we're a success, I want the credit." Gleason went on to oversee and control every aspect of the show, from the writing to the music (which he composed by humming to a trained musician) to the actual credits themselves.

Gleason grabbed audiences with short character sketches, comical portraits he had been developing since his burlesque days: the Poor Soul, a Chaplinesque failure; the garrulous Joe the Bartender; the vain, pompous Reginald Van Gleason III. By the third episode, he told his writers that he wanted to add a domestic skit. (This was not uncommon; Sid Caesar had done something similar on his show.) But, as was typical, Gleason barked his orders to his writing staff, reportedly telling them that his domestic couple "got a little flat in Brooklyn. Flatbush Avenue, maybe. Cold-water flat. Third or fourth floor. Hell, I lived in these joints. . . . Make it real. Make it the way people really live. If it isn't credible, nobody's going to laugh. The guy at home has got to be able to look at it and say, 'That's the way my old lady sounds.'" This identification factor was crucial to Gleason—he always called the domestic skit "a nudge act. Somebody's always out there in the audience nudging his partner, saying there's Uncle Charlie." The recurring skit was called "The Honeymooners."

"The Honeymooners" snowballed concurrently with Gleason's success on *Cavalcade*. Originally, the sketch just consisted of Ralph Kramden, a harried, bombastic bus driver (at one point Ralph was going to be a cop), and his no-nonsense wife, Alice, who had to put up with plenty of nonsense. Soon, neighbors were added, with Gleason's comrade in arms and supporting cast member Art Carney playing the loony, preternaturally unflappable Ed Norton. The length and complexity of "The Honeymooners" varied from evening to evening; popular though it was, it was only one segment out of many.

Gleason's popularity was such that he was lured away to CBS in 1952 and eventually given a three-contract deal that amounted to $11 million, making him far and away the most highly paid comedian on television. It was enough money to run a small country, and Gleason ran the newly dubbed *The Jackie Gleason Show* like a dictator. Audrey Meadows was the new Alice on CBS, and even though she was a glamorous, elegant woman in real life, she magnificently channeled the housewife's weary acceptance of her lot. She also had, according to Lily Tomlin, "great timing—you went out whistling her timing." Between the third episode of *Cavalcade* in 1950 and 1955, Gleason and Co. played in seventy-five "Honeymooners" sketches; then Gleason decided to break out the sketch as its own thirty-minute episode, filmed in a new process called Electronicam, which would allow the series to be repeated and syndicated. That proved to be yet another audaciously brilliant Gleason move.

The "Classic 39" episodes of *The Honeymooners* quickly entered the pantheon of legendary television comedies. They had a marvelous predictability to them—Ralph jumps incautiously on a get-rich-quick scheme, aided and abetted by the clueless Norton; he fails and is upbraided by the long-suffering Alice. "We worked from a possible—though perhaps not probable—premise, like Ralph's weaknesses and proceeded from there," said one writer, reaffirming the show's unremitting devotion to reality. The setting and set itself reflected that; as Joyce Randolph, who also signed on in 1952, recalled, "The set felt real to us and I'm sure it felt real to Jackie; he wanted the set to look very poor and bedraggled. When fans sent us curtains for the windows, he said, 'No, no. Give them to a hospital or something. We don't want any curtains here.' So I guess he grew up without curtains."

At the center of the comedy was the intense conjugal struggle between Ralph and Alice. When Ralph discovers that there's only $3.31 in the bank, he wails, "What do you do with all the money, Alice?" "I put it in the bank," she curtly responds, letting the reality of Ralph's $62 per week salary hang silently in the air. Of course, Ralph would frequently threaten to sock Alice so hard that she would go—*bang, zoom*—straight to the moon, but audiences knew it was just Ralph "acting out." "I wonder if many a husband doesn't feel the same way that Ralph does when Alice puts one over on him," observed Gleason when critics raised their eyebrows at the idea of wife beating as far back as 1955. "It's evidence of the simple frustrations and suppressions that we all have. And it's funny because, knowing Ralph's character, we realize Ralph won't hit her at all." Gleason and Meadows were capable of careening from comedy to anger to pathos to comedy again with the skill of Olympic slalom skiers.

You're gonna get yours:
Audrey Meadows getting even with Gleason; Everyman working man.

Offstage, it was Meadows who was frequently tempted to send Gleason to the moon. No despot ever ruled with more disdain for the needs of others than Gleason. "Jackie Gleason did not like to rehearse," said Randolph. "He said comedy is not funny if it's over-rehearsed, and boy, we weren't over-rehearsed. We saw him only Saturday, the day of the show. We went through the show with him once. Just once." Sometimes they were lucky to get even that. The cast frequently had to go to his apartment or country house just to get a line-through. Gleason, who far preferred to tuck into a cocktail or two than spend hours memorizing his lines, would breezily encourage everybody to buck up: "We'll get down to the studio pretty soon and shoot another one of 'em—Civil War style." While Meadows was suffering through the two episodes that the cast shot every week in front of a live audience, wondering what would come out of Gleason's mouth, a production assistant asked if he could bring her anything. "Yes," she replied, "a cake with a file in it."

For a large man, Gleason was incredibly adept at walking a tightrope—especially while tight. Garry Marshall, who observed filming one day, remembered:

> They had written this whole skit where he's talking to a baby. Jackie took a drink once in a while, and would come in late. And he came in and he had never read the script, it was too late, and they were going on live. He was supposed to be talking to this bundle, the baby, a doll, and the greatest thing I ever saw him do was he just dragged this bassinet out on the stage, and he says, "I'll do it this way"—and he put the script in the bassinet! He would be talking and acting, but he was reading from the script! But you couldn't tell he was reading it. Then when he had to turn the page, he went, "Coochy coochy coo!" And he'd turn the page! So, Jackie never missed a line.

Meadows must have simply shrugged at his genius; in that same episode, where the Kramdens try to adopt the baby, she said, "the live audience cried so much that we ran out of time with the performance uncompleted."

Ironically, once *The Honeymooners* broke out on its own, it diminished in popularity. Gleason pulled the plug in 1956, after thirty-nine episodes. "The excellence of the material could not be maintained and I had too much fondness for the show to cheapen it," he told the press. By the early 1960s, Gleason had moved his variety show to Miami Beach and reinvented *The Honeymooners* in a dozen different ways—as a musical segment, as a color segment, in an ongoing miniseries where the Kramdens and Nortons travel to Europe together. Even the casts changed, with Carney as the only other constant; hardly a way to "maintain the excellence of the material" (and fans can barely bring themselves to refer to these cheesy excursions), but then Gleason always did what he wanted.

Livin' large:
Gleason picks up the tab at pal Toots Shor's bar.

Years before the phrase was coined, Jackie Gleason lived large. There hardly seemed to be any showbiz perquisite he disdained—a house with three swimming pools and twelve separate bars, a private train—and he built his own television empire. In reality, he achieved the kind of epic grandiosity to which poor Ralph Kramden always aspired. In some kind of bizarre reversal of the Horatio Alger myth, Gleason used his considerable clout and fortune to reconstruct his faded brown childhood poverty in Bensonhurst. It was the most impressive get-poor scheme in television history. Comedian Richard Lewis, who was once heckled by Gleason in a Miami nightclub, still admired his genius:

> Gleason was just, you know, one of a kind. He, as they say, "owned the stage." He ate the stage, the scenery, the audience, he was the monster that ate Cleveland. He was able to play this poor bastard who so loved his wife and so wanted to pull through, but he was such a dramatic loser. So, you wanted him to be as arrogant as he could be. That combination of being a loser and arrogant—he pulled it off like nobody I know in history.

He was the greatest.

Even if *The Dick Van Dyke Show* had been nothing more than a link in the evolutionary chain between *Your Show of Shows* and *The Mary Tyler Moore Show*, it would still have been a seminal event in the history of television. But it was much more than that; it was arguably the quintessential 1960s situation comedy.

"OH, ROB!"
THE DICK VAN DYKE SHOW

The program did have its roots in *Your Show of Shows*, or more specifically, with the show's key writer and performer, Carl Reiner. After the various incarnations of Sid Caesar's programs left the air, Reiner found himself billed as a "not-so-special guest star" on *The Dinah Shore Chevy Show* as the 1960s began. Feeling stuck between the demise of the variety genre and unimpressed by the sitcom pilots that were offered to him, Reiner had an epiphany at, of all places, the Ninety-sixth Street exit of the East River Drive: "I asked myself, 'What piece of ground do you stand on that nobody else stands on?' Oh, wait a minute, I live in New Rochelle, I'm married, I have a kid, I worked on a comedy variety show with Sid Caesar and the *Show of Shows*. I'll write about that." Reiner worked like a demon in the summer of 1959 to grind out thirteen scripts about a television writer who commuted between the Westchester suburbs and his job in Manhattan. It resembled Reiner's life in the 1950s in nearly every detail, except "I used three writers because seven writers is too expensive."

The show was called *Head of the Family* and starred the one actor who could perfectly capture Carl Reiner's world: Carl Reiner. Unfortunately, he wasn't right for the part and the pilot was shot down. Then series producer Sheldon Leonard stepped in and told Reiner to buck up: "We won't fail. We'll get a better actor to play you." The two final choices to play Rob Petrie were an up-and-coming game-show host named Johnny Carson and an up-and-coming song-and-dance man from Danville, Illinois, named Dick Van Dyke. Van Dyke was currently starring in *Bye Bye Birdie* on Broadway. "I had a couple of scripts of another series I wanted to do and Carl sent me eight scripts he had written and I just threw mine out the window. The writing was so great. And I said, 'I'm with you from now on.'" Reiner and Leonard recruited the rest of the cast from every corner of show business. For Rob's cowriters, they got Rose Marie, who had been in vaudeville since the age of five, and Morey Amsterdam, a comic and gag writer who had performed in every possible venue. For Rob's wife, they chose a nearly unknown television actress whose previous distinctions had been her shapely pair of legs: Mary Tyler Moore. Compared to her cohorts, she had next to no comedy experience, but according to one of the show's writers, Garry Marshall, "She became a great comedian by osmosis. You can learn, if you're smart and you can follow."

One of Reiner's major innovations was the split focus of the comedy:

> Some very bright critic wrote, "This is the first time that we know what the man does. When he says 'Honey, I'm home!' we know where he's home from." When we first took it to the network and they said, "Couldn't he be, like, an insurance salesman?" I said, "Insurance salesman? Are you not aware that when our people talk about their work they're talking about jokes? What do you talk about when you work in insurance? Your fiduciary plan?"

The home / work dichotomy was so important to the show's identity that, for a while, it was called *Double Trouble*.

However, by the time the show was picked up and debuted on CBS in October of 1961, it was called *The Dick Van Dyke Show*, largely by default—besides, even though no one had heard of Van Dyke, if the show was a hit, audiences would certainly know who he was. It took awhile for the series to catch on, and its popularity was added to immeasurably when CBS chose, as its lead-in, the sophisticated show's absolute opposite, *The Beverly Hillbillies*. If audiences watched closely, and eventually they did, they could recognize the important

The Boss:
Van Dyke and Rose Marie placate the irate Alan Brady—played by the off-camera boss, Carl Reiner.

WE HIT EVERYTHING THAT WAS FORBIDDEN. *THAT* PEOPLE DIDN'T REALIZE.

—Rose Marie

innovations of the show. According to Rose Marie, "We hit everything that was forbidden. *That* people didn't realize. We had a show where the neighbor had crab-grass, and everybody was mad at him because he wouldn't cut it. It was real. You believed it."

A large part of the show's appeal was the adult charm shared by its leads. Before *The Dick Van Dyke Show*, claims Reiner, "the comedies that really worked were husband against wife. Battle of the sexes. Instead of two against each other, we had two against the world. They had mutual problems they solved differently. But they were obviously in love with each other. There was a sexuality between Dick and Mary that was very apparent." But Reiner also brought a unique vision to the often contrived universe of the television sitcom; it seems odd that it would take so many years for a program to realize it, but the best way to reach millions of viewers was actually to focus on what happened to one person. "Carl used to bring the writers in and you'd sit around, and you'd just talk about how things happened to you that were either so silly or so embarrassing," said Marshall. "He said much of our show is based on embarrassing moments you had and then you write 'em and transfer 'em to Rob Petrie." And one other grace note, as recognized by Van Dyke: "Carl said at the outset, 'I don't want to ever mention anything that's in news. I don't want to hear any current slang. Any of that stuff, because it will date the show.'"

Even so, *The Dick Van Dyke Show* represented, for many, the perfect time capsule of Camelot and the Kennedy era, with its youthful, good-looking, stylish leading couple. Certainly the program captured the aspirations of a new generation trying to make things go right in a changing world; the Petries had inherited the future—now what were they going to do with it? "My favorite thing about Rob," said Van Dyke, "was he was educated and bright and very nice but he had a fear of authority that he had had from childhood. And he always began to stammer when he was around a cop or a judge or anybody like that. So we had a lot of fun with that insecurity of his." Nowhere was that more apparent than with two groundbreaking episodes that brought the Petries face-to-face with the ramifications of the burgeoning civil rights movement. One, broadcast in 1963, called "That's My Baby?" had the Petries convinced they had brought the wrong baby home from the hospital—until they discover, in the end, that the supposedly mistaken baby's parents are black. In 1965, in the course of "A Show of Hands," the Petries accidentally dye their hands black while making a Halloween costume for their son, hours before they are supposed to appear at a community banquet celebrating racial equality. In both cases, the climax of the shows showcased Rob and Laura's genuine shame at their preconceptions in front of African American characters—a rare and noble gesture in the early 1960s.

But fittingly, considering the rubber-band contortions of its titular hero, *The Dick Van Dyke Show*'s greatest asset was its elasticity. Nearly anything could happen on the show, and did. Reiner's basic concept allowed for some first-class vaudeville and song-and-dance turns from his cast whenever *The Alan Brady Show*-within-a-show called for them. It bounced ideas off of sex education and civil rights and science fiction fantasies—it even, improbably, featured a grown man getting bar mitzvahed in a later episode. For its five seasons, *The Dick Van Dyke Show* lived within the parentheses of Carl Reiner's borscht belt sense of humor and Dick Van Dyke's midwestern affability; between the show's creator and his alter ego, there was a composite of everything Americans found amusing and likable on the home front of the New Frontier.

New Frontier:
Van Dyke and Mary Tyler Moore; Kennedyesque glamour and presidential fiber.

"YOU CAME RIGHT STRAIGHT OUT AND CALLED ME COLORED" NORMAN LEAR AND ALL IN THE FAMILY

Jerry Lewis had reduced Norman Lear to tears. In 1950, Lear was a fresh young writer on Martin and Lewis's television showcase, *The Colgate Comedy Hour*, and Lewis had actually gone ahead and demolished one of Lear's carefully written sketches to an explosion of comic shenanigans.

It's a changing world, Arch. What're you gonna do?
—Mike (Rob Reiner), "Meet the Bunkers"

"I thought the sketch had some Everyman kind of meaning—don't ask me what the meaning was, I can't remember—but Jerry had destroyed the meaning and I was devastated because I thought that the piece had something to say," recalled Lear. "I never wrote anything that didn't come from a serious mind."

Nearly two decades later, Lear had evolved into a successful writer, director, and producer, teaming with another *Colgate* alum, Bud Yorkin, to create Tandem Productions. They had made some successful film comedies, but their accountant warned them that if they wanted to keep up their standards of living, they were going to have to go back to television, where the money was. The trouble was there was nothing on television that appealed to Lear: "*The Beverly Hillbillies, Petticoat Junction*—those were the shows on the air—the biggest problem anybody faced was the boss coming to dinner and the roast beef got burned, you know?" Not the kind of thing for a serious mind. Lear had heard about a BBC comedy called '*Till Death Do Us Part* in which a hardnosed, bigoted dockworker lived with his nagging wife, his daughter, and her sponging husband. It seemed like just the kind of uncompromising view of a family that Lear thought was missing from the networks—and the kind of family he recognized from his childhood.

Lear's father was a Jewish appliance salesman in the middle of Connecticut who frequently complained about his hard-knock life, disparaged *schwartzes*, put down his son, Norman, as "the laziest white kid he ever met," and told his wife to "stifle" herself when she got on his nerves, which was often. "My family lived at the end of their nerves," said Lear.

MY FAMILY LIVED AT THE END OF THEIR NERVES.

Bundle from Britain:
Warren Mitchell as Alf Garnett and his American counterpart, Archie Bunker (Carroll O'Connor).

Once Lear and Yorkin screened the BBC comedy, they knew some changes were in order to make the show more palatable for American audiences—but not too palatable. They thought they should bring the pilot script to ABC, which was in such desperate straits in the late 1960s that they would try anything. *Those Were the Days*, as the pilot was called, starred two relatively unknown actors with stage and film backgrounds: Carroll O'Connor and Jean Stapleton. In one of the luckiest breaks in television history, Mickey Rooney had turned Lear down for the role of the character who was originally called "Archie Justice." When Lear brought O'Connor in to read, "He looked at his script which I had sent him, read a half a page, and that was it. Archie grew to be a combination of what we put on paper and what he invented, not by way of story, but by way of language, on the spot, when he slipped into the character." O'Connor was not sanguine about the project—"There is a saying that satire is what closes on Saturday night. I thought the American public was too dour to laugh at itself"—but the forty-five-year-old actor was not inundated with prospects.

Lear was emboldened, in the pilot episode called "Meet the Bunkers," to show things that happened in millions of homes across America, but just never on their actual television sets. Archie was a working-class veteran of WWII ("the Big One," he'd remind people) with a bigoted view of anyone and everyone outside his constricted circle—"Hebes" or "spics" or "coloreds" or "fags," as he called them. Archie was, as it were, an archconservative. His wife, Edith, was a literal-minded chatterbox with a heart of gold, whom Lear based on several of his aunts. ("She would come from love. Whatever the subject, whatever the difficulty, she came from love," he said.) The Bunkers' daughter, Gloria, had married an eternal college student, the "bleeding heart liberal" Mike, who was forced, out of economic necessity, to, well, bunk with the Bunkers. They brought a healthy dose of real sexuality to the show. Although Mike and Gloria were not as colorful as their parents, they were a crucial aspect of the program, a balancing act and a lens through which the audience could judge Archie's more outrageous pronouncements.

Yet however desperate ABC may have been for noteworthy programming, they passed on both versions of the "Meet the Bunkers" pilot that they had Lear film for them, for a total of $250,000. Luckily, the president of CBS, Robert D. Wood, was getting as frustrated as Lear was with the evergreen cornball comedies on his network. A combination of demographics and greater creative freedom in the movies made *Those Were the Days* suddenly appealing to the network. According to television historian Gerard Jones, "There was a genuine desire to make TV a little more relevant to what was going on, particularly since so many of the older, very wholesome shows were dying right and left. We had to do something to look younger, if we wanted to get young people to stay home from the movies and watch a TV show. I'm sure they smelled big ratings, as well." CBS gave Lear the green light for a mid-season replacement, with two provisions: change the name to something that sounds less old-fashioned, and don't broadcast the incendiary pilot as the first episode.

But Lear stuck to his guns. The pilot episode, with its barrage of ethnic slurs and clear intimation of sexual intercourse between Mike and Gloria, was the perfect way to introduce the world to the Bunkers. "You jump into a swimming pool, you can't get wetter than wet," Lear told the network. "And this gets Archie all wet, three hundred and sixty degrees of him, so this is the one we're gonna do." The fight between Lear and the network went all the way up to the night before the January 12, 1971, initial broadcast, when William Tankersley, head of CBS Program Practices, called up Lear and told him, "You've got your way, Norman. You're gonna blow your whole series, but you go right ahead." CBS ran a disclaimer—something about "a humorous spotlight on frailities, prejudices, and concerns"— and ordered extra phone operators to deal with the expected onslaught of complaints.

King Lear:
Norman Lear gives notes to his hard-working cast on the set of *All in the Family* (Rob Reiner, Sally Struthers, Jean Stapleton and O'Connor).

The calls never came. *All in the Family* was barely a blip in the prime-time lineup when the first thirteen episodes aired, but it was getting a lot of press, and by the time it returned to the fall lineup in 1972, buoyed by three Emmy Awards, including Outstanding Comedy Series, it had become a national phenomenon, eventually becoming the number one show for five years in a row. Some of that popularity had to do with the enormous amount of press and editorial coverage the show received. Some of it had to do with the provocative themes and elements of the show: Archie's epithets, Mike's politics, episodes that included Edith's bout with menopause, Gloria's bout with PMS, Mike's bout with impotence, Archie's bouts with anyone black, Jewish, gay, transsexual, or pro-McGovern (these

ARCHIE: **If God had meant for us to be together, he'd a put us together. But look what he done. He put you over in Africa and put the rest of us in all the white countries.**

SAMMY DAVIS: **Well, he must've told 'em where we were because somebody came and got us.**

were all separate events), miscarriage, breast cancer, draft dodging, infidelity, and so on. There would be no point in listing a catalog of the television taboos busted by the Bunkers—just figure on one groundbreaking event every other episode for the first six seasons. But as Gerard Jones pointed out, "No one'll stay for racial epithets for five years; audiences wanted to know what was going to happen to these people."

Indeed, *All in the Family*'s strongest suit was its nuclear family, no matter how often it detonated. Mike and Gloria, recast for CBS from the ABC pilots with Rob Reiner and Sally Struthers, constantly deflated Archie's retrograde pronouncements, which allowed his comments to be tolerated without being endorsed, his character to be beloved without being admired. Stapleton's Edith was no Gracie Allen–style dingbat but rather the emotional center of the household, always loyal, tender, and brave under fire (and the show's writers put her under fire a lot, including a rape attempt). But her reversals could be shocking, too, and moving, especially when she once fired back at Mike for complaining about Archie's treatment of him:

> Do you wanna know why Archie yells at you? Archie yells at you because Archie is jealous of you. You're going to college. Archie had to quit school to support his family. He ain't never gonna be any more than he is right now. Now you think that over.

O'Connor's Archie was one of television's great creations, an instance of an actor perfectly understanding his character. As he told the *New York Times* in 1972:

> Archie's dilemma is coping with a world that is changing in front of him. He doesn't know what to do, except lose his temper, mouth his poisons, look elsewhere to fix the blame for his own discomfort. He's isn't a totally evil man. He's shrewd. But he won't get to the root of his problem, because the root of his problem is himself and he doesn't know it.

Archie's fear of losing control, especially in the early 1970s, when all bets were off when it came to honoring the traditions of an earlier generation, drove every aspect of his behavior, including his sexism, his racism, and, yes, his dedication to his family. "This was America, there were enough Americans who were like Archie," said Lear. "Of all the comments we got through the years, the biggest was, 'Oh, my God, that's my dad, that's my uncle. You can't believe how close Archie was to this person, that person in my life.' "

Perhaps the greatest explosion of all of Archie's contradictory impulses came in February of 1972, in the second season, when Sammy Davis Jr. guest-starred on the show. Davis was a huge fan of the program, even rescheduling his concert tour on Saturday nights to catch the program in his dressing room, and wanted somehow to appear on it. Since Lear and his staff placed a high value on realism, Davis had to appear as himself—some contrived plotline about Davis picking up a lost briefcase at the Bunker house—and when they put a black, Jewish, one-eyed celebrity in the same room with Archie, the sparks flew everywhere. Archie devolved into a quivering mass of obsequiousness around Davis but was unable to control his basic instincts: "I know you was born colored, Mr. Davis, there, you couldn't help that, but I always wanted to know, what made you turn Jew?"

The series got a bad rap for sending ethnic slurs out into the ether, but the writers were always careful never to let Archie say "nigger" on the show. It was left to Davis to put the word out there for the first time. Archie asks Davis if he "figures" him for a prejudiced guy:

DAVIS: You prejudiced, Mr. Bunker? Why, if you were prejudiced, Archie, when I came into your house, you would have called me "nigger" or "coon" or something like that. Not you. I heard you clear as a bell. You came right straight out and called me "colored." If you were prejudiced you'd go around saying you were better than anyone else in the world, but I can honestly say, after spending these marvelous moments with you— you ain't better than *anybody*.

When, at the show's climax, Archie begs for a snapshot with Davis, Sammy does him one better by planting a big kiss on Archie's cheek as the flash bulb goes off. Lear considered it one of the largest laughs he ever heard.

The basic framework of *All in the Family* was so strong that it set off every character who walked through the doors of 704 Hauser Street into comedic relief. Two months before Sammy Davis entered the Bunker household, actress Beatrice Arthur arrived as Archie's cousin Maude, as excessively liberal as Archie was reductively conservative. Lear said that "Maude was the flip side of Archie in that I always saw Archie as a horseshit conservative and Maude was the same as a liberal. She didn't know what the hell she was talking about most of the time but she had these instincts, these feelings, and she *espoused* them." The fireworks between Arthur and O'Connor were so intense that CBS immediately ordered a *Maude* sitcom for the following fall, which Tandem also produced. For Lear, it was a question of bringing up "somebody in the minor leagues that ought to come up to the majors."

If it was all in the family for Maude and Archie, it was all in the family for Lear, too, who based the character of Maude on his wife, Frances. According to Yorkin, Lear said, "I got a whole season just out of problems with my wife." "So he saw Maude as his wife and he copied her behavior and based it on her and she knew it." For her part, Frances Lear appeared to the media to be perfectly sanguine about it; she told the *New York Times*, "A great deal of Maude comes from my consciousness being raised by the [feminist] movement and from Norman's consciousness being raised by mine." Maude Findlay lived with her fourth husband, Walter, in an upscale Westchester suburb and had no compunctions about forcing her liberal positions and liberated lifestyle down other people's throats. According to Arthur, "The character of Maude was simply this woman dedicated to being politically correct, who always, I think the expression is, stepped in shit; it always came around and

Timely, as ever.
Maude (Beatrice Arthur), a liberal addition to the Norman Lear stable; *The Jeffersons* (Sherman Helmsley and Isobel Sanford, with Lear) was more mainstream.

TENACITY IS NORMAN'S MIDDLE NAME.

she was always made to look the fool."

The show, which ran for six seasons, was nearly as successful as *All in the Family*, and what few taboo subjects weren't brought up by *All in the Family*, Maude was happy to oblige. In one major controversy, the 47-year-old Maude discovers she's pregnant and, in consultation with Walter, decides to have an abortion, which had only recently been made legal in New York State. Anti-abortion activists lay down on the pavement outside the CBS Manhattan headquarters. At the end of another episode, a furious Maude calls Walter an unprecedented "a son of a bitch"—a character decision that had Lear screaming with Program Practices to retain. He won. "Tenacity is Norman's middle name," conceded Bill Tankersely, CBS's chief warrior against Lear.

Just Shoot Me:
Stapleton and O'Connor.

Lear was to require more of it. In 1975, the three networks worked together ("conspired" according to some), under the influence of Congress, to create a "Family Viewing Hour"—devoid of controversy, bad language or bad behavior—from 8pm to 9pm. Since this was the exact time slot for *All in the Family* and *M*A*S*H*, another groundbreaking series, this notion would have proved calamitous. Lear spearheaded a lawsuit against the Family Hour and, within a year, the courts declared the restriction unconstitutional.

For moral support, Lear and Bud Yorkin brought other teams up from the minors; *Good Times* was the first spin-off of a spin-off, featuring Esther Rolle, who had previously played Maude's black maid, Florida Evans. Florida was given a husband and a family in the Chicago projects for a comedy series—liberally sprinkled with social meaning—that lasted five seasons. In 1975, another spin-off from *All in the Family* featured the Bunkers' black neighbors, the Jeffersons, who struck it rich in their dry-cleaning business and moved on up from Queens, to Manhattan and, famously, "their de-luxe apartment in the sky." *The Jeffersons* had the longest tenure of the original Tandem sitcoms and, like *Good Times*, was not without its controversies. Although both spin-offs were applauded as groundbreaking African-American-oriented programs (along with their cousin, *Sanford and Son*), there was criticism that some of the characters and situations—namely the irascible George Jefferson and Florida's eye-popping slickster son, J.J.—were throwbacks to the minstrel era. Small changes were wrung in both programs to make them more palatable, but they were still more mainstream than *All in the Family*, where it all began.

What Archie Bunker would have made of the fact that he gave birth to three more shows—starring an outspoken feminist and two black families—is anybody's guess. It's doubtful that he would have been at a loss for words; Archie's racist epithets are what made him famous. For his creator, Norman Lear, "It was difficult getting those words on television in the first place, but back then one could hear them in a playground, you know? This was America, there were enough Americans who were like Archie. But, those words—it seems more difficult thinking about getting them on the air today than back then. . . "

Critical reaction to *All in the Family*

On September 12, 1971, author Laura Z. Hobson wrote an article about *All in the Family* for the *New York Times*. It provoked hundreds of responses. What follows are excerpts from Hobson's article, two typical letters to the editor, and an excerpted version of Norman Lear's response to Hobson.

"As I Listened to Archie Say 'Hebe' . . ."
Laura Z. Hobson
I have a most peculiar complaint about the bigotry in the hit TV comedy, "All in the Family." There's not enough of it.

Hebe, spade, spic, coon, Polack—these are the words that its central character Archie Bunker is forever using, plus endless variations, like jungle bunnies, black beauties, the chosen people, yenta, gook, chink, spook and so on. Quite a splashing display of bigotry, but I repeat, nowhere near enough of it.

Had Norman Lear never realized that what bigots really called Jews was kike or sheeny? Then why did Norman Lear, in this honest portrayal of the bigot next door, never say either?

And that other word. Where was that one, among the spades and coons and jungle bunnies and black beauties?

Don't even print it. Nigger.

Everybody knows it. Then why doesn't this honest show use the real words that real bigots always use?

Don't risk it. Don't tell it like it is. Clean it up, deterge it, bleach it, enzyme it, and you'll have a how about a lovable bigot that everybody except a few pinko atheistic bleedin' hearts will love.

Well, I differ. I don't think you can be a bigot and be lovable. And I don't think the millions who watch this show should be conned into thinking that you can be.

And there you have the basis for my particular complaint. How about showing the real thing for a while, before accepting any more praise for honest shows and honest laughter? What about laying it on the line about bigots and then seeing whether CBS switchboards light up with nothing but cheers?

To The Editor:
We feel that "All in the Family" is based on a false premise. We do not believe that it is possible to combat bigotry by laughing at a central bigoted figure who evokes the sympathy of the audience. We feel the show sanctions the use of derogatory epithets. When the program is over the listener has had a good time and he has enjoyed the bigotry of Archie rather than feeling a sense of revulsion.

I share with Mrs. Hobson her premise that if the show went all the way and used terms like "nigger" and "kike," the viewer might reject the bigotry. It is most regrettable that a very funny program makes light of the vicious ethnic slur and makes the bigot tolerable.

    –Benjamin R. Epstein, National Director, Anti-Defamation League
    of B'nai B'rith, New York City

To The Editor:
As a comedy writer who has practiced the art from Fred Allen in the thirties down through Bob Newhart in the sixties, I can assure Mrs. Hobson that what's funny about Archie is that he doesn't know he's a bigot—along with too many millions of his real-life prototypes. Indeed, the funniest

moments on the show derive from the exasperation and frustration of his family when they can't make him see his bias.

If Archie objected to "niggers moving in next door," as Mrs. Hobson proposes, he'd be damning himself out of his own mouth, and he's much too amusingly self-righteous for that. He wouldn't get any laughs either, not because, as Mrs. Hobson suggests, it would be too real, but because we'd stop believing the very real character his creators have developed. If Mrs. Hobson had ever written comedy, she would know that without credibility there is no risibility.

    –Roland Kibbee, Woodland Hills, Calif.

"As I Read How Laura Saw Archie . . ."
Norman Lear
Mrs. Hobson asks: "Had Norman Lear never realized that what bigots really call Jews was kike and sheeny? ...Then why did Norman Lear, in his honest portrayal of the bigot next door, never say either?"

Because, Mrs. Hobson, Norman Lear was presenting what to him, out of his knowledge and life experience, was his honest portrayal of the bigot next door.

If kike and sheeny were all that bigots called Jews, why was I so enraged at age 8 that I tackled a kid twice my size because he called me "a dirty Jew"? And as a G.I. in Italy, why did I spend a day in the brig for punching a stranger whose voice cut through me like a knife when I heard him discussing "those lousy Hebes"?

If kike and sheeny were the words that bigots really called Jews, as Mrs. Hobson insists, I wasted a lot of tears and some blood in my lifetime on such pleasantries as yid, Hebe, and dirty Jew.

The important thing about bigots and their choice of expression, however, is that unless they are conversing with other known bigots, they will always tread very carefully, testing, before coming out directly.

Archie Bunker does that. A bigot motivated not by hate, but by fear—fear of change, fear of anything he doesn't understand—he knows that Mike and Gloria will jump his every bigoted remark, which indeed they do, so he tries forever to sneak them by.

My hope is that the public won't discount Archie Bunker at all. According to Mrs. Fay Love, who heads a Lutheran affiliated social service agency for children and families in Harrisburg, Pa., there is little danger of that. Viewers there see Archie as "a lovable bigot who helps us all to laugh at ourselves and view our own behavior with new insights."

The thing about bigots, and this includes Archie Bunker, is that they do not know they are prejudiced. If prejudice were to disappear at noon tomorrow from the hearts of all the good people in the world, there would be no real problem at all.

"All in the Family" simply airs it, brings it out in the open, and has people talking about it.

"WE'RE ALL OUT OF CORN FLAKES: F.U."
THE ODD COUPLE

The trouble between Tony Randall and Jack Klugman began on the first day of shooting *The Odd Couple*. "I was in the limo smoking my cigar," recounted Klugman, "and Tony gets in and says, 'You can't smoke.' 'Well, I do smoke.' He said, 'Well, you can't smoke.' So I said, 'I quit.' I got out and I said, 'I can't work with this guy,' and he came out the other end of the limo and 'I can't work with him. He smokes!' So our producer Garry Marshall said, 'We'll get two limos.' "

The trouble between Randall and Klugman also ended on the first day of shooting. Over the course of five seasons and 114 episodes of the ABC sitcom, Randall and Klugman set a high-water mark for comic chemistry, playing, respectively, the compulsive Felix Unger and the indolent Oscar Madison, two divorced men thrown together in the same New York apartment, trying to get on with their lives "without," as the famous prologue had it, "driving each other crazy." "They knew how to make the dialogue work. And you can't have two people talking at once unless you have chemistry. It's an art form and they understood it, Tony and Jack," said Garry Marshall, the man who brought Neil Simon's Broadway smash to the small screen.

Danny and Neil Simon were a brother writing team who made their mark in the early days of television on such hits as *Your Show of Shows* and *The Phil Silvers Show*. In 1961, Neil wrote his first play, *Come Blow Your Horn*, a decent-sized hit. Danny, in the meantime, had been thrown out of the house by his wife and roomed for a time with another divorced friend, Roy Gerber. The impossible situation of two divorced men sharing an apartment struck Danny as being good raw material for a play of his own; unfortunately, he couldn't figure his way through it. "I don't know what to do with it," he reportedly lamented to his brother, according to Klugman. "So Neil says, 'Let me write it, I'll give you ten percent.' " Paramount Pictures had become so infatuated with Simon after his 1963 hit *Barefoot in the Park* that they made an offer to buy the screen rights for his next play, sight unseen—as long as he could provide an outline. He sent a brief précis of the divorced roommate idea and Paramount wrote an advance check that amounted to $600,000. Now all Simon had to do was write the play.

He sent the first two-thirds of the comedy to Walter Matthau, who accepted the role of Oscar on the spot, on the strength of the first two acts. "It was very funny without making you suspend your disbelief," said Matthau, who drove Simon crazy over lunch one day by suggesting that he should play the role of Felix instead. Thankfully, in the end, Matthau was matched with Art Carney as Felix, and under the expert direction of Mike Nichols, *The Odd Couple* opened in March of 1965. It was such a smash that it repaid its investment within a month and went on to run nearly a thousand performances. Matthau repeated his role as Oscar in the 1968 screen version, opposite an enervatingly Chekhovian performance by Jack Lemmon. *The Odd Couple* would spawn scores of productions and replacement casts around the world, including a London version featuring Jack Klugman as Oscar and a Chicago tour with Tony Randall.

When Paramount decided to reconfigure the play into a situation comedy for ABC, they hired Garry Marshall and Jerry Belson to produce the series. Marshall lured Randall and Klugman back to prime time and created what was, to many minds, the best Felix / Oscar combination of all time. The two actors were indeed opposites in a variety of ways—Randall was an opera connoisseur, while Klugman's hobbies consisted of betting on the ponies—but they were also experienced stage actors whose early training came out of the Method-orient-

FELIX: **When I die, I'd like a regimental flag draped across my coffin. And then—I hope this isn't pretentious—I'd like it to be drawn by a team of white horses, while the band plays the Grand March from *Aida*, because that's my favorite opera. And I'd like it to go round and round the cemetery three times. What would you like?**
OSCAR: **I'd like to be there.**

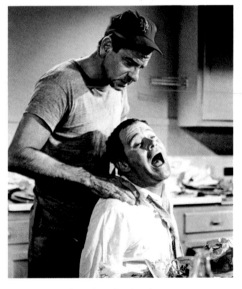

The cooking, the crying, the cleaning: Tony Randall and Jack Klugman (opposite); their movie ancestors, Walter Matthau and Jack Lemmon.

OSCAR: I can't take it any-more, Felix, I'm cracking up. Everything you do irritates me. And when you're not here, the things I know you're gonna do when you come in irritate me. You leave me little notes on my pillow. Told you 158 times I can't stand little notes on my pillow. "We're all out of cornflakes. F.U." Took me three hours to figure out F.U. was Felix Ungar!

Oscar, Oscar, Oscar...
Randall is lucky he can even find Klugman.

ed disciples of the Group Theater. Randall and Klugman were admired but they were not television stars. ABC was dubious.

Even Simon had his doubts. According to Klugman, "Neil said, 'How many neat and sloppy jokes can you do?' Well, he didn't know us. We went beyond that." Indeed, they did. Although the first season somewhat slavishly mined all of the play's possible scenarios, by the second season, when Klugman and Randall also insisted that Paramount ditch the laugh track and perform the show in front of a live audience, the show achieved liftoff. Sure, there were still jokes about Oscar's horrendous habits—his favorite meal was to take one Chinese TV dinner and one Italian TV dinner, mush them together, and shake well—and Felix's fastidiousness: "Everyone thinks I'm a hypochondriac. It makes me sick." But eventually *The Odd Couple* worked harder and worked deeper for its jokes. Marshall gave the credit to his stars: "Tony Randall said, 'We don't want to be embarrassed, Jack and I. We'll be at the home for the old funny people soon, and people will visit and we will play them these shows because what else are we gonna show them? And we don't want to be embarrassed. So let's do better.' And they forced all the writers to write a little better."

Klugman's Oscar was all id, taking no responsibility for his health, his love life, his laundry, his income tax, or his paycheck. He was the kind of guy you'd love to play softball with and have a beer with (but stand back when he opened the can), only never, *never* trust him to put your insurance premium in the mail. Randall's Felix was the embodiment of the superego, the ultimate control freak who thought that all of life's messiness—including ambition, love, marriage, devotion—could be micromanaged and arranged as neatly as a table service. He would go to pieces when human nature exploded all around him. A male Jewish mother (Randall was born Leonard Rosenberg), Felix, in the words of Klugman, "didn't want you to be neat because he wanted it, but because it would help you—*you'd* live your life more if you were neat." In their near-Jungian tangle, Randall and Klugman presented not only the impossibility of being roommates, not even simply of being married, but the essential impossibility of coexistence in human society. Sounds heavy, but it made for a lot of laughs.

The show was never a big hit during its network run, though both stars eventually won Emmys. ABC was always nervous that viewers would perceive Felix and Oscar as a homosexual couple and threw many girlfriends and ex-wives into the episodes. (Again, to the show's credit, it was a pioneer in producing a conclusive final episode after its cancellation: Felix remarried his beloved ex-wife Gloria.) The writers often twitted the studio executives with some outlandish possibilities, never filmed. Randall once recalled, "We had a script where Oscar was doing an article on homosexuality in sports, and I come across the article on his desk and I think he's writing about *himself*. We had the wonderful line, 'Gee, if it was either one of us, you'd think it would be *me*!' " *The Odd Couple* was also a quintessential urban show—while it hovered in the national basement of TV ratings, it was always in the top ten in New York City, and cultivated the fame and admiration it truly deserved when it went into syndication.

Randall and Klugman remained good friends after the series came to an end in 1975; Randall helped nurse Klugman through a near-fatal bout of throat cancer and Klugman gave his all to support Randall's pet project, a repertory theater company in New York. The simple answer to Randall and Klugman's on-camera chemistry was clearly that they were so good at driving each other crazy because they were so crazy about each other.

"DAD CAN I?"
BILL COSBY

One of the things you learn when you become a parent is the horrible thought and the reality that your children will be your children for the rest of your life! That's why there's death. –Bill Cosby

When Bill Cosby made this kind of trenchant remark about children on *The Tonight Show* in the spring of 1984, he had already been one of America's best-regarded comic voices on the nature of parenthood for more than two decades. The next fall, Dr. William H. Cosby, Ed.D, would graduate to the head of class with *The Cosby Show*, one of the most influential and popular television programs of all time. It would be fair to say that Cosby had been studying for his role of developmental counselor since the day he was born.

That was July 12, 1937. Cosby was born and raised in one of the poorer sections of Philadelphia. His father left the household when Bill was a youngster. He remembered Christmas as so cheerless that his family barely had enough stockings for their feet, let alone for Santa; young Bill made a Christmas tree by painting an orange crate with some watercolors. He kept on the straight and narrow during his adolescence, working as a shoe-shine boy, for fear that if he got arrested for the kinds of things his pals were up to, "Who'll look out for Mom?" Eventually, he went into the navy and enrolled at Philadelphia's Temple University, to become a physical education instructor. He knew he had a funny way with a line, and to make some additional cash, played some nightclubs in Philly and New York. To his surprise, it all went very well, and by 1962, he was playing the New York scene with confidence and gaining a following.

For most black entertainment pioneers in the 1960s, the road to fame could be rocky. Not quite so with Cosby. According to Joan Rivers, who was also starting out at the same time, in the same clubs:

> I always said Bill suffered terribly from the time he got in the train in Philadelphia to when he got off in New York—maybe he didn't get a seat—because he was very successful immediately in New York. He was colorless. It had nothing to do about black or white. And that's why he was so accepted immediately because everybody would go, "He's just funny." They didn't have to make a decision with him.

Just Cos:
As a popular stand-up; and as an acclaimed TV espionage agent in *I Spy*.

Early on, Cosby was tempted to bring race into the picture, mostly because in the early 1960s that was expected from black entertainers. One early gag went, "Can you imagine the first black president? 'For Sale' signs in the yards of every home up and down Pennsylvania Avenue," but he soon dropped the pose in favor of what he knew best—the life of Bill Cosby. Fellow Philadelphian Jack Klugman remarked that "He wouldn't tell jokes, he would tell stories about his family: his father, his mother, and he would create attitudes. He would create these characters and he would make them real."

Whether he was talking about shivering under the covers as a kid listening to a horror show on the radio or getting hammered after school with a "slush ball" or trying to relate Noah's incredulity at being chosen to save the human race, Cosby connected immediately with his audience. Perhaps the most revolutionary thing he did in the frenetic 1960s was to take his time. As he told an interviewer: "I am not the kind of person who enjoys line, line, line, laugh, laugh, laugh. I think that people get on a roll from a thought, a picture, an idea, or something preconceived, and they go with it." He was able to expand his gift for portraiture on a series of record albums in the mid-1960s. He was taken under the considerable wing of Allan Sherman, who gave Cosby his first late-night shot when he guest-hosted *The*

Tonight Show and then convinced Warner Bros. to sign Cosby for a record contract. Cosby would go on to win six consecutive Grammys from 1964 to 1969, and his LPs brought him his first legion of fans, including a young Jeff Foxworthy: "He was just a great storyteller. He was always clean, so you didn't have to worry about listenin' to it in front of somebody or retellin' it."

But again, in the mid-1960s, it would be disingenuous for a major black entertainer to assume he could be divorced from racial issues. Still, Cosby assiduously stuck to his mantra, which he repeated for hundreds of interviewers:

> I'm tired of those people who say "You should be doing more to help your people." I'm a comedian, that's all . . . my humor comes from the way I look at things. I see things the way other people do. . . . A white person listens to my act and he laughs and he thinks, "Yeah, that's the way I see it, too . . . that must mean that *we are alike.*" *Right?*

Cosby's profile only increased when, in 1965, he became the first black performer with a starring role in a network series since *Amos 'n' Andy* had been canceled in 1953. *I Spy* was a tongue-in-cheek espionage buddy drama that ran for three seasons—and Cosby copped the Emmy for Outstanding *Leading* Actor in a Series each year. During the 1970s, Cosby expanded his profile further, going solo and either appearing in or creating five new series for television, including two separate variety shows and a charming sitcom, *The Bill Cosby Show*, which featured him as a low-key inner-city phys-ed instructor.

But truth to tell, by the time the 1980s began, it seemed as if many trends in entertainment had passed him by. Everyone acknowledged Cosby was the preeminent black comedian—of an earlier generation. Richard Pryor and Eddie Murphy were giving black and white audiences cutting-edge comedy (and, in his stand-up act, Murphy used his devastating imitation of Cosby to portray his mentor as an uptight old fogey), and there had been several successful black sitcoms on the air—*The Jeffersons*, *Good Times*, *Sanford and Son*, and so on. Yet, for Cosby, the tone of the black explosion was all wrong. He blamed much of the decline of civility on *All in the Family*: "People don't want Mr. Nice Guy. They want Archie Bunker. A lovable bigot." As he told Phil Donahue in 1985, "My opinion is that the man never apologized for anything. [He] became a hero to too many Americans for his shortsightedness, his tunnel vision. And I'm really a believer that the show never taught or tried to teach anybody anything."

And so Bill Cosby set out to create a show that might teach somebody something. NBC executive Brandon Tartikoff was impressed with Cosby's family-friendly routines on *The Tonight Show*, but when Cosby approached the network about developing those ideas into a show, they were uneasy. Sitcoms were on their way out, and Cosby's record on TV—a spate of big-time commercials notwithstanding—was mixed at best. They gave a half-hearted fall commitment to Cosby for a handful of episodes; he countered their ambivalence by demanding that the show be taped live, and in a studio in Brooklyn. The network figured it had little to lose, and so *The Cosby Show* debuted in September of 1984.

"I did this show because I was confused," Cosby said during a retrospective. "When I became a parent I had certain thoughts and things didn't go according to plan. You'd think a person having been a child would understand how to raise one—but it really doesn't work that way. You would think that these small people—who we're feeding, getting

Pudding Pop:
Father of a beloved TV family; Phylicia Rashad is to the right of Cosby.

I DID THIS SHOW BECAUSE I WAS CONFUSED.

clothing for, saving the life of—you'd believe that every now and then that they'd believe you every once in a while when you gave them some information. Not so, said the brown turtle." There was nothing turtlelike in Cosby's pace in controlling his show. He told his staff, "This is how it's going to be"—just the way that Jackie Gleason did—and according to one producer, the show was built around "Bill's philosophy, universal in its message, that we were all alike when it comes to parenthood and children."

I DID NOT HAVE CHILDREN SO THAT YOU CAN CHANGE MY NAME TO "DAD CAN I?"

Cosby's take on his television family was radically retrograde. He starred as Dr. Cliff Huxtable, a successful gynecologist who lives with his wife, a successful attorney (cannily played by Phylicia Rashad), and their five children in a tastefully decorated brownstone in Brooklyn. (Cosby, by the way, also had a wife and five children.) Along the way, the Huxtables would make sure that any family conflict was tastefully and respectfully handled and that the children (and occasionally the parents) would grow and learn from whatever mishaps or misapprehensions occurred. Cosby also situated the Huxtables in a vibrant world of African American culture; jazz music was heard, the portraits of historically important black figures were seen on the walls, the civil rights movement was discussed, and great black artists, such as Lena Horne, B.B. King, Dizzy Gillespie, and Sammy Davis were featured in guest spots. All of these grace notes were conducted under Cosby's controlling gaze.

What he could not—and did not—predict was the commercial and critical reaction to his show. Its success with viewers was immediate; after its first season, the series finished third in the ratings. For the next four seasons in a row, it landed at number one. It pulled NBC immediately out of the ratings cellar and made it the most successful network on the air. What was more difficult was how *The Cosby Show* was dividing critics and creating criticism within the black community. Dick Gregory, a racial pioneer if ever there was one, pointed out that "Ninety-nine percent of white folks never saw a black doctor or a black lawyer! Where would they see one? And so Bill Cosby every week brought a black doctor and a black lawyer into your living room." But many African Americans felt that Cosby's view was simply too contrived. One black respondent to a focus group expressed that the Huxtables were "the type of blacks who have made it, everybody's happy, the don't-worry-be-happy type of black people; again, it's a total farce, and they don't represent what the black masses in this country are really like." While another respondent thought that "it was good that black people and whites could see that we don't all live in ghettos and projects and kill each other," one critical journal called the show "*Father Knows Best* in blackface."

Cosby himself was bewildered by the response. Echoing a sentiment that he had espoused decades earlier, he said, "I don't think you can bring the races together by joking about the differences between them. I'd rather talk about the similarities, about what's universal in their experiences." What never—*never*—was mentioned in any of these debates was, simply, what a great comedian Cosby was. True, his honorable intentions made him a wider target for social moralists who demanded more; "I have a problem with the fact that the show will build a thirty-minute episode around [Cliff] building a hero sandwich—why aren't we dealing with some real issues that are confronting the black middle class?" wrote one audience member. But no one was funnier at building that hero sandwich than Bill Cosby.

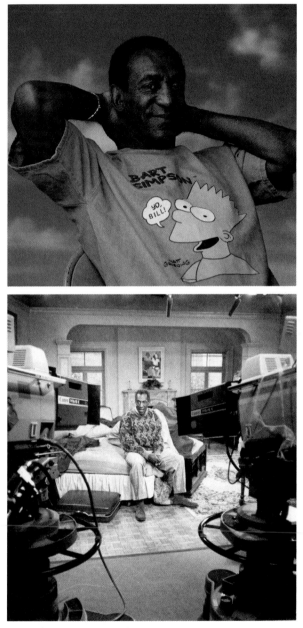

Cosby was a great, elastic clown on his show. He could be clumsy while dancing and graceful while cooking. He could be imperious to a five-year-old and reduced to infancy by his wife. His incredible timing and his way with a one-liner were priceless; when he told his intransigent son, Theo, "I am your father—I brought you in to this world and I'll take you out," he captured all the braggadocio, fierceness, and love inherent in that statement. As a producer and star, he was smart enough to allow for an ad-lib-friendly environment on the show that encouraged many of his best moments—"Leave it open and catch the funny" was his motto.

"I think you and I should get up, get in the car and go. Let 'em have the house," said Cliff to his wife, Clair, in one episode, and in the final one, in April 1992, they did nearly that, dancing together across the set, into the audience, and out of the studio. The two hundred episodes of *The Cosby Show* earned the highest syndication fee of its time, and there were more sitcoms on television after the show called it quits than at any time in network broadcast history. Tommy Davidson said that *The Cosby Show* "gave us a warm, loving, value-system-oriented lifestyle of the African American experience. We couldn't ask for more out of Bill Cosby. He made that foundation in society for us."

Catching the funny:
Cosby, with the one kid he couldn't charm; ruler on the set.

It's a shame, in a way, but it was perhaps unavoidable that the differences between whites and blacks adhered to Cosby, despite how determinedly he chose to step away from them. But there was always a greater dichotomy in his work than even race. Bill Cosby embodied both parent and child; each inhabited his body simultaneously and never stopped squabbling with the other. That was the comedic struggle in his soul and he told us it was eternal; he seemed a very credible expert on the subject. In a later episode of *The Cosby Show*, his eldest daughter, Sondra, had just given birth to twins, and told her father, "I just hope I do as good a job with my children as you did with us." "Well, let me tell you something," responded Cosby. "It's impossible."

"SO WHAT'RE YOU GONNA DO BUT LAUGH?"
ROSEANNE

ROSEANNE: Dan, how was work today?

DAN: Well, today was a special one for me. It was the 179th day in a row where I did exactly the same thing.

If you stumbled into Bennigan's in Georgetown, Colorado—about twenty minutes west of Denver—sometime between eight at night and two in the morning, in, say, the fall of 1980, and you ordered a gin and tonic, you might be lucky enough to have it served to you by a saucy waitress the locals called Rosie. "That's six bucks for the drinks, another three bucks for me to take them off the tray and give them to ya," she'd say. Rosie, short for Roseanne Barr, a housewife with three kids, working the night shift to bring in some money for the bills, was a pistol, all right. "My best line was," said Roseanne years later, "this guy, he kept coming and I guess he liked me or something and he said that he was looking for somebody who was married and wanted to fool around and, you know, didn't want to get too serious. Did I know anybody like that? And I said, 'I do. Your wife.' "

Blue-collar blues:
With John Goodman and family.

At Bennigan's, Roseanne would get good tips for speaking her mind. Less than a decade later, she'd earn a million dollars a week for it. Her mouth would often be a liability, but commercially and comically, it was her greatest asset: "I have a big mouth and I want to use it as much as I can against what I think is wrong. Creative speech is a weapon against evil, so you gotta use it or lose it."

Roseanne knew what it was like to be in the minority from the moment she was born into a Jewish family in Salt Lake City in 1952. Her family was descended from Holocaust survivors, and she grew up in a frightened, neurotic household. She married at eighteen and had four children by the age of twenty-six. After her rounds at Bennigan's, she turned to the local stand-up scene as a kind of spiritual salvation. Roseanne had immersed herself in feminist literature but hadn't yet reconciled her politics with her onstage manner, and it was a rocky road at first. She used to close her nascent act by saying, "People say to me, 'You're not very feminine.' Well, they can *suck my duck*." As she told *Playboy* magazine, "I used to be the most foulmouthed comic. But I figured out how to take a radical thought and make it mainstream through wording and packaging. Men became the butt of my jokes, only I tried not to be mean-spirited. For packaging, I used the cover of being everyone's fat mother, fat neighbor. I used a funny voice."

By the time she made her debut appearance on *The Tonight Show* in 1985, she had refined both the wording and the packaging. Chewing gum, with a nervous laugh and a fluttery hand, she was actually charming. And incisive:

I'm a housewife. I never get out of the house. I sit home all the time; I never do anything. I hate that word. I prefer to be called Domestic Goddess—after all, it's more descriptive. . . . Still, stuff bugs me. This bugs me the worst. That's when the husband thinks that the wife knows where everything is, huh? Like they think the uterus is a tracking device.

"They didn't want me to say the word *uterus*—it had never been said on late-night telly or something," she recalled. "That was pretty symptomatic of what it was like to be a woman comic at the time." It may have been Roseanne's first encounter with the authority of network television; it wouldn't be the last. Her appearance with Johnny Carson made her an overnight sensation, which led to an HBO special in 1987. It caught the attention of two producers, Marcy Carsey and Tom Werner, who were developing a series about working-class moms called *Life and Stuff*.

At first, Roseanne and the new series seemed like a perfect fit—once, of course, the other two moms in the script were jettisoned in favor of Our Heroine. Debuting in October of 1988 on ABC, *Roseanne* showcased a new kind of family for television viewers: a real one. Roseanne Conner and her husband, Dan (played with an ursine amiability by John Goodman), lived in the blue-collar neighborhood of fictional Landford, Illinois, with their

two girls and one son (which paralleled Barr's own family structure). In the initial season, Roseanne worked an intensely boring job at Wellman Plastics and Dan was a building contractor, but as the eight seasons wore on, life affected the Conners much as it had affected many working-class families during the Reagan era: Roseanne was fired from her union job and worked double shifts to make ends meet (including a waitressing gig) while her husband tried starting his own business, only to watch it fail. Their kids got into puberty's real predicaments, dated creeps, got depressed and locked themselves in their rooms, were embarrassed by their parents, and, of course, never put their stuff away. The Conners' living room looked either like a megaton bomb had been detonated in it or looked simply like millions of viewers' living rooms or both. *Roseanne* was referred to in the press as the exact opposite of *The Cosby Show*.

ROSEANNE: Hey! Black people are just like us. They're every bit as good as us and any people who don't think so is just a bunch of banjo-picking, cousin-dating, barefoot embarrassments to respectable white trash like us!

Unlike those in many sitcoms, the characters in *Roseanne* were aware how at odds they were with a typical sitcom; when Dan is about to make some paternal pronouncement, Roseanne sneers, "What is this, the Ward Cleaver speech?" Eldest daughter Becky wants a new dress for the school dance, but the one she wants costs $79.99 at the mall. A helpful mall worker suggests that the dress could eventually be worn by the younger daughter. "Yeah," drawls Roseanne, "but for eighty bucks, it had better fit the whole family." When some financial and logistical calamities back up against each other, Roseanne tells Dan, "Well, hell, it can't get any worse. So, what're you going to do but laugh?"

Millions of Americans did. The show catapulted to number two in the annual Nielsen rankings and remained in the top five for its first six seasons. According to Jeff

Foxworthy, "Somebody said to me early on, when I first started trying to write the first redneck book, 'Well, you're talking about the lowest common denominator.' And I said, 'No, I'm not, I'm talking about the most common denominator.' And that's who *Roseanne* appealed to. People watched that show and they saw their relationship with their kids and their relationship with their sister, they saw something in it that they made a connection with and that's why it worked." Roseanne increasingly modeled the show after her own style and preoccupations, including ongoing subplots with homosexual characters, mirroring her own gay brother and lesbian sister. And if the Conner family slung around put-down zingers like the best Catskills comics, that was okay, too. *Roseanne* increasingly became the text on which the real Roseanne rewrote her life story, but in the beginning, it maintained its crucial relationship to real life. As she said about the series:

> If you really want to get big and philosophical about it, it was just life. It was a working-class woman. She lost her union job and it was about losing your union job and, basically, all the union benefits. So, it pretty much documented the destruction of the working class and that's what I always meant to do.

But, like Job, whose family was in even direr straits than the Conners, Roseanne was born unto trouble, as the sparks fly upward. The soundstage for her show quickly turned into a battlefield as she seized more and more control of the writing, the production, the direction of the material. Heads rolled faster than anything seen since the French Revolution, and even Carsey and Werner, the show's producers, voluntarily exiled themselves from the set for fear of agitating their apoplectic star further. At one point, Roseanne was the most powerful woman in television, but by the time the show wound down in 1997, she had spent a good deal of her likability capital.

Still, likability, tolerance, and deference were never in her self-created job description. Her fierce commitment to the real world is what put her on top in the first place. "I think it's the comedian's job to be controversial and explode—to afflict the comfortable and comfort the afflicted," she said, compounding an earlier quote:

Hear me roar:
Many guises, versions, and series later, Roseanne still can work a room.

> ## Look, I'm a comic. I'm not the fucking president. Everything comics do is to expose hypocrisy and dishonesty, so why wouldn't I be honest, for Christ's sake?

"I'M COUNTING YOUR SHRIMP!"
SEINFELD

Larry and I were at the cash register at one of those Korean delis, and there's a lot of products that you don't know where they're from—they're just wrapped in cellophane and sometimes there's a Post-it note on it or something like "fig bar." So we would talk about it and he said, you should do a show like this. And that was it.

–Jerry Seinfeld

The "show like this" that two stand-up comics, Jerry Seinfeld and Larry David, discussed in an all-night Korean deli one evening in New York at the tail end of the 1980s would evolve into "nothing"—a magical nothing that fueled the most popular television comedy of the next decade.

Seinfeld, born in 1954, was raised in the Long Island town of Massapequa (which, he claimed, was an American Indian word for "near the mall") and grew up listening to the yarn-spinning albums of Bill Cosby. As soon as he graduated from Queens College, he was taking the subway or the Long Island Rail Road into Manhattan, trying to make his name at the various stand-up clubs that had proliferated in the late 1970s. Seinfeld was a disciplined comedian, able to seclude himself for hours on end to develop his material, and he cultivated a genial gift for observation. As a teenager, Judd Apatow, a fellow Long Islander, also obsessed with comedy, used to catch his act:

> I used to go see him at Caroline's in New York and he was just one of those guys where the entire act was perfect and every joke was as strong as any observational joke you had ever seen and it seemed like your friend making observations. There was something very warm about it and it wasn't angry, but annoyed.

Seinfeld himself concurred in an interview: "I'm annoyed. But if you're not cranky and annoyed, you can't be a comedian. Even I, though I might not seem to be, am constantly irritated."

Seinfeld may well have been irritated that his career wasn't moving ahead faster, but a debut appearance on *The Tonight Show* on May 6, 1981, put him in the express lane, when Johnny Carson gave Seinfeld a rarely conferred OK sign after his monologue. For the next decade, Seinfeld did the stand-up route in clubs across America, often working three hundred nights a year, but he and his managers searched long and hard to find the right vehicle for his gifts. The television sitcom *Benson*, however, wasn't it. Seinfeld had the small part of a publicist but was fired after two episodes—a fact he discovered only when he showed up for work one day and everyone in the cast had a script but Jerry.

After that debacle, he returned to New York and hooked up with Larry David, and their wanderings through a Korean grocery store inspired a pitch to NBC. With Roseanne Barr's success, there seemed to be a run on stand-up comics whose work could transform into a series. Seinfeld and David's first idea was a TV special that would follow Jerry through his day and end with the nightclub material inspired by it, but it ultimately became a series, originally called *Stand-up.* Its concept was unique, to say the least; according to Seinfeld, "That was the concept behind the show: no concept." The show would focus on the random peregrinations of Jerry and his three friends caroming around Manhattan in an unfocused search for love, fame, and a place that served good cold sesame noodles. The executives at NBC admitted they didn't get it. Seinfeld's case was not helped by David and his obsessive perfectionism; he refused to change one word of the material—even though the network hadn't made the slightest commitment to the show.

Eventually a pilot was stitched together, but it was a hardly an auspicious debut. "Our test results were the worst test results in comedy history," recalled Jason Alexander,

The most famous shirt in TV history: Seinfeld with Michael Richards as Kramer.

who joined the cast as Jerry's school chum George Constanza. "I mean, they basically said, 'Now we have to throw out our TV sets because this was on the screen for a moment.'" Seinfeld concurred: "My favorite [test result report] was the one that said, 'Contemporary, unusual, appealing to young adults—and therefore something we don't want.'" The executives thought it might be salvaged if Seinfeld's character married his friend Elaine Benes and ditched the loser, George, and the weirdo, Kramer, but Seinfeld and David stuck to their guns—not that anyone was particularly impressed by such integrity. Characteristically, only David was buoyed by the bad news. "Once the network said they weren't gonna run the show, I just thought, 'Oh, well, it must be very unusual for them not to run it,' so it became a little more special in my eyes once they said that."

Seinfeld's manager, George Shapiro, kept badgering the network executives about getting what was then called *The Seinfeld Chronicles* on the air. NBC shrugged its collective shoulders and stuck the show in as a summer one-shot, then ordered a few isolated episodes, then a larger commitment in a rotten time slot. It was being crushed in the ratings by a detective show called *Jake and the Fat Man*. NBC president Brandon Tartikoff saw his worst doubts confirmed: "Who's going to care about the four Jews running around New York City?" Comedian and director David Steinberg came to Seinfeld and David's defense. "I ran into Brandon Tartikoff and told him, 'You know these guys, they're not doing the comedy that you expect on purpose. This was the only way that they know how to do their comedy.'"

Eventually, *Seinfeld* found its audience and its voice around its sixteenth episode in May of 1991, called "The Chinese Restaurant," where Jerry, George, and Elaine (Kramer wasn't leaving his apartment much at this point) wait unsuccessfully for a table at a local Chinese restaurant. The idea was David's: "A show is what, twenty-three minutes? So, I thought, let's have them wait for the whole twenty-three minutes." The wait provided the kind of painful choices and solipsistic inequities that were uniquely characteristic of the show's main characters. Jerry won't leave because "I don't want to go to a bad movie by myself. Who am I going to make sarcastic remarks to?" They reluctantly decide to bribe the restaurant's recalcitrant host with a twenty-dollar bill, which only leads to more bickering.

For all of its innovative structure, *Seinfeld* followed a tradition that went back to *The Jack Benny Program*: Jerry Seinfeld, stand-up comedian, played a stand-up comedian named Jerry Seinfeld. According to Alexander, "Jerry always says that the strangest thing in his life was he would come to work in a pair of jeans, take off those jeans, put on an identical pair of jeans to play the character, and then take those off to go home as himself." Like Benny, Seinfeld also surrounded himself with a memorable ensemble, a trio of gifted comic actors: Alexander, Julia Louis-Dreyfus, and Michael Richards. And also like Benny, Seinfeld was extremely generous with his playmates, giving away some of the best parts of the show, often because, never confident of his acting abilities, he thought they could be served up better by his supporting cast.

But where Jack Benny's repertory company was composed of amiable wiseguys, Seinfeld's friends were pathologically self-indulgent, capable of cheating not only innocent

Who's waiting on line first?
Modern-day Bud and Lou: Seinfeld and Jason Alexander.

ELAINE: Let's just slip him money.
JERRY: Do they do that kind of thing? How do we split it? Three ways.
GEORGE: How about seven and seven and six–I'm not a big eater.
Jerry: I'm counting your shrimp!

bystanders and small children but each other as well. Unlike other sitcoms, which were drenched in sentimentality, *Seinfeld*'s dictum was "no hugging, no learning." In fact, there was no evolution at all on the show; like the movie *Groundhog Day*, each episode seemed to reboot the series. Yes, there were recurring characters that came, interacted as best they could with the leads, and then went their merry way, but they never appeared to have any effect on Jerry and his friends. That principle was in immense defiance of television sitcom rules, and that's largely because there were never any children featured on the show—except, of course, Jerry, George, Elaine, Kramer, and the Bubble Boy.

Despite—or perhaps because of—the characters' basic unlikabilty, *Seinfeld* became television's most successful comedy over the course of nine seasons. Because of episodes like "The Chinese Restaurant," the "show about nothing" moniker was frequently hung around the show's neck, but as King Lear might have said, that nothing didn't come from nothing. Actually, the show's episodes became more and more intricately plotted, brilliantly weaving four or more plotlines together per episode. Often, the plots were so complex that a strand or two had to be resolved as the closing credits played—and there were still one or two left spinning in the air. Alexander marveled at the effect:

Goodbye Yellow Brick Road
When the series departed from the airwaves, it was a national event.

> The reason people think the show is about nothing, which is so interesting considering how uniquely and intricately plotted each of those episodes were, is that, in any episode, regardless of what the story lines were, if there was a funny run, if it was tangential, we still did it. Because funny ruled the day. Is it funny? If it's really funny, let's do it. And if it's not, let's kill it.

In 1998, Seinfeld decided to kill the show itself. At NBC corporate headquarters in New York, he was offered a rumored $110 million for a tenth season. As his manager, George Shapiro, recounted, Seinfeld took a walk around Central Park after being made the offer:

> Jerry sits down. He said, "As a stand-up comedian, you feel you're getting a standing ovation. And that's the time to leave. You don't want to stay on, like, another fifteen minutes so they say, 'Oh, he was good but he was on a little long.'" He said, "My deepest gut, you know, is to leave now, despite the offer and everything else."

For a show that began with a whimper, the end of its run turned into a big bang. On May 14, 1998, the last episode was watched by more than 76 million viewers, concluding a two-part episode where Jerry and Co. get thrown into prison. The final tag referred back to an ongoing gimmick discarded after the fourth season—Jerry doing bits of his stand-up act as bookends to the episode—and featured Seinfeld, in orange prison garb, trying to crack jokes in front of a pretty tough crowd.

JERRY: So, what is it with the yard? You'd think the weights and the sodomy would be enough . . .

HECKLER'S VOICE: Hey, Seinfeld—you suck!!

The voice of the heckler who was giving Jerry a hard time—a deranged criminal serving consecutive life sentences for serial killings, no doubt—was Larry David's.

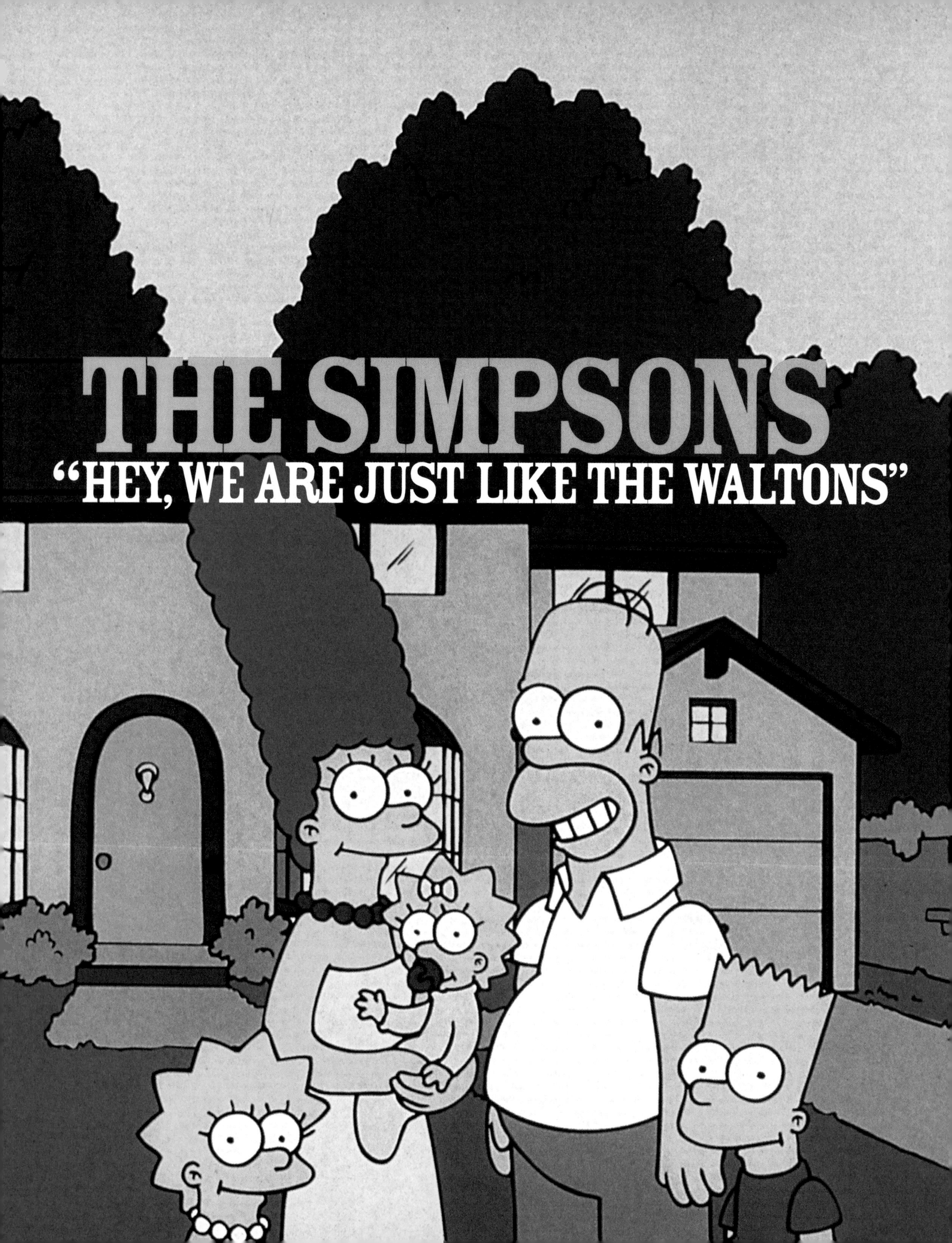
THE SIMPSONS
"HEY, WE ARE JUST LIKE THE WALTONS"

HOMER: I'm sorry, Marge, but sometimes I think we're the worst family in town.

MARGE: Maybe we should move to a larger community.

HOMER: D'oh!

BART: Don't have a cow, Dad.

LISA: The sad truth is, all families are like us.

In the fall of 1990, there were two typical American parents who were tormented by a very unruly and irresponsible son. Their names were George and Barbara Bush, and Mrs. Bush, who was first lady of the nation at the time, gave an interview to *People* magazine, where she discussed the latest television craze: *The Simpsons*. "It was the dumbest thing I've ever seen," she said, "but it's a family thing and I guess it's clean."

Two years later, while running for reelection, her husband, George, couldn't let the matter drop: "We need a nation closer to the Waltons than to the Simpsons," he declared at the Republican National Convention. In an episode that aired two days after the speech, the Simpsons were shown sitting around the living room, watching the president on TV. Bart objects to the criticism: "Hey, we *are* just like the Waltons. We're praying for an end to the Depression, too." Bush picked on the wrong family; within a few months, he was out and the Simpsons are still on television (and *his* son hasn't gotten any better behaved, either).

The idea for *The Simpsons* had been hatched in 1997, when film and television producer James L. Brooks was making the TV variety series *The Tracey Ullman Show* for the fledgling Fox network. Brooks was a fan of local cartoonist Matt Groening and had one of Groening's original cartoons—from the syndicated comic strip called *Life in Hell*—hanging on his office wall. Brooks invited Groening to discuss turning his strip into a series of animated short films to use in the show. While Groening was waiting in the reception area of Brooks's office, he had a change of heart: "I had this good gig going with my weekly comic strip, and I was afraid that if the animated cartoon didn't work out, there would be a taint on my weekly comic-strip job. So I created *The Simpsons* on the spot, thinking that if it did fail, I could just go back and draw rabbits, and no one would be the wiser."

I'd like to thank the Academy . . . Matt Groening with his hellspawn.

Groening proposed a cartoon featuring a dysfunctional American family in a typical American town, "a family on television that watches television." He was inspired by a show that *he* used to watch on television, *Leave It to Beaver*:

> The best character was not Beaver, not his brother, but Eddie Haskell. Eddie Haskell was this mean, sarcastic, two-faced teenager who just made me vibrate with happiness every time he was on-screen. And I thought, wouldn't it be neat to make a disobedient bad character the main character of a show? "Son of Eddie

Haskell," and really that's what *The Simpsons* is. Bart Simpson is the son of Eddie Haskell, flash forward thirty years later.

Bart is, of course, not the son of Eddie Haskell, but of the self-involved, donut-devouring Homer Simpson and his long-suffering, silver-lining-looking wife, Marge. They live with their overachieving daughter, Lisa, and silent toddler, Maggie, in the mythical town of Springfield, intentionally named after the suburban utopia at the center of *Father Knows Best* (and there are Springfields in half the states in the Union). Once one got under the fluorescent yellow skin of the Simpson family, they actually seemed to be pretty utopian themselves. This, according to chief writer George Meyer, was a conscious choice:

> We can get away with a little more on *The Simpsons* because the setup is so traditional. The Simpsons are an intact family unit, which is something you hardly ever see on television anymore. Homer works nine to five, and Marge stays at home, and they have a boy and a girl and a baby, and they live in the standard middle–class house even though it would seem that they probably couldn't afford that house. It was a smart choice to be very traditional, and then make the execution odd and quirky. Because people can take only so much before their heads explode.

The crudely animated five-minute cartoons premiered on *The Tracy Ullman Show* on April 19, 1987, and managed to explode quite a few heads—in a good way—nationwide. At a Christmas party for the Ullman show, a staff member came up to Brooks and "just told me with such passion—almost with tears springing from his eyes—how much everybody like him was waiting for a prime-time animated series on network television again. And the passion of that really impacted me, so producer Sam Simon, Matt, and I set about converting it into a half-hour show." It would be the first animated prime-time series since *The Flintstones*, nearly a quarter of a century earlier. Within weeks, *The Simpsons* would become the bedrock of the Fox network, cracking the Nielsen top ten in its first year. Bart Simpson quotes became catchphrases, appearing on millions of T-shirts across the country. *TV Guide* proclaimed *The Simpsons* to be "TV's hot new prime-time family."

BART: According to Creationism, there were no cavemen.

HOMER: Good riddance! Their drawings suck and they look like hippies.

"We always hide behind 'It's just a cartoon!'" said Groening, and that allowed *The Simpsons* to tackle a wide range of topics that would have been taboo in a regular sitcom series, let alone an animated show. Everything from the Moral Majority to nuclear regulation to chemical dependency to homosexuality to Broadway musicals (well, those two aren't such a big leap from each other) could be tackled by *The Simpsons*' aggressively elastic style and format. Meyer, mixing metaphors, said the show "is like a Trojan horse that gets past people's radar because it's superficially conservative. The show's subtext, however, is completely subversive and wild." Audiences didn't even know that rules were being broken; they were enjoying themselves too much. As Groening pointed out:

> There are all these little unspoken rules on TV: characters can't smoke; everyone has to wear their seat belt; drinking is frowned upon. And on *The Simpsons*, of

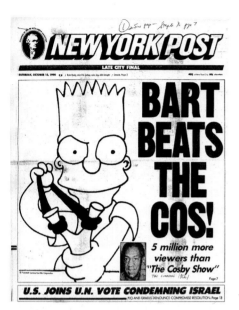

Sorry about that.
The Simpsons outdrew the final episode of *The Cosby Show*; (far right) Groening, James T. Brooks and Sam Simon, the creators.

course, our characters drink and smoke, don't wear seat belts, and litter. On the other hand, right-wingers complain there's no God and religion on TV. Not only do the Simpsons go to church every Sunday and pray, they actually speak to God from time to time. We show Him, and God has five fingers. Unlike the Simpsons, who only have four.

But without an emotional core, *The Simpsons* would just have been inefficiently policed anarchy. That's where the show "played both sides of the street," as Sid Caesar referred to the balance between comedy and seriousness. "We wanted you to believe these people were real," said Brooks. "We've got to make you experience the stories and feel something." Conan O'Brien, who was briefly a writer for the series, remembered that "Sam and Jim and Matt stressed that *this is a family*. And that can start to sound pretty treacly, but you can't have an episode where Homer sells Bart, or harvests his organs." At the center of the series' ethos was Homer himself, a TV dad who has gone beyond "Father Knows Least" and regressed to "Father Knows Worst":

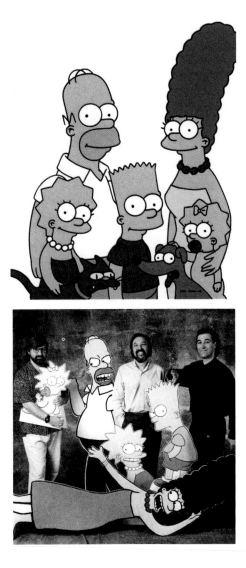

MARGE: Well . . . it's not that I don't love the guy, I'm always sticking up for him, it's just that he's so self-centered. He forgets birthdays, anniversaries, holidays. He chews with his mouth open, he gambles, he hangs out at a seedy bar with bums and lowlifes.

HOMER: Oh, it's true!

MARGE: He blows his nose on the towels and then puts them back in the middle!

HOMER: I only did that a couple of times!

Brooks defends his hero: "Let's just say that he's a father who teaches you to assume that love is there, without any concrete act to substantiate it on his part. I guess if you can raise kids with the thought that a person mistreating them in the moment might actually love them, it wouldn't be altogether bad."

In 2007, *The Simpsons* aired its four hundredth episode, making it the longest-running sitcom in American television history, and no end is in sight. Even the legions of *Simpsons* imitators recognize its mythic dominance; a 2002 episode of *South Park* was titled "*The Simpsons* Already Did It!" Its creators seem overwhelmed: "The whole experience of *The Simpsons* is now so much more than any of us," said Brooks. "It's a culture, it's a little city; we all go to work there every day. It has its own rules and laws. It's out there to be served." But the success story of *The Simpsons* wouldn't be complete without a moral. Matt Groening supplies it:

> *The Simpsons*' message over and over again is that your moral authorities don't always have your best interests in mind. Teachers, principals, clergymen, politicians—for the Simpsons, they're all goofballs, and I think that's a great message for kids.

CHAPTER SIX

WHEN I'M BAD, I'M BETTER

THE GROUNDBREAKERS

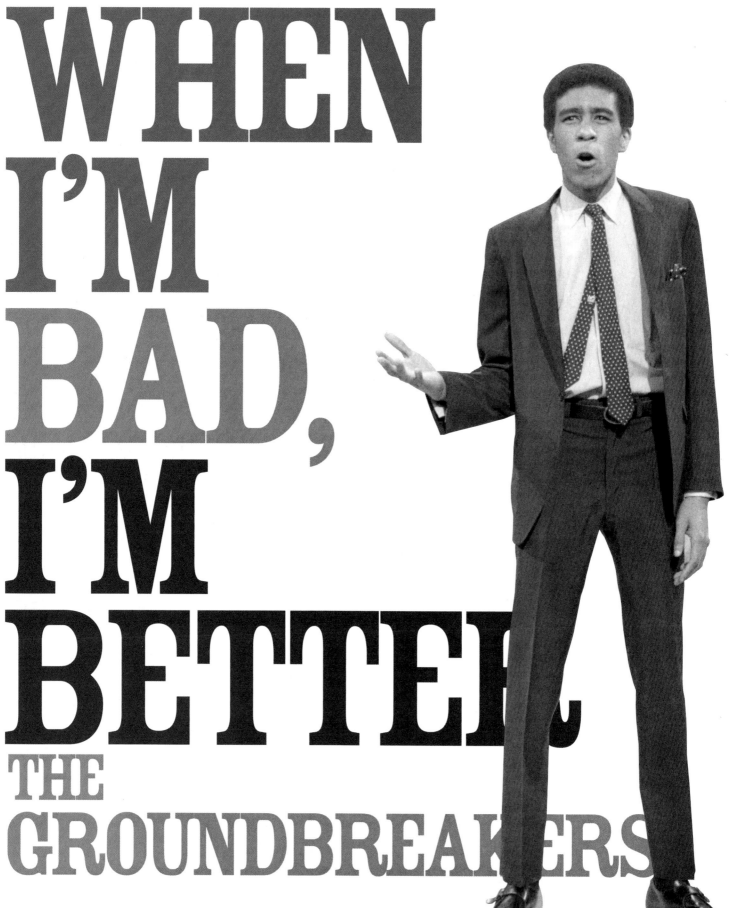

The Puritan streak in
America runs deep. We
seem to accept every sort
of depraved aspect of
human nature, except
the more natural things.
There has always been
bathroom humor and sex
jokes; those are the two
most irresistible urges.
–George Carlin

THE BIG(GER) PICTURE

When the Puritans arrived in America in the early seventeenth century, they brought with them a high regard for freedom of expression, but comedy, apparently, didn't make the cut. This country's complex relationship between expression and repression stretches back to that arrival at Plymouth Rock. In fact, a majority of America's early colonists, despite their insistence on religious freedom, drew the line at all forms of entertainment: theatrical presentation, singing, dancing. During most of the colonial era, comedy in America—in the northeast in particular—was left out in the cold. (Although, perhaps, it gave rise to that old joke: "Why do Puritans forbid sex?" "It could lead to dancing.")

This essential tension would unleash a turbulent undercurrent in American popular culture for five centuries. While it seems inherent to the American character to provide access to sexual, political, and religious freedom to as many people as possible in a democratic society, it is equally inherent in our character to limit that access. The popular arts have always drawn fire from a multitude of forces throughout our existence, and those forces have normally been lumped in the catchall term of that great boogeyman of freedom of expression: censorship.

But censorship in America is as complex and multivaried as the country itself. When we say a work of art or a performer has been censored, that censorship rarely comes from the same source twice, or for the same reasons, or by the same standards.

In our democracy, the process of censorship has been torn between two opposing but unequal forces: freedom of expression, ostensibly guaranteed in the First Amendment as every American's right, and access to that freedom, which is subjected to the ever-changing forces of the marketplace and technology. This struggle is often boiled down to the argument "If you don't like it, you can turn the knob." But the counterargument, as legal historian Fred W. Schauer put it, is "you can't turn the knob until you've heard what it is that you want to turn the knob off from." Advocates of restriction have often pointed to the concept of material "unforeseen, unbidden, and unwelcome" entering their homes—or their cars, for that matter. A broadcast of some George Carlin material over a car radio in 1973 became the basis for a censorship case that went as far as the Supreme Court.

Unfortunately, even the highest court in the land—"the Big Daddy," as Lenny Bruce put it (alas, performing in front of it was one gig he never got)—is inconsistent regarding issues of obscenity and indecency. Comedy has been regulated, more often than not, by legal precedents that involve pornography, obscenity, and indecency, and standards for these issues have never remained written in stone for very long. As an example, it was up to the Court to define pornography, the exhibition of which could be a criminal offense, in a famous 1957 case, *Roth v. United States*. The Court ruled that Congress could ban material "utterly without redeeming social importance," or in other words, "whether to the average person, applying contemporary community standards, the dominant theme of the material taken as a whole appeals to the prurient interest." That sounds reasonably clear, but who is an "average person"? What is a "contemporary community standard"? There has never been, and probably never will be, one gold standard for censorship.

Of course, state and local authorities have their own respective standards, and most of the censorship cases in this country, certainly as they affect the performance of comedy, come from the state or local level. New York City, oddly enough, brought forth some of the most high-profile censorship cases. In the 1920s, Mayor James Walker was one of the town's most beloved reprobates; he managed to hold back the tide of the New York Society for the Suppression of Vice, but then he went on vacation in 1927 and all hell broke loose—or rather all hell was locked up. Under the acting mayor, the police raided three Broadway shows, including one starring Mae West. This kind of moral crusade was not lost on another New York mayor, Fiorello La Guardia, who took office in 1934.

In his ardor to remove all kinds of corruption from New York, La Guardia put burlesque on the same level as gambling, graft, and organized crime. "There will be no let-up on the part of the city in this situation. It will be a bitter fight to the finish against incorpo-

First Amendment rights:
Lenny Bruce enters an opinion.

rated filth!" he proclaimed. When the city refused to renew the licenses of all burlesque theaters on May 1, 1937, it was curtains for burlesque. Nearly thirty years later, Lenny Bruce would be busted in New York for violating Section 1140-A of the Penal Law (Immoral Shows and Exhibitions). His New York arrest would lead to his only criminal conviction. (Interestingly, although Bruce, George Carlin, Richard Pryor, and Mae West were all arrested at one time or another for violating a local obscenity law, only West ever went to prison.)

But the governmental figurehead of censorship is only the most obvious source of censorship. Outrage usually begins at the grass roots level. Citizens all over America have formed groups to represent their community interests—special interest groups, they are now called. Often, they have been formed in religious communities or by citizens with religious affiliations, but these groups are not bound to any one denomination. Indeed, they are not even necessarily part of the mainstream. The NAACP was highly vocal in its disapproval of both the radio and television versions of *Amos 'n' Andy* and that led to the show's eventual removal from the air, even though it was ostensibly enjoyed by millions of white people.

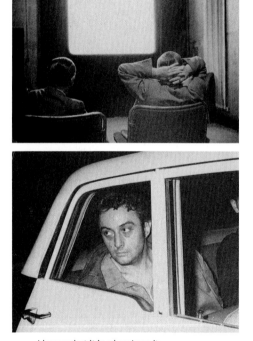

I know what it is when I see it: Joseph A. Breen (right), screening for the Code; Bruce on an obscenity bust.

The power of the pocketbook has a far greater influence on censorship than is generally credited. When interest groups have boycotted a film or a performance or raised enough bad publicity to convince others to do so, self-censorship follows quickly. The emergence of radio in the early 1920s and sound film in 1927 also ushered in fresh approaches to singing, dancing, joke telling—and sex. As soon as these freedoms appeared in the media, there came a battalion of moralists and interest groups, largely Catholic, lobbying Hollywood to police its product. Hollywood accepted a self-imposed nonbinding list of dos and don'ts as early as 1930 but largely flouted the criticism of the moralists and continued to portray sin and seduction. The Depression had made it harder to bring in audiences, and sex and violence sells—not an ingenious discovery. The Catholic Legion of Decency was organized to stamp its formal disapproval on certain movies. Faced with a boycott during hard times at the box office, Hollywood swallowed hard and adopted the suggestions of the Production Code in 1934. The Code forbade the depiction of "lustful and licentious acts," among other "sinful" acts. The highly devout Catholic enforcer of the Code, Joseph A. Breen, once proclaimed that "Cockeyed philosophies of life, ugly sex situations, cheap jokes, and dirty dialogue aren't wanted. Decent people don't like this sort of stuff and it's our job to see that they get none of it." These values, and their concomitant restrictions, lasted more than three decades.

Commerce exerted even greater pressure in the early days of radio and television. The broadcast media realized fairly early on that material that could be piped directly into your living room was different from material that a person had to go out and purchase a ticket to see. In 1927, the Hoover administration created the Federal Radio Commission, which proclaimed that the public owned the airwaves and that the public deserved both protection and freedom. (It was transformed into the Federal Communications Commission in 1934.) It was inevitable, however, that the commercial sponsor would be more sensitive to the issue of broadcast material than the government. Shows were sponsored by one commercial company per program, and an offensive joke or remark reflected directly on that sponsor; each gaffe or risqué comment meant a hundred fewer washing machines sold or a thousand fewer bars of soap. Those add up. Now, of course, "sponsors" are called "advertisers," and there are many more of them, and the force with which they can wield their combined cudgels is considerable.

When television came into being by 1948, it became clear that the FCC would have to take jurisdiction of this potentially more explosive broadcast medium. By and large, television simply adopted the moral values of the Hollywood Production Code; sitcoms of the 1950s and 1960s are rife with bedrooms containing two twin beds. When Senator Estes Kefauver chaired a Senate Subcommittee on Juvenile Delinquency in 1954, the focus became violence on television. As a result, each of the three major broadcast networks set up a Standards and Practices office (although CBS called theirs Program Practices) to review, suggest, and often enforce emendations to submitted material. The work of the internal censor is an arcane art, a mysterious force that derives much of its power from its very mystery. Standards and Practices units referred to themselves as "editors" rather than as censors. Producers could object, compromises could be reached, creative solutions arrived at, but the editors' objections were not necessarily proscribed in formal, accessible ways; a comedian often didn't know if he was going to cross a line until he had.

This is what George Carlin was getting at when he came up with his classic "Seven Words You Can't Say on Television" routine. He wasn't attacking the censors, really, or even the networks; he was expressing his frustration at the FCC, which never published, or made accessible, a list of objections. This is the great paradox in American censorship: practically every ruling or set of standards fell short of objective truth; each age, time, and community brings along its own subjective standards. Sex was not always the major offender, either. It could just as easily be politics or racism. One decade's outrageousness becomes the next generation's collective shrug. Even all "seven words" are no longer necessarily proscribed from network television—*piss*, *tits*, and even *shit* have made substantial progress.

Of course, with the advent of cable television, any attempt at broadcast restrictions seems quaint, if not ridiculous. The FCC has pointedly recused itself from interfering with the content of cable networks on the grounds, presumably, that the consumer has paid good money for control of that particular "knob." It comes back to the idea of access; technology has outpaced our ability to police our content. In December of 2006, *Saturday Night Live* debuted a digital short featuring a song called "Dick in a Box." Apparently *dick* is an honorary eighth word—it was bleeped out sixteen times. Producer Lorne Michaels did the next best thing; he posted the short on YouTube in its unexpurgated entirety. It has become one of the most popular Internet downloads of all time. It also provides a, well, potent metaphor—censors have been trying to put dicks in boxes for nearly a century, but they do tend to pop out anyway.

Perhaps more disturbing than the ineffectual attempts to put comedy in a box is the essential double standard in American censorship—that violence is okay, but sex and laughter are not. It seems appropriate to give Lenny Bruce the final summation on the subject:

Ne'er the twain shall meet:
Separate beds, per Standards and Practices.

Here come da judge!
Pigmeat Markham's legendary jurisprudence.

"Over-emphasis of sex and violence will be a deterrent to your child"—what he sees now, he will do later on. Good logic. Correct. If so, I'd rather my kid see stag movies than *King of Kings*. I don't want my kid killing Christ if he comes back. Did you ever see a stag film where it ends with someone killed in the end, or slapped in the mouth? Well, for the kids to watch killing, *King of Kings*—yes. *Shtupping*—no.

"GOODNESS HAD NOTHING TO DO WITH IT"

MAE WEST

It's hard to be funny when you have to be clean....On love and sex, I take it out in the open and laugh at it.
–Mae West

When Mae West sashayed down the steps of the Santa Fe *Chief* in June of 1932, at the height of the Great Depression, she already had a lot of scandal behind her—and what was in front of her was wide open. If that sounds like a Mae West line, it's because just about any sentence, spun in her inimitable way, sounds like one. It also happens to be the truth. West had never made a motion picture before, she was nearing forty, she was not a conventional sex symbol, and censors and moralists had been wagging their fingers at her since she was a kid. And yet within three years of her arrival in Hollywood, she would become the highest-paid woman in the country.

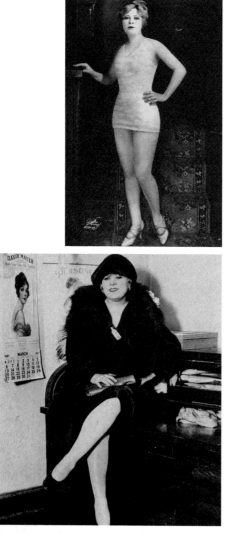

Hootchie-cootch:
Young Mae in vaudeville; looking her best, on trial in 1927.

MAN: I'd like to take you away from all this.
MAE WEST: All this? Oh, I get you. For a long time I was ashamed of the way I lived.
MAN: You mean to say you reformed?
MAE WEST: No, I got over being ashamed.

"I was born on August 17 at 10:30 p.m. on a cool night of a hot month, so I can expect anything." That is a real Mae West line. Her childhood in Brooklyn (she was born in 1893) was, in many ways, a perfect example of the rough-and-tumble mixture of high-art aspirations and low-art realities of popular entertainment at the beginning of the twentieth century. Mary Jane West's Bavarian-born mother, Matilda, thought that a stage career filled with singing and dancing lessons would be the way out of a lower-class existence. While such refinements helped Mae get onstage, her heart belonged to her daddy, "Battlin' Jack" West, a former bare-knuckle featherweight fighter, who, when he wasn't tending bar or mucking out stables, could be found at the racetrack. One could argue that her future stage persona rendered the rough truth of her father's world through the elegance of her mother's pretensions.

Her sentimental education came from her magpie talents at borrowing the most useful aspects of popular culture available to her. She made her stage debut at five, and she had little use for the sentimental blarney performed at the time; as a young girl she sang risqué songs, such as the one about a nice Italian girl who winds up dancing the "hootch-a-ma-kootch" at Coney Island. As she climbed the ladder of small-time vaudeville, she appropriated African American slang and attitudes and came away with her own idiosyncratic but highly effective way of singing the blues. By the mid-1920s, it was clear to West that she would be the best custodian of her talent, and with a colleague she adapted a third-rate one-act play into a Broadway vehicle specifically crafted for her. She would play Margie LaMont, a prostitute who winds up as the love object of the heir to a family fortune from Montreal. The story alone would have raised eyebrows; audiences were also taken aback by West's references to daddies, dames, dolls, and dirty rats. This was no lady of the camellias—West didn't play at the demimonde, she lived it. If her intentions weren't clear enough in the play, all audiences had to do was read the title of it: *Sex*.

***Sex* opened on Broadway in April of 1926**, and although some of the press was not amused (the *New York Times* refused to carry advertising for it), it enjoyed a run into the next year. But in early February 1927, acting mayor Joseph V. "Holy Joe" McKee, vulnerable to the campaigning of the New York Society for the Suppression of Vice, ordered the police to raid three Broadway shows (another was a serious look at lesbianism called *The Captive*), and their respective producers and performers were arrested. West, in her dual role as author and star, was charged with "corrupting the morals of youth, or others." West was particularly vulnerable because she had written a new show, trying out in Connecticut, called *The Drag*, a garishly realistic look at transvestism in vaudeville.

When the *Sex* trial began a week after the arrest, Mae West was featured on the front page of every tabloid in town. "I enjoyed the courtroom as just another stage, but not as amusing as Broadway," she later wrote. Stymied to find any lines or scenes that could be definitively obscene, the assistant D.A. went after West's performance and contended that her mannerisms, gestures, and personality were obscene. The attempt to prove this was ludicrous. West herself recounted what happened on the stand:

> I performed the dance fully clothed, wearing a tight metallic evening gown. . . . The prosecutor questioned one of the arresting officers in detail about this dance. The officer blushed and testified.

"Miss West moved her navel up and down and from right to left."

"Did you actually see her navel?" my lawyer asked him.

"No, but I saw something in her middle that moved from east to west."

The court room roared.

The final verdict wasn't quite so amusing: Judge George E. Donnellan declared that even though "New York is the most moral city in the universe, the show would have made a terrible impression upon the youth of our city" and sentenced West to ten days at the Welfare Island Woman's Workhouse on obscenity charges. Ironically, West's sentence was shaved off by a day for good behavior, and when the reporters surrounded her on her release, she told them, "A few days in the pen 'n' a $500 fine ain't too bad a deal. The publicity alone is worth a million dollars."

She returned to the stage in another vehicle, *Diamond Lil*, which placed her comfortably in the Victorian era, where her portrait of a scarlet woman had some aesthetic distance. When Paramount Pictures called for her in 1932, it was less concerned with her checkered past than with what her future could do for their checkbooks. There was a brief window of permissiveness in Depression-era Hollywood, and audiences were curious about these new fallen women, gangsters, and vampires. The film industry was not about to strangle the goose that was laying what few golden eggs could be had; Hollywood was going to get in what few good lays it had left.

And so, Mae West made her film debut in the fall of 1932, playing a supporting role in *Night After Night*. Her entrance was one of the most famous in film history. As the ex-mistress of nightclub owner George Raft, she wafts past a girl at the coat check:

COAT CHECK GIRL: Goodness, what beautiful diamonds.

MAE WEST: Goodness had nothing to do with it, dearie.

Even more audacious than her screen entrance was her studio entrance; she didn't much like the script and offered to quit and return her salary until she was given permission to rewrite the part for herself. *Variety* noted that "Miss West's dialogue is always unmistakably her own. It is doubtful if anyone else could write it." As George Raft put it, "She stole everything but the camera." She was such a success that Paramount optioned *Diamond Lil*, a property that had been put on a "banned" list two years earlier by the Hays Office, so West was asked first to submit her screenplay to the picture, now called *She Done Him Wrong*. It came back scrawled with blue pencil marks. It was all part of West's strategy:

Delectable digits:
With W.C. Fields in *My Little Chickadee* (1940); screen debut in *Night After Night* (1932).

> When I knew that the censors were after my films and they had to come and okay everything, I wrote scenes for them to cut! Those scenes were so rough that I'd never have used them. But they worked as a decoy. They cut them and left the stuff I wanted. I had these scenes in there about a man's fly and all that, and . . . then they'd say "cut it" and not notice the rest.

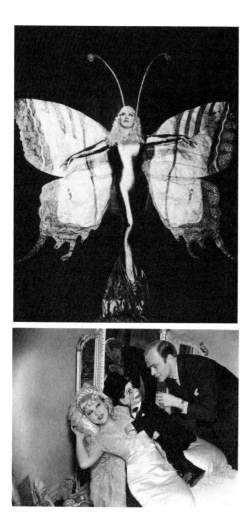

But she drifted:
Like flames to a moth; on the radio with Bergen and McCarthy; in color.

Unlike what led up to the *Sex* trial, there was little censors could say about West's appearance or performance. As one critic put it, any chorus girl in any Warner Bros. musical showed much more skin than West. Playing Lady Lou, "one of the finest women who ever walked the streets," West never lifted anything but her eyebrow. It was her way with a line that made Mae West special—and no censor could put his finger on *that*. Mae West made an even bigger splash in her second film, prompting a reporter to ask if West thought that there would now be an epidemic of smiling sinners who triumph at the end of movies. "Copy my stuff?" she replied. "Say, they can put all the scarlet women they like on the screen, and all the tenderloin stories. It's my clowning they can't copy, and it's the laughs that make me different." F. Scott Fitzgerald thought she was "the only Hollywood actress with an ironic edge and a comic spark." Her 1933 follow-up *I'm No Angel* made her part of popular culture; her biggest fans were young women, and even little girls were being entered in Mae West look-alike contects sponsored nationwide, each purring her frequently recycled catchphrase "Come up and see me sometime" (introduced in *She Done Him Wrong*).

JACK CLAYTON: You were wonderful tonight.

WEST: Yeah, I'm always wonderful at night.

JACK CLAYTON: Tonight, you were especially good.

WEST: Well . . . When I'm good, I'm very good. But, when I'm bad . . . (*winks at Jack*) I'm better.

As radio host Joe Franklin put it, "By being blue, she took Paramount out of the red." Indeed, she had saved the film studio and was on her way to becoming the highest-paid woman in America. She was a pioneer master (mistress?) at manipulating the media; she always had a wisecrack at the ready, and even though in real life she neither drank nor smoked (she was, however, an ardent enthusiast of the enema), West was smart enough to hide such inconsistencies from the public. Even a brief marriage in 1911 was expunged from her collective consciousness. In her unexpurgated state, she even appealed to people who professed to know better. After *I'm No Angel* was released, a film distributor in Louisiana wrote:

> Did the best business of the year with this one. Whether they like her or not, they all come out to see her. The church people clamor for clean pictures, but they all come out to see Mae West and stay as far away as they can from the clean ones.

A year later, the clamor from the church people turned loud enough to alter her career permanently. In July of 1934, Hollywood hired Joseph A. Breen to adopt and uphold a new Production Code. This one meant business; there would be no loopholes, no appeals, and certainly no sense of humor. While the new Code was being introduced, West was in production for her fourth Paramount picture, titled *It Ain't No Sin*. Breen and his enforcers questioned just what exactly was the "It" of the title, and—sin or no—the picture was retitled *Belle of the Nineties*. The handwriting was on the wall; such relentless tinkering and objections from the Production Code offices began to wear down Mae West. By end of 1935, the torch of the female box office star had been passed to six-year-old Shirley Temple. One couldn't ask for a more potent metaphor.

West had a few more cards up her Victorian sleeve. She appeared on the radio with Edgar Bergen and the ventriloquist dummy, Charlie McCarthy. Bantering with the little fellow, she remarked, "Charles, I remember our date and have the splinters to prove it." This comment, along with a sketch in which she played Eve in the Garden of Eden, drove NBC to distraction; she was banned from radio for the next twelve years. "She could make the phone book sexy," said Hugh Hefner, who would know. "It was all innuendo. They couldn't really censor her because it wasn't the lines, it was the way she read 'em." The rest of her movies during this period (she only made eight from 1932 to 1940) were pale imitations, and being forced to share screen time with W. C. Fields in *My Little Chickadee* was more of a chore than an inspiration. As historian Leonard Maltin said, "It's hard to tell whether the need to sanitize the stories and characters helped kill off Mae West's popularity or if the novelty wore off."

She thought of her persona as a trademark, like Coca-Cola, and resisted any attempt to change or update it. She refused to play Norma Desmond in the film *Sunset Boulevard*—that would have required transformation. She revived *Diamond Lil* for the stage and created a Las Vegas muscleman review. Joe Franklin remembers interviewing her during that engagement: "A man comes to the door and says, 'There were twelve musclemen here tonight.' And she says, 'Tell one to go home, I'm tired.' " In the 1970s, after a three-decade absence, she made two cinematic embarrassments, *Myra Breckenridge* and *Sextette* (which she also wrote), continuing to play the same flirtatious character even though she was now eligible for Social Security. "I met her at the end of her life," said Joan Rivers, "and she could not sit down at a dinner table unless you had adjusted the lights. She was so artfully conceived, and she was so smart. Mae, to the day she died, was Mae."

That day was November 22, 1980. Though Mae West herself ultimately became fixed in time, all you have to do is scratch the icon, and her saucy humor drips through:

WEST: You know, it was a toss-up whether I go in for diamonds or sing in the choir. The choir lost.

CARY GRANT: They always seem so cold to me. They have no warmth, no soul. I'm sorry you think more of your diamonds than you do of your soul.

WEST: I'm sorry you think more of my soul than you do of my diamonds. Maybe I ain't got no soul.

CARY GRANT: Oh, yes, you have, you just keep it hidden under a mask. Haven't you ever met a man who could make you happy?

WEST: Sure, lots of times.

Never tamed:
With Cary Grant, and as Tira, the lion tamer in *I'm No Angel* (1933).

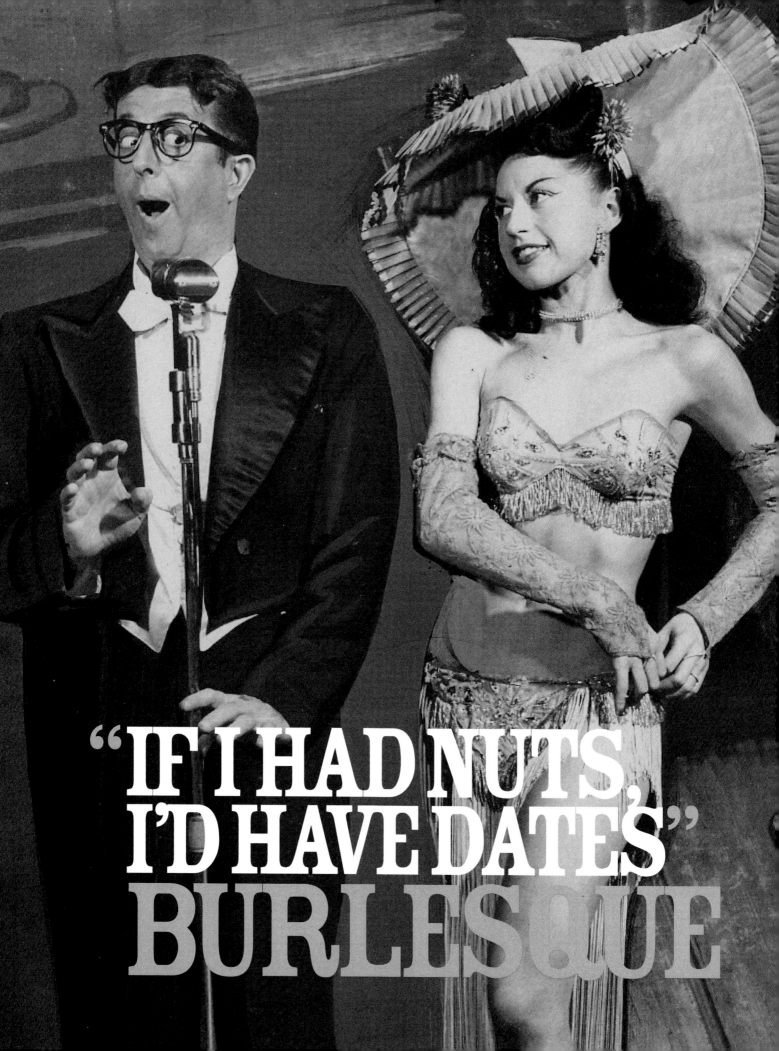

"IF I HAD NUTS, I'D HAVE DATES"
BURLESQUE

(Stooge enters, all bandaged up, with crutch)

STRAIGHT MAN: What happened to you?

STOOGE: I was living the life of Riley.

STRAIGHT MAN: Then what?

STOOGE: Riley came home.

You'd think if you had an entertainment form that catered to half the population, you'd be doing pretty well—and for a few decades, burlesque did pretty well.

Burlesque had its roots in the all-male, blackface minstrel shows of the nineteenth century, and its comedy was based on poking fun at, or burlesquing, current tastes or politics by having blacked-up comics imitate more established figures or stereotypes. Often the comics would be paired off, in what was called a double-act, which traded on wordplay and double-talk. In the late nineteenth century, a clever producer appropriated the structure of the minstrel show but threw out the male singing and dancing and replaced it with a chorus of beautiful girls. Blackface was out, too, but the corny jokes and double-talk remained; and that's how, as Stephen Sondheim once wrote in his lyrics to *Gypsy*, burlesque was born.

It was an effective and relatively inexpensive way to entertain an audience, and very much in contrast to vaudeville, it was constructed to appeal exclusively to the male population. Borrowing the touring structure of vaudeville, the first burlesque circuit (or "wheel") was created in 1905. There was nothing subtle about burlesque—it was low gags and tall gals. Initially, the spotlight of the burlesque show was on the comic. Burlesque comedians had to plug into the stock conventions that preceded them—even the scenery they joked in front of was just that: curtains or drops pulled from stock.

> Convention, not innovation, was the founding principle of burlesque comedy. The ritual was immutable. A fat comic did not bend over simply to tie his shoelace. He bent over to provide a target for the straight man's toe. . . . If none of these things were done, it was not ritual, and people who paid to see burlesque were gypped and would ask for their money back.
>
> —Rowland Barber, *The Night They Raided Minsky's*

At the center of burlesque comedy was the double-act borrowed from the minstrel show—the straight man and the stooge, otherwise known as the first and second banana. The stock situations included doctor's offices where incompetent physicians bullied credulous patients or hotel rooms where assignations were routed by intransigent hotel clerks or courtrooms where a percussive judge would bring down his gavel—usually on someone's head—at the least provocation, or simply a street corner where some poor boob was harassed, beaten, or robbed while asking the directions to Floogle Street, the mythical destination of every third burlesque sketch. To separate the sketches, there were the lightning-fast bits in front of the curtain: the blackout. And in all cases, sex was the not-so-submerged undercurrent; a double entendre would have been considered too much work for the men in the audience; a single one would do. Even the classroom was not immune from burlesque's salacious touch:

TEACHER: Where's little Mickey?

TOP BANANA: Here I am. I'm sorry I'm late, but mother was late packing my lunch. Here it is.

(Shows bag.)

TEACHER: Do you have nuts?

TOP BANANA: No.

TEACHER: Do you have dates?

TOP BANANA: If I had nuts, I'd have dates.

There were a thousand different routines out there, and to survive, a comic had to

Top bananas:
(previous) Phil Silvers in full burlesque mode; Jackie Gleason, with a spritz from his past; (opposite) the end of Minsky's Burlesque, 1937, thanks to Mayor La Guardia, crusader against vice.

pick up a cue and launch into one at a moment's notice. As the critic Leonard Maltin said, 'Burlesque, like vaudeville, was very demanding work because you didn't just do one performance a day, you did many. So performing the same routines over and over and over again was crucial to any comedian's development. There were old standby routines that every burlesque comic knew and you could just refer to them by the shorthand descriptions and everybody knew what you meant."

As the 1920s began, and there was more competition from vaudeville and motion pictures, burlesque had a more difficult time holding on to the exclusively male audience who would shuffle into the theaters for the two to four daily shows. And so, not for the first time in American culture and certainly not for the last, they resorted to sex. Shows got "bluer," first by putting the girls in the spotlight and having them display more of their pulchritude and, second, by pushing the comics' material further and further to the edge.

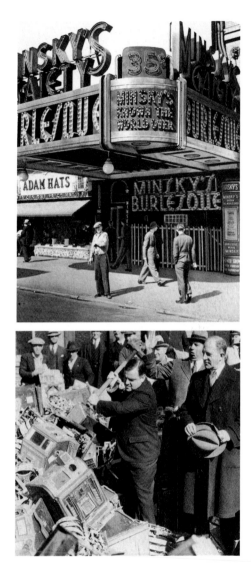

TEACHER: **All right, Jimmy, you're so smart. Use the words** *honor* **and** *offer* **in a sentence.**

COMIC: **That's easy. She offered her honor. He honored her offer. And all night long, he was on her and off her.**

When the Depression hit, the strippers took center stage from the comics—which upended (as it were) the whole comic premise of burlesque. Whereas before, the comic could make antic hay out of playing bits with, or off, a pretty girl, the pretty girl was now the main attraction, with the comics filling the time between G-string changes. As Phil Silvers remembered, "Burlesque was about the only steady work in 1932. To seize the attention of the predominantly male audience, a comedian had to make his presence felt. And fast. The management was not interested in how funny you were. Just how *often* you were funny."

Just as burlesque was getting racier, it bought itself a higher profile—and it was a mixed blessing. After operating several burlesque houses in New York City, the Minsky family decided to invade the citadel of the Theater District and open for business in the Republic Theater on West Forty-second Street in 1931. The Minskys banked on the hopes that their swanky surroundings might make their product seem classier, but they did little to alter the content of their shows. It was hard to know what was worse—the content of the shows or their leering titles, such as "Eileen Dover from Aiken." Whatever other emotions Minsky's burlesque roused in the city's male populace, it roused the ire of the new mayor of New York, Fiorello La Guardia, who shut down burlesque by 1937. It was about time to bring down the ragged curtain on burlesque anyway; the jokes were getting as old as the scenery.

Still, burlesque limped along as an American institution. It was a profitable training ground for comedians like Mickey Rooney, Red Buttons, Jack Albertson, Jackie Gleason, Abbott and Costello, and Phil Silvers. Nothing in American humor could be more childish, more cheap, more smutty than burlesque—but nothing could give more simple, unadorned pleasure, either. It cast a very long shadow. Whenever Johnny Carson arched an eyebrow at the buxom Carol Wayne during "The Mighty Carson Art Players," or whenever Jerry Seinfeld and George Costanza tied themselves into linguistic pretzels, the sweet sounds of the seltzer bottle could be heard spritzing in the distance.

"I DON'T EVEN KNOW WHAT I'M TALKING ABOUT"

ABBOTT AND COSTELLO

LA GUARDIA TO COSTELLO: What are you doing here?

COSTELLO: Here's your pass for tonight's rally.

LA GUARDIA: Do you mean to say I need a ticket to get into my own park? Does your wife know you're on tour?

COSTELLO: I think she does.

LA GUARDIA: Well, she must be having a good time.

(Costello begins to doff his jacket to sock him one.)

LA GUARDIA: Who do you think you are—a City Councilman?

When New York's mayor, Fiorello La Guardia engaged in some horseplay with Lou Costello for the newsreel cameras on the steps of City Hall on August 26, 1942, both men could afford to be good natured. La Guardia was coming to the end of his pioneering tenure as mayor, having, among many other civic initiatives, effectively eradicated burlesque from New York's stages in 1937. Costello, who began his comedy career with partner Bud Abbott on those very burlesque stages a year earlier, was now half of Hollywood's most successful comedy team.

They had made eight full-length features in the previous two years, nearly all of them hits. Abbott and Costello were on their way to earning a $1-million-a-year paycheck, a far cry from the $150 a week they were making playing in burlesque only five years earlier. But as the saying might go, you could take the boys out of burlesque, but no one ever really took the burlesque out of Abbott and Costello.

Lou Costello was born in a working-class New Jersey neighborhood in 1906. A natural athlete and a boxer, he kicked around Hollywood as a stuntman before returning to the East Coast just as the 1930s began, to try his hand as a burlesque comic. William Alexander "Bud" Abbott grew up—literally—on the Coney Island boardwalk and began his burlesque career as a ticket taker. He moved up to producing his own show and became an efficient jack-of-all-trades. One night, Abbott fired the straight man at one of his shows and took over himself, saying, "Why am I paying this guy fifty dollars a week when I can do the same thing myself?"

The origins of Abbott and Costello's actual partnership are shrouded in the mists of showbiz legend, rendered even murkier by the fact that, when they got together, no one really noticed. Both men had been playing the Manhattan burlesque circuit along West Forty-second Street with other partners; perhaps one of Costello's partners tanked or fell sick one afternoon and Abbott filled in. Perhaps, admiring each other's work from the wings, they decided to walk out onstage together for one show. Every comedian knew all the routines anyway, and no one in the audience was going to object if the headliner didn't show up. And so, Abbott and Costello glided out of the wings one matinee, clicked, and became headliners themselves.

They soon found themselves starring in *Life Begins at Minsky's* at the Republic Theater on the other end of Forty-second Street. Apparently, Abbott and Costello worked "clean"—which makes sense, considering they partnered up in the heyday of La Guardia's crackdown—but whether or not Costello was, as he liked to shriek, "a b-a-a-a-d boy" in burlesque, the handwriting was on the wall. As Lou's daughter, Chris Costello, maintained, "To most audiences in New York at the time, they were clearly known as burlesque comedians and, in order for their careers to continue, they had to clean up their act or get out of burlesque completely, or both. And both is exactly what they did." Bud and Lou needed to break into another venue. On February 3, 1938, Abbott and Costello appeared on *The Kate Smith Radio Hour* to no great acclaim (although the show's producer asked Costello to raise the pitch of his voice so that audiences could distinguish between the two partners—*that* was a good idea). On March 24, Abbott and Costello vexed the producer by performing their favorite burlesque routine on the air; he didn't think it was very funny, but everyone else did. "Who's on First?" made its debut in front of a national audience, and the switchboards lit up. No one can claim the exact provenance of "Who's on First?" either. Such wordplay stretched all the way back to the minstrel show, but it hardly matters; the effortlessness of such back-and-forth was in Abbott and Costello's genes and, as film historian Leonard Maltin put it, "Nobody made of that material what they did, and nobody scored such a tremendous impact with the public as they did with that variation on this stock idea."

Abbott and Costello kept performing on Smith's program, stole the show in a

That's what I'm tryin' to find out!
Abbott and Costello as stage stars in *The Streets of Paris* (1939); film debuts in *One Night in the Tropics*.

1939 Broadway revue called *The Streets of Paris*, and made their film debuts as supporting comedians in a patchwork quilt of a musical called *One Night in the Tropics* in 1940,
where they shoehorn in five of their burlesque sketches. That movie didn't make a huge

impression, but Abbott and Costello's timing,
always impeccable, couldn't have been better,
when, the next year, they made one of the first
"service" comedies of the 1940s: *Buck Privates*, a
spoof of life in an enlistment center. The movie
was released just months after the Selective
Training and Service Act of 1940 and struck a
nerve across the country. Abbott and Costello's
slapstick byplay, such as a drill instructor
sequence borrowed from their burlesque days,
turned the low-rent comedy into one of the
biggest hits of 1941: made for $20,000, *Buck
Privates* earned $4.7 million.

Throughout their more than three dozen
features, fifty television show episodes, and innumerable personal, radio, and variety appearances,
Abbott and Costello worked only the slightest variations on their essential burlesque personas. As
Maltin puts it, "Lou was sort of the childlike patsy

Home run:
Reprising their famous bit in *The Naughty Nineties*
(1945).

and Bud was the slickster, the con man, always getting the better of Lou. They never sat
down and analyzed it. I don't think they could if you begged them." Their lives off-camera were not all laughs; Bud Abbott suffered from debilitating bouts of epilepsy, often
while in the middle of a routine. Lou Costello fought a bout of rheumatic fever at the
height of their careers, only to lose his infant son in an accidental swimming pool
drowning months after.

Abbott and Costello clowned through the inevitable feuds, breakups, and rap-
prochements over a twenty-year partnership. Their film producers, usually Universal,
picked them up and dropped them down in every possible genre picture or situation:
haunted houses, safaris, tropical islands, the Wild West—even the American
Revolution. You could wind Abbott and Costello up and watch 'em go. When their
stock dipped a bit after World War II, some genius at Universal thought of teaming
them up with the studio's stock of monsters. *Abbott and Costello Meet Frankenstein*
proved a lightning bolt to their careers in 1948, and soon they were teamed with mum-
mies, invisible men, mad doctors, and berserk swamis. Perhaps their most imaginative
turn was on their weekly sitcom from the early fifties, *The Abbott and Costello Show*,
where they vaguely impersonated two out-of-work actors named Bud Abbott and Lou
Costello. Comedians who grew up in the 1950s, such as Robert Klein and Jerry Seinfeld,
fondly remember the disjointed make-believe aspect of the show, where Bud and Lou
reprised their old routines once again, only now in a concentrated form that superseded anything as irrelevant as narrative. They even adopted a chimp—as their son.

It didn't end with as many laughs as it had begun. They fought more and more

LOU: Tomorrow throws the
ball and the guy gets up
and bunts the ball.
BUD: Yes.
LOU: So when he bunts the
ball, me being a good
catcher, I want to throw
the guy out at first base,
so I pick up the ball and
throw it to who.
BUD: Now that's the first
thing you've said right!
LOU: I don't even know
what I'm talking about!

often with each other, Costello wanting to expand or go solo while Abbott wanted to hold on to the same shtick. According to film historian Stephen Cox:

> Unfortunately, they were heavy gamblers and they put their financial affairs in other people's hands. A lot of bad decisions were made over a period of time and at the end of their careers, the IRS came and kind of swallowed them whole, really. It was very sad because both of them died broke, for the most part. It was kind of the American dream gone sour.

The intelligentsia never loved Abbott and Costello; only audiences did. They kept one of America's great comedy traditions alive for decades beyond its demise; lost in a desert, a harem, or a haunted house, you could be assured that Abbott and Costello would carry a burlesque routine along in their supply kit. Most significantly, they met their mainstream audience at exactly the right time. They were a new team just when some of older teams and comedians of the 1930s had waned, and, best of all, they could be relied upon to distract an anxious wartime public. As Shelley Berman put it, "They gave us wonderful nonsense, utter nonsense! And they came in World War Two, and they gave us such laughter, because they were such nonsense, they had nothing to do with reality."

In hot water:
Raking in the dough; with Glenn Strange in
Abbott and Costello Meet Frankenstein (1948).

THEY GAVE US WONDERFUL NONSENSE, UTTER NONSENSE!

Fifty percent of what I write ends up in the toilet... practically everything is taboo and we end up with ersatz subject matter and ditto humor. –Fred Allen

"HELL OR THE COLUMBIA BROADCASTING SYSTEM"

FRED ALLEN

In the Golden Age of Radio, whoever paid the pipeline really called the tune. These were the days before programming was parceled out by network ad executives to an abundance of advertisers. Radio had sponsors, corporate commercial entities who paid for the entire hour or half-hour program, hoping to create audience identification with their companies, rather than a specific product. Therefore, it was of the greatest importance that a sponsor liked the performer who hosted their show—it was the sponsor, not the network, who wrote

the checks. With a comedy show, it was especially crucial to have an amiable personality hawking the product. Comedians became nearly synonymous with their sponsors: Edgar Bergen and Charlie McCarthy with Chase and Sanborn; Bob Hope with Pepsodent ("This is Bob 'Pepsodent' Hope, saying that if you brush your teeth with Pepsodent you'll have a smile so fair that even Crosby will tip his hair!"); Jack Benny with Jell-O. But the golden rule was that you could be funny *around* the product, but you could never make fun *of* the product.

Probably no one on radio was less disposed to respecting his sponsor than Fred Allen. Allen thought the whole obsequious relationship between comic and sponsor was ridiculous, and in a world "fraught with politeness," he was the only one who stuck up for the truth. "The vice president of an advertising agency is a bit of executive fungus that forms on a desk that has been exposed to conference," he once said. Allen came by his saturnine cynicism honestly. He had toiled in vaudeville for years, where he was billed as

The sap is in Hollywood:
Fred Allen trading barbs with his good friend, miser Jack Benny.

"The World's Worst Juggler." Like W. C. Fields, he left a broken home and an alcoholic father to rise through the ranks and made a name for himself in a series of comic revues on Broadway. He started his own radio career in 1932 and wound up hosting seven different shows for five major sponsors, including *The Linit Batch Club Revue*, named for a bathing lotion, and *The Salad Bowl Revue*, sponsored by Hellmann's mayonnaise. Allen also wrote most of each hour-long comedy show—an impressive feat then, as it would be now—and once claimed that he was "the only man who has written more than he could lift." He had a great gift for parody and created a sequence specifically for that purpose called "The Mighty Allen Art Players," which was appropriated years later by Johnny Carson. Frequently his humor hinged on a mind-boggling pun or turn of phrase. Playing a Charlie Chan clone called One Long Pan, Allen solved the murder of a circus contortionist shot while twisted into the letter *R*; his wife shot him, Allen/Pan concluded, because she didn't want him to make an *S* out of himself.

The various sponsors seemed scared to death that Allen's humor, which was blissfully over the heads of the lowest common denominator, would somehow sneak in something dirty or insulting. The censors forced him to delete words like *saffron*, *a woman's lavaliere*, *Rabelaisian*, and *titillate*. Allen wasn't paranoid; sponsors could wield a heavy cudgel. One of Allen's shows was *The Sal Hepatica Revue* (*The Hour of Smiles*), promoting a laxative made by Bristol Myers, and when Allen once made a pejorative reference to Scottish frugality, several hundred Scotsmen from the Pittsburgh area sent a letter threatening never again to use the sponsor's product. Allen made a grudging apology: "The prospect that they will go through life constipated so frightened the agency that they made me apologize."

He could also frighten the sponsors by willfully disregarding the time constraints of the program by throwing in ad-libs and other unscripted asides. According to one critic, "it seems likely that Fred Allen used the expression 'We're a little late, folks, so good night' more than any other performer." Despite the restraints on his comedy, Fred Allen's programs had a weekly audience of 20 million, or three out of four radio sets. He hit his stride during the war, when he introduced one of radio's greatest comic ensembles, the dotty denizens of "Allen's Alley," a beloved feature of a new half-hour program now called *The Fred Allen Show*. They included the New York Jewish housewife Mrs. Pansy Nussbaum ("You vair egspecting mebbe Cecil B. Schlemiel?"); a hick from the sticks in Maine, Titus Moody ("Effen I ain't a rube, I'll do till one gets here"); and the most famous, the Southern windbag, Senator Beauregard Claghorn ("That's a joke, son!").

Despite Allen's fame and ratings bonanzas, he was still dogged by the antsy advertising reps. In 1947, NBC threw him off the air for making fun of the radio executives who cut shows off the air when they ran long—something, of course, that Allen's shows did all the time. Peeved beyond endurance, he told a studio audience:

> If by chance any of you folk are in the wrong place, you still have ten minutes to get the heck out of here. Heck, incidentally, is a place invented by the National Broadcasting Company. NBC does not recognize Hell or the Columbia Broadcasting Company. When a bad person working for NBC dies, he goes to Heck.

He became one of the first radio comedians to try the new medium of television. Where Allen's relationship with radio was tempestuous, it was at least successful. Television was an unmitigated disaster. Some critics blamed Allen's hangdog sourpuss as being untelegenic; others thought his radio comedy depended greatly on the listener's imagination. Indeed, at one point, on television's *Colgate Comedy Hour*, some genius had the idea of replacing the actual "Allen's Alley" gang with marionette versions. How Allen ever agreed to that is lost to history—but after four episodes, Allen was given the gate.

Allen and television were a marriage made in Heck, anyway. He hated the bright lights, the cue cards, the cameras, the makeup, all the stuff he didn't need and never used on radio. He thought the giveaway quiz shows were for morons (especially when they replaced his programs) and that television itself was "a device that permits people who haven't anything to do to watch people who can't do anything." If television did anything for Fred Allen, it gave him a prime target. His verbal jabs at television, lobbed with the true venom of the wounded, far surpass anything he did on it. "I've decided why they call television a medium. It's because nothing in it is well done," he famously said in 1950. For the next six years, until his death in 1956, he stumbled around the tube, trying to find an inviting home. It never happened. How could it? This was a comedian who proclaimed:

> We are living in the machine age. For the first time in history the comedian has been compelled to supply himself with jokes and comedy material to compete with the machine. . . . Television is the triumph of machine over people. . . . Whether he knows it or not, the comedian is on a treadmill to oblivion.

We're a little late, folks:
Fred Allen, professional curmudgeon.

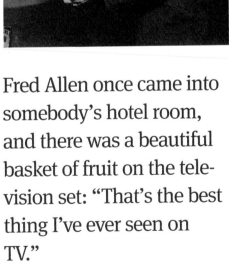

Fred Allen once came into somebody's hotel room, and there was a beautiful basket of fruit on the television set: "That's the best thing I've ever seen on TV."

"ASK SOMEONE OLDER THAN ME" MOMS MABLEY

There's nothing an old man can do for me 'cept get on a bicycle and bring me a message from a young man! —Jackie "Moms" Mabley

"Black people never had to worry about what to say onstage—we were always segregated, on the chitlin circuit," said Chris Rock in the 2005 film *The Aristocrats*. "We never had to worry about how to appeal to white audiences." For forty decades, while the biggest white comedians in the business were being tripped up by the slightest innuendo, a black woman would thrive outside the mainstream as one of the most outrageous comedians of all time. She was one of the great stealth comics, hiding her ribald honesty under the guise of a benevolent grandma: Jackie "Moms" Mabley.

Full circuit:
Jackie Mabley in the 1940s, her glamour years; in the mid-1970s, when she could enjoy a good smoke after a long career.

"I gots something to tell you . . ." she often began a story. Moms's own story stretched across a fifty-year career in show business, a long road that began as far back as the Civil War. Loretta Mary Aiken was born on March 19, 1894, in Brevard, North Carolina, one of sixteen children. Her grandmother was one of the first freed slaves in the state—she lived long enough to be Loretta's role model:

> This is the truth. My granny lived to be 118 years old. Granny hipped me. One day she was sitting on her porch, and I said, "How old does a woman have to be before she don't want no more boyfriends?" She said, "I don't know, honey, you have to ask someone older than me."

At eleven, Loretta was raped by an older black man and raped again by the local sheriff two years later. She gave birth both times and both children were given away; her father made her marry a much older man. The most shop-worn gag of her act had its basis in a sad truth:

This *old*—d-e-a-d, p-u-n-y, m-o-l-d-y—man. I mean an OLD man. I was fifteen, he was eighty-four. My daddy liked him, so I had to marry that old man. My daddy should have married him; he the one that liked him.

Show business proved the only way out. Back then, the only showcase for black performers was in segregated vaudeville, commonly known as the chitlin circuit. Officially, it was called the "TOBA," for Theater Owners Bookings Association. The hardworking performers it employed gave it another definition: Tough on Black Asses. While on the "Toby," Loretta took the stage name of Jackie Mabley and toured through the Depression in the Deep South, up north and back again, telling jokes and singing songs. One night, traveling through the South by train, she looked out the window and saw a lynch mob surround a black man: "They were gonna burn him, so I pulled down the shade," she later said.

It wasn't until the 1930s that Mabley adopted her "Moms" character, which was inspired—or "hipped," as she might say—by her grandmother. As a maternal figure, she gained the confidence of her audience; and in mocking herself in a dumpy, frowsy getup with a garish housedress, oversize slippers, and a floppy hat, she gave herself a clown mask that allowed her to speak the truth. Eventually, friends and colleagues started calling Jackie Mabley "Moms" because of her warmth and support of other entertainers. (And is it any coincidence that the greatest black male entertainer, also gravelly voiced and frequently salty, was called "Pops"?—Louis Armstrong.) She shot to the head of the chitlin circuit, rubbing elbows with the best in black entertainment:

Everybody loves Cab Calloway. But Cab Calloway treats me like an old dog; that's the truth. Even calls me an old dog, an old dog, yeah. Sometimes I wish I *was* an old dog. And Cab Calloway was a tree.

Better late than never:
"Moms" enjoying a television career, on the *Ed Sullivan Show*; and a variety special.

The mecca of the circuit was Harlem's Apollo Theater, and Moms performed there more times, and at a higher salary, than any other act, comedy or otherwise. The only thing she didn't like at the Apollo was the way the microphones came up out of the floor: "God damn microphone be shootin' up out of the floor," she said. "One of them got me right up tight." Her act was simple, salty, and satisfying. She would tell a few off-color jokes, sing a song or two (usually changing the lyrics to suit her persona), and always wind back to her gently exasperated remarks about the inequity of being an older sexual being in a male-dominated, youth-dominated world. It was also radical for her to suggest to her audience that a black man was something other than infallible or sexually potent:

> I thought he would never die. I shouldn't talk like that about him, though. He's dead. They say you shouldn't say nothing about the dead unless you can say something good. He's dead: GOOD! I know he's dead 'cause I had him cremated; I burnt him up—I was determined he was gonna get hot *one* time. . . .

Moms zigzagged through some minor "race films" in the late 1940s but didn't really meet a larger audience until 1956, when she began to put some of her routines down on vinyl. This led to breakthrough engagements at Chicago's Playboy Club, where she played to her first white audiences. They were often slow to "get it," but once they did, Moms expanded her career into mainstream network television. She appeared on *The Smothers Brothers Comedy Hour*, *The Merv Griffin Show* (sharing a slot with Woody Allen), *The Flip Wilson Show*, and *The Ed Sullivan Show*. Bill Cosby cast her as his grumpy aunt in a guest appearance during his first sitcom. There was something immensely appealing about this utterly unglamorous figure who padded onto the stage—and simply took her time.

Moms was aided immeasurably by white audiences' curiosity about black culture in the late 1960s, and on network television she gave them a piquant but unchallenging view of race relations. As Whoopi Goldberg put it, "Moms was able to do a lot of what she did because the people [in charge] recognized that she was telling the truth—they let her do certain things they wouldn't let other comedians do, because they understood Moms was reaching out to everyone." Away from the confines of network television, onstage, in concert (she performed at both the White House and Sing Sing), Moms—to appropriate a later phrase—spoke the truth to power:

> (*Sung to the tune of "Fascination."*)
> Oh, segregation—it's sneaky.
> They'll work side by side with you weekly,
> But they can't hardly wait till Friday comes due—
> 'Cause they don't have to spend the weekend next to you.

And even though Moms was rumored to be a lesbian, there was nothing sacred about it in her act:

> Two old maids was layin' in bed
> Bout four o'clock, I heard one of 'em said:
> "Now, I'm going to be frank with you—"
> The other said, "No, you was Frank last night, I'm gonna be Frank tonight."

By the early 1970s, she was on her way to becoming a household word, starring in a film comedy, *Amazing Grace*, and appearing on the 1974 Grammy Awards ceremony. She could now command $5,000 a week in clubs but lived modestly and contributed a great deal to her church charitites. "All this success and now I'm too old to enjoy it," she lamented before her death in 1975. Her influence is felt both in the easy laughs mined by a salty old black grandma in a housedress—Eddie Murphy in *The Nutty Professor*, Martin Lawrence in *Big Momma's House*—and in the comforting shoulders lent by mature black women on television talk shows—Oprah Winfrey and Whoopi Goldberg. Like other comedians, usually male, Moms Mabley displayed a large libido for laughs; what she also displayed, which other comics didn't, was a huge heart. In many ways, her warmth was more revolutionary than her saltiness; it certainly went a long way to endear her to audiences for half of the twentieth century.

Don't you children let old people sit around and tell you nothing about the "good old days." What good old days? When? I was there. Where were they at? You are living in the greatest day that ever was and ever will be right now, children, in this atomic age. Go where you want to go; do what you want to do; love who you want to love; marry who you want to marry.

Maybe the Russians will steal all our secrets, then *they'll* be three years behind. —Mort Sahl

"ARE THERE ANY GROUPS I HAVEN'T OFFENDED?"
MORT SAHL

That joke about the Russians was a pretty provocative remark in the middle of the Eisenhower Administration, Cold War era and it worked very well for Mort Sahl. Only it wasn't Mort Sahl's line to begin with. "Now that joke actually came to me from Milton Berle," recalled Sahl. "And he said to me 'Mort, you can have it because they wouldn't accept it from me. They don't think I'm smart enough.' Very realistic."

When Mort Sahl appeared in a nightclub in San Francisco on Christmas night, 1953, he ushered in a new, smart, realistic era for American comedians. He was everything that Milton Berle and the other big nightclub comics of the postwar years weren't. As a fellow pioneer, Shelley Berman, put it: "Mort came into the nightclub era without jokes. We'd always had comedians who told jokes; good one-line strong jokes, with a setup and a slam, good punch line. And he wasn't doing that, he was making commentary on our lives, on our social life, and on our political thinking, making fun of us in some way, or showing us our silliness, and the lies we were telling." Historian Gerald Nachman put it more simply: "Nobody saw Mort Sahl coming."

NOBODY SAW MORT SAHL COMING.

Morton Lyon Sahl first came along in 1927, born in Montreal and raised in Los Angeles from the age of seven. He developed an early fascination with the military and left high school to join the army. Stationed in Anchorage, Alaska, he created a post newspaper called *Poop from the Group*. His satirical editorials about military payoffs earned him an eighty-three-day KP sentence. He returned to college at USC but got swept up in the jazz joints, coffeehouses, and free expression that were burbling to the surface in Southern California.

Sweater boy:
Sahl's graduate student apparel set him apart from the tuxedoed entertainers of the 1950s.

Sahl soon discovered "I had to talk. . . . A writer has no voice in America, but any hooligan can get an audition. The solution for the writer is simple—he smuggles in his ideas as a performer." A girlfriend from Berkeley suggested he try out his ideas at a small nightclub favored by the folk-song crowd in San Francisco:

> She said, "Go to the hungry i. If they understand you, we'll have a better life. And if they don't understand you, they'll laugh anyway because they'll think you're quaint." So I loaded the night I was gonna try out with all my friends. And I got the job for a week at seventy-five dollars. But my friends couldn't come every night. So then it got brutal.

The nightclub's owner, Enrico Banducci, convinced him to abandon the coat and tie—every comedian's badge of respect—open his collar, and put on a cardigan sweater. His new persona would be, as Sahl called it, "a perpetual grad student," complete with loafers and black chinos. Performing for a subculture of perpetual grad students, he became a hero. He also carried a newspaper onstage; initially, it was a prop to hide some of the lines he'd written, but the newspaper eventually became an oracle and Sahl its diviner. He talked about the headlines, he read *between* the headlines, and immediately connected with anyone living in the real world of the late 1950s.

Remember, I started in the fifties and it was a button-down, clean generation pretending to hear no evil. Like anybody worth his salt in America, I was hoping that what the movies were saying was true. When they took the guys that dreamed that stuff up, the Hollywood Ten, and they put them in jail, I thought someone should say something. So I had a little platform in San Francisco with eighty-five seats, and I said it.

His breakthrough line came in 1954, a remark about an Eisenhower jacket, which had zippers all over, including "a big zipper here that went all the way across." But, Sahl continued, "Ah! They have a new jacket called the *McCarthy* jacket, and it zips up the side, and over the mouth." By then, Joseph McCarthy was nearly through, but no comic would have dreamed of taking on the infamous House Un-American Activities Committee. Sahl was branded with the sobriquet "Rebel without a Pause," and there wasn't an exposed wound of political hypocrisy in the late 1950s that he didn't poke at. "For a while, every time the Russians threw an American in jail, the Un-American Activities Committee would retaliate by throwing an American in jail, too." Or "Nixon's been on the cover of every magazine except *True*." When Little Rock exploded in 1957, Sahl picked up on a comment Hubert Humphrey made about the country's golf-obsessed president: "Humphrey said, 'Why doesn't Eisenhower go down to Alabama where Governor Wallace is, with all the discrimination, and take a black girl by the hand and lead her into the school, by example?' And I said, 'Eisenhower's making a policy decision on whether to use an overlapping grip.'"

Sahl's most quoted comments came from the world of politics, but in his act, he would also take on social trends, books, cars, stereo hi-fis, movies. At the premiere of Otto Preminger's bloviated three-and-a-half-hour film of Israeli independence, *Exodus*, Sahl cried, "Otto, let my people go!" Sahl was compared to Will Rogers, but he, characteristically, would have none of it: "I never met a man I didn't like until I met Will Rogers," he quipped. As his political diatribes were quoted everywhere, he became a media sensation. When he made the cover of *Time* magazine in August 1960, it was official; Sahl was the ringleader of a new gang that had transformed American comedy.

Start the revolution: Ringleader of the "sick comics"; never giving up.

Everybody was ready for the revolution, but some guy had to come along who could perform the revolution and be great. Mort was the one. He changed the rhythm of the jokes. He had different content, surely, but the revolution was in the way he laid the jokes down . . . with such guile.
–Woody Allen

Sahl burnished his persona as the quintessential "hip cat" with a sharp tongue, the perfect MC to usher in the Kennedy years. "Nixon wants to sell the United States, and Kennedy wants to buy it," he cracked as the 1960 election began. Little did he know that Kennedy's ascension to the presidency would provide the first of many shocks to Sahl's system. One day, Sahl got a phone call from JFK's father, Ambassador Joseph Kennedy:

> He said to me, "I want you to write for Johnny." That's what he called him. "Because all these guys available to me use a bludgeon on the enemy. I want you because you have the skill to put the stiletto between the fifth and sixth rib." And they liked me because it was nonconformist.

Sahl did write some material for Kennedy—one time a reporter asked Kennedy what he was doing for women. "Not enough, I'm sure" was the snappy response. But once the election was successful, the Kennedy camp hadn't reckoned on the basic contrariness of a political satirist. As Gerald Nachman said, "Mort Sahl always said, 'If there were two people left on the planet, I would have to oppose you. That's my job.'"

I'll tell you what I've learned. You can rock the boat. I'm not afraid to take on anyone. You can have your say in America and really survive.
—Mort Sahl

When Sahl, naturally, started making barbed comments about the new president, his liberal fans were shocked. Sahl found himself getting vague threats relayed to him through an old manager. However, these threats, real or imagined, faded next to the horrible events of November 22, 1963. The Kennedy assassination would impact Sahl's career in a way that no one could have predicted. The Warren Commission report obsessed Sahl, and he devoted four years of his life to uncover the conspiracy behind Kennedy's murder. No one was interested—certainly not as fodder for comedy—and Sahl watched his income drop from $1 million a year to $13,000. He could, occasionally, find humor in his predicament. On a 1968 program, *Playboy After Dark*, he told Hugh Hefner, "I don't go out much anymore, because I am busy saving America. Sometimes I go out. The last four girls I went out with fell asleep listening to the Warren Report."

Still, such knowing zingers were of little help in rehabilitating his career. The 1970s and 1980s were filled with canceled series, aborted projects, and limited bookings. But if the exposure diminished, the Sahl spirit didn't: "Nixon's the kind of guy that if you were drowning fifty feet offshore, he'd throw you a thirty-foot rope. Then Kissinger would go on TV the next night and say that the president had met you more than halfway."

Sahl provided the atomic fission of the Cold War era of comedy that provides nuclear explosions—Jon Stewart, Bill Maher, Stephen Colbert—to this day. He used to close his act with the following lines: "Are there any groups I haven't offended? And I want to thank you all for individual perceptions." Few comedians' perceptions were more individual than Mort Sahl's.

"THE FAULT LIES WITH THE MANUFACTURER"
LENNY BRUCE

Chicago is fantasyland. Chicago is so corrupt, it's thrilling. Chicago's the only city where the autopsy comes in—"he wouldn't listen..." –Lenny Bruce

The Gate of Horn was a Chicago nightclub at 1036 North State Street, used to hosting folksingers and improv acts for a hip crowd. Shortly after midnight on November 5, 1962, the spotlight turned on America's hippest comic, making his first Windy City appearance in nearly three years. The MC put it simply: "Ladies and gentlemen, Lenny Bruce . . . let the buyer beware."

Lenny Bruce rocked the house with the routines already known to some of the insiders in the audience:

> Christ and Moses standing in the back of St. Pat's, looking around, confused, Christ is, at the grandeur of the interior...because his route took him through Spanish Harlem, and he was wondering what the hell fifty Puerto Ricans were doing living in one room, when that stained glass window is worth ten G's a square foot?

Suddenly, a policeman stood up in the middle of the crowd. What followed was recounted by one of the audience members that night—George Carlin:

> He actually said the classic policeman thing, he said, "The show's over. Alright, the show's over." As I get to the door, the policeman said, "ID, let's see your ID." I said, "I don't believe in ID." He took me by the neck collar and kind of half-trotted me out. And I got into this truck, oh this—like a paddy wagon. And Lenny was in there. He knew me—I'd visit him a little bit backstage—and he says, "What did you do, what are you here for?" I said, "I told him I didn't believe in ID." And he said, "Schmuck."

Schmuck was a pretty useful word for Lenny Bruce. Sometimes he'd get a laugh with it, sometimes it would get him arrested:

> I don't think any Jew ever neologized and said, "You're acting like a man's penis!" Did you? No, it's "We drove in from Yonkers. Who did all the driving?" "*Me*, like a *schmuck*." Now, "*Me*, like a *schmuck*" doesn't mean "Me *like* a schmuck"— unless you're a faggot Indian.

The obscenity bust in Chicago was trouble, but Bruce was always comfortable with trouble. He was born in 1925 into a working-class neighborhood on Long Island as Leonard Alfred Schneider. Show biz was part of his life from an early age; his mother, Sally Marr, raised Lenny after she divorced his father by performing as a dancer and nightclub comic herself. She brought him to a burlesque show when he was twelve; the owner objected but Sally claimed that Bruce "had a good time." Bruce ran away from home at fifteen and soon served a three-year stint in the navy. "And he found that he didn't like the navy anymore, and so he started dressing as a WAVE. A WAVE was the Women's Auxiliary Volunteer something. He got into drag. And I don't think it worked for him. But he met some nice people," recalled writer Larry Gelbart, who, years later, based the Klinger character from *M*A*S*H* on Bruce's antics.

In fact, Bruce was discharged from the navy for dressing in drag. He started hanging out at the clubs where his mother performed and fell in love with the guffaws of an audience. By 1948, he was trying out his own shtick—doing imitations and the like on such mainstream shows as *Arthur Godfrey's Talent Scouts*. In the late forties, a promising, inventive comic like Bruce might work his way up to the best clubs, or a Broadway revue, or even his own 15-minute show in the new medium of television. But by 1953, Bruce found himself schlepping at a series of strip joints in Southern California.

His show-biz nightmare was to wind up like the ninth-rate hack he created, a desperate loser named Frank Dell:

> I got twenty-four minutes of dynamite, absolute dynamite . . . I've got it down now.

Let the lady dance: In a Hawaii strip club; (opposite) up against the wall.

I work to Jewish people—I've learned how to say "toe-kiss." When I work for musicians, I do a bit called "Hep Smoked the Reefer." I work to the Italian people—I've got the mamma mia bit—I got it all down. I got a Jolson bit, kills them, they don't want to let me off—

And so, out of desperation or inspiration or both, Bruce began to take a new approach to his comedy, inspired by the improvisational musicians that were becoming the new voice of jazz. Bruce's perceptions about life came out as something else: "riffs." He was redefining the nature of comedy for the "Beat Generation."

The comic mind of Lenny Bruce was a kaleidoscopic juke box of corny '40s movies, Yiddish shtick, knock-out impressions, and current events filtered through an incisive distaste for cant and hypocrisy. But Bruce was never happy simply doing Bela Lugosi imitations and he soon ventured into what was, in the 1950s, the Forbidden Realm of religion:

You and I know what a Jew is—"One Who Killed Our Lord....We did this 2,000 years ago, 2,000 years of Polish kids whacking the shit out of us on our way home from school...Alright, I'll clear the air once and for all, and confess. Yes, we did it. I did it, my family. I found a note in my basement. It said: "We killed him, (signed), Morty."

Tough stuff, but even Jewish jokes like this were within certain boundaries if you were a Jewish comedian, but Bruce was an equal opportunity offender. As long as religious hypocrisy was around, it became a frequent target. Bruce's investigations into establishment hypocrisy were laced with words that were used by real people and real situations. The four-letter words—and ten-letter words—and *twelve*-letter words that Bruce used in his act were beginning to polarize the audience and the critics. He was branded "The Man from Outer Taste." In 1959, Broadway columnist Burt Boyar limped to his defense. "I accept the dirty words...although they have 'made him' they will hold him back. He will reach his highest peaks when they are completely gone." Bruce responded to the criticism. "I don't use words to get laughs. I use them for color—a big bold stroke. And people do talk that way. My conversation is the argot of the gangster, the hipster, and Yiddish."

While Bruce was not at a loss for words, the critical community was. There was no word to describe Bruce's brand of comedy—until *Time* magazine put a label on it in 1959: "sicknick." Bruce, they declared, "dispenses social criticism liberally laced with cyanide with jolly ghoulishness. [He is] the high priest of the sick comedians." Hugh Hefner, who booked Lenny Bruce into his Chicago Playboy Club, put it into the proper context: "Lenny was a truth-teller, and when you're commenting on the follies and foibles of our time, that could be perceived in some quarters as sick. But he wasn't a sick comedian, he was commenting on a sick society."

And that society was changing rapidly. In June of 1957, just as Bruce was beginning his ascent to national fame, what constituted "dirty words" would no longer be a matter of personal opinion: it would become a matter of legal opinion. That summer, the Supreme Court ruled that obscenity had to be "utterly without socially redeeming importance," implying that even an idea of slightest importance had the full protection of the First Amendment. Now, for a performer like Lenny Bruce, the subjectivity of this definition opened up a number of happy loopholes, but those loopholes soon transformed into a net—and that was the net which trapped Lenny Bruce.

I'm going to do a science fiction picture...These two weirdos, they've got this monster they're making, you know, and he's a really a horrendous looking creature and they send him up to Coney Island...and he goes back down:

"Well, did you make it? What was the scene?"
"I bombed."
"Well, did you do all the bits? Did you do 'AAAAAARRRGGHH!'"
"Yeah."
"Did you do 'GRAAAAAGGGH!'"
"Yeah."
"What did they say?"
"They said I was doing Jerry Lewis."

In the fall of 1961, seven months after Bruce played a sold-out midnight concert at Carnegie Hall in the middle of a fierce snowstorm, he was caught in a snowstorm of his own—a narcotics bust in Philadelphia for possession of heroin. Charges were dropped, but a week later, he was arrested at a San Francisco club for violating Section 311.6 of the California penal code—his first obscenity charge. The word that brought Bruce to court— "cocksucker"—seemed an unlikely one to upset the "community standards" of hip San Francisco, but the trial put Bruce's brand of humor on full public view. Bruce's defense seemed unassailable—"Generally, I try to make my audience laugh and it seems to me that my point of view has been consistently that I am inconsistent and that we all are."—and he was acquitted by a jury six months later.

Over the next three years, he would be charged with six more obscenity offenses in three different cities. He was always getting busted for the same relentless litany of dirty words: *shit*, *piss*, *fuck*, *cocksucker*, *motherfucker*, *tits*, and *shtupp* (the last for cultural diversity, one assumes). Bruce always felt the "fix" was in: "I guess what happens if you get arrested in Town A and then in Town B with a lot of publicity, then when you get to Town C, they have to arrest you, or what kind of shithouse town are *they* running?" But, the one word that really brought Bruce down in the end was *disrespect*.

> The Pope does not know about American Catholics. He doesn't know
> how to gear down a Porsche, he can't work a cigarette machine, doesn't
> know about Bank Americard—doesn't know about any of your problems.
> And the big issue, contraceptives?—he never makes it with anybody!

Standing up to authority: A gig in San Francisco; (opposite) reading from a trial transcript; poster for his final gig, the Filmore West, 1966.

The way George Carlin saw it, "The Catholic Church didn't like Lenny Bruce because he talked about God and the Pope. And the Irish police forces of New York and the Chicago police were the instrument of the Church. And they executed the Church's wishes: 'We have to silence this man, he's questioning very sacred and very basic things.'" Since even the most ardent Catholics on the judicial bench couldn't legally censure Bruce for making profane remarks about the Pope, they branded him with the one transgression that could stick in a courtroom: obscenity. Bruce had his own, brilliantly argued, perspective on his material: "If you have any of the superstitions, if anyone of the audience believes that God made his body and your body is dirty—the fault lies with the manufacturer. He made it all—it's all clean or it's all dirty."

By 1964, Bruce was shuttling from the West Coast to the East Coast to the Midwest, embroiled in litigation among three different cities so he had to appear at whatever nightclubs dared to hire a comedian busted on an obscenity rap. Television, of course, would hardly touch Bruce by now. A 1964 appearance on *The Steve Allen Show* was pulled by the NBC censors at the last minute and never aired, but he did get a chance to get define "obscenity" on his terms:

> I have a reputation for being sort of controversial and irreverent. These are the
> words that offend me. Let's see: Governor Faubus, segregation, the shows that
> exploit homosexuality, narcotics, and prostitution under the guise of helping these
> social problems. Late night shows...

The beginning of the end came that spring in New York, when he was busted twice in the same week while appearing at the Café-a-Go-Go. For many in New York, which was in the throes of a moral retrenchment by the Catholic Church, Bruce had gone too far with a riff on President Kennedy's recently widowed wife and a *Time* magazine report that said, during Kennedy's assassination, she was trying to help him: "That's a dirty lie. Jackie Kennedy hauled ass to save her ass." All of Bruce's obscenity cases in California and Chicago would eventually be dismissed or the convictions reversed. In New York—that most liberal of cities—it would prove to be a different story. On Christmas week, 1964, Bruce was found guilty by a three-judge panel, on a count of 2 to 1, on obscenity charges. For the first time in his criminal career, he was sentenced: four months in the workhouse. The conviction shocked him: " What does it mean to be found obscene in New York? This is the most sophisticated city in the country. If anyone is to be found obscene in New York, he must feel utterly depraved." He immediately appealed, but his appeal would be caught in the court treadmills for years. The legal struggles occasioned a shift in Bruce's public persona; he now spent most of his rare stage time reading legal transcripts of his trials aloud and commenting on his victimization.

In the four years since his 1961 obscenity bust in San Francisco, his annual earnings had plummeted from $108,000 to $10,963. His decade-long heroin habit was getting worse and getting him into more trouble. He became philosophical, morbid—realistic, maybe:

> I was thinking about Marilyn Monroe. You know, when Marilyn Monroe did herself in—no, she didn't—when she *died*, a lot of friends of mine said, "Are you going to do any jokes about her? What are you, chicken shit?" No, it's just that she was really pretty and I don't feel very humorous about it. Now, if I were ever to do a bit about doing myself in, I would like to be unique.

In the end, it wasn't that unique: on August 3, 1966, he was found dead of acute morphine poisoning from an accidental overdose in his Hollywood home. "The story is," said George Carlin, "among those who care about those stories, that the dose of heroin that he bought, that killed him was a deliberate 'hot shot.' They just wanted to, I guess, make an example—they wanted to eliminate a very powerful voice." Within a few years, Bruce became something between a cult figure and a martyr. There were books, plays, album reissues, documentaries and films about his life. Mort Sahl was, characteristically, unimpressed with the hagiography:

> Lenny is misperceived. He was not profound. He did movie imitations. He liked dope and he liked girls and he liked jazz. But he was used as a metaphor by a group of people who want to turn their social cowardice into prudence.

As Shakespeare wrote, "the evil that men do lives after them." Bruce was never able to appeal his New York conviction during his lifetime, so it was never reversed. Even as a dead man, he was still sentenced to four months of hard labor. That all changed in March of 2003, when, after being petitioned by a group of prominent comedians, New York governor George Pataki pardoned Lenny Bruce posthumously. The ambivalent press statement read, in part: "The holiday season is a time when we are reminded of the true meaning of compassion . . . and I hope this pardon serves as a reminder of the precious freedoms we are fighting to preserve as we continue to wage the war on terror."

Whether or not Lenny Bruce had the last laugh is a metaphysical question, but surely he would have found the idea of co-opting his pardon to support the war on terror a brilliant stroke of hypocrisy—the kind of hypocrisy that was always right up his neon-fringed, litter-strewn alley.

Without the censors we would all be at the mercy of the warped minds of the television industry and Deity only knows what you would see, probably some of the most foul, nasty, disgusting, vulgar, funniest, greatest stuff in the world.

–Pat Paulsen, regular on *The Smothers Brothers Comedy Hour*

"IT'S WRITTEN IN CRAYON"
THE SMOTHERS BROTHERS

At the height of the Vietnam War, with the rebellious hippie generation agitating daily against the White House, two young men from California declared war on the censorship policies of a major broadcast network. The irony was that the clean-cut Smothers Brothers looked like they were "conservative, Bible-carrying ultraconservatives," according to Tommy, the elder. When they made a guest appearance on one of Jack Benny's final programs in 1965, Benny thought they had mistakenly wandered into the studio from "an eighth-grade dancing class."

In reality, the Smothers Brothers were the secret weapon of the counterculture, cloaked in matching preppy red blazers to sneak in under the radar. They were always different from the image they presented to their public. They were born not in the Midwest, as audiences assumed, but on a military base in New York Harbor (Tom was born in 1937, Dick in 1939). Their army dad died as a POW in World War II, and the brothers grew up in Southern California, respecting military authority and entering San Jose State as energetic frat boys. Their musical talents—Tommy on guitar, Dick on bass—brought them into the coffeehouse circles of the "folk song army," but eventually they switched their focus to comedy. They contrived a successful double-act, with Dick utilizing an urbane affability to undercut his brother's blockheaded befuddlement.

TOM: Mom always liked you best. Mom always liked my brother best.

DICK: Why do you always keep telling me that? Every time you get mad, you always whine, "Mom always liked you best."

TOM (beat): Oh, yeah . . . ?

DICK: Well, she did always like me best. Would you like to know why?

TOM (beat): I didn't know she liked you best. . . .

DICK: Well, she did. And why wouldn't she? After all, I'm an only child. (beat)

TOM: Touchy, touchy . . .

DICK: That's touché, touché.

They were young and extremely likable, so they rose pretty far in the mid-1960s. A failed sitcom didn't do much for them, but it was the possibility of capturing a younger audience that induced CBS to offer the Smothers Brothers a prime-time variety show in February of 1967. There was one catch: *The Smothers Brothers Comedy Hour* would be opposite television's number-one hit show, *Bonanza*, on Sunday nights on NBC. Nine other shows had failed against the cowboy drama; it was known as the kamikaze slot. In concert with a team of young, unconventional writers in their twenties and early thirties, which eventually included Steve Martin and Rob Reiner, the brothers began to expand the boundaries of the stale musical variety format.

Even the show's guests demonstrated the eclectic interests of the Smothers Brothers. At one point, Jack Benny and George Burns shouldered guitar and bass to portray the Geritol version of the Smothers Brothers. "All of the people we looked up to, all my heroes, we got to work with. And all the new people that are happening," said Tommy. "We were sitting in a balance position." The brothers wanted to stay topical, and in 1967, "topical" meant a host of worrisome social issues: "Voter registration was taking place. The riots. Bobby Kennedy was shot. Martin Luther King, Kent State. Democratic convention riot—all that happened while we were with a television show and had a platform. There it was. So we were at the scene of the accident and we kept reflecting it," said Tommy. Soon, overt commentary on gun control, the draft, peace marches, and civil rights were incorporated into the brothers' routines, and even the supporting cast snuck in references to the youth movement and their drugs of choice. One ongoing sketch, "A Little Tea with Goldie," featured cast member Leigh French as the ultimate flower child: "Now, you housewives out there, if you're tired of coming across roaches in your living room, just send them to me. I'll happily accept all the roaches you have to spare." "That was all right at first," said their eventual nemesis, William Tankersley, CBS Vice President of Program Practices, "until they came to do more drug jokes, more risqué jokes, and gradually became obsessed with the Vietnamese war."

SECRET WEAPON OF THE COUNTER-CULTURE

The Smothers Brothers
WHO CONTROLS TV

The boys next door:
(previous): Clean-cut stealth warriors, Tommy, left, and Dick Smothers; (above) hot water; during a rehearsal break.

DICK: We've come a long way since that first Thanksgiving in Plymouth, when the Pilgrims sat down at the table with the Indians to eat turkey.

TOM: Boy, I'll say we've come a long way. Now we're in Paris sitting down at a table with the Vietcong, eating crow.

The executives at Standard Practices were working overtime on the show. "Tommy claimed that, that we edited maybe seventy-five percent of their scripts," said Tankersley. "And I said that's not right. A hundred percent would be more accurate. They gave us something to object to in every script." A sketch in the ninth episode, written by Elaine May, in which May and Tommy played a pair of self-important movie censors, provoked an angry response and was removed from the broadcast. "Never tell a comedian not to do something," said Tommy. "Because sure enough, they'll probably do it. This attitude, it comes from the deepest part of the American soul, which is Don't tread on me. Don't mess with me. Don't push me. And when you get pushed, a comedian has some tools." One of the tools that Tom Smothers—the more aggressive of the brothers—had was control of the closed-circuit tape of the show that had to be sent from the Los Angeles studio to the New York executives for proper vetting. Those tapes would become political footballs.

Before that, however, whether because of the controversy or in spite of it, *The Smothers Brothers Comedy Hour* proved to be a ratings bonanza of its own, and knocked the cowboy show down a few notches in the ratings. The brothers' success made them that much harder to control. Frequent cast member David Steinberg reprised one of his comic sermons one night. "When God tells Moses, 'I am that I am,'" Moses coughed politely and said, "Thanks for clearing that up." Innocuous, but no comedian dared to take on either Testament on national television. "A week later," recounted Steinberg, "Tommy called me up very excited and he said, 'You gotta come over.' And I came over, and I opened one of the office doors, and there were duffel bags, duffel bags of mail. And I said, 'What is it?' I said. 'That's your hate mail.' And he said it, like, *gleefully*."

As the show moved into its second, then third successful season, the memos between Tom Smothers on the West Coast and the censors on the East Coast were flying fast and furious. "I demanded to see a list of what we were doing wrong. I was trying to get them to define their rules; I didn't see that we were breaking any rules, I didn't read them in the FCC guidelines. I wanted to see it in writing," said Tommy. CBS Program Practices ultimately demanded to see a full closed-circuit tape of each episode days before its broadcast and that only made the Smothers Brothers and their supporting crew want to stick it to the censors even harder. The fight began to appear on the air:

DICK: Tommy, what have you got there?

TOM (*perusing a slim yellow pamphlet*): Oh, this, this is the guide to the official CBS Program Practices rule book. This book has a lot of things. Wow. I've seen the light, I know I've overdone things, but I've learned to watch my mouth in my travels. In America, this book—

DICK: Well, they lived a lot longer. They know things.

TOM: They really do. Listen, America, these men are guardians of our country, of pure, adult thought. They are learned men, scholars, PhDs, and sober judgment is their call. The censors' handbook right here. It's changed my life, that's for sure. Now, I've got to get back to reading it. See, it's here—

DICK: But, Tommy, it's only a tiny yellow book there, why is it taking so long to read it?

TOM: It's written in crayon.

The Johnson administration never found much of this amusing; the political waters became choppier when Richard Nixon came into office in 1969 and the censors were even more terrified of interference from the White House. "They were on the right side of the angels," said Tankersley, "but they picked the wrong place to do it. The First Amendment gives them the right to free speech. But it doesn't give them the right to make us give them an audience." The closed-circuit football came into play in April 1969. Tom Smothers refused to surrender that week's tape to the East Coast on the appointed hour. There was no time for CBS to edit it, then turn it over to its affiliates. "Our own affiliates think we're not in charge anymore," recounted Tankersley. "In effect, they fired themselves. There was no alternative." One week before the end of the season, *The Smothers Brothers Comedy Hour* would be thrown off the air.

According to Steve Martin, who was writing and occasionally appearing on the show, "I think that CBS was really under pressure from the government, from the administration, from the political climate, and they just couldn't bear it, because the Smothers Brothers were doing what in America it's okay to do theoretically, which is, to do satire." (Tankersley denies direct government interference.) For millions of television viewers who didn't know any better, the on-stage Tommy Smothers seemed incapable, in Lyndon Johnson's colorful phrase, of "pouring piss out of a boot into the ocean," in real life, he was a smart cookie who took the whole business personally and seriously:

The battle against censorship is always going on. And the greatest danger is we start to anticipate it and start to censor ourselves in the name of staying on the straight and narrow. Some people say that freedom is a very thin line. I always thought it was a broad highway.

It took several years for the Smothers Brothers to settle their differences with the network; a California court eventually awarded them nearly three-quarters of a million dollars from a breach of contract suit. For three brief seasons, these unlikely "boys next door" were a political conscience in prime time, and received the battle scars to prove it. As Tommy postulated, perhaps had they not been born into such a clean world, things might have been different:

If Dickie and I started in the nineties, instead of the late fifties, and to be successful, if we'd have been just like everybody else, we'd have been, you know, "Mom always liked you best," "Oh, yeah? Well, fuck you." Then they can say that the Smothers Brothers have set foot in the twenty-first century.

Times, they are a-changin':
Tom and Dick adopt a hipper style; by the 21st Century, they have evolved into the longest-running comedy team in American history.

The Sketch That Couldn't Be Done

by Elaine May

*This is the first part of a three-part sketch that Miss May wrote for her
and Tommy Smothers for* The Smothers Brothers Comedy Hour. *It was ruled out for "bad taste."*

SCENE: Two censors are watching the end of a movie. As the movie ends and the lights go on they refer to notebooks that they've been making notes on during the showing.

SHE: There are several scenes I think could be cleaned up. First of all I think the . . . uh . . . the word "breast" should be cut out of the dinner scene. I think that . . . "breast" is a tasteless thing to say while you're eating . . . and I'd like it out.

HE: (*writing*) "Take the word breast out of the dinner scene."

SHE: There's only one "B" in breast.

HE: Oh, yes . . . (*He erases*) Sorry.

SHE: Tell them they can substitute the word "arm." Arm has the same number of syllables as . . . "breast" and I just think it's a more acceptable word to use at the dinner table.

HE: But won't that sound funny? "My heart beats wildly in my arm whenever you're near?"

SHE: Why? Oh, I see. You mean because . . .

HE: Yes. The heart isn't in the arm.

SHE: Where is the heart exactly?

HE: Audrey, we're alone here. The heart is in the breast. Maybe it shouldn't be, but it *is* in the . . . .

SHE: All *right*. Don't keep saying it.

HE: So what do we do?

SHE: Let's change "heart." Can we change "heart" to "pulse"?

HE: "My pulse beats wildly in my arm whenever you're near?"

SHE: Isn't there a pulse somewhere in the arm?

HE: Not that I've noticed.

SHE: (*Suddenly*) What about the wrist?

HE: (*Excitedly*) That's it!

BOTH: "My pulse beats wildly in my wrist whenever you're near."

SHE: Oh, that's marvelous.

HE: I think it's better than the original.

SHE: We could write as well as they do.

HE: Oh, easily.

SHE: What else should we change?

HE: Let's take the word "heterosexual" out of the biology class scene.

SHE: Is that the scene where the professor explains to a group of college students how earthworms reproduce?

HE: Yes. And while we're at it let's take out the word "reproduce."

SHE: (*Writing*) "Reproduce."

HE: What words can we substitute?

SHE: Well, the professor can just say, very frankly, that earthworms are male *and* female, and multiply by laying eggs.

HE: (*Begins to write. Looks up.*) Is that true?

SHE: Is what true?

HE: That earthworms lay eggs?

SHE: Yes.

HE: I thought they just divided.

SHE: Oh, if only.

HE: You mean they . . .

SHE: They mate, Ed. And frankly I don't think it's necessary to put that fact into a scene where there are a lot of young college students.

HE: Isn't that something. So earthworms mate.

SHE: (*Consulting notebook*) Now let's see . . . we've taken out "heterosexual," we've taken out "reproduce," we've substituted "pulse" and "wrist" for "heart" and "breast" . . .

HE: (*Still incredulous . . . to himself*) Earthworms *mate*.

SHE: Oh, Ed . . . If only we had been here when the Lord created man. We could have cut out so many unnecessary parts.

HE: I'll tell you one thing. It would have been a cleaner world.

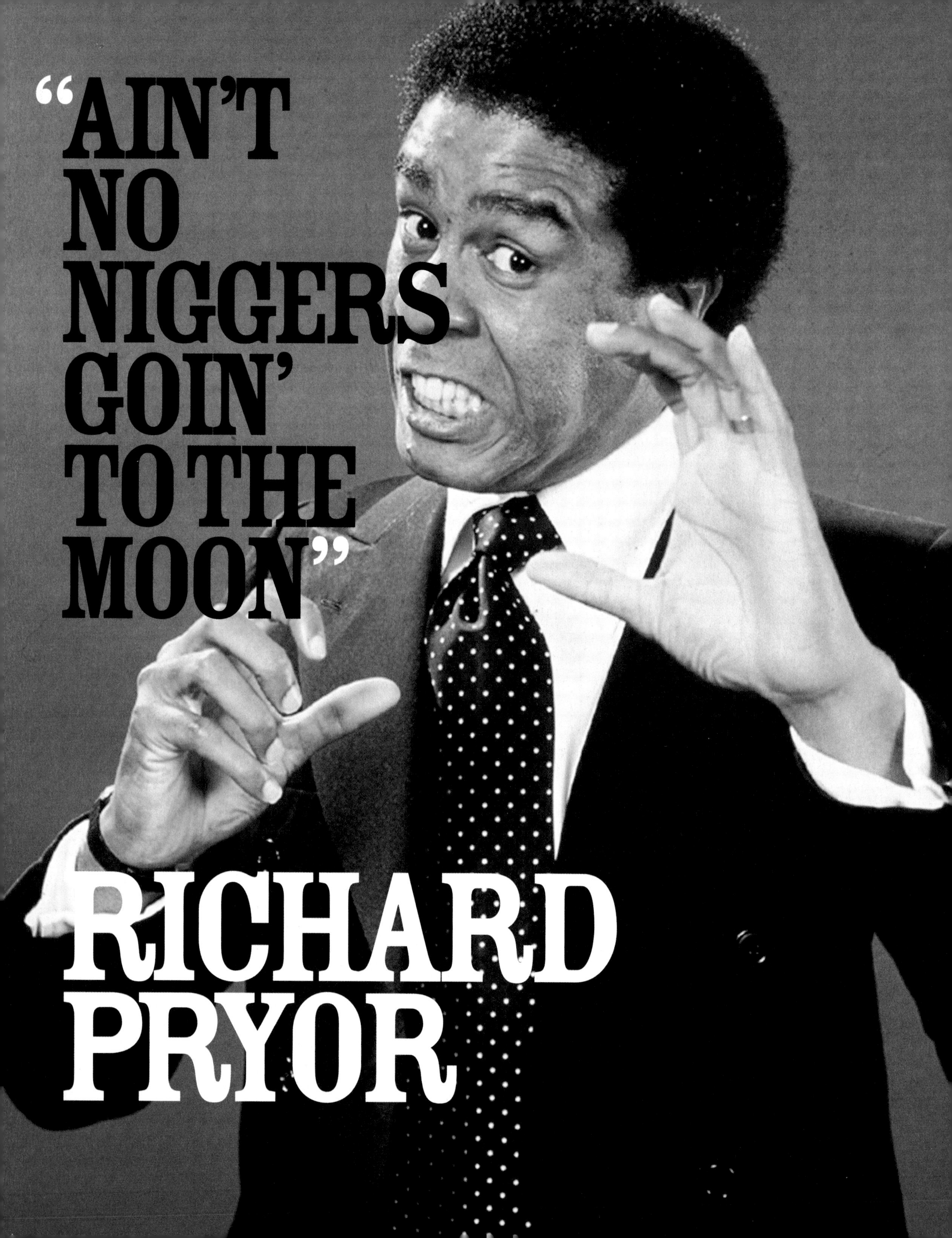
"AIN'T NO NIGGERS GOIN' TO THE MOON"
RICHARD PRYOR

In 1977, NBC cut off Richard Pryor's balls. Literally. Actually, it would be more truthful to say that Pryor cut off his own balls. He was the hottest comic in America, and he had been given his own prime-time variety show. Addressing the camera at the beginning of the first episode, he said, "Over the past few months, there's been a lot written about me doing the show or not doing the show. I really don't know what the problem is. People seem too concerned about me doing television—worried that I might have to give up something. . . ." The camera pulled back to reveal Pryor's naked body—with his genitals completely air-brushed out. The censors never allowed that opening to be aired. Ironic, as Pryor was probably the ballsi-est—in the sense of honesty—comedian of the twenti-eth century.

Pryor was born on December 1, 1940, into a set of circumstances that were difficult even by a comedian's standards. His father was a former boxer in the black ghetto of Peoria, Illinois, and his mother was a prostitute who continued turning tricks even after they married. His friend and colleague Paul Mooney remembered, "His grandmother, who he loved dearly, was a madam in a whorehouse, and his mother was a prostitute, and the father was a pimp, so Richard saw and heard things a child shouldn't have seen or heard. But that's part of it, too; that's what makes the genius of an artist. To have to go through all that pain."

Pryor was a nervy kid, a cutup who amused the denizens in his ghetto neighborhood, but his raw talent went unnoticed until he enrolled at the Carver Community Center at age fifteen and was mentored by Juliette Whittaker, the drama coach. Still, he drifted about, became a father himself at age seventeen, and, like Lenny Bruce before him, enlisted in the service as a way out. It proved to be a mistake, and by his early twenties, and without any real training for it, he settled on a career as a pianist, then as a comedian. In 1963, he read an article about Bill Cosby in *Newsweek*. He was fascinated with Cosby's success and was desperate to cross over into the big time. Pryor put it succinctly:

"Goddamn it, this nigger's doin' what I'm fixing to do. I want to be the only nigger. Ain't room for two niggers."

Pryor restraint:
A young comedian in the early 1960s; (opposite) making nice on *The Ed Sullivan Show*, 1965; a shift in the wind, post 1969.

He arrived in New York City in the early sixties to develop his act and made his television debut in 1964 on Rudy Vallee's show, of all things. He did fine but was almost unrecognizable in his desire to please. To watch him joining George Carlin in some dumb production number from *The Kraft Music Hall* summer special is almost unbearably depressing. Pryor climbed all the obligatory rungs in the ladder of success for a 1960s nightclub comic, but even as one of the few black comedians of the mid-1960s, his material was still safe, conventional, vanilla. As Black Power assumed greater prominence in America, Pryor was losing his own identity:

> One time, early in my career, I was in New York with Redd Foxx—we'd just been doing a show with Merv Griffin—and after the show we went uptown and everyone was hollering "Zorro!"—that was his nickname— "Redd!"—they all knew him; not many uptown people knew me. When we were downtown, white people knew me, liked what I was doing. Nothing wrong in that; but I wanted my own people to like me. I had to get a grip on that.

Pryor's confusion became a crisis during a 1967 appearance at the Aladdin Hotel in Las Vegas, a first-class gig for any rising comic. The evening has been recounted by many people, in many different ways, but Pryor eventually gave his own account. "I looked out at the audience. The first person I saw was Dean Martin . . . staring right back at me. I looked back at Dean, who was still looking at me, waiting for something, you know? I imagined what I looked like and got disgusted. . . . In a burst of inspiration, I finally spoke to the sold-out crowd: 'What the fuck am I doing here?' Then I turned and walked off the stage." His career didn't exactly come to a crashing halt—but close. He kicked around some minor gigs, failed to show up for an *Ed Sullivan* appearance, and one day, moved all his gear out of Los Angeles and up to Berkeley, the seat of the Black Power movement, where he sought the counsel and inspiration of the poets and politicians of the movement.

By the time he had reemerged on the national scene in the early 1970s, there was a new Richard Pryor—whom he discovered by tapping into the *old* Richard Pryor. Paul Mooney remembered the Pryor of this period:

> He was a caterpillar who became his own butterfly. And he finally got the message of who he was. I used to tell him all the time who he was, and he would say sometimes to me, "I'm not Martin Luther King; I can't have that responsibility." But you have it whether you want it or not. You've been chosen.

As he was breaking out, according to Pryor, "An agent said to me, 'Be the kind of colored guy we'd like to have over to our house.' And I'm buying this shit. They were gonna try to help me be nothing as best they could." He was determined to get as far away from "nothing" as possible. George Carlin observed that "There was so much pain in Richard's work. That was wonderful, because it was working through the pain. And using it. And of course he had great skills delivering it." Pryor tapped into his gift for community, creating a street-corner sage named Mudbone; he carried on conversations between two, sometimes three, different characters; he indulged his remarkable gift for mimicry, imitating hookers, vampires, exorcists, dogs, white people—even his own heart. But one word kept appearing and reappearing. When Lenny Bruce said it in his act, it was shocking. When Pryor used it, it was an authentic statement:

> Ain't no niggers goin' to the moon, you know that. First of all, ain't no niggers qualified, so you all tell us. . . . Niggers was hip, they help y'all get to the moon. "Hey, man, let's organize and help these white motherfuckers get to the moon, so they leave us alone."

Chris Rock put it into context: "He wasn't doing this so white people could hear him—he never thought white people were going to hear it. He didn't do all that so, you know, he could sit next to Bob Hope or something." Pryor was bold enough to put the word in the title of his third comedy album in 1974, and *That Nigger's Crazy* defied all industry expectations. It crossed over to a white audience, went gold, and won the Grammy. The same year, Pryor—whose routines were studded with every conceivable profanity—received his first and only nightclub bust in Virginia, for "disorderly conduct."

> The white man who owned the club there called another man and had me busted. Why? Because they're white and they had nothing else to do that weekend. "That nigger talks about Jesus!" They just thought I was a smart nigger, and wanted to shut me down, but they can do that because they white. And the niggers who were booking me said they loved my albums.

By the end of 1974, Pryor had cowritten the smash hit movie *Blazing Saddles*, was popular enough to cohost the conventional *Mike Douglas Show* for an entire week, and received an Emmy as a writer for a Lily Tomlin TV special. Tomlin recalled trying to sign him up:

Finding the voice:
Getting to his roots; Pryor in *Live from the Sunset Strip* (1982).

He knew me from *Laugh-In* or whatever, but still, I kind of had to prove myself to him, that I was enough of a soulful person. So he made me go to a porno movie with him. And I said, "Okay, but I'm paying my own way." And then, he took me down in the neighborhood, and when he saw that a lot of black folks knew me and liked me from *Laugh-In*, then that was pretty good and affirming.

Inevitably, Pryor made his long-awaited debut on the hottest comedy show on TV two weeks before Christmas, 1975, and brought his knack for controversy with him. *Saturday Night Live* wanted something cutting edge from Pryor and this job application-word association sketch fit the bill:

CHEVY CHASE: Spear-chucker.

PRYOR: White trash.

CHASE: Jungle bunny!

PRYOR: Honky.

CHASE: Spade.

PRYOR: Honky-honky.

CHASE: Nigger.

PRYOR: *Dead* honky.

It would be the first time a white man called a black man a "nigger" on a nationally televised comedy sketch.

During the following year, Pryor's film career was on the express track, with three hits that year, including *Silver Streak*, which earned $30 million, making it one of the top fifty films of its time. The next year, NBC came calling again and produced *The Richard Pryor Special?* in prime time. The show was so successful that NBC wooed him for a prime-time series commitment. Pryor demurred and deferred but eventually agreed to a ten-episode variety show and was given $2 million by the network. The variety show featured scathing sketches, but for all its groundbreaking social commentary, it trailed well behind *Happy Days* and *Laverne and Shirley* in the ratings. The network standards and practices department blue-penciled much of Pryor's work; sick of it all, he pulled the plug after only four of ten scheduled episodes. "One week of truth on TV could straighten out everything," Pryor said. "But they're not going to write shows about how to revolutionize America. The top-rated shows are for retarded people."

In his entire career, Lenny Bruce never made more than a handful of television appearances. Pryor walked away from a comedian's dream—a showcase in front of millions of viewers weekly. He wanted to reach his audience in his own way, no censors, no compromises. In 1979, he got his chance with *Richard Pryor: Live in Concert. Live in Concert* was the first successful film of its kind: nothing but a comedian, a mike, an audience. To avoid an X rating, the film has a disclaimer: "WARNING: This picture contains harsh and very vulgar language and may be considered shocking and offensive."

Isn't it funny that Richard Pryor uses badder language than almost anybody else and yet for him, in that situation, it was appropriate. You were never shocked because he was talking about his life and his experience. And I was never shocked by the four letter words that Richard Pryor used because he was such an artist and so brilliant. He communicated what it felt like to be a black man in his time.

–Dick Van Dyke

As the eighties began, Pryor's career was, to use the title of one of his film hits, bustin' loose, but so was his personal life. He was seriously addicted to cocaine. In the middle of a benefit for gay rights in the Hollywood Bowl, he turned on the audience, telling them that "You Hollywood faggots can kiss my rich, happy, black ass." Months later, he shot his own Mercedes Benz with a Magnum .38 into the bargain. "He was enormously self-destructive," said Robert Klein, "and he did not take good care of himself, but then he was so honest about talking about it—these self-confessions, but they were so funny that they weren't self pitying." He could be full of surprises: after a visit to Africa, he decided to give up using the word *nigger* in his act. "It can't make you feel good, because when the white man calls us that, it hurts no matter how strong we try to be about," he said.

For all of his rollercoaster publicity, his career was riding high. And then, in June of 1980, it all went up in smoke. It would be six years before Pryor told the public the full truth. Paranoid after a hit of freebased cocaine, he had tried to commit suicide by setting himself on fire. For any other celebrity, the publicity alone would have been devastating. Perhaps one or two brave comedians might have mentioned it again in their acts. But as anyone who saw Pryor's next concert film, *Live from the Sunset Strip*, can attest, no one else could have made the incident so heart-breakingly hilarious. The sight of Pyror equating himself with a lit match—"Richard Pryor running down the street . . ." —remains one of comedy's most brilliant moments.

Pryor moved in and out of movies, some of which were worthy of him, many that were not. In 1986, he suffered another setback; a bout of multiple sclerosis. It was difficult for friends and colleagues to watch his decline, and most shockingly, his silence. Every now and then, there were sparks of the old flame:

> They had a program called *The American Comedy Awards*. We went to a press function afterward and we were sitting there and Richard turned to me, he said, "I stole your album." I said, "What, Richard?" He said, "I stole your album. In Peoria. I walked into the record store and I put it inside my jacket, and I walked out." That's about as high a compliment as you can receive, that Richard Pryor stole your album.
>
> —Bob Newhart

Still, Pryor's disease, and his death from a heart attack in 2005, could never diminish the distance that he had pushed the American public. One of the many black comedians influenced by Pryor, Tommy Davidson, called it: "Richard Pryor had the most authentic black voice in America probably still to this day. But it was a black voice not only filled with rage but insight. The dignity in him was second nature because it wasn't about explaining who these people were; it was about expressing what these people were about." As Pryor once said, in the voice of his "truth-teller" Mudbone:

> I knowed that boy . . . see. He fucked up. See, that fire got on his ass and it fucked him up upstairs. Fried what little brains he had. 'Cause I 'member the motherfucker—he could make a motherfucker laugh at a funeral on Sunday Christmas Day.

Dark star:
Allergic to network censorship; with buddy Gene Wilder in *Stir Crazy* (1980).

KISS MY RICH HAPPY BLACK ASS

"**YOU CAN PRICK YOUR FINGER, BUT YOU CAN'T FINGER YOUR PRICK**"

GEORGE CARLIN

I love words. . . . I want to tell you something about words that I think is important. They're my work, they're my play, they're my passion. Words are all we have really. So be careful with words—some can hurt, some can heal.... –George Carlin, *Class Clown*

George Carlin was fascinated by words from the moment he was born in 1938 into an uptown New York Irish neighborhood; he called it "White Harlem" because "it sounded *bad*." Carlin was raised almost single-handedly by his mother. "My father was absent," he said, "but he was very gifted verbally. He was an after-dinner speaker. He won the Dale Carnegie nationwide public speaking contest in 1935 against twelve hundred entrants. So, as they say in Ireland, 'I didn't lick it off the rocks,' you know?" His mother "drove home to me the Irish gift of language, whatever that is, by sending me to the dictionary."

Like Mort Sahl and Lenny Bruce before him, Carlin left home at an early age to join the service. Appropriately, he was deployed to drop bombs—by the Strategic Air Command, serving as a mechanic on B-47 bombers trained for nuclear exercises. Also like Sahl and Bruce, he proved to be too much of a cutup for the service. He was following a pattern. During his relatively brief existence, he had already been kicked out of the Boy Scouts, the altar boys, the choirboys, and summer camp. By 1957, the twenty-year-old Carlin wanted to be "an actor/comedian/impersonator/disc jockey/trumpet player." He teamed with a comedy partner named Jack Burns, and by 1960, they were turning up on national television, performing an act that was rebellious and snarky but not quite original enough to become big.

Carlin went solo in 1962 and pursued a single-minded mission: he toned down his act so he could get more television gigs and use the television gigs to get parts in movie comedies. He borrowed riffs from his disc jockey days and mixed them in with "observation comedy," still employing his fascination for words. He developed a small following with his character Al Sleet, the "Hippy Dippy Weatherman": "Tonight's forecast: Dark." He hit all the big variety and talk shows. By the late sixties, Carlin had become a regular on a jovial middle of the road variety show called *The Kraft Summer Music Hall with John Davidson*. His career dream had come true—only now it was beginning to look like a nightmare:

> It's great to do a Perry Como special 'cause you're gonna do a stand-up on an important show. But then you're in the bunny number. And you're in the pirate number. And, you know, in all this moron stuff. Hey, I thought, I'm wasting my time with these people, I don't like these people—I'm entertaining the enemy. I had to get in touch with the comedian who says fuck you, who says you can't do that.

Just when it looked like his career was going to bell-bottom out, Carlin played the prestigious Frontier Hotel in Vegas in 1970; he saw the whites of the enemy's eyes—and fired at them:

> I had a little routine I did in Vegas where I said the word "shit." I said, "You know I don't say 'shit.' I don't say 'shit.' Redd Foxx says 'shit' right down the street. Buddy Hackett says 'shit' over and across the boulevard there. I don't say 'shit.' I'll *smoke* a little of it. . . ." And it got its laugh, but after that show they just said, "That's it. You're fired—and you don't get the money." So that was the thing that broke the mold completely.

Carlin grew out his beard, grew his hair longer, junked his white polyester bell-bottoms for jeans, and left the lounge crowd for good. "I'll go to the colleges—

Dippy, not yet hippy:
Carlin as comedy relief in *With Six, You Get Eggroll* (1968); straight-laced comic on the variety scene.

We have more ways of describing dirty words than we have dirty words...that seems a little strange:

bad, dirty filthy foul, vulgar, coarse, unseemly, locker room language, bawdy, naughty, saucy, raunchy, obscene, off-color, risqué, cursing, cussing.

that's where my audience is," he told his wife. "If all I ever do is fill coffeehouses all weekend—Thursday, Friday, Saturday, Sunday—I'll be happy." The stripped-down Carlin was immediately apparent on the cover of his new 1972 album *FM/AM*. It was a dress rehearsal for his shift from comfortable—AM-comedian—to provocative: FM-comic. His second album of 1972, *Clown Class*, was opening night.

> I wanted a list—that's the problem, nobody gives you a list. Wouldn't that make sense, if they didn't want you to say something, they'd give you a list. Nobody even tells you when you're a kid what the words are you're supposed to avoid. "Shit." *Pow!!* I wanted to know the words that were always filthy.

The routine "Seven Words You Can Never Say on Television" was the natural extension of Carlin's innocent childhood fascination with words. The words themselves were anything but innocent.

> The left brain in me wanted to tell the people that there were some words you could say on television that were not considered nice depending on how you used them. Depending on the meaning, there were some words you could use. And one I used the most delightfully, I felt, was, "You can prick your finger, but you can't finger your prick." But there are seven words I've been able to find that have no redeeming meanings. And they are: *shit*, *piss*, *fuck*, *cunt*, *cocksucker*, *motherfucker*, and *tits*.

The album was a hit, went gold, and won the Grammy. "Seven Words" became a signature bit for Carlin and he expounded further with "Filthy Words" on his next album. Blockbuster albums, sold-out college concerts—he was finally connecting with the audience he was always searching for. It was a far cry from the persecution of Lenny Bruce. "Some people have erroneously connected me with Lenny because of profane language," Carlin once said. "He was the first one to make language an issue and suffered from it. I was the first one to make language an issue and succeed from it." Carlin's concert career became hugely successful by the fall of 1973, helped in no small measure by his albums, but in October, the "Filthy Words" routine went from being famous to being infamous. WBAI-FM, a Pacifica Foundation listener-supported station in New York, broadcast a program called *Lunchpail*, a show about language with a disclaimer that "Filthy Words" would be played and that some listeners might find it offensive. As Carlin recounted:

> There was a complaint. One complaint to the FCC, in a city the size of New York, think of all the radio receivers, counting cars, there would be at that time. One complaint to the FCC by a kind of professional moralist. He was in the car with his son, and he had his son listen to it. I'm not sure the son was morally corrupted by the experience. But, because this guy wanted to do his moral agitator thing, he made a complaint. The FCC fined the station just a hundred dollars.

But the FCC also voted to censure WBAI, which was a serious mark against a station for its license renewal application. The station fought the censure and won on appeal, but the FCC took the case to a higher court—the "Big Daddy," as Lenny Bruce called it—the Supreme Court. The case, *FCC v. Pacifica Foundation*, was in the courts for five years, and the ruling handed down in July of 1978 upheld the FCC action, by a vote of five to four, ruling that the routine was "indecent but not obscene." Justice Brennan though the opinion was "misguided" and wrote in his dissent:

> Pacifica explained that "Carlin is not mouthing obscenities, he is merely using words to satirize as harmless and essentially silly our attitudes towards those words." In confirming Carlin's prescience as a social commentator by the result it reaches today, the Court evinces an attitude toward the "seven dirty words" that many others besides Mr. Carlin and Pacifica might describe as "silly." Whether today's decision will similarly prove "harmless" remains to be seen. One can only hope that it will.

" 'Indecent but not obscene,' " said Carlin, "was kind of a new category of filth for me, initially for me. The only case in the Supreme Court based on a comedian." Carlin himself was not a party to the lawsuit, nor did he testify in any way, but "I knew it would validate the piece of material and the thought behind the piece of material which was the center of my identity and act—'Let's all feel a little freer, and not be bound up with all this crap that religion and the culture put on us.' " And in a sign of some kind of progress, Carlin's routines were at least broadcast in his lifetime. More than a year before the Supreme Court ruling, Carlin found himself triumphing in another arena, where his language was beyond the reach of the FCC—cable television. Carlin did his first HBO special in 1977, then continued to perform on the network for thirty more years, a dozen specials in all.

By the end of his exceptional decade of the 1970s, Carlin had become a kind of elder statesman of comedy for a younger generation. He hosted the first episode of *Saturday Night Live* in 1975. But the decade exacted a price from Carlin: Like his hero Lenny Bruce, he had a series of substance abuse addictions—cocaine, painkillers—as well as two heart attacks, which sidelined him in the early 1980s. In the late 1990s, Carlin branched out into publishing some of his perceptions, thoughts, and routines. His last book, *When Will Jesus Bring the Pork Chops?*, was full of Carlin's fascination with euphemism:

> Television news channels will often present some guest they identify as a "terrorism expert." But you can take one look at him and see . . . he's a guy in a suit who obviously works in an office. And I say he's not a terrorism expert. You wanna know who's a terrorism expert? Osama bin Laden.

Wal-Mart pulled the book off its shelves in 2004, claiming that Carlin's books never did well with its customers. Censorship? Salesmanship? It's all in the words:

> Listen, when I was growing up, I was taught to look up to and respect policemen, soldiers and sailors, and baseball players and athletes. And, then I found out how they all talk. These words didn't morally corrupt them, because I was taught to look up to them. So, if the words didn't hurt them, they can't hurt me, and they can't hurt anyone.

In the summer of 2008, Carlin's much-abused heart finally gave out. The next day, in the *New York Times*, Jerry Seinfeld tucked himself in—along with millions of fans—with a fond remembrance:

> As a kid it seemed like the whole world was funny because of George Carlin. His performing voice, even laced with profanity, always sounded as if he were trying to amuse a child. It was like the naughtiest, most fun grown-up you ever met was reading you a bedtime story.

"SHIT." POW!! I WANTED TO KNOW THE WORDS THAT WERE ALWAYS FILTHY.

Cable Television

The cable that revolutionized television had nothing to do with getting 500-plus channels.

In the early days of television, nearly all of the major broadcasting came out of New York, and most of the comedy and variety shows—*Admiral Broadway Revue*, *Texaco Star Theater*, *Colgate Comedy Hour*—were performed live in front of the cameras from different studios throughout the city's Theater District. Then these signals were sent over telephone wires to Chicago, which was as far west as they could be transmitted. In Chicago, a tape would be made of these broadcasts, then sent on to the West Coast, which would broadcast the show anywhere from four days to a week after its initial broadcast on the East Coast. Not an efficient way to bring the whole country together around a new entertainment medium.

All that changed in the fall of 1951, when the first transcontinental coaxial cable was laid (no jokes, please) by AT&T. Coaxial cable, a method of sending signals through cable rather than through the ether, allowed for live broadcasts to originate from either coast. By the end of September 1951, *The Colgate Comedy Hour*, hosted by Eddie Cantor, became the first network series to originate from the West Coast. The next month, *I Love Lucy* was able to transmit its half-hour filmed episodes via the coaxial cable from its Hollywood studio to homes across the country.

The cable created an enormous change in doing business. As Bud Yorkin, one of the original producers of *Colgate*, observed, performers such as Martin and Lewis saw the cable as a lifeline to their California lifestyles. "So the minute that [the cable] happened, all these performers that were complaining that they didn't want to leave their swimming pools and their golf courses and everything and come to New York to rehearse [could now stay in Los Angeles]. All of us that were involved in television in New York, we had to move, too, because everything was coming out here." Carl Reiner suggested that the coaxial cable, and its nationwide access, was the beginning of "dumbing down" the programming that came out of New York, a change that was crucial to his program, *Your Show of Shows*.

Flash forward nearly a quarter of a century: after battling the FCC and the broadcast network on the numerous legal technicalities for

decades, a pay cable network makes its debut in 1972. Home Box Office, based in New York, feeds a live NHL game to its East Coast subscribers. By 1975, HBO was able to access satellite technology and spread its reach nationwide. What HBO was able to offer—at a time when there were only three major networks and, at best, an additional six or seven local stations in most urban markets—was what all broadcast competition wants: unique access. With Home Box Office, as its name suggests, audiences at home were allowed direct, unfiltered access to what audiences "on the town" could get: sports events, movies, music concerts—and comedy concerts. As Carolyn Strauss, the former president of HBO Entertainment, put it: "Comedy was something that we could do in a way that followed in the footsteps of showing uncensored movies—programming that could exist in its pristine form."

HBO initially broadcast a Robert Klein concert in 1975, but for its 1977 program *On Location*, HBO went after the best possible uncensored comedian they could find, the man who defined "censored," George Carlin. For Carlin, the new venue couldn't have come a moment too soon.

You're never the fastest gun in town forever. [In 1977,] I did not have a place because my albums were cooling down, and the heat and the fire were off, you know. I didn't have a focal point for who I was anymore. And then cable came along in 1977. Now, it didn't happen instantly for me. I more or less recycled things from the previous four years, but what cable did for me, it replaced recordings as a way for me to reach a mass audience and [still do my act the way it was].

Carlin's first HBO concert, *On Location: George Carlin at USC*, even used an opening disclaimer about the language he used, "which of course is kind of quaint now when you look at it," Carlin reflected. When he was showcased in *On Location: George Carlin at Phoenix* a year later, he cemented his reputation as cable's signature comic.

On Location allowed television audiences access to something they had never seen before—a front-seat view of what comics really do in front of real people. Said Strauss, "While it's great to watch somebody on Johnny Carson, you hear that sort of disembodied laughter. We were able to bring the television audience into the seats of a theater audience, and you could watch the comic and respond to the comic in concert with everybody else who was sitting in the audience." The show wound up turning the spotlight on hot new comics, like Steve Martin, Robert Klein, Billy Crystal, and Roseanne Barr, while providing unadulterated versions of old-timers who had been forced to screen out some of the best stuff for *Ed Sullivan* and *Merv Griffin*: Phyllis Diller, Redd Foxx—even borscht belt pioneer Myron Cohen.

In 1992, HBO opened a window—or pulled back a rope line—onto an entirely different kind of comedy with *Russell Simmons' Def Comedy Jam*, which lasted five seasons in its original incarnation. It was a breakout show, introducing both white audiences and, not incidentally, white producers into the raucous world of a black comedy club. Although, as Strauss admits, "there were some people who were better than others," the hip-hop atmosphere brought artists like Martin Lawrence, Cedric the Entertainer, Steve Harvey, and D. L. Hughley to a mass audience and to huge film and concert careers.

Such success spawns eager imitation, and the proliferation of basic cable networks in the late 1980s made imitation easy to come by. By the end of the decade, it seemed as though every other cable network was putting a comedian against a brick wall; given only a few minutes to score, the talent would often rely on material that was raunchy for raunchy's sake, hoping to make either an impact or a deal for a sitcom or feature film. As Tommy Davidson put it: "I've seen a lot of comics resort to that because it's just quicker, cheaper laughs, sort of like McDonald's food compared to Ruth's Chris Steak restaurant. You know it's faster food, but it's not as good for you."

In 1991, two rival cable channels, The Comedy Channel and HA!, merged to become Comedy Central on, aptly, April Fool's Day. Originally, its dance card was filled with recycled movies, British comedies (*Absolutely Fabulous*), and bargain basement shows (*Mystery Science Theater*), but it quickly became a media powerhouse when it was able to turn to original programming. Now, it houses some of the pioneers of the field: *The Daily Show with Jon Stewart*, *Chappelle's Show*, *Reno 911!*, *The Sarah Silverman Show*, as well as numerous roasts, tributes, and documentaries. The crown jewel of their programming, if that's the right phrase to use for a show that raises a piece of poop to glorified heights, is *South Park*, which debuted in 1997. *South Park*, a kind of vile version of *Peanuts* with the most rudimentary animation (part of its charm, partisans would claim), has become not only Comedy Central's most popular

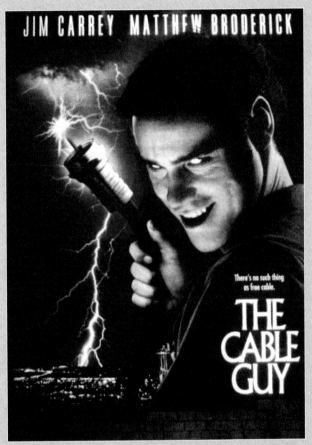

show but one of cable's most reliable lightning rods for controversy. Still, its filth has a disarming disingenuousness; at the opening of each episode, a disclaimer reads, in part: "the following program contains coarse language and due to its content it should not be viewed by anyone." Considering that, in one episode, *South Park* used the word *shit* 162 times and, in another, the word *nigger* 42 times, the disclaimer seems, if anything, to be an understatement.

What cable has clearly given the world is a verbal (and visual) freedom for comedy; the FCC still does not regulate cable programs, although considering the fact that more and more homes will acquire basic or pay cable programming, the kind of censorship endured by the broadcast networks seems inevitable. Whether such freedom is a good or bad thing remains a constant source of debate. Largely through shows like *South Park*, cable has taken a lot of heat for the kind of material that now reaches audiences in every hamlet in America. For connoisseurs of comedy, it largely boils down to a matter of taste. As *Laugh-In*'s producer George Schlatter says, "The minute you drop the f-bomb in the middle of a show, you can't be funny after that because you've already gone as far as you can go." Strauss defends the kinds of programs made accessible by cable: "Certainly cable didn't invent the blue comic. The blue comic has been around forever. So it certainly allowed a little more expression for people than it would have on network television."

For Budd Friedman, the founder of the Improv Comedy Club, it's not a matter of taste, tone, or material, it's a matter of ubiquity—an unexpected consequence of unique access:

Somebody just asked me the other day, "Does doing *The Tonight Show* with Jay Leno get [comics] the same respect that it used to when they did Johnny?" I say, "Absolutely not." Nothing to take away from Jay, but when *The Tonight Show* was on, there was no cable. Now, Leno, or the comic on Leno, has so much competition from cable and other shows that it's impossible to make the impact that they did back then. Because, now, people see comics every minute of the day.

"THE ONLY GUY WHO WHO GOT FIRED FOR 9/11"
BILL MAHER

Far be it from me to criticize religion. But just remember one thing: if the Pope was, instead of a religious figure, merely the CEO of a nationwide chain of daycare centers where thousands of employees had been caught molesting kids and then covering it up, he'd be arrested faster than you can say "Who wants to touch Mister Wiggle?"

—Bill Maher

Bill Maher is as competitive as any comedian, and it's always nice to win an award of some kind—any kind. In 2003 the Catholic League, the nation's largest Catholic civil rights organization, declared Maher "the number one bigot in America." Criticism of—and by—organized religion is a crucial part of the Bill Maher playbook. Still, the League's denunciation may have torn Maher in half—he has an Irish-Catholic father and a Jewish mother (a fact he didn't learn about until he was in his teens)—but Maher constantly courts controversy, and controversy seems to have no problem returning his phone calls.

Even the title of his first television show, *Politically Incorrect*, was a gauntlet thrown down to conventional morality. Cable television proved to be the perfect arena for his vociferous, vitriolic panel show, and HBO hosted the program when it debuted in 1993. It proved so popular that Maher was wooed away by the commercial broadcast network ABC—although his show had to be shown late at night, when the kiddies were presumably asleep.

In the days after the 9/11 tragedy, comedy was in short supply. Criticism was even scarcer, until Maher ignited a firestorm on *Politically Incorrect*. On September 17, 2001, he said, "We have been the cowards lobbing cruise missiles from two thousand miles away. That's cowardly. Staying in the airplane when it hits the building, say what you want about it, it's not cowardly." Although such unlikely colleagues as Rush Limbaugh came to Maher's defense, ABC sponsors FedEx and Sears, Roebuck pulled their advertising dollars, and some affiliates dropped the show. By June of 2002, ABC pulled the show from its lineup.

Mission accomplished:
Maher, pillar-ied on *Politically Incorrect*; (opposite) kissing and making up with the Decider.

On the final broadcast of *Politically Incorrect*, Maher told his audience, "I do not relinquish, nor should any of you, the right to criticize, even as we support, our government. This is still a democracy, and feelings are gonna get hurt so that actual people won't, and that will be a good thing." Six days later, on June 22, 2002, Maher was awarded the L.A. Press Club's President's Award, its highest honor, for "championing free speech." Accepting the award, Maher said, "Isn't there something wrong when I'm the *only* guy in the country that got fired for 9/11?"

For a while, it seemed as if 9/11 was the last barrier for accepted comedy. But even Bob Newhart stepped up to the plate "a couple of months later":

> I did my first 9/11 joke, which was, when they quit asking you at the airport if, if someone, if some stranger had handed you something to take aboard the plane— they stopped asking that because they realized if, if you were a terrorist, that you might lie. "Comedy is tragedy plus time," and, and that's when you find out that people are ready to laugh, they move beyond it. You couldn't do it the next day, there's no question about that.

After Maher made his 9/11 comments, the White House Press Secretary, Ari Fleischer, said, "They're reminders to all Americans that they need to watch what they say, watch what they do. This is not a time for remarks like that." For Maher, that was quite a compliment: "It was rather flattering to be, at that moment in history when we were under attack by real enemies, to be receiving this sort of attention from an administration that really should have been focusing on Al Qaeda, instead of what I was saying."

Maher may have been fired, but he was not out of work for long. Cable welcomed him back in 2003 with a new HBO show, *Real Time with Bill Maher*, where, apparently, he is free to offend whomever he chooses:

> It made me understand that you have to fight for your position especially in this "gotcha" culture. The truth is, there are a lot of things wrong with this country, but there is totally free speech. Yes, you have to fight for it a little, but you have to fight for anything that's worthwhile. Any country that lets me run my mouth the way I do is still worth saving.

Maher's childhood idol was Johnny Carson, and Carson still casts a long shadow over his work, but Maher departed from the late-night guru in one critical way: "When I started doing *Politically Incorrect*, I remember critics saying, 'You can't really last on television if you let people know what side you're on.' That was the Johnny Carson playbook. But I thought, 'Well, I'm going to break that rule. If I don't last, then I guess they were right.' But they're obviously wrong." Even though Maher came out for Barack Obama during the 2008 Democratic primary season, it didn't keep him from poking fun at the candidate:

> Never play a sport in public that you suck at. To connect with Pennsylvania's blue-collar voters, Barack Obama went bowling and scored a 37. And the right wing had a field day. Joe Scarborough said he bowls like a four-year-old. And Ann Coulter offered to loan him one of her balls. But you know who's a good bowler? George Bush. His specialty is preemptive strikes.

For his constant courage under ire, Maher has earned the respect and loyalty of millions of viewers, including Roseanne Barr:

> I call him the bravest man in the world. He still has his blind spots, but I think he's the bravest person on television now. I mean, the level of corruption that we live with now, it's the enemy of freedom of speech and comedy. Anybody right now who has the ethics to speak out while we still can—Rosie O'Donnell is as brave as anybody's ever been. She even makes Bill Maher look a little bit like a pussy.

PUNCH LINE

What's the punch line? Where is comedy headed in the twenty-first century?

Chief of the future?: Chris Rock in *Head of State* (2004).

Some comedians, like Joan Rivers, like a socko finish. Some, like Andy Kaufman, did away with punch lines entirely. The future probably lies between the two. What's clear is that comedy has earned an exalted place in American culture, and as the nation gets more complex and problematic, we will turn to comedy as a way of both avoiding and reflecting our problems.

Comedy will be delivered to us in different ways, through the Internet and websites, bypassing the need for the communal experience of a living room or a nightclub. The magicians of computer technology will continue to amaze us with the extreme physical manifestations of their imaginations. Politicians will continue to give satirists and late-night monologists the gift that keeps on giving—incredible acts of ineptitude, immorality, and idiocy. New genres in popular culture, as yet unmaterialized and unperformed, will serve as fodder for the next generation of parodists. As the American family keeps reconfiguring and redefining itself, it will be captured on television comedies in brand-new ways. And the fearless comedians will keep testing the boundaries of taste and taboo. Whether it's Margaret Cho, or Dave Chappelle, or Sarah Silverman, rather than bend our preconceptions, these comedians prefer to break them. As Chris Rock put it, "Hey, I'd love to do a nice, clean act and be on the networks or whatever, there's definitely more money in that. But that wouldn't work for me. I wouldn't make a dime doing that 'cause I'm not funny that way. I gotta do what works for me. I gotta do the thing that, you know, will get my mother a house."

One predictable punch line of the future is that new groups will keep arriving on our shores, bringing their own cultural perspectives to reflect and refract what it means to be an American through a sense of humor. One contemporary comedian interviewed for our series, Dean Obeidallah, is an Arab-American which makes him a pioneer—but not for long: "You know, sadly, Arabs, Muslims in America—we are the new enemy. We have replaced the new Soviet Union. And we are stuck here until somebody replaces us. That's why I am begging all of you to help me taunt North Korea as much as possible."

Yet for all the unstable elements in the future of American comedy, Jerry Seinfeld pointed to some eternally relevant pioneers:

> There's a periodic chart of comedy: Woody, Carlin, Chaplin, Keaton, Groucho, you know, Carson, "Who's on First?" These are pure elements—you can't break them down any further, do you know what I mean? You can't take a piece off them, it's like [they've] already been broken down to what's essential.

Perhaps the really big finish is that a comedian's work is never finished—at least not if comic genius is hotwired into your DNA. Chris Rock has the last, best word on the subject:

> I'm almost never comfortable. Like, literally, in my whole life, I can count on maybe two hands, the moments in life where I felt comfortable. I'm never comfortable. And I think most comedians have this thing where we're just not comfortable. We're just kinda too aware of things. They always say, "Ignorance is bliss." So what's the opposite? To be aware of every little thing, to notice everything? It's Hell.

BIBLIOGRAPHY

There are many joke books, but there are not too many book jokes. Here's one, courtesy of Professor Irwin Corey:

> A guy goes to the library and he wants to buy a book on suicide. The librarian says, "You'll find it in aisle one under the letter *S*."
>
> He goes and looks and looks. He says, "There's nothing here." She says, "I know, they never bring 'em back."

What follows is a list of books certainly worth keeping. A particular nod of appreciation must go to three authors, each of whom, coincidentally, has a name beginning with *Ma*. Leonard Maltin was interested in the great comedians and cartoons of the past long before it became fashionable; I was lucky enough to meet him at a Sons of the Desert convention when I was a teenager, and I was hooked. His books are exemplary history and his enthusiasm is infectious. Steve Martin's latest book, *Born Standing Up*, is the best account of being a comedian in the modern world, elegantly written and moving, as well. For an account of being a comedian in the not-so-modern world, Groucho Marx's reminiscences in *The Marx Brothers Scrapbook* can't be beat. The book took a lot of heat when it came out in 1973 because it was unexpurgated and some dreary litigation ensued. Too bad; thirty-five years later, I can still recall some of Groucho's on-target perceptions about the mendacity and crudity of show business and they always make me weep with laughter.

–LM

Adamson, Joe. *Groucho, Harpo, Chico and Sometimes Zeppo: A Celebration of the Marx Brothers*. New York: Simon & Schuster, 1973.

Ajaye, Franklin. *Comic Insights: The Art of Stand-Up Comedy*. Los Angeles, CA: Silman-James Press, 2002.

Allen, Fred. *"All The Sincerity in Hollywood . . .": Selections from the Writings of Radio's Legendary Comedian*. Golden, Co,: Fulcrum Publishing, 2001.

—. *Much Ado about Me*. Boston, MA: Little, Brown, 1956.

Allen, Ralph. *The Best Burlesque Sketches*. New York: Applause Books, 1995.

Allen, Steve. *Funny People*. Briarcliff Manor, NY: Stein & Day, 1981.

Anobile, Richard J., with introduction by Groucho Marx. *Why a Duck? Visual and Verbal Gems from the Marx Brothers Movies*. New York: Darien House, 1971.

Arce, Hector. *Groucho*. New York: G. P. Putnam's Sons, 1979.

Baker, William F., and George Dessart. *Down the Tube: An Inside Account of the Failure of American Television*. New York: Basic Books, 1998.

Barber, Rowland. *The Night They Raided Minsky's*. New York: Simon & Schuster, 1960.

Barr, Roseanne. *Roseanne: My Life as a Woman*. New York: Harper & Row, 1989.

Beatts, Anne. *Titters: The First Collection of Humor by Women*. New York: Collier Books, 1976.

Beck, Jerry, ed. *Animation Art: From Pencil to Pixel, the History of Cartoon, Anime & CGI*. New York: Harper Collins, 2004.

Benny, Jack, and Joan Benny. *Sunday Nights at Seven: The Jack Benny Story*. New York: Warner Books, 1990.

Berg, Gertrude. *Molly and Me: The Memoirs of Gertrude Berg*. New York: McGraw-Hill Book Company, 1961.

Berger, Phil. *The Last Laugh: The World of the Stand-Up Comics*. New York: Limelight Editions, 1985.

Bogle, Donald. *Prime Time Blues: African Americans on Network Television*. New York: Farrar, Straus & Giroux, 2001.

Bonney, Jo, ed. *Extreme Exposure: An Anthology of Solo Performance Texts from the Twentieth Century*. New York: Theatre Communications Group, 2000.

Brownlow, Kevin. *The Parade's Gone By. . . .* Berkeley and Los Angeles: University of California Press, 1968.

Bruce, Lenny. *How to Talk Dirty and Influence People: An Autobiography*. New York: Fireside, 1963.

Burnett, Carol. *One More Time: A Memoir*. New York: Random House, 1986.

Burr, Lonnie. *Two for the Show: Great 20th Century Comedy Teams*. New York: J. Messner, 1979.

Byron, Stuart, and Elisabeth Weis. *The National Society of Film Critics on Movie Comedy*. New York: Grossman Publishers, 1977.

Cader, Michael. *Saturday Night Live: The First Twenty Years*. Boston: Houghton Mifflin, 1994.

Caesar, Sid, with Eddy Friedfeld. *Caesar's Hours: My Life in Comedy, with Love and Laughter*. New York: PublicAffairs, 2003.

Cahn, William. *The Laugh Makers: A Pictorial History of American Comedians*. New York: Bramhall House, 1957.

Cantor, Eddie. *My Life Is in Your Hands & Take My Life*. Boulder, CO: Cooper Square Press, 2000.

Carlin, George. *When Will Jesus Bring the Pork Chops?* New York: Hyperion, 2004.

Carter, Joseph. *The Quotable Will Rogers*. Layton, Utah: Gibbs Smith, 2005.

Chaplin, Charles. *My Autobiography*. New York: Penguin Books, 1964.

—. *My Life in Pictures*. London: The Bodley Head, 1974.

Cohen, John. *The Essential Lenny Bruce*. New York: Bell Publishing Company, 1967.

Coleman, Janet. *The Compass: The Improvisational Theatre That Revolutionized American Comedy*. Chicago: University of Chicago Press, 1990.

Collins, Ronald K. L., and David M. Skover. *The Trials of Lenny Bruce*. Naperville, IL: Sourcebooks, 2002.

Comte, Michel, ed. *Charlie Chaplin: A Photo Diary*. Germany: Steidl, 2002.

Corio, Ann. *This Was Burlesque*. New York: Madison Square Press, 1968.

Cosby, Bill. *Cosbyology: Essays and Observations from the Doctor of Comedy*. New York: Hyperion, 2001.

Costello, Chris. *Lou's on First?* New York: St. Martin's Press, 1981.

Cox, Stephen. *Here's Johnny: Thirty Years of America's Favorite Late-Night Entertainer*. Nashville, TN: Cumberland House, 2002.

Cox, Stephen John and Lofflin. *The Abbott & Costello Story*. Nashville, TN: Cumberland House, 1990.

Crichton, Kyle. *The Marx Brothers*. Garden City, NY: Doubleday & Company, 1950.

Curtis, James. *W. C. Fields, A Biography*. New York: Alfred A. Knopf, 2003.

Dale, Alan S. *Comedy Is a Man in Trouble: Slapstick in American Movies*. Minneapolis: University of Minnesota Press, 2000.

David, Jay. *The Life and Humor of Robin Williams: A Biography*. New York: Quill, 1999.

Davidson, Telly R. *TV's Grooviest Variety Shows of the '60s and '70s*. Nashville, TN: Cumberland House, 2006.

Davis, Madelyn Pugh, with Bob Carroll Jr. *Laughing with Lucy: My Life with America's Leading Lady of Comedy*. Cincinnati, OH: Emmis Books, 2005.

Dewey, Donald. *The Art of Ill Will: The Story of American Political Cartoons*. New York and London: New York University Press, 2007.

Diller, Phyllis. *Like a Lampshade in a Whorehouse: My Life in Comedy*. New York: Jeremy P. Tarcher, 2005.

Dolan, Deirdre. *Curb Your Enthusiasm: The Book*. New York: Gotham Books, 2006.

Dougherty, Barry. *A Hundred Years, a Million Laughs: A Centennial Celebration of the Friars Club*. Cincinnati, OH: Emmis Books, 2004.

Edwards, Elisabeth. *Lucy & Desi: A Real-Life Scrapbook of America's Favorite TV Couple*. Philadelphia: Running Press Book Publishers, 2004.

Ely, Melvin Patrick. *The Adventures of Amos 'n' Andy: A Social History of an American Phenomenon*. New York: Free Press, 1991.

—. *Mixed Nuts: America's Love Affair with Comedy Teams from Burns and Allen to Belushi and Aykroyd*. New York: PublicAffairs, 2004.

Epstein, Lawrence J. *The Haunted Smile: The Story of Jewish Comedians in America*. New York: Public Affairs, 2001.

Everson, William K. *The Art of W. C. Fields*. New York: Bonanza Books, 1967.

Faith, William Robert. *Bob Hope: A Life in Comedy*. New York: G. P. Putnam's Sons, 1982.

Fein, Irving A. *Jack Benny: An Intimate Biography*. New York: G. P. Putnam's Sons, 1976.

Florenski, Joe, and Steve Wilson. *Center Square: The Paul Lynde Story*. New York: Advocate Books, 2005.

Ford, Gerald R. *Humor and the Presidency*. New York: Arbor House, 1987.

Forrester, Jeff. *The Three Stooges: The Triumphs and Tragedies of the Most Popular Comedy Team of All Time*. Los Angeles: Donaldson Books, 2002.

Foxx, Redd. *The Redd Foxx Encyclopedia of Black Humor*. Pasadena, CA: W. Ritchie Press, 1977.

Fretts, Bruce. The Entertainment Weekly *Seinfeld Companion: Atomic Wedgies to Zipper Jobs, An Unofficial Guide to TV's Funniest Show*. New York: Warner Books, 1993.

Furmanek, Bob, and Palumbo, Ron. *Abbott and Costello in Hollywood*. New York: Perigee, 1991.

Gabler, Neal. *Walt Disney: The Triumph of the American Imagination*. New York: Alfred A. Knopf, 2006.

Gehring, Wes D. *Groucho and W. C. Fields, Huckster Comedians*. Jackson: University Press of Mississippi, 1994.

Gelbart, Larry. *Laughing Matters*. New York: Random House, 1998.

Gelbart, Larry, et al. *Stand-Up Comedians on Television*. New York: Harry N. Abrams, 1996.

Gregory, Dick. *Nigger*. New York: Simon & Schuster, 1964.

Groening, Matt. Ray Richmond, ed. *The Simpsons: A Complete Guide to Our Favorite Family*. New York: HarperCollins, 1997.

Hamilton, Marybeth. *When I'm Bad I'm Better: Mae West, Sex, and American Entertainment*. Los Angeles: University of California Press, 1995.

Hayes, Kevin J., ed. *Charlie Chaplin Interviews*. Jackson: University Press of Mississippi, 2005.

Henderson, Amy. *On the Air: Pioneers of American Broadcasting*. Smithsonian Institution Press, Washington, DC, 1988.

Hill, Doug, and Jeff Weingrad. *Saturday Night: A Backstage History of Saturday Night Live*. New York: Vintage Books, 1987.

Hirsch, Foster. *Love, Sex, Death, and the Meaning of Life: The Films of Woody Allen*. Cambridge, MA: Da Capo Press, 2001.

Hoberman, J., and Jeffrey Shandler. *Entertaining America: Jews, Movies, and Broadcasting*. Princeton, NJ: Princeton University Press, 2003.

Hope, Bob, with Melville Shavelson. *Don't Shoot, It's Only Me: Bob Hope's Comedy History of the United States*. New York: G. P. Putnam's Sons, 1990.

Jacobs, Frank. *The Mad World of Wiliam M. Gaines*. New York: Bantam Books, 1973.

Jenkins, Henry. *What Made Pistachio Nuts? Early Sound Comedy and the Vaudeville Aesthetic*. New York: Columbia University Press, 1992.

Jones, Chuck. *Chuck Amuck: The Life and Times of an Animated Cartoonist*. New York: Farrar, Straus & Giroux, 1989.

Jones, Gerard. *Honey, I'm Home! Sitcoms: Selling the American Dream*. New York: St. Martin's Press, 1992.

Kanfer, Stefan. *Ball of Fire: The Tumultuous Life and Comic Art of Lucille Ball*. New York: Alfred A. Knopf, 2003.

—. *Groucho: The Life and Times of Julius Henry Marx*. New York: Alfred A. Knopf, 2000.

Keaton, Buster, and Charles Samuels. *Buster Keaton: My Wonderful World of Slapstick*. New York: Doubleday, 1960.

Keaton, Eleanor, and Jeffrey Vance. *Buster Keaton Remembered*. New York: Harry N. Abrams, 2001.

Kercher, Stephen E. *Revel with a Cause: Liberal Satire in Postwar America*. Chicago: University of Chicago Press, 2006.

Kerr, Walter. *The Silent Clowns*. New York: Alfred A. Knopf, 1975.

Klein, Robert. *The Amorous Busboy of Decatur Avenue*. New York: Simon & Schuster, 2005.

Klugman, Jack. *Tony and Me: A Story of Friendship*. West Linn, OR: Good Hill Press, 2005.

Knelman, Martin. *Jim Carrey: The Joker Is Wild: The Trials and Triumphs of Jim Carrey*. Richmond Hill, ONT: Firefly Books, 2000.

Knopf, Robert. *The Theater and Cinema of Buster Keaton*. Princeton, NJ: Princeton University Press, 1999.

Krassner, Paul. *Impolite Interviews*. New York: Seven Stories Press, 1999.

Lahr, John. *Show and Tell: New Yorker Profiles*. New York: Overlook Press, 2000.

Laurie, Joe. *Vaudeville: From the Honky Tonks to the*

Palace. Port Washington, NY: Kennikat Press, 1972.

Lax, Eric. *Conversations with Woody Allen: His Films, the Movies, and Moviemaking*. New York: Alfred A. Knopf, 2007.

—. *Woody Allen: A Biography*. Cambridge, MA: Da Capo Press, 1991.

Leamer, Laurence. *King of the Night*. New York: Avon Books, 2005.

Leider, Emily Wortis. *Becoming Mae West*. Cambridge, MA: Da Capo Press, 1997.

Lenburg, Jeff, and Joan Howard Maurer, et al. *The Three Stooges Scrapbook*. Secaucus, NJ: Citadel Press, 1982.

Leonard, Maurice. *Mae West: Empress of Sex*. New York: Birch Lane Press, 1991.

Levy, Shawn. *King of Comedy: The Life and Art of Jerry Lewis*. New York: St. Martin's Press, 1996.

Lewis, Jerry. *The Total Film-Maker*. New York: Random House, 1971.

Lewis, Paul. *Cracking Up: American Humor in a Time of Conflict*. Chicago: University of Chicago Press, 2006.

Littleton, Darryl. *Black Comedians on Black Comedy: How African-Americans Taught Us to Laugh*. New York: Applause Books, 2006.

LoMonaco, Martha. *Every Week, A Broadway Revue: The Tamiment Playhouse, 1921-1960*. New York: Greenwood Press, 1992.

Louvish, Simon. *Mae West: It Ain't No Sin*. London: Faber & Faber, 2005.

—. *Man on the Flying Trapeze: The Life and Times of W. C. Fields*. London: Faber & Faber, 1999.

Maltin, Leonard. *The Great American Broadcast: A Celebration of Radio's Golden Age*. New York: Dutton, 1997.

—. *The Great Movie Comedians: Updated Edition from Charlie Chaplin to Woody Allen*. New York: Harmony Books, 1982.

—. *Movie Comedy Teams*. New York: New American Library, 1974.

—. *Of Mice and Magic: A History of American Animated Cartoons*. New York: McGraw-Hill, 1980.

Marc, David. *Comic Visions: Television Comedy and American Culture*. Malden, MA: Blackwell, 1997.

Marshall, Garry. *Wake Me When It's Funny: How To Break into Showbusiness and Stay There*. New York: Newmarket Press, 1995.

Marshall, Peter, and Adrienne Armstrong. *Backstage with the Original Hollywood Square*. Nashville: Rutledge Hill Press, 2002.

Martin, Steve. *Born Standing Up: A Comic's Life*. New York: Scribner, 2007.

Marx, Bill. *Son of Harpo Speaks! A Family Portrait*. Albany, GA: Bear Manor Media, 2007.

Marx, Groucho, and Richard Anobile. *The Marx Bros. Scrapbook*. New York: Darien House, 1973.

Marx, Groucho. *The Groucho Phile: An Illustrated Life*. New York: Pocket Books, 1976.

Marx, Harpo, with Rowland Barber. *Harpo Speaks!* NJ: Limelight Editions, 1962.

Mast, Gerald. *The Comic Mind: Comedy and the Movies*. Chicago: University of Chicago Press, 1979.

McClay, Michael. *I Love Lucy: The Complete Picture History of the Most Popular TV Show Ever*. New York: Warner Books, 1995.

McCrohan, Donna. *The Honeymooners' Companion: The Kramdens and the Nortons Revisited*. New York: Workman Publishing, 1978.

Meade, Marion. *Buster Keaton: Cut to the Chase*. Cambridge, MA: Da Capo Press, 1997.

Meglin, Nick, and John Ficarra, ed. *MAD about the Movies*. New York: MAD Books, 1998.

Merton, Paul. *Silent Comedy*. London: Random House, 2007.

Minsky, Morton, and Milt Machlin. *Minsky's Burlesque*. New York: Arbor House, 1986.

Mitchell, Glenn. *The Marx Brothers Encyclopedia*. London: B. T. Batsford, 1996.

Museum of Broadcasting, ed. *The Many Worlds of Carol Burnett*. New York: Museum of Broadcasting, 1995.

Nachman, Gerald. *Raised on Radio*. New York: Pantheon, 1998.

—. *Seriously Funny: The Rebel Comedians of the 1950s and 1960s*. New York: Back Stage Books, 2004.

Neibaur, James L., and Ted Okuda. *The Jerry Lewis Films: An Analytical Filmography of the Innovative Comic*. Jefferson, NC: McFarland & Co., 1994.

Neuwirth, Allan. *They'll Never Put That on the Air: An Oral History of Taboo-Breaking Comedy*. New York: All-worth Press, 2006.

O'Neill, Ellen, ed. *Jack Benny: The Radio and Television Work*. New York: HarperCollins, 1991.

Oliver, Donald. *The Greatest Revue Sketches*. New York: Avon Books, 1982.

Parish, James Robert. *It's Good to Be the King: The Seriously Funny Life of Mel Brooks*. Hoboken, NJ: Wiley, 2007.

Radner, Gilda. *It's Always Something*. New York: Simon & Schuster, 1989.

Reidelbach, Maria. *Completely MAD: A History of the Comic Book and Magazine*. Toronto: Little, Brown, 1991.

Reiner, Carl. *My Anecdotal Life*. New York: St. Martin's Press, 2003.

Rickles, Don, and David Ritz. *Rickles' Book: A Memoir*. New York; Simon & Schuster, 2007.

Rivers, Joan, with Richard Meryman. *Enter Talking*. New York: Delacorte, 1986.

Robinson, David. *Charlie Chaplin, Comic Genius*. New York: Harry N. Abrams, 1996.

—. *Chaplin: His Life and Art*. New York: McGraw-Hill, 1985.

Rogers, Will. *The Wit and Wisdom of Will Rogers*. New York: HarperCollins, 1991.

Rourke, Constance. *American Humor: A Study of the National Character*. New York: Harcourt Brace, 1931.

Sahl, Mort. *Heartland*. New York: Harcourt, Brace, Jovanovich, 1976.

Schickel, Richard. *Woody Allen: A Life in Film*. Chicago: Ivan R. Dee, 2003.

Schickel, Richard, ed. *The Essential Chaplin: Perspectives on the Life and Art of the Great Comedian*. Chicago: Ivan R. Dee, 2006.

Schlissel, Lillian, ed. *Three Plays by Mae West*. New York: Routledge, 1997.

Shales, Tom, and James Andrew Miller. *Live from New York: An Uncensored History of Saturday Night Live as Told by Its Stars, Writers, and Guests*. Boston, MA: Little, Brown, 2002.

Shout! Factory, ed. *Lenny Bruce: Let the Buyer Beware*. Los Angeles Retropolis, LLC / Shout Factory, 2004.

Shydner, Ritch, and Mark Schiff. *I Killed: True*

Stories of the Road from America's Top Comics. New York: Crown, 2006.

Sicilia, Gail, ed. *Zingers from The Hollywood Squares*. New York: Popular Library, 1974.

Sikov, Ed. *Screwball: Hollywood's Madcap Romantic Comedies*. New York: Crown, 1989.

Silverman, Stephen M. *Funny Ladies: 100 Years of Great Comediennes*. New York: Harry N. Abrams, 1999.

Silvers, Phil, and Saffron, Robert. *This Laugh Is on Me: The Phil Silvers Story*. Englewood Cliffs, NJ: Prentice Hall, 1973.

Simon, Neil. *Rewrites: A Memoir*. New York: Simon & Schuster, 1996.

Skretvedt, Randy. *Laurel and Hardy: The Magic Behind the Movies*. Beverly Hills, CA: Past Times Publishing, 1987.

Slide, Anthony. *The Vaudevillians: A Dictionary of Vaudeville Performers*. Westport, CT: A Westport, CT: Arlington House, 1981.

Smith, Bill. *The Vaudevillians*. New York: Macmillian, 1976.

Smith, Ronald L. *Who's Who in Comedy: Comedians, Comics, and Clowns from Vaudeville to Today's Stand ups*. New York: Facts on File, 1992.

—, ed. *The Stars of Stand-Up Comedy: A Biographical Encyclopedia*. New York: Garland, 1986.

—. *Comedy On Record: The Complete Critical Discography*. New York: Garland, 1988.

Sobel, Bernard. *A Pictorial History of Vaudeville*. New York: The Citadel Press, 1961.

Staveacre, Tony. *Slapstick! The Illustrated Story of Knockabout Comedy*. Sydney, Australia: Angus & Robertson, 1987.

Stein, Charles W., ed. *American Vaudeville As Seen by Its Contemporaries*. New York: Alfred A. Knopf, 1984.

Steinberg, David. *The Book of David*. New York: Simon & Schuster, 2007.

Sterling, Bryan B., and Frances N. Sterling. *Will Rogers: A Photo-Biography*. Dallas, TX: Taylor Publishing Company, 1999.

—. *Will Rogers Speaks*. New York: M. Evans, 1995.

Stewart, Jon. *America (The Book): A Citizen's Guide to Democracy Inaction*. New York; Warner Books, 2004.

Stock, Rip. *Odd Couple Mania: All You Ever Wanted to Know About Felix and Oscar—and One of the Great TV Shows of All Time*. New York: Ballantine, 1983.

Stone, Laurie. *Laughing in the Dark: A Decade of Subversive Comedy*. Hopewell, NJ: The Ecco Press, 1997.

Sweeney, Don. *Backstage at the Tonight Show: From Johnny Carson to Jay Leno*. Lanham, MD: Taylor Trade Publishing, 2006.

Sweeney, Kevin W., ed. *Buster Keaton Interviews*. Jackson: University Press of Mississippi, 2007.

Taraborrelli, J. Randy. *Laughing Till It Hurts: The Complete Life and Career of Carol Burnett*. New York: William Morrow., 1988.

Taylor, Robert Lewis. *W. C. Fields: His Follies and Fortunes*. Garden City, NY: Doubleday, 1949.

Trav S. D. *No Applause, Just Throw Money, or, The Book That Made Vaudeville Famous*. New York: Faber and Faber, 2005.

Turner, Chris. *Planet Simpson: How a Cartoon Masterpiece Defined a Generation*. Cambridge, MA: Da Capo Press, 2004.

Tuska, Jon. *The Complete Films of Mae West*. New York: Carol Publishing Group, 1992.

Tynan, Kenneth. *Show People: Profiles in Entertainment*. New York: Simon & Schuster, 1979.

Vance, Jeffrey. *Chaplin: Genius of the Cinema*. New York: Harry N. Abrams, 2003.

—, and Suzanne Lloyd. *Harold Lloyd: Master Comedian*. New York: Harry N. Abrams, 2002.

Waldron, Vince. *Classic Sitcoms: A Celebration of the Best Prime-Time Comedy*. New York: Collier Books, 1987.

Watkins, Mel. *On the Real Side: Laughing, Lying, and Signifying—The Underground Tradition of African American Humor That Transformed American Culture, from Slavery to Richard Pryor*. New York: Simon & Schuster, 1994.

Watts, Jill. *Mae West: An Icon in Black and White*. New York: Oxford University Press, 2001.

Weatherby, W. J. *Jackie Gleason: An Intimate Portrait of the Great One*. New York: Pharos Books, 1992.

Weintraub, Joseph, ed. *The Wit and Wisdom of Mae West*. New York: G. P. Putnam's Sons, 1967.

Weissman, Ginny, and Coyne Steven Sanders. *The Dick Van Dyke Show: Anatomy of a Classic*. New York: St. Martin's Press, 1983.

West, Mae. *Goodness Had Nothing to Do with It*. New York: Manor Books, 1976.

Wilde, Larry. *Great Comedians Talk About Comedy*. New York, Citadel Press, 1968.

Wilk, Max. *The Golden Age of Television: Notes from the Survivors*. New York: Delacorte Press, 1976.

Williams, Elsie A. *The Humor of Jackie Moms Mabley: An African American Comedic Tradition*. New York: Garland, 1995.

Williams, John A., and Dennis Williams. *If I Stop I'll Die: The Comedy and Tragedy of Richard Pryor*. New York: Thunder's Mouth Press, 1991.

Winters, Jonathan. *Winters' Tales: Stories and Observations for the Unusual*. New York: Random House, 1987.

Yagoda, Ben. *Will Rogers: A Biography*. New York: HarperCollins, 1993.

Zoglin, Richard. *Comedy at the Edge: How Stand-Up in the 1970s Changed America*. New York: Bloomsbury, 2008.

Zweibel, Alan. *Bunny, Bunny: Gilda Radner: A Sort of Romantic Comedy*. New York: Applause Books, 1997.

VIDEOGRAPHY

Fred Allen once dismissed TV as permitting "people who haven't anything to do to watch people who can't do anything." If you find yourself with nothing to do, the following programs offer some people worth watching.

Our intent was never to analyze comedy, but to help contextualize it. In other words, if you don't understand the setup for a Depression era joke, you won't enjoy the punch line, either. Though nowadays you often have to click past innumerable maggot-loving reality shows to find a television documentary on comedy, there is actually a huge amount of material available. Much of that which helped to inform our series can be found within the archives of the Paley Center for Media (formerly the Museum of Television and Radio) based in New York and Los Angeles. What follows is a brief sampling of germane documentaries.

–MK

American Masters programs on PBS:
Charlie Chaplin: Unknown Genius (1986)
Buster Keaton: A Hard Act to Follow (1987)
Harold Lloyd: The Third Genius (1989)
Neil Simon: Not Just for Laughs (1989)
Preston Sturges: The Rise and Fall of an American Dreamer (1990)
Will Rogers: Rediscovering Will Rogers (1994)
Nichols and May: Take Two (1996)
Danny Kaye: A Legacy of Laughter (1996)
Jack Paar: As I Was Saying (1997)
Vaudeville (1997)
Billy Wilder: The Human Comedy (1998)
Lucille Ball: Finding Lucy (2000)
Bob Newhart: Unbuttoned (2005)
Carol Burnett: A Woman of Character (2007)

Robert Weide has produced a number of landmark films, including:
The Marx Brothers in a Nutshell (1982)
The Great Standups: Sixty Years of Laughter (1984)
W. C. Fields, Straight Up (1986)
Mort Sahl: The Loyal Opposition (1989)
Lenny Bruce: Swear to Tell the Truth (1998)

Other notable documentaries, most of which are available on home video, include:
Alan King: Inside the Comedy Mind (1991)
The College of Comedy with Alan King (1997)
The Aristocrats (2005)

Smothered: The Censorship Struggles of the Smothers Brothers Comedy Hour (2002)
The Stooges: The Men Behind the Mayhem (2004)
Mr. Warmth: The Don Rickles Project (2007)

My personal favorite is *Comedian* (2002), the cinema verité documentary that chronicles Jerry Seinfeld creating new material. When you watch this film, while laughing, you will also understand why dying is easy but comedy is hard.

Finally, a wealth of insightful material is now available online.

CharlieRose.com features his compelling interviews with innumerable comic greats.

http://www.emerson.edu/comedy is the home page for the American Comedy Archives, which was founded by "José Jimenez" himself, Bill Dana. Interviews include everyone from Jack Carter to "Weird Al" Yankovic.

Finally, the Archive of American Television, administered by the Academy of Television Arts and Sciences, was extremely helpful to our project. http://www.emmys.tv/foundation/archive/ is the home page for this entity, which posts many of its rare interviews (with comedy greats like Norman Lear

ACKNOWLEDGMENTS

THE SERIES

During the presidential election campaign of 2004, I was inspired to create a documentary series on the history of American comedy. At the time, nothing seemed particularly funny, apart from the partisan bickering that was lampooned nightly on *The Daily Show*'s "Indecision 2004" segments. It seemed to me that PBS viewers could use a good solid six-hour laughfest, and in exploring America's most popular comedy, we might learn a little bit about who we are collectively as a people.

Make 'Em Laugh: The Funny Business of America, in both film and book form, grew out of my conversations with Larry Maslon, with whom I have been working for more than six years now. On this project, Larry proved a combination of Carl Reiner, Larry Gelbart, Selma Diamond, Mel Tolkin—just imagine all of the writers from all of Sid Caesar's various shows rolled into one human being, and you'll then appreciate the kind of energy and wit that Larry has brought to our work.

Beginning in 2005, the team at Thirteen/WNET began to work its considerable magic. Most important to this project was executive producer David Horn, who not only used his savvy to lock down critical financing for the series but protected us "creative types" from the blustery winds that for years now have buffeted all who choose to work on documentaries about the arts. Supervising producer Bill O'Donnell helped to improve every rough assembly and oversaw every interaction with PBS, and also ensured that every word of our various grant applications was carefully chosen. The executive team at Thirteen/WNET, first led by the passionate vice president for national programming, Tamara Robinson, under president emeritus Bill Baker, and then by vice president of production Stephen Segaller under president and CEO Neal Shapiro, voiced confidence in our work daily over the past three years. As with our series *Broadway: The American Musical*, the design by B. T. Whitehill was superb; the legal wisdom of Arlen Appelbaum was invaluable; the musical know-how of John Adams, Rosie Fishel, and Emily Lee made our series "sing," and indispensable production manager Jane Buckwalter always made sure that we stayed off the "Losers' List" by keeping our expenses in order and our budget on track.

The "second bananas," who actually created the film series, will no doubt continue to distinguish themselves in all their future endeavors. Cinematographers Mead Hunt, Ulli Bonnekamp, Alan Palmer, and Buddy Squires brought their keen eyes to our high definition interviews, just as Jayme Roy, Bob Schuck, Mark Mandler, John Zecca, Mark Roy, and other sharp-eared sound recordists made sure everything funny was audible.

Editors on documentary films are like Olympic decathaletes—they need to do everything well and in record time. Kris Liem and I shared the same sense of humor, and we constantly wondered why no one else laughed at our jokes; Jed Parker was always surprising, which is the key to good comedy; Ed Barteski is even funnier now that he moved away from the nastiest dog on Long Island; and Pam Arnold was our fourth editor, batting cleanup and hit every straight pitch out of the park. Christy Denes artfully shaped our presentation reels and laid the foundation for our Mae West and Sid Caesar sections, and Eric Treiber and Irene Kassow worked long nights, rotating among four AVID editing systems when there was no one else with whom to share a laugh.

There is no way to properly thank coproducer Sally Rosenthal for the years of commitment and dedication she has brought to this project, not to mention the ton of ribald wisecracks that she has shared with the staff. Erika Frankel was a calm port in the footage storm, and Amy Gottung on still photos, Jason Kouzikas on production, and Matt Tischler (on everything!) poured their hearts into this project. Comedy is all about timing, and our music directors, Peter Millrose, Steve Ulrich and Larry O'Keefe brought the episodes alive with their timely and underappreciated melodies. We always look forward to working with sound editor Deborah "Deserves the Emmy" Wallach and audio mixer Ed "This Is His Fifth Emmy Award" Campbell on this and every future project.

The *Make 'Em Laugh* series was blessed with a devoted team of collegial consultants, including Jeff Abraham, Anne Beatts, Barry Dougherty, Rachel Dratch, Eddy Friedfeld, Michael Frisch, Barry Goldsmith, Gerald Nachman, Allan Neuwirth, Mel Watkins, Elisabeth Weis, Max Wilk, and Don Wilmeth. Never too busy to meet a deadline and offer cogent suggestions, these teachers, writers, and funny folks kept us on track and improved our work immeasurably with every script meeting.

The nasty business of comedy was never a challenge for accountant Larry Brown, and once again Jim Kendrick's sage counsel made even the harshest negotiations somewhat joyful with his wry humor.

More so than on any project I've ever worked on, the supporters of public television deserve a special thanks. First and foremost, the series would not have been possible without the major support of CPB and PBS, as well as the steadfast support of the National Endowment for the Arts. As most New Yorkers know, even if they rarely enter a museum or visit Lincoln Center or watch Thirteen/WNET, Dorothy and Lewis Cullman are philanthropists with real heart and soul; Larry Condon and Jay Beckner at the LuEsther T. Mertz Charitable Trust have likewise been longtime supporters to whom we are profoundly grateful; Judy Resnick is not only a most generous angel, but she is funny as well; and continued support from Mike Strunsky of the Ira and Leonore Gershwin Philanthropic Fund and Al Cardinali of the DuBose and Dorothy Heyward Memorial Fund was critical to the project. Beth Kobliner Shaw was commended by Bill Clinton in his book *Giving*, and I hope she and David E. Shaw know how much their support meant to this ambitious work. Everywhere he goes, whether at the Friars or at the 92nd Street Y, Buddy Teich spreads joy, and I am ever grateful for his friendship and support. Rounding out the roster of key supporters and patrons at the time this book went to print are Mary and Marvin Davidson, the Starr Foundation, the Vital Projects Fund, Susan R. Malloy and the Sun Hill Foundation, the Carson Family Charitable Trust, and the Mary Duke Biddle Foundation. And finally, a major thanks to John Beug and everyone at Rhino Records, as well as to David Jackson and Tina Fletcher at BBC Music, Arts & Performance, and our partners at ABC-Australia.

Comedians are notorious for becoming jaded and listening to someone else's routine without laughing and saying, "That's funny." This happened to me at one point, and thankfully, Emma, Sacha and Twyla were always there to make me laugh.

Finally, in every interview I conducted, I asked, "Who was the funniest person you ever knew?" Answers ranged from Bill Cosby to W. C. Fields to Larry David. My answer is Kathy Landau. She cracks me up, even when she calls me Mr. Faputznik. Thank God she is Mrs. Faputznik.

Michael Kantor

THE BOOK

From a young age, I was always particularly fond of comedy double-acts: Carl Reiner and Mel Brooks, the Smothers Brothers, Felix and Oscar, Groucho and Chico. My favorite double-act of the last eight years has been Michael Kantor and me. Michael's inspiration and leadership on this project and his vision for making these beloved chestnuts accessible, entertaining, and enlightening to a whole new audience are exemplary. To accomplish what he has on this series, over such a short amount of time with so many subtle obstacles, is impressive indeed. To do so and still maintain a sense of humor is remarkable.

I also want to thank the staff of *Make 'Em Laugh* at Channel Thirteen for their patience and assistance: Sally Rosenthal, Erika Frankel, Jason Kouzikas, Amy Gottung, and Jared Rosenberg in particular. The panel of advisers assembled for the documentary project over the fast few years has been challenging and inspiring; I want to recognize Anne Beatts, Mel Watkins, and Gerald Nachman as being especially insightful.

In the early stages of the publishing part of the project, Karyn Gerhard and Lisa Halliday were immensely helpful. We owe a tremendous debt to literary agents Andrew Wiley and Jeffrey Posternak, who believed in our work from the first day we visited their office, and who steered us, with careful guidance and discretion, into the arms of the incomparable Jonathan Karp and his team at Twelve. Jonathan relishes a great story, wields a sharp but judicious pen, but most of all brings a keen sense of humor to every comment he offers. Pamela Schechter steered the production of the book through each phase with a sure hand, and the patient and awesomely talented designer Roger Gorman handled our material with artistry and a sense of humor—in his hands, a picture often was worth more than a thousand words. Bob Castillo was thoroughly a gentleman and a thorough one.

My assistant, Jennifer Ashley Tepper, has come through once again with incredible diligence and grace under pressure. Ron Mandelbaum at Photofest provided his characteristic encouragement. The Tamiment Archives at New York University was a great resource, as was Bobst Library itself. Brad Rosenstein of the San Francisco Performing Arts Library & Museum generously shared the pearls of his hungry i exhibit. Jeffrey Vance and Bonnie Rowan provided key research items. Emma O'Neill did an expert job of photo coordination.

I want to thank several people for their inspiration and guidance. Michael Perillo, Steve Rotterdam, and Dave Silberger were the original geek chorus of comedy enthusiasts from four decades ago, and their collective spirit can be found everywhere in the manuscript of this book. At New York University, two of my colleagues, Jim Calder and David Costabile, provided rare insight into the world of physical comedy; if among my many supportive students I single out Nyambi Nyambi and Julie Sharbutt, it's because of their specific enthusiasm for Richard Pryor and *The Simpsons* respectively. Fritz Brun, Tom Lindblade, Don Wilmeth, and Anne Kaufman Schneider constantly encouraged the project and provided their continually provocative insights. A special nod to my father, Gerald Maslon, who always made sure I watched the Marx Brothers on TV and took me to see Jack Benny when, at the age of nine, I begged him to drive me to the Westbury Music Fair. And I hope my brother Henry shares the laughs in this book with his friends and coworkers.

Just as this book was going to press, my great friend George Furth passed away. Besides being a profound influence on my life and work, he would joyously feed me his favorite lines by Gracie Allen, Jack Benny, and Bob Hope on a weekly basis. Many of them made it into this book; it grieves me that he's not around to read it.

My dearest wife, Genevieve Elam, has provided me with love, support, and patience. She provides three laughs a day, guaranteed, and has even delivered another potentially ardent comedy fan, our newly arrived son, Miles. I'm incredibly grateful for all of these gifts—and hopeful that Miles will someday sit with me and laugh at the Marx Brothers, just the way I did with my dad.

Laurence Maslon

INDEX

Abbott, Bud, 22, 266, 320-24

Abbott and Costello Meet Frankenstein (movie), 63, 323

ABC network, 254, 278, 279, 362

Academy Awards, 212, 215

Actors Equity, 205

Adamson, Joe, 33, 37

Addams Family, 195

Admiral Broadway Revue, The (TV show), 76, 84, 358

advertising. See sponsors

African Americans. See blacks

Aladdin (movie), 15, 244

Albee, E.F., 156

albums, 228-29

alcohol, 83, 136, 139-40

Alexander, Jason
  on Allen (Woody), 226
  on Brooks (Mel), 110
  on David (Larry), 188, 189
  on *Seinfeld* show, 130, 132, 297-98
  on Silvers (Phil), 132, 164, 166

Allen, Fred, 325-27, 370
  background, 326
  and Benny (Jack), 153-54
  on comedy piracy, 156
  on vaudeville, 157

Allen, Gracie, 260-64

Allen, Woody, 223-27
  background, 224
  Cavett on, 224, 226
  as combination of nerd and hip, 195-96
  on Hope (Bob), 210, 211
  on Sahl (Mort), 334
  Sahl on, 225

All in the Family (TV show), 254, 276-83, 289

Al Qaeda, 362

American Humor (Rourke), 8

Amos 'n' Andy (radio/TV show), 160-61, 265, 308

Amsterdam, Morey, 274

Anderson, Eddie, 152, 154

Animal Crackers (show), 145

animation, 14, 15, 36-39, 300-303

Apatow, Judd, 56, 197, 297

Apollo Theater (N.Y.), 330

Arbuckle, "Fatty," 24-25

Arnaz, Desi, 46, 48, 253

Arthur, Beatrice, 281

As Thousands Cheer (revue), 63

Atlas, Charles, 194

Avery, Tex, 14, 37-38, 57

Aykroyd, Dan, 115, 116

Ball, Lucille, 43, 44-48
  background, 46
  and Burnett (Carol), 48, 103
  comedy style, 13
  I Love Lucy, 46, 47, 252-53, 358
  and Keaton (Buster), 46, 47
  and Marx (Harpo), 34, 35
  with prop, 15

Ballard, Kaye, 153

Banducci, Enrico, 84, 333

Barnum, P.T., 129, 131, 133

Barr, Roseanne, 255, 292-95
  background, 293
  on Ball (Lucille), 46
  on Burnett (Carol), 100
  on Carson (Johnny), 95
  on Maher (Bill), 363
  Roseanne, 294-95

Beatts, Anne, 66, 115, 116, 117, 225, 238, 239

Behar, Joy, 170

Bellboy, The (movie), 52

Belson, Jerry, 285

Belushi, John, 114, 116, 117, 193

Belzer, Richard, 117, 153

Benny, Jack, 9, 131, 150-51
  background, 152
  and Burns (George), 264
  casual atmosphere of show, 266
  concerts for servicemen, 195
  generosity, 132
  as idol of Carson, 92
  parody of *Gaslight*, 63
  radio show, 152-55
  repertory company, 152, 298
  sight gags, 265
  and Smothers Brothers, 343, 344
  on variety shows, 156
  vaudeville act, 156

Benny, Joan, 152, 153, 154, 155

Berg, Gertrude, 255, 256-59

Berg, Lew, 258

Bergen, Edgar, 265, 266, 315

Bergman, Ingmar, 224

Bergson, Henri, 13

Berle, Milton, 27, 156, 266, 333

Berlin, Irving, 63, 65, 137, 145

Berman, Shelley, 84, 228, 324, 333

Best, Willie, 194

Beverly Hillbillies, The (TV show), 254, 274

bigotry, 283

Black Power, 350

blacks
  on *All in the Family*, 280-81, 282
  Cantor and, 204

chitlin circuit, 329

Cosby and, 288, 289, 290-91

first mainstream black comedian, 207

Foxx's depiction of, 177

on *In Living Color*, 123-24

on *The Jeffersons*, 282

Murphy as most successful black performer, 186

Murphy's imitation of black performers, 184

as opposite of hyperwhites, 196

as outsiders, 193

Blaine, David, 133

Blake, Eubie, 160

Blanc, Mel, 37

Blazing Saddles (movie), 110, 111, 351

Born Standing Up (Martin), 366

Boyar, Burt, 339

Breen, Joseph A., 308, 314

Brennan, Justice, 357

Brice, Fanny, 193

Brillstein, Bernie, 83, 115, 117, 239

Broadway comedies, 157

Broadway revues, 157, 168, 251

Brooks, James, 255, 301, 303

Brooks, Mel, 67, 106-11
  background, 108
  on Carson (Johnny), 93
  at Catskills resorts, 84
  The Producers, 110, 111, 158
  2000 Year Old Man, 107, 119

Bruce, Lenny, 219, 336-41, 352
  albums, 229
  background, 338
  and Carlin (George), 338, 340, 341, 356-57
  and Catholic Church, 340, 341
  drug use, 341, 357
  and obscenity, 307, 308, 309, 339-41
  Rivers on, 180

Bucholtz, Mary, 196

Bugs Bunny, 37-38

burlesque, 164, 165, 307-8, 316-19, 322

Burnett, Carol, 48, 56, 79, 100-105

Burns, Biff, 267

Burns, George, 109, 157, 214, 260-64, 344

Burrows, James, 246, 247, 255

Bush, Barbara, 301

Bush, George H.W., 301

Bush, George W., 61, 363

Buzzi, Ruth, 98

Bye Bye Birdie (show), 168

cable television, 309, 357, 358-59

Caesar, Sid, 66, 74-79, 274

background, 76
on balance between comedy and
    seriousness, 303
and Brooks (Mel), 108
Caesar's Hour, 224
Your Show of Shows, 63-64, 76-79, 119
Camp Tamiment (Pa.), 84, 224, 227
Cantor, Eddie, 203-6, 358
    Americanization, 194
    background, 204
    film at Palace Theater, 157
    on radio, 265, 266
    Yiddishisms, 193, 194
    at Ziegfeld Follies, 193, 204-5
Cantor, Ida, 206
Carell, Steve, 126
Carlin, George, 305, 350, 354-57
    book, 357
    on Bruce (Lenny), 338, 340, 341
    on Carson (Johnny), 94
    censorship issues, 307, 308, 309
    comedy recordings, 229
    on Kaufman (Andy), 246
    on old radio shows, 266
    On Location shows, 358
    on Pryor (Richard), 351
Carlson, Tucker, 127
Carmichael, Stokely, 177
Carne, Judy, 98
Carney, Art, 271, 285
Carol Burnett Show, The (TV show), 103-5
Carrey, Jim, 54-57
Carsey, Marcy, 294, 295
Carson, Johnny, 90-91, 113, 274, 326
    background, 92
    on Benny (Jack), 153
    on Chase (Chevy), 116
    influence of burlesque, 319
    as Maher's idol, 362
    political neutrality on stage, 94-95, 363
    and Seinfeld (Jerry), 297
    Tonight Show, 93-95, 297, 359
Carter, Jimmy, 116
cartoons. See animation
Catholic Church, 340, 341
Catholic League, 361
Catskill Mountain resorts, 83-84, 108
Cavalcade of Stars (TV show), 270
Cavett, Dick
    on Allen (Woody), 224, 226
    on Carson (Johnny), 92, 94
    and/on Groucho, 33, 145, 148
    on Hope (Bob), 214
    on Kaufman (George), 145

on Silvers (Phil), 166
CBS network, 279, 280, 281
censorship
    of broadcast networks, 359
    of Bruce (Lenny), 307, 308, 309
    and Carlin (George), 307, 308, 309
    from government, 308, 346
    and Smothers Brothers, 343, 345, 346
    of West (Mae), 315
Chaplin, Charlie, 16-21
    animators' study of, 14-15
    background, 18
    in feature films, 14
    grace of, 20
    The Immigrant, 193
    Keaton on, 27
    Lewis's admiration of, 52, 53
    Lloyd and, 199-200, 201
    music hall troupe, 29
    Tramp character, 19
    in vaudeville, 13
Chaplin, Sydney, 18
Chase, Chevy, 66, 114, 116
Cheech and Chong, 229, 230-32
Cher, 133
Chicago (Ill.), 337, 338, 358
children, 251
Chong, Tommy, 231
Clampett, Bob, 37
Clifton, Tony, 246-47
coaxial cable, 358
Coca, Imogene, 77, 78, 79
Cocoanuts (movie and show), 145, 149
Cohan, George M., 205
Cohen, Myron, 359
Cohn, Harry, 42
Colbert, Stephen, 61, 67, 126, 127
Colgate Comedy Hour (TV show), 206,
    224, 277, 358
color, 14
Columbia Pictures, 42-43
comedian(s)
    knockabouts, 10-35, 40-57
    in nightclubs and resorts, 83-85
    outsiders, 9, 192-96, 207
    stand-up, 13, 85, 188, 189, 297
    in vaudeville, 156-57
    wiseguys, 9, 128-89
    See also specific comedians
comedy
    albums, 228-29
    on cable, 358-59
    domestic, 9, 250, 251-53, 266, 267
    influence of nightclubs and resorts on, 83

physical, 9-57
prop, 15
radio, 152-53, 265-67
satire and parody, 9, 58-127
screwball, 251
situation, 253-55, 258, 299, 309
stage, 157-58, 251
in twenty-first century, 364-65
Comedy Central channel, 359
commedia dell'arte, 9, 12, 13
Commodore Records, 119
communism, 193, 259
Compass Players, 84
computer animation, 15
conformity, 192
Congreve, William, 133
con men, 130-31, 132, 160, 161, 166
Cook, Peter, 67
Coolidge, Calvin, 72
Cooper, James Fenimore, 62, 67
Copacabana (N.Y.), 83
Corey, Irwin, 366
Correll, Charles, 160, 265
Cosby, Bill, 119, 184, 229, 287-91, 330, 350
Costello, Chris, 322
Costello, Lou, 22, 266, 320-24
Coughlin, Father, 206
Coulter, Ann, 363
Coward, Noël, 251
cowardice, 194, 210
Cox, Stephen, 43, 324
Crosby, Bing, 212, 213
Crystal, Billy, 118-21
Curb Your Enthusiasm (TV show), 188, 189

Daffy Duck, 37
Daily Show, The (TV show), 125-27
Daniels, Bebe, 200
David, Larry, 132, 133, 165, 187-89, 297-99
Davidson, Tommy, 56, 123, 124, 176,
    186, 291, 353, 359
Davis, Sammy Jr., 206, 276, 280-81
Day, Dennis, 152
de Cordova, Fred, 94
DeGeneres, Ellen, 196-97
"Dick in a Box" (song), 309
Dick Van Dyke Show, The (TV show), 273-75
Diller, Phyllis, 195, 211, 220-22
Dillingham, Charles, 137
disguise, 132, 185
Disney, Walt, 15, 36, 37
domestic comedy, 9, 250, 251-53, 266, 267
Donald Duck, 37
Douglas, Mike, 169

drugs, 231-32, 244, 340, 341, 353, 357
Duck Soup (movie), 34
Dumont, Margaret, 133, 146
Durante, Jimmy, 156, 157

Ebersol, Dick, 114, 117, 119
Edwards, John, 126
Eisenhower, Dwight D., 334
Elliott, Bob, 267
Epstein, Benjamin R., 283
Essanay Studios, 19
experimentation, 12

Fairbanks, Douglas, 21
families, 249-52, 255
FCC. See Federal Communications
Commission
FCC v. Pacifica Foundation, 356-57
Federal Communications
   Commission (FCC), 308, 309, 356, 358, 359
FedEx, 362
Felix the Cat, 36
Fibber McGee and Molly (radio show),
   265, 266-67
Fields, Ronald, 136
Fields, W.C., 146, 315
   on Chaplin, 21
   distrust of producers, 176
   in Follies, 71, 137, 204
   on humor, 21
   and Marx Brothers, 143
   on radio, 266
   and Rogers (Will), 71
   as wiseguy, 131-34, 136-41
Fine, Larry, 42, 43
First Amendment, 9, 127, 307, 346
First Family, The (album), 229
Fitzgerald, F. Scott, 314
Fleischer brothers, 36, 37
Fleming, Erin, 148
Flintstones, The (TV show), 38, 39
Florensi, Joe, 170
football, 193
Ford, Gerald, 66, 116
Foxworthy, Jeff, 9, 249, 289, 294-95
Foxx, Redd, 132, 161, 172-77, 184, 229, 350
Franklin, Joe, 205, 206, 314, 315
freedom of expression, 307
French, Leigh, 344
Freshman, The (movie), 193, 196, 200, 202
Friedman, Budd, 85, 242, 246, 359
*Funny Thing Happened on the Way to
   the Forum, A* (show), 158

Gaines, William, 64
Garry Moore Show, The (TV show), 224
Gaslight (movie), 9, 63
Gelbart, Larry, 75, 77-79, 108, 155, 211, 266, 338
Gerber, Roy, 285
Gibson Girl, 192
Gish, Lillian, 27
glasses, 200
Gleason, Jackie, 255, 268-72, 290
Goldberg, Whoopi, 330
Goldbergs, The (radio/TV show), 252, 256-59
Goldwyn, Samuel, 71, 201, 205
Gone with the Wind (movie), 104
Goodman, John, 294
Gore, Al, 127
Gosden, Freeman, 160, 265
Gould, Elliott, 116
Goulding, Ray, 267
Grange, Red, 193
Granz, Norman, 228
Gregory, Dick, 85, 173, 195, 290
Grier, David Alan, 124
Groening, Matt, 301, 302, 303
groundbreakers, 9, 304-65
   Abbott and Costello, 320-24
   Allen (Fred), 325-27
   Bruce (Lenny), 336-41
   Carlin (George), 354-57
   Mabley (Jackie "Moms"), 328-31
   Maher (Bill), 360-63
   Pryor (Richard), 348-53
   Sahl (Mort), 332-35
   Smothers Brothers, 342-47
   West (Mae), 307, 310-15
Guest, Christopher, 67

Hanna and Barbera, 38
Happy Days (TV show), 242-43
Harburg, E.Y., 131
Hardy, Oliver, 28-31
Harris, Phil, 152
Hart, Moss, 63, 251
Hawn, Goldie, 98
Hayman, Joe, 228
HBO (Home Box Office), 357, 358-59, 362
Healy, Ted, 41-42
Hefner, Hugh, 315, 339
"Hello, Mudduh. Hello, Faddah"
   (song), 86, 88
Henning, Paul, 254
Henrie, Joe, 42
Hiken, Nat, 165
hipsters, 195, 196
Hitler, Adolf, 43, 108, 111

Hobson, Laura Z., 283
Hollywood Production Code, 139, 308, 314
Hollywood Squares (TV show), 169, 170, 171
Home Box Office. See HBO
homosexuality, 170, 255, 286
Honeymooners, The (TV show), 268-72
Hoover, Herbert, 69-70
Hope, Bob, 38, 147, 208-14
   background, 156, 210
   casual nature of show, 266
   charity, 155
   cowardly act, 194
   Diller on, 211, 221
   influence on Allen (Woody), 210, 224, 225
   one liners, 215
   Road pictures, 212-13
   USO tours, 213-14
Houdini, Harry, 24
Houseman, John, 242
Howard, Curly, 42, 43
Howard, Moe, 42, 43
Howard, Shemp, 42, 43
hucksters. See con men
Humphrey, Hubert, 99, 334
hungry i (San Francisco), 84, 333
hyperwhites, 196

I Love Lucy (TV show), 46, 47, 252-53, 358
Immigrant, The (movie), 18, 193
I'm No Angel (movie), 314
improv (N.Y.), 85
individualism, 251
In Living Color (TV show), 123-24
Irwin, Bill, 13, 15, 56, 57

Jack Benny Program, The (radio show), 152-55
Jacobs, Frank, 64, 65
Jeffersons, The (TV show), 282
Jerk, The (movie), 236
Jews
   in Allen's jokes, 195
   Berg's portrayal of, 258, 259
   and Brooks (Mel), 108, 109, 110-11
   Bruce on, 339
   from Eastern Europe, 193
   Lear on terminology for, 283
   and Sherman (Allan), 87-88
Johnson, Arte, 98
Jones, Chuck, 37, 38
Jones, Gerard, 166, 279, 280
Jones, Spike, 228
Jordan, Jim and Marian, 266
Juilliard School, 242

Kanter, Hal, 53, 140, 212, 213, 214

Karno American Company, 18-19, 29

Kaufman, Andy, 245-47, 364

Kaufman, George S., 263

  Cocoanuts, 145

  and Marx Brothers, 33, 145, 146

  Roman Scandals, 205

  satires, 62, 157

  Woody Allen's admiration for, 224

  You Can't Take It With You, 251

Kaufman, Irving S., 65

Keaton, Buster, 22-27, 53, 201-2

  background, 24

  and Ball (Lucille), 46, 47

  gags, 14

  Maltin on, 27

  and Marx Brothers, 34

  with prop, 15

  as stand-up comedian, 13

  Van Dyke on, 25

Keith, B.F., 156

Kelly, Walt, 65

Kennedy, John F., 66, 209, 229, 335, 341

Kennedy, Joseph, 335

Kenwith, Herbert, 47

Kerr, Walter, 202

Keyes, Paul, 99

Keystone Studios, 19

Kibbee, Roland, 283

Kilborn, Craig, 126

King, Alan, 120

Kissinger, Henry, 335

Klein, Robert

  on Abbott and Costello, 323

  on Chase (Chevy), 66

  on Foxx (Redd), 177

  HBO concert, 358

  on *Saturday Night Live*, 66, 114

  in Second City ensemble, 85

  on Three Stooges, 43

  on Winters (Jonathan), 218

Klugman, Jack, 284-86

knockabouts, 10-35, 40-57

  Ball (Lucille), 34-35, 44-48

  Carrey (Jim), 54-57

  Chaplin (Charlie), 13-21, 27, 29

  Hardy (Oliver), 28-31

  Keaton (Buster), 13-15, 22-27

  Laurel (Stan), 18, 28-31, 52

  Lewis (Jerry), 15, 38, 49-53, 56, 186

  Marx Brothers, 32-35, 42, 142-49

  Three Stooges, 13, 40-43

Kohan, Buz, 103, 104

Kohan, David, 255

Krassner, Paul, 64

La Guardia, Fiorello, 135, 307, 319, 321

Lahr, John, 211

Lantz, Walter, 37

L.A. Press Club, 362

Laurel, Stan, 18, 28-31, 52

Lax, Eric, 225

Lear, Frances, 281

Lear, Norman, 9, 175, 254, 255, 276-83

Legion of Decency, 308

Lehrer, Tom, 67, 80-82

Lemmon, Jack, 285

Leno, Jay, 359

Leonard, Sheldon, 274

Lewinsky, Monica, 95

Lewis, Jerry, 38, 49-53, 56, 225

  admiration of Chaplin, 52, 53

  background, 51

  comedy style, 14, 53

  at the Copa, 83

  as idol of Murphy (Eddie), 186

  and Lear (Norman), 277

  with prop, 15

Lewis, Richard, 67, 126, 188, 189, 272

Liebman, Max, 75-76, 79, 84

Limbaugh, Rush, 362

Lindbergh, Charles, 193, 205

Little, Rich, 56, 60, 61

Little Nemo in Slumberland series, 36

Livingstone, Mary, 152

Lloyd, Harold, 198-202

  Allen on, 225

  background, 200

  The Freshman, 194, 196, 200, 202

  as physical comedian, 14, 15

Lloyd, Suzanne, 193, 200, 201

Loeb, Philip, 259

long-playing records, 228

Louis-Dreyfus, Julia, 298

Lucy Show, The (TV show), 48

Lynde, Paul, 132, 167-71

Mabley, Jackie "Moms," 328-31

Mackie, Bob, 104

MAD Magazine, 64-65, 66

Maher, Bill, 92, 94, 127, 360-63

Malcolm X, 174

Maltin, Leonard

  on Abbott and Costello, 322, 323

  on animation, 14, 36, 39

  on Benny (Jack), 152

  books, 366

  on burlesque, 319

  on Cantor (Eddie), 205

  on Chaplin and Keaton, 14, 20, 27

  on Crosby and Hope, 213

  on Fields (W.C.), 138, 139

  on Laurel and Hardy, 30

  on West (Mae), 315

Marin, Cheech, 160, 219, 229, 231

Marshall, Garry

  ABC shows, 254

  on *Dick Van Dyke Show*, 274, 275

  on Gleason (Jackie), 272

  Happy Days, 242-43

  on Lucy and Desi, 46

  on Moore (Mary Tyler), 274

  as producer of *The Odd Couple*, 285, 286

  on Silvers (Phil), 165

Martin, Dean, 50, 51, 83, 350

Martin, Dick, 98, 99, 213, 263

Martin, Steve, 233-36, 246

  albums, 229

  background, 234

  Born Standing Up, 366

  on Carson (Johnny), 96

  and hecklers, 83

  on Lehrer (Tom), 82

  on Lewis (Jerry), 53

  on Radner (Gilda), 239

  on *Saturday Night Live*, 115, 235

  on Smothers Brothers, 346

  Stone on, 196

Martin, Tony, 80

Marx, Bill, 34, 35

Marx, Chico, 13, 33, 34, 132, 144-48

Marx, Groucho, 13, 142-49, 176

  background, 144

  and Harpo, 33, 34, 35

  and Keaton (Buster), 34

  Marx Brothers Scrapbook, 366

  on radio, 266

  as wiseguy, 131, 132, 133

  You Bet Your Life, 147-48

Marx, Gummo, 144

Marx, Harpo, 13, 15, 32-35, 87, 144, 148

Marx, Minnie, 144, 152

Marx, Zeppo, 144, 152

Marx Brothers, 33, 42, 143-46, 152

Mask, The (movie), 57

Matthau, Walter, 285

Maude (TV show), 281-82

Maugham, Somerset, 251

May, Elaine, 65, 84, 344, 347

McCarthy, Joseph, 334

McCay, Windsor, 36

McEvoy, J.P., 138

McKean, Michael, 29, 67, 202
McKee, Joseph V. "Holy Joe," 312
Meader, Vaughn, 65, 229
Meadows, Audrey, 271, 272
mechanization, 13, 15
Melville, Herman, 131
Mencken, H.L., 72
Meyer, George, 302
Michaels, Lorne, 112, 114-17, 119, 120, 238, 309
Mickey Mouse, 36
Minsky's burlesque, 319
minstrel shows, 62, 318
Mooney, Paul, 175, 176, 350, 351
Moore, Garry, 103
Moore, Mary Tyler, 254, 274, 275
Moore, Tim, 159, 160, 161
Moranis, Rick, 57
Mork and Mindy (TV show), 243
Morris, Howard, 77
Mostel, Zero, 158
Murphy, Eddie, 15, 182-86
    background, 184
    cutting-edge comedy, 289
    imitation of black performers, 184
    as most successful black performer, 186
    as nerd, 196
    and Pryor, 177, 184
    on Saturday Night Live, 117, 184
    Wayans (Keenen) on, 123
    as wiseguy, 131, 132
Murray, Bill, 239
Murrow, Edward R., 258
musical comedy, 157, 158
Music Box, The (movie), 30
music halls, 156
Mutchnick, Max, 253, 255
Mutual Film Corporation, 18, 21
Myers, Mike, 67

Nachman, Gerald, 154, 219, 226, 333, 335
National Lampoon magazine, 66
National Lampoon's Animal House
    (movie), 196
NBC network, 290, 327
nerds, 195-97, 202
Newhart, Bob, 84, 93, 96, 103, 228, 235, 353
Newsweek magazine, 350
New York City, 307-8, 319, 341, 358
Nichols, Mike, 65, 84, 285
Night at the Opera, A (movie), 146
nightclubs, 83, 85, 229
Nixon, Richard M., 98, 99, 116, 335, 346

Obama, Barack, 363

Obeidallah, Dean, 365
O'Brien, Conan, 303
obscenity, 338-41
O'Connor, Carroll, 278, 280, 281
Odd Couple, The (TV show), 284-86
O'Donnell, Rosie, 363
O'Donoghue, Michael, 66
O'Hara, John, 71
On Location (TV show), 358
On the Waterfront (movie), 63-64
Oppenheim, Jess, 46
Oropeza, Vincente, 70
outsiders, 9, 192-96, 207

Paar, Jack, 93, 216, 218, 242
Page, La Wanda, 176
Palace Theater (N.Y.), 157
pantomime, 14, 15, 18
Paramount Pictures, 146, 285, 313
parody. See satire and parody
Pastor, Tony, 156
Pataki, George, 341
Pepsodent Show (radio show), 211, 212, 213
Perelman, S.J., 146
Phil Silvers Show, The (TV show), 165, 166
physical comedy, 9-57
    See also knockabouts; specific comedians
Pickford, Mary, 21
Piscopo, Joe, 117
Playboy Club (Chicago), 85
Politically Incorrect (TV show), 362, 363
political satire, 61-62
pornography, 307
Preminger, Otto, 334
Prinze, Freddie, 132
Producers, The (movie and show),
    110, 111, 158
Prohibition, 135
prop comedy, 15
Pryor, Richard, 9, 110, 348-53
    album, 229
    arrest, 308
    background, 350
    cutting-edge comedy, 289
    Murphy and, 177, 184
    on Sanford and Son, 176
    on Saturday Night Live, 115, 352
    Van Dyke on, 352-53
    Wilmore on, 185
punch lines, 364
Puritans, 305-6

Quayle, Dan, 95

racial stereotypes, 186
radio, 152-53, 160, 206, 228, 229, 252, 265-67
    See also specific shows and performers
Radner, Gilda, 116, 237-39
Raft, George, 313
Randall, Tony, 284-86
Randolph, Joyce, 270, 271
Rashad, Phylicia, 290
Reagan, Ronald, 117
Reeve, Christopher, 194
Reiner, Carl
    on Burns (George), 264
    on Carson (Johnny), 93
    on coaxial cable, 358
    on Dick Van Dyke Show, 275
    on Liebman (Max), 76
    on Martin (Steve), 235, 236
    sitcoms, 255
    2000 Year Old Man sketches, 107-9, 119
    Your Show of Shows, 77, 78, 274
Reiner, Rob, 67, 280
Revenge of the Nerds (movie), 196
revues, 157, 168, 251
Rey, Reynaldo, 174, 175, 176, 177
Rhymer, Paul, 267
Richards, Michael, 298
Richmond, Bill, 51, 52, 53
Rivers, Joan, 178-81, 364
    background, 180
    on Ball (Lucille), 47
    on Carson (Johnny), 93
    on Cher, 133
    on Cosby (Bill), 288
    on Diller (Phyllis), 221
    at Second City, 85
    on Taylor (Elizabeth), 133
    on West (Mae), 315
    as wiseguy, 132
Roach, Hal, 29, 198, 200
Road pictures, 212-13
Rock, Chris, 133, 329, 351, 365
Rogers, Will, 68-73
    background, 70
    and Cantor (Eddie), 204, 206
    compared with Allen (Woody), 226
    compared with Sahl (Mort), 334
    and Fields (W.C.), 71
    Roosevelt and/on, 72, 73
    Yagoda on, 62, 70
Rolle, Estelle, 282
Rollins, Jack, 120
Roman Scandals (show), 205
Rooney, Mickey, 278
Roosevelt, Franklin D., 72, 73

Roseanne (TV show), 294-95

Rose Marie, 9, 139, 164-65, 168, 170, 274, 275

Rosen, Arnie, 105

Rosenberg, Edgar, 181

Ross, Jeffrey, 232

Roth v. United States, 307

Rotoscope, 36

Rourke, Constance, 8

Rowan, Dan, 98

Rowan & Martin's Laugh-In, 97-99

Russell Simmons' Def Comedy Jam
   (TV show), 359

Ruth, Babe, 193

Ryskind, Morrie, 33, 145

Sahl, Mort, 224-26, 228, 332-35, 341

Sandrich, Jay, 47

Sanford, Fred, 132, 174

Sanford and Son (TV show), 175-76, 177

satire and parody, 9, 58-127, 157

Saturday Night Live (TV show), 105, 112-17
   David as writer for, 188
   debut episode, 119, 357
   vs. *In Living Color*, 124
   Kaufman on, 246
   Martin on, 235
   Murphy on, 117, 184
   parodies, 66-67
   Pryor on, 352
   Radner on, 237-39
   short on YouTube, 309

Scarborough, Joe, 363

Schauer, Fred W., 307

Schickel, Richard, 225

Schlatter, George, 98, 99, 242, 359

Schlosser, Herb, 114

screwball comedy, 251

Sears, Roebuck, 362

Second City, 65, 84, 180

Sedgewick, Eddie, 46

Seinfeld, Jerry, 296-99, 319
   background, 297
   on Carlin (George), 357
   on comedy pioneers, 365
   and David (Larry), 188, 298, 299
   memory of Abbott and Costello, 323

Seinfeld (TV show), 189

Seldes, Gilbert, 204

Sennett, Mack, 19, 138

Sex (show), 312

Shandling, Garry, 239

Shapiro, George, 56, 246, 247, 298, 299

Shatner, William, 116

Shavelson, Mel, 211

Shean, Al, 33, 144

She Done Him Wrong (movie), 313, 314

Sherman, Allan, 35, 86-89, 229

Sherwood, Robert E., 205

Shore, Dinah, 103

Shrek (movie), 39

sight gags, 265

silent films, 14, 25, 202

Silvers, Phil, 132, 162-66, 319

Simon, Danny, 285

Simon, Neil, 158, 285, 286

Simon, Sam, 302, 303

Simpsons, The (TV show), 39, 300-303

situation comedy, 253-55, 258, 299, 309

Skelton, Red, 27

slackers, 196

slapstick. *See* knockabouts; physical comedy

smart-alecks. *See* wiseguys

Smith, Kate, 322

Smothers, Dick, 264, 342-46

Smothers, Tommy, 98, 342-47

*Snow White and the Seven
   Dwarfs* (movie), 37

social Darwinism, 194

songs, 228

Sorkin, Dan, 228

sound, 14, 30, 36-37, 42-43, 251

South Park (TV show), 359

speakeasies, 83

Spiegel, Sam, 64

sponsors, 308, 326

Stadlen, Lewis J., 108, 144, 146, 147, 148

stage comedy, 157-58, 251

stagehands, 15

Stalling, Carl, 37

stand-up comedians, 13, 85, 188, 189, 297

Stapleton, Jean, 278, 280

Steamboat Bill, Jr. (movie), 26

Steamboat Willie (short), 36

Steinbeck, John, 213

Steinberg, David
   on Benny (Jack), 153
   on Burns (George), 263
   on Carson (Johnny), 91
   on comedy albums, 229
   on *Curb Your Enthusiasm*, 189
   on Nixon, 94-95
   on Seinfeld, 298
   on Smothers Brothers, 345
   on Stewart (Jon), 127
   on *You Bet Your Life*, 148

Stewart, Cal, 228

Stewart, Jon, 125-27

Stone, Laurie, 196

Strauss, Carolyn, 358-59

Struthers, Sally, 280

substance abuse. *See* alcohol; drugs

success, 192

Sullivan, Ed, 27, 152

Superman, 194

Tandem Productions, 278

Tankersley, William, 267, 279, 282, 344, 346

Tartikoff, Brandon, 188-89, 289, 298

Tashlin, Frank, 34, 37, 38, 52

Taxi (TV show), 246, 247

Taylor, Elizabeth, 133, 181

television
   animation on, 39
   cable, 309, 357, 358-59
   domestic comedies on, 252
   live shows on, 76-77, 114
   moral values, 309
   satire and parody on, 63, 66
   situation comedy on, 253-55, 258, 299, 309
   violence on, 309
   See also specific shows and performers

Texaco Star Theater (TV show), 358

Thalberg, Irving, 146, 147

"Thanks for the Memory" (song), 210

Three Stooges, 13, 40-43, 231

Thurber, James, 219

'Till Death Do Us Part (TV show), 278

Time magazine, 47, 214, 334, 339

Tobias, Patricia, 24, 25

Tolkin, Mel, 77

Tolstoy, Leo, 250

Tom and Jerry series, 38

Tomlin, Lily, 47, 98, 263, 271, 351

Tonight Show, The (TV show), 93, 95, 359

TV Guide, 102

Twain, Mark, 62, 67, 219

United Artists, 21

United Booking Office, 156

USO tours, 213, 214

Vance, Jeffrey, 13

Vance, Vivian, 48

Van Dyke, Dick
   on Benny (Jack), 154
   Carrey's admiration of, 56, 57
   Dick Van Dyke show, 273-75
   on Kaufman (Andy), 245
   Kaufman on variety series, 246
   on Keaton (Buster), 25
   on Laurel and Hardy, 30
   on Lynde (Paul), 168, 169

on Martin and Lewis, 51
on Pryor (Richard), 353
on Silvers (Phil), 165-66
vaudeville, 70, 143, 156-57, 265, 318, 319
Vic and Sade (radio show), 267
violence, 309

Walker, Dan, 70
Walker, Jimmy, 205, 307
Wallis, Hal, 52
Ward, Jay, 39
Warner Bros., 37, 38, 228
Watkins, Mel, 160
Wayans, Damon, 122-24
Wayans, Keenen Ivory, 56, 122-24
Wayne, Carol, 319
WBAI-FM, 356
Werner, Tom, 294, 295
West, Mae, 307, 308, 310-15
White, Jaleel, 196
White, Jules, 42, 43
White, Slappy, 175, 176
White House Correspondents Dinner, 60
Whittaker, Juliette, 350
Whoopee! (musical comedy), 205
Wilde, Oscar, 62
Wilder, Gene, 110, 239
Williams, Bert, 193, 204, 207
Williams, Robin, 15, 219, 240-44
Wilmore, Larry, 123, 124, 126, 161, 185
Wilson, Demond, 175
Wilson, Don, 152
Wilson, Steve, 170
Winters, Jonathan, 9, 216-19
    background, 218
    on "freaks," 195
    influence on Crystal (Billy), 119
    Klein on, 218
    Nachman on, 219
    Paar and/on, 216, 218
    on radio, 266
    and Williams (Robin), 242, 243-44
wiseguys, 9, 128-89
    Benny (Jack), 9, 63, 92, 131, 132, 150-55
    David (Larry), 132, 133, 165, 187-89
    Fields (W.C.), 10, 21, 71, 131-41
    Foxx (Redd), 132, 161, 172-77
    Lynde (Paul), 132, 167-71
    Marx (Groucho), 13, 33-35, 131-33, 142-49
    Murphy (Eddie), 131, 132, 182-86
    Rivers (Joan), 132, 133, 178-81
    Silvers (Phil), 132, 162-66
women, 193, 221, 222
Wonder, Stevie, 184

Wood, Robert D., 279
Woollcott, Alexander, 145
Wynn, Ed, 265

Yagoda, Ben, 62, 70
Yankee peddler, 131
Yankovic, "Weird Al," 80
Yorkin, Bud, 175-77, 278, 281, 282, 358
You Bet Your Life (TV show), 147-48
You Can't Take It With You (play
    and movie), 251-52
You Natzy Spy! (movie), 43
Young Frankenstein (movie), 110, 111
Your Show of Shows (TV show), 63-64, 76,
    78, 79, 108, 119, 274, 358
youth movement, 193

Ziegfeld, Florenz
    Broadway revues, 157
    and Cantor (Eddie), 204-5
    death, 73
    and Fields (W.C.), 136, 137, 141
    and Marx Brothers, 145
    and Rogers (Will), 70-71, 73
    and Williams (Bert), 207
Ziegfeld Follies, 136, 137, 193, 204-5, 207
Zweibel, Alan, 115, 188, 189, 224, 238, 239

FILM CREDITS

Directed and Produced By
Michael Kantor

Written By
Michael Kantor
Laurence Maslon

Produced By
Sally Rosenthal

Edited By
Kris Liem
Jed Parker
Pam Arnold
Ed Barteski

Hosted by
Billy Crystal

Narrated By
Amy Sedaris

Special Material Written by
Jon Macks

CoProducer
Erika Frankel

Production Coordinators
Amy Gottung
Matt Tischler

Production Associate
Jason Kouzikas

Cinematography
Mead Hunt
Ulli Bonnekamp
Allan Palmer

Assistant Editors
Eric Treiber
Irene Kassow

Music
Peter Millrose
Steven Ulrich
Larry O'Keefe

Voiceover
Keith Carradine

Additional Cinematography
Richard Chisholm
Steve Kazmierski
Rick Malkames
Buddy Squires
Jeff Sutch

Assistant Camera & Grip
Chris Barron
Damon Bundschuh
Luke Deikis
Ian Eastman
Craig Feldman
Stan Fyfe
Tim Gordon
Sharra Jenkins

Alex Klymkl
John Nastase
Gerald Russell
Kipjaz Savoie
Keith Sikora
Katie Strand
Lieven van Hulle
Marc Wall

Sound Recording
Lisa Gage
Jim Jack
Steve Longstreth
Mark Mandler
Roger Phenix
Ben Posnack
Jayme Roy
Mark Roy
Bob Schuck
Bob Silverthorne
Jay Ticer
Merce Williams
John Zecca

Hair & Makeup
Janet Arena
Marissa De Leon
Lea Nettles
Michelle O'Callaghan
Stacey Stempler
Stacy Halax
Shannon Hughey
Brenda Todd
Sachi Worrall

MediaLogging
Christina Aceto

Interns
Lindsay Blatt
Nicole Cumminskey
Nicolas Edelbach
Daniel Goodwin
Charles Hershow
Susan Johnson
Neha Kumar
Eliora Noetzel
Jon Rhymes
Lauren Betsy Riley
Jared Rosenberg
Shweta Suratkar
Hannah Tamminen
Matthew Tischler
Will Wiseheart
Lande Yoosuf

Board of Advisors
Eddy Friedfeld
Jeffrey Abraham
Anne Beatts
Barry Dougherty
Rachel Dratch
Michael Frisch
Barry Goldsmith
Gerald Nachman
Allan Neuwirth
Mel Watkins
Elisabeth Weis
Max Wilk

Supervising Sound Editor
Deborah Wallach

Assistant Sound Editor
Angela Organ

Dialogue Editor
Branka Mrkic

Re-Recording Mixer
Ed Campbell

Online Editor
Alan Miller

Graphics/Stills Animation
Asterisk
Brian O'Connell
Richard O'Connor

**Post Production
Supervisors**
Sean Riordan
Jeff Dockendorff

Title Design
B.T. Whitehill

**Coordinator, Program
Information**
Michael Weinstein-Reiman

Music Services
John Adams
Emily Lee
Rosie Fishel

Business Affairs
Arlen Appelbaum

Production Manager
Jane Buckwalter

Supervising Producer
Bill O'Donnell

Executive Producer
David Horn

**For Ghost Light Films
Legal Services**
James Kendrick

Accounting
Lawrence Brown

**Bookkeeping/Computer
Services**
Robert Spinner

A six-part series for public television, *Make 'Em Laugh: The Funny Business of America* is a production of Ghost Light Films and Thirteen/WNET New York in association with the BBC. For more information on the series, visit www.pbs.org or www.thirteen.org.

Funding for the *Make 'Em Laugh: The Funny Business of America* of America was provided by:

The Corporation for Public Broadcasting (CPB)
The Public Broadcasting Service (PBS)
Dorothy and Lewis B. Cullman
The LuEsther T. Mertz Charitable Trust
The Starr Foundation
The National Endowment for the Arts
David E. Shaw and Beth Kobliner Shaw
The DuBose and Dorothy Heyward Memorial Fund
Judith B. Resnick
Marvin and Mary Davidson
The Vital Projects Fund
The Carson Family Charitable Trust
The Ira and Leonore Gershwin Philanthropic Fund
Susan R. Malloy and the Sun Hill Foundation
Buddy Teich
The Mary Duke Biddle Foundation